FOURTH EDITION

LONGMAN
Preparation Series for the
NEW TOEIC® Test

Introductory Course

Lin Lougheed

PEARSON
Longman

Longman Preparation Series for the New TOEIC® Test, Introductory Course, Fourth Edition

Pearson Education, 10 Bank Street, White Plains, NY 10606

Staff credits: The people who made up the *Longman Preparation Series for the New TOEIC® Test, Introductory Course* team, representing editorial, production, design, and manufacturing, are listed below:

Jennifer Adamec
Rhea Banker
Angela M. Castro
Dave Dickey
Pam Fishman
Nancy Flaggman
Patrice Fraccio
Margo Grant
Michael Mone
Edie Pullman

Cover design: Barbara Sabella
Text design: Pat Wosczyk
Text composition: TSI Graphics
Text font: 11/15 Palatino

Photo Credits appear on page vi.

Library of Congress Cataloging-in-Publication Data

Lougheed, Lin, 1946–
    Longman preparation series for the new TOEIC test: Introductory course / Lin
        Lougheed. — 4th ed.
        p. cm.
    ISBN 0-13-199319-4 (with answer key) — ISBN 0-13-199320-8 (without answer key)
    1. Test of English for International Communication—Study guides.   2. English language—Business English—Examinations—Study guides.   3. English language—Textbooks for foreign speakers.   I. Lougheed, Lin, 1946—Longman preparation series for the TOEIC test. Introductory course.   II. Title.

PE1128.L646 2006
428.0076—dc22

2005037523

Printed in the United States of America
2 3 4 5 6 7 8 9 10–BAH–10 09 08 07

LONGMAN ON THE **WEB**

Longman.com offers online resources for teachers and students. Access our Companion Websites, our online catalog, and our local offices around the world.

Visit us at **longman.com.**

CONTENTS

PHOTO CREDITS

CORBIS

cover (right) © Darren Modricker; cover (left) © Lucidio Studio, Inc.

CORBIS/Royalty-Free

page 98 (top); page 99 (bottom); page 212 (bottom); page 214 (bottom); page 252 (bottom); page 253 (top); page 254 (bottom)

Educational Testing Service

pages 2; 94; 210; 250

Getty Images

cover (center) © Triangle Images

Instructional Design International, Inc.; Washington, D.C.

page 4; page 10; page 13; page 17; page 20; page 26; page 30; page 31; page 33 (both); page 34 (both); page 35 (both); page 36 (both); page 95 (both); page 96 (both); page 97 (top); page 98 (bottom); page 99 (top); page 211 (both); page 212 (top); page 213 (both); page 214 (top); page 215 (both); page 247 (both); page 251 (both); page 252 (top); page 254 (top); page 255 (both)

O'Toole, Steve

page 7; page 23; page 32 (both); page 97 (bottom); page 253 (bottom)

INTRODUCTION

TO THE STUDENT

The new TOEIC® (Test of English for International Communication) test measures your ability to understand English. It also measures your ability to take a standardized, multiple-choice test. In order to score well on the new TOEIC test, you must have two goals: improve your proficiency in English and improve your test-taking skills. The *Longman Preparation Series for the new TOEIC® Test* will help you do both.

Goal 1: Improving your proficiency in English

The *Longman Preparation Series for the New TOEIC® Test* will help you build your vocabulary. It will introduce you to words that are often used on the new TOEIC test. These are words that are used frequently in general English and also in business English contexts. You will learn words used by businesspeople involved in making contracts, marketing, planning conferences, using computers, writing letters, and hiring personnel. You will learn the words to use when shopping, ordering supplies, examining financial statements, and making investments. You will also learn general English terms often found in business contexts. This includes words used for travel and entertainment and for eating out and taking care of one's health.

The *Longman Preparation Series for the New TOEIC® Test* will help you review English grammar. The grammar items commonly tested on the new TOEIC test are reviewed here. You will learn grammar structures in TOEIC contexts.

Goal 2: Improving your test-taking skills

The *Longman Preparation Series for the New TOEIC® Test* will teach you to take the new TOEIC test efficiently. It will help you understand what a question asks. It will help you analyze the test items so you will know what tricks and traps are hidden in the answer choices. It will familiarize you with the format of the test so you will feel comfortable when taking the test. You will know what to expect. You will know what to do. You will do well on the new TOEIC test.

TO THE TEACHER

As a teacher, you want your students to become proficient in English, but you know your student's first goal is to score well on the new TOEIC® test. Fortunately, with the *Longman Preparation Series for the New TOEIC® Test,* both your goals and the students' goals can be met. All activities in the Longman Preparation Series match those on the actual new TOEIC test. Every practice exercise a student does prepares him or her for a similar question on the test. You do not, however, have to limit yourself to this structure. You can take the context of an item and adapt it to your own needs. I call this teaching technique "LIPP service": Look at; Identify; Paraphrase; Personalize. LIPP service makes the students repeat the target words and ideas in a variety of ways. Repetition helps students learn English. Variety keeps them awake. Here are some examples on how LIPP service can "serve" you in your classroom for each of the seven parts of the new TOEIC test.

Part 1: Photos

L   Have the students look at the photo.

I   Have the students identify all the words in the photo. Have them determine who is in the photo, what they are doing, and where they are standing. If there are no people, have them determine what is in the photo and describe it.

P   Have the students paraphrase the sentences they used when identifying the people or objects in the photo. This can be very simple, but it teaches the versatility and adaptability of language. For example, the students identify in the picture a man getting on the bus. Paraphrase: *A passenger is boarding the bus.* The students can also enrich the sentence by adding modifiers: *A young man is about to get on the city bus.*

P   Have the students personalize their statements. Start with simple sentences such as *I am getting on the bus* and expand to short stories: *Every morning, I wait for the bus on the corner. The bus stop is between Fifth and Sixth Street on the west side of the street. There are often many people waiting for the bus, so we form a line.*

Part 2: Question-Response

L   Have the students listen to the question and three responses.

I   Have the students identify all the words in the question and three responses. They can take dictation from the audio program or from you.

P   Have the students paraphrase the question or statement they hear. *You're coming, aren't you?* can be paraphrased as *I hope you plan to come.* Options such as, *Yes, of course.* can be paraphrased as *Sure.*

P Have the students personalize their statements. The students can work in pairs and develop small dialogues: *You're coming to my house tonight, aren't you? No, I'm sorry. I have to study.*

Part 3: Conversations

L Have the students listen to the conversations and look at the three questions and answer options in the book.

I Have the students identify all the words in the short conversations, the three written questions, and possible answers.

P Have the students paraphrase the sentences. The method is the same as for Parts 1 and 2. The students will demonstrate their understanding of the individual sentences by providing a paraphrase.

P Have the students personalize their statements. If the conversation is about dining out, the students can make up their own short conversation about a dining experience that they had. They should work in pairs or small groups for this exercise.

Part 4: Talks

L Have the students listen to the talks and look at the question(s) and answer options in the book.

I Have the students identify all the words in the talks, the written question(s), and possible answers.

P Have the students paraphrase the sentences.

P Have the students personalize their statements. Have them work in pairs or groups to create a similar talk. Have different individuals from the same group stand and give the talk. It will be interesting to see which vocabulary and grammar patterns they choose to share.

Part 5: Incomplete Sentences

L Have the students look at the statement and four responses.

I Have the students identify all the words in the statement and four responses.

P Have the students paraphrase the statement. They can also create sentences with the answer options that did not complete the blank in the original statement.

P Have the students personalize their statements. The students may find it difficult to find something in common with the whole statement, but they might be able to isolate one word and create some personal attachment. For example, in *Our clients are satisfied with their computer system*, your students may not have clients, but they will probably have a computer: *I am satisfied with my personal computer.*

Part 6: Text Completion

L Have the students look at the statement and four answer options.

I Have the students identify all the words in the statement and the four answer options.

P Have the students paraphrase the statement. They can also create sentences with the answer options that did not complete the blank in the original statement.

P Have the students personalize their statements. For example, in *Our offices are modern and spacious*, your students may not work in offices, but they probably live in apartments: *My apartment is modern, but it's not very spacious.*

Part 7: Reading Comprehension

L Have the students look at the passage.

I Have the students identify all the words in the passage.

P Have the students paraphrase the passage. If the passage is an advertisement, have them create a new advertisement for the same product. If the passage is a timetable, have them put the timetable in a different format.

P Have the students personalize the passage. Advertisements can be turned into a student's personal classified ad. A diary can be turned into a student's own schedule. A report can be turned into a student's essay on the same subject. With a little imagination, you can find a way to personalize almost any reading passage.

ABOUT THE NEW TOEIC® TEST

The new Test of English for International Communication (TOEIC) is a multiple-choice test of English for adult, nonnative speakers of the language. The test uses the language of international business. It has two sections: Listening Comprehension and Reading.

Listening Comprehension	Part 1 Photos	10	45 minutes
	Part 2 Question-Response	30	
	Part 3 Conversations	30	
	Part 4 Talks	30	
	TOTAL	100	
Reading	Part 5 Incomplete Sentences	40	75 minutes
	Part 6 Text Completion	12	
	Part 7 Reading Comprehension		
	• Single Passages	28	
	• Double Passages	20	
	TOTAL	100	

The TOEIC test is scored on a scale of 10 to 990. Only correct responses count toward your score. These correct responses are added and converted to a TOEIC score.

Tips for Taking the New TOEIC Test

- **Be familiar with the directions before you take the exam.**
  The directions are the same on every exam. If you study the directions in this book, which are identical to those on the actual new TOEIC, you don't need to read them on the day of the exam. Instead you can study the photos, read the answer options, and take more time to answer the questions themselves.

- **Work rapidly, but carefully.**
  Train yourself to work quickly. Train yourself to be thorough.

- **Guess.**
  If you do not know the answer, guess. You are not penalized for wrong answers, and you may get it right.

- **Mark only one answer per question.**
  Any question with more than one answer blackened will be counted as wrong.

- **Use the strategies and tips that you learned in this book.**
  This book was written so you can score higher on the new TOEIC test. Use these strategies and tips for success.

NEW TOEIC® TEST DIRECTIONS

General Directions

These directions are provided by the Educational Testing Service (ETS) and are reprinted here with their permission. Read them and make sure you understand them. These directions are the same on every test.

Test of English for International Communication

General Directions

This test is designed to measure your English language ability. The test is divided into two sections: Listening and Reading.

You must mark all of your answers on the separate answer sheet. For each question, you should select the best answer from the answer choices given. Then, on your answer sheet, you should find the number of the question and fill in the space that corresponds to the letter of the answer that you have selected. If you decide to change an answer, completely erase your old answer and then mark your new answer.

Specific Directions

Each part of the new TOEIC test begins with specific directions for that part. In this book, you will find these directions at the beginning of each study section and in the Practice Tests. Read them and be sure you understand them.

NEW TOEIC® TEST ANSWER SHEETS

The Answer Sheets used in this book are similar to those used in the new TOEIC test. The precise format of the Answer Sheets varies from test site to test site.

To record a response to a test question, examinees should find the number on the answer sheet that corresponds to the test question and make a solid mark with a pencil, filling in the space that corresponds to the letter of the answer they have chosen.

LISTENING
COMPREHENSION

In the first section of the new TOEIC® test, you will be tested on how well you understand spoken English. There are four parts to this section with special directions for each part:

Part 1   Photos

Part 2   Question-Response

Part 3   Conversations

Part 4   Talks

Each part contains activities to help you practice these strategies. Each part ends with a Strategy Review consisting of questions similar to those on the new TOEIC test. In this part of the **Introductory Course** for the new TOEIC Test, you will learn strategies to help you on the Listening Comprehension section.

PART 1—PHOTOS

These are the directions for Part 1 of the new TOEIC® test. Study them now. If you understand these directions now, you will not have to read them during the test.

LISTENING TEST

In the Listening test, you will be asked to demonstrate how well you understand spoken English. The entire Listening test will last approximately 45 minutes. There are four parts, and directions are given for each part. You must mark your answers on the separate answer sheet. Do not write your answers in the test book.

PART 1

Directions: For each question in this part, you will hear four statements about a picture in your test book. When you hear the statements, you must select the one statement that best describes what you see in the picture. Then find the number of the question on your answer sheet and mark your answer. The statements will not be printed in your test book and will be spoken only one time.

Example   *Sample Answer*

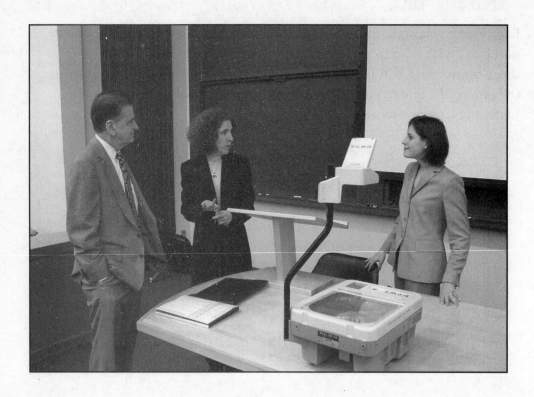

Statement (C), "They're standing near the table," is the best description of the picture, so you should select answer (C) and mark it on your answer sheet.

In this part you will learn how to look at photographs. These are the types of photographs you will see:

- photos of people
- photos of things

PHOTOS OF PEOPLE

You will see photos of people in Part 1. You will hear statements about the people that may give information about:

- Who are they?
- Where are they?
- What are they doing?
- What do they look like?

PHOTO 1

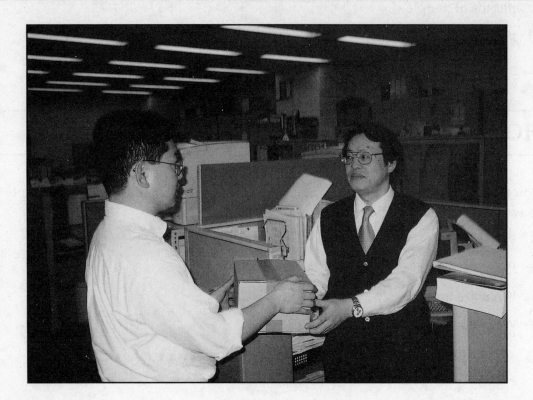

A. WHO ARE THE PEOPLE? Look at the photo above. Make assumptions about the occupation or relationship of the people in the photo.

Write Y (Yes), N (No), or ? (Unsure) beside the following relationships or occupations.

1. _____ brother and sister

2. _____ father and son

3. _____ boss and worker

4. _____ employees

5. _____ colleagues

6. _____ workers

7. _____ clerks

8. _____ repair personnel

9. _____ landlords

10. _____ shipping agents

11. _____ dentists

12. _____ mechanic and customer

B. WHERE ARE THE PEOPLE? Try to determine the setting. Pay attention to the prepositions such as *next to*, *in front of*, and *at*.

Write Y (Yes), N (No), or ? (Unsure) beside the following locations.

1. _____ in an office

2. _____ on the job

3. _____ at home

4. _____ next to a school

5. _____ on the bus

6. _____ at work

7. _____ in the street

8. _____ in a hallway

9. _____ behind a desk

10. _____ by a work station

11. _____ in front of a window

12. _____ in a conference room

C. WHAT ARE THE PEOPLE DOING? Identify the appropriate action.

Use these words to complete the sentences:

     facing   giving   sitting   taking   touching

1. The man on the right is _____ a box from the man on the left.

2. The man on the left is _____ a box to the man on the right.

3. Both men are _____ one another.

4. Neither man is _____ down.

5. Both men are _____ the box.

D. WHAT DO THE PEOPLE LOOK LIKE? How would you describe these people?

Write Y (Yes) if the description is true. If it is not, rewrite the sentence to make it true.

1. _____ Both men are wearing jackets.

2. _____ The man on the right is wearing a tie.

3. _____ Both men are wearing glasses.

4. _____ One man has a watch on his right hand.

5. _____ There are a lot of people in the office.

6. _____ Both men are wearing dark shirts.

7. _____ The box is big and heavy.

8. _____ The man on the left is wearing a vest.

PHOTO 2

A. WHO ARE THE PEOPLE? Look at the photo above. Make assumptions about the occupation or relationship of the people in the photo.

Write Y (Yes), N (No), or ? (Unsure) beside the following relationships or occupations.

1. _____ father and son

2. _____ brothers

3. _____ colleagues

4. _____ speaker and panelist

5. _____ master of ceremonies and speaker

6. _____ employer and employee

7. _____ political opponents

8. _____ construction managers

9. _____ architects

10. _____ service technicians

11. _____ teacher and administrator

12. _____ teacher and student

B. WHERE ARE THE PEOPLE? Try to determine the setting. Pay attention to the prepositions such as *next to, in front of,* and *at.*

Write Y (Yes), N (No), or ? (Unsure) beside the following locations.

1. _____ under the painting

2. _____ on the desk

3. _____ behind the podium

4. _____ between the two tables

5. _____ at the table

6. _____ next to one another

7. _____ across the street

8. _____ at the podium

9. _____ in front of the podium

10. _____ between the paintings

11. _____ behind the microphones

12. _____ above the water pitchers

C. WHAT ARE THE PEOPLE DOING? Identify the appropriate action.

Use these words to complete the sentences:

addressing   expressing   listening   sitting   standing

1. The man at the podium is _____ an audience.

2. The man _____ to the speaker has his elbow on the table.

3. The speaker is _____ at the podium.

4. The honoree is _____ his thanks.

5. The next speaker is _____ at the table beside the podium.

D. WHAT DO THE PEOPLE LOOK LIKE? How would you describe these people?

Write Y (Yes) if the description is true. If it is not, rewrite the sentence to make it true.

1. _____ Both men are wearing suits.

2. _____ Only one man is wearing a tie.

3. _____ Only one man is wearing glasses.

4. _____ One man is dressed casually.

5. _____ The man behind the podium is wearing a hat.

6. _____ One man is wearing a dark suit.

7. _____ Both men have a lot of hair.

8. _____ The man sitting down has a handkerchief in his suit pocket.

PHOTO 3

A. WHO ARE THE PEOPLE? Look at the photo above. Make assumptions about the occupation or relationship of the people in the photo.

Write Y (Yes), N (No), or ? (Unsure) beside the following relationships or occupations.

1. _____ husband and wife

2. _____ brothers

3. _____ construction workers

4. _____ file clerks

5. _____ lawyer and client

6. _____ metal workers

7. _____ computer technicians

8. _____ doctor and patient

9. _____ building inspectors

10. _____ assembly line workers

11. _____ circus performers

12. _____ dock hands

B. WHERE ARE THE PEOPLE? Try to determine the setting. Pay attention to the prepositions such as *next to, in front of,* and *at.*

Write Y (Yes), N (No), or ? (Unsure) beside the following locations.

1. _____ at a construction site

2. _____ in a basement

3. _____ on the roof

4. _____ on a girder

5. _____ at the drug store

6. _____ at the payroll office

7. _____ on a support beam

8. _____ in a clinic

9. _____ by a telephone pole

10. _____ near a bridge

11. _____ on a trolley

12. _____ around back

C. WHAT ARE THE PEOPLE DOING? Identify the appropriate action.

Use these words to complete the sentences:

    constructing   following   holding   walking   watching

1. The construction workers are _____ where they are going.

2. They are _____ a new building.

3. They are _____ on to a support wire.

4. One man is _____ the other.

5. The workers are _____ across the support beam.

D. WHAT DO THE PEOPLE LOOK LIKE? How would you describe these people?

Write Y (Yes) if the description is true. If it is not, rewrite the sentence to make it true.

1. _____ Both men are wearing hard hats.

2. _____ Both men are wearing similar construction uniforms.

3. _____ One man is not wearing shoes.

4. _____ One man is wearing gloves.

5. _____ The man in front is wearing a sport coat.

6. _____ The man behind is wearing light colored pants.

7. _____ Both men have dark hard hats.

8. _____ Both men are wearing shorts.

PHOTO 4

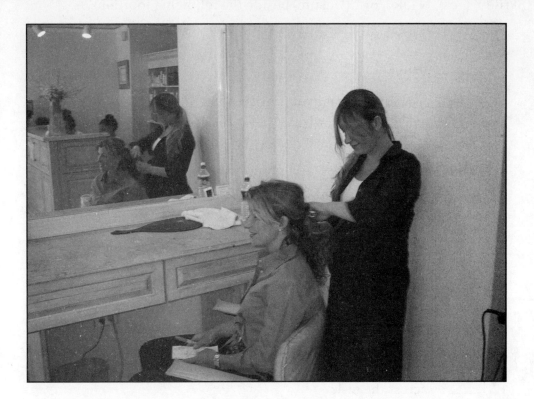

A. WHO ARE THE PEOPLE? Look at the photo above. Make assumptions about the occupation or relationship of the people in the photo.

Write Y (Yes), N (No), or ? (Unsure) beside the following relationships or occupations.

1. _____ aunt and niece

2. _____ mother and daughter

3. _____ customer and salesperson

4. _____ pharmacist and client

5. _____ doctor and patient

6. _____ TV technician and actress

7. _____ student and teacher

8. _____ security guard and electrician

9. _____ insurance salesperson and health care provider

10. _____ hairstylist and client

11. _____ strangers

12. _____ carpenter and homeowner

B. WHERE ARE THE PEOPLE? Try to determine the setting. Pay attention to the prepositions such as *next to, in front of, behind,* and *at.*

Write Y (Yes), N (No), or ? (Unsure) beside the following locations.

1. _____ in a chair

2. _____ behind the client

3. _____ in front of the mirror

4. _____ behind the door

5. _____ in the corner

6. _____ on top of the cabinet

7. _____ next to the shelf

8. _____ under the drawers

9. _____ beside the stylist

10. _____ at the hair salon

11. _____ inside the supermarket

12. _____ across the aisle

C. WHAT ARE THE PEOPLE DOING? Identify the appropriate action.

Use these words to complete the sentences:

     having   holding   looking   sitting   styling

1. The stylist is _____ the client's hair.

2. The client is _____ her hair styled.

3. The woman is _____ a pen and paper.

4. The haircutter is _____ at her client.

5. The customer is _____ in the chair.

D. WHAT DO THE PEOPLE LOOK LIKE? How would you describe these people?

Write Y (Yes) if the description is true. If it is not, rewrite the sentence to make it true.

1. _____ Both women are wearing white dresses.

2. _____ The stylist is wearing a dark skirt.

3. _____ Both women have hair across their eyes.

4. _____ Only one woman has long hair.

5. _____ The woman on the right is wearing a dark shirt.

6. _____ The woman on the left is wearing white pants.

7. _____ Both women are wearing glasses.

8. _____ The woman sitting down has dark hair.

PHOTOS OF THINGS

You will see photos of things in Part 1. You will hear statements about the things that may give information about:

- What are they?
- Where are they?
- What was done to them?
- What do they look like?

PHOTO 5

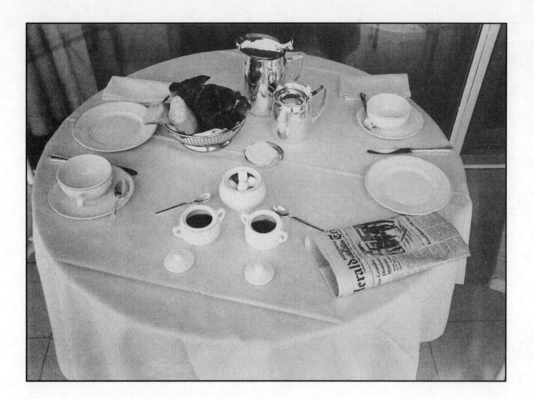

A. WHAT ARE THE THINGS? Look at the photo above. Make assumptions about what you see.

Write Y (Yes), N (No), or ? (Unsure) beside the following assumptions.

1. _____ There are flowers on the table.

2. _____ The newspaper is beside a plate.

3. _____ There are two napkins on the table.

4. _____ The coffee cups are to the left of the plates.

5. _____ There are three coffee cups.

6. _____ There is no tablecloth on the table.

7. _____ The table is set for breakfast.

8. _____ There is a basket of bread on the table.

9. _____ There are two lids on the table.

10. _____ There is a fork by the coffee cup.

11. _____ There is only one spoon on the table.

12. _____ There is a sugar bowl near the center of the table.

B. WHERE ARE THE THINGS? Pay attention to the prepositions such as *next to*, *in front of*, and *at*.

Write Y (Yes), N (No), or ? (Unsure) beside the following locations.

1. _____ The cups and saucers are on the table.

2. _____ The spoons are under the saucer.

3. _____ The newspaper is beside the coffeepot.

4. _____ The place settings are opposite one another.

5. _____ The bread basket is close to the newspaper.

6. _____ The sugar bowl is between two pots of jam.

7. _____ The lids are on the jam pots.

8. _____ The small pitcher is beside the large one.

9. _____ The tablecloth is beside the table.

10. _____ The knife is between the plate and the saucer.

11. _____ The napkins are both to the right of the saucers.

12. _____ The sugar bowl is near the center of the table.

C. WHAT WAS DONE TO THESE THINGS?

Use these words to complete the sentences:

     filled   folded   placed   set   took off

1. The _____ newspaper is on the table.

2. Someone _____ the lids to the jam pots.

3. The table is _____ for breakfast.

4. The basket is _____ with bread.

5. The spoons were _____ on the saucers.

D. WHAT DO THE THINGS LOOK LIKE? How would you describe these things?

Write Y (Yes) if the description is true. If it is not, rewrite the sentence to make it true.

1. _____ The saucers are smaller than the plates.

2. _____ Both cups are the same size.

3. _____ The pitchers are the same size.

4. _____ The table is square.

5. _____ The tablecloth is a dark color.

6. _____ The bread basket is full.

7. _____ The coffee cups are empty.

8. _____ The plates are dirty.

PHOTO 6

A. WHAT ARE THE THINGS? Look at the photo above. Make assumptions about what you see.

Write Y (Yes), N (No), or ? (Unsure) beside the following assumptions.

1. _____ A television is in the corner.

2. _____ A dresser drawer is open.

3. _____ The window is open.

4. _____ A screen covers the window.

5. _____ There is a floor lamp beside the chair.

6. _____ There is a table lamp on the coffee table.

7. _____ There is a coffeepot on the dresser.

8. _____ There is an armchair beside the dresser.

9. _____ There are clothes on the floor.

10. _____ A suitcase is open on the bed.

11. _____ The television is off.

12. _____ The floor is carpeted.

B. WHERE ARE THE THINGS? Pay attention to the prepositions such as *next to, in front of,* and *at.*

Write Y (Yes), N (No), or ? (Unsure) beside the following locations.

1. _____ A floor lamp is beside the armchair.

2. _____ The television is in the center of the room.

3. _____ The dresser is against the wall.

4. _____ The table lamp is on the dresser.

5. _____ The television is on a stand.

6. _____ The bed is across from the dresser.

7. _____ The coffee table is in front of the armchair.

8. _____ The armchair is behind the floor lamp.

9. _____ There is an article of clothing on the bed.

10. _____ The TV is in front of the dresser.

11. _____ The stand is under the TV.

12. _____ The sitting area is next to the bed.

C. WHAT WAS DONE TO THESE THINGS?

Use these words to complete the sentences:

cleaned   made up   opened   placed   turned on

1. The television set was _____ by the porter.

2. The drawers of the dresser were _____ by the guests.

3. The carpet was _____ before the guests arrived.

4. The bed was _____ for the guests.

5. The coffeepot was _____ on the dresser.

D. WHAT DO THE THINGS LOOK LIKE? How would you describe these things?

Write Y (Yes) if the description is true. If it is not, rewrite the sentence to make it true.

1. _____ The television is larger than the dresser.

2. _____ The lamps are all the same size.

3. _____ The bed is not made.

4. _____ The chair doesn't have any arms.

5. _____ The windows are covered with screens.

6. _____ The dresser is made of wood.

7. _____ The carpet is not wall-to-wall.

8. _____ The coffee table has four legs.

PHOTO 7

A. WHAT ARE THE THINGS? Look at the photo above. Make assumptions about what you see.

Write Y (Yes), N (No), or ? (Unsure) beside the following assumptions.

1. _____ A bicycle is resting against the side of a wall.

2. _____ The house is several stories tall.

3. _____ There are three windows in the picture.

4. _____ There are many signs on the wall.

5. _____ The road passes in front of the house.

6. _____ There are signs in the windows.

7. _____ There is a basket on the bicycle.

8. _____ There are shingles on the roof.

9. _____ The bicycle has two wheels.

10. _____ There are flowers in the garden.

11. _____ Only one person lives in this house.

12. _____ The house is in a small city.

B. WHERE ARE THE THINGS? Pay attention to the prepositions such as *next to, in front of,* and *at.*

Write Y (Yes), N (No), or ? (Unsure) beside the following locations.

1. _____ The bicycle is parked between two windows.

2. _____ The street address is written on the sign.

3. _____ The bicycle is directly below the signs.

4. _____ The hours of operation are written on the signs in the window.

5. _____ The roof is above the windows.

6. _____ The bike is in front of the windows.

7. _____ The wall between the windows is blank.

8. _____ The bench is against the wall.

9. _____ There are signs in the windows.

10. _____ The bicycle is kept in a garage.

11. _____ There are two signs to the right of a window.

12. _____ The motorbike is beside the bicycle.

C. WHAT WAS DONE TO THESE THINGS?

Use these words to complete the sentences:

closed   hanging   leaning   made up   painted

1. The bike is _____ against the wall.

2. The "open" sign is _____ below the shop sign.

3. The windows are _____.

4. The roof is _____ of shingles.

5. The wall was _____ white.

D. What do the things look like? How would you describe these things?

Write Y (Yes) if the description is true. If it is not, rewrite the sentence to make it true.

1. _____ A small sign hangs below a larger sign.

2. _____ There are no curtains hanging in the windows.

3. _____ The small "open" sign is straight.

4. _____ The road is a dirt road.

5. _____ The windows are different shapes.

6. _____ The front wheel of the bicycle is smaller than the rear wheel.

7. _____ The window on the right is lower than the one on the left.

8. _____ There is a basket on the handlebars of the bike.

PHOTO 8

A. WHAT ARE THE THINGS? Look at the photo above. Make assumptions about what you see.

Write Y (Yes), N (No), or ? (Unsure) beside the following assumptions.

1. _____ There is a bridge across a canal.

2. _____ There is a walkway beside the canal.

3. _____ Many people are walking on the walkway.

4. _____ The canal is lined with trees on both sides.

5. _____ The canal is used to transport goods.

6. _____ There are some streetlamps along the canal.

7. _____ People are walking beside the water.

8. _____ The buildings are reflected in the water.

9. _____ Electric wires run underground.

10. _____ There are four lanes on the road.

11. _____ Many boats are in the canal.

12. _____ The water is very deep.

B. WHERE ARE THE THINGS? Pay attention to the prepositions such as *next to, in front of,* and *under.*

Write Y (Yes), N (No), or ? (Unsure) beside the following locations.

1. _____ The canal passes under the bridge.

2. _____ The fence is between the canal and the walkway.

3. _____ There is a small park to the right of the canal.

4. _____ There is a tall building beyond the park.

5. _____ There are two bridges in the distance.

6. _____ A fence separates the road from the walkway.

7. _____ Electric poles and wires run along the road.

8. _____ A dotted line runs down the middle of the road.

9. _____ The first bridge crosses over the road.

10. _____ There are no buildings on the right side of the road.

11. _____ There are ladders on both sides of the canal.

12. _____ There is a small strip of earth between the walkway and the fence on the right.

C. WHAT WAS DONE TO THESE THINGS?

Use these words to complete the sentences:

    divides   planted   runs   separates   strung

1. Water _____ through the canal.

2. A fence _____ the walkway from the canal.

3. The park was _____ with trees.

4. Electric wires are _____ along the poles.

5. A dotted line _____ the lanes on the road.

D. WHAT DO THE THINGS LOOK LIKE? How would you describe these things?

Write Y (Yes) if the description is true. If it is not, rewrite the sentence to make it true.

1. _____ The walkway and the canal are on the same level.

2. _____ The park on the left has many trees.

3. _____ The bridge further away is smaller.

4. _____ The canal curves through the city.

5. _____ The fence is a solid fence.

6. _____ The building beyond the bridge is about seven stories tall.

7. _____ Both the road and the walkway are paved.

8. _____ The road is full of cars.

STRATEGY REVIEW

In the exercises for Part 1, you learned what to ask yourself when analyzing a photo. Knowing what to ask yourself will help you choose the right answer.

For photos of people, ask yourself:

Who are they?
Where are they?
What are they doing?
What do they look like?

For photos of things, ask yourself:

What are they?
Where are they?
What was done to them?
What do they look like?

In the exercises for Part 1, you saw how certain answer choices try to confuse you. Here are the ways that choices may seem correct to you.

■ words that sound like the correct answer

■ words related to the correct answer

■ words used out of context

■ incorrect details provided

■ incorrect inferences made

Look at the examples on the following pages.

Example 1

(A) The carpenter is hammering a nail.   (correct answer)
(B) The snail is crawling up the wall.   (similar sound *snail/nail*)
(C) The carpet is nailed to the wall.   (similar sound *carpet/carpenter; nail*
                                          and *wall* used in a different context)
(D) The handyman is putting away   (*handyman* and *tools* related to
     his tools.   correct answer)

Example 2

(A) The tourist is buying some postcards.   (*tourist* used in a different context)
(B) The passenger is checking his bags.   (incorrect inference)
(C) The traveler is pushing his luggage   (incorrect detail)
ahead of him.
(D) The man is pulling his suitcase   (correct answer)
behind him.

STRATEGY PRACTICE

DIRECTIONS: Look at these photos and listen to the four statements. Choose the statement that most closely matches the photo. Listen again and see if you can recognize how an answer choice tries to confuse you.

1.

Ⓐ   Ⓑ   Ⓒ   Ⓓ

2.

Ⓐ   Ⓑ   Ⓒ   Ⓓ

3.

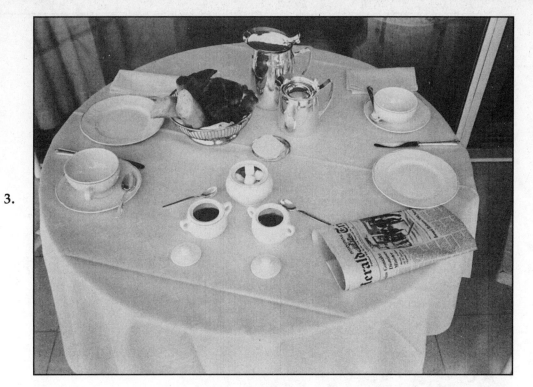

Ⓐ   Ⓑ   Ⓒ   Ⓓ

4.

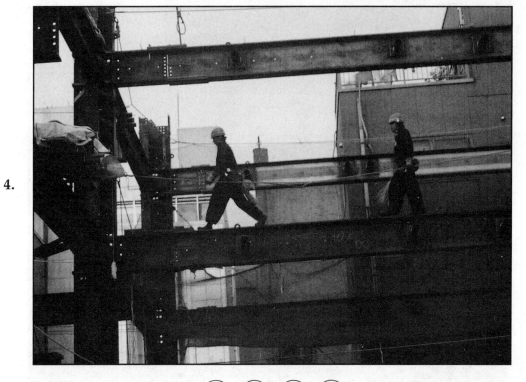

Ⓐ   Ⓑ   Ⓒ   Ⓓ

5.

Ⓐ　Ⓑ　Ⓒ　Ⓓ

6.

Ⓐ　Ⓑ　Ⓒ　Ⓓ

7.

Ⓐ   Ⓑ   Ⓒ   Ⓓ

8.

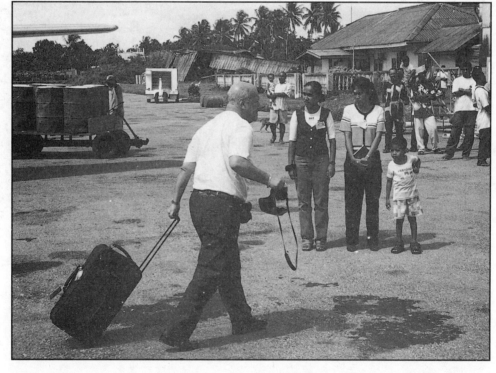

Ⓐ   Ⓑ   Ⓒ   Ⓓ

9.

Ⓐ   Ⓑ   Ⓒ   Ⓓ

10.

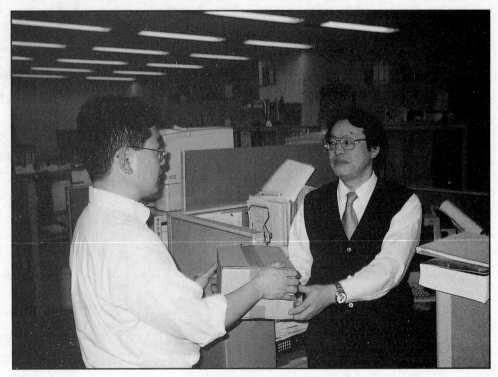

Ⓐ   Ⓑ   Ⓒ   Ⓓ

PART 2—QUESTION-RESPONSE

These are the directions for Part 2 of the new TOEIC® test. Study them now. If you understand these directions now, you will not have to read them during the test.

PART 2

Directions: You will hear a question or statement and three responses spoken in English. They will not be printed in your test book and will be spoken only one time. Select the best response to the question or statement and mark the letter (A), (B), or (C) on your answer sheet.

Sample Answer

Example

You will hear: Where is the meeting room?

You will also hear: (A) To meet the new director.
(B) It's the first room on the right.
(C) Yes, at two o'clock.

Your best response to the question "Where is the meeting room?" is choice (B), "It's the first room on the right," so (B) is the correct answer. You should mark answer (B) on your answer sheet.

In this chapter you will learn how certain words will help you identify the purpose of a question. These are the purposes you will learn about:

- identifying time
- identifying people
- identifying an opinion
- identifying a choice
- identifying a suggestion
- identifying a reason
- identifying a location

IDENTIFYING TIME

You will hear questions that ask about time. Some questions will begin with *When* or *How long*. Others will be *yes/no* questions. The answer to a *yes/no* question is sometimes a statement without *yes* or *no*.

Example 1

When did she leave for work?
- (A)   About an hour ago.
- (B)   It doesn't work.
- (C)   As soon as he's ready.

The correct answer is (A). Choice (B) tries to confuse you by repeating the word *work*. Choice (C) tries to confuse you by changing the tense to present and the person to *he*.

Example 2

Haven't you filled out the application yet?
- (A)   They filled the jet with fuel.
- (B)   I've been too busy.
- (C)   I applied it over the surface.

The correct answer is (B). Note the *no* is implied in the response. The person was too busy to take the time to complete the application. Choice (A) tries to confuse you by repeating the word *filled* and using the similar-sounding word *jet* for *yet*. Choice (C) tries to confuse you by using *applied* with a different meaning.

Example 3

We'll leave at 5, so try to be on time.
- (A)   That leaves five of us.
- (B)   I'm never late. I'll be there at 4:59.
- (C)   The plane is on time.

The correct answer is (B). The speaker suggests that the listener will not be on time, but the listener responds that he/she is never late and will in fact be there one minute early. Choice (A) tries to confuse you by repeating the word *leave* but with a different meaning. The word *five* is repeated, but here it means *people* not *time of day*. Choice (C) repeats the phrase *on time* but in a different context.

These are some words you might hear in questions about time:

when	early
how long	morning, noon, afternoon, evening, night
what time	at 1:00, 2:30 . . .
yet	today, this week, this month, this year
still	yesterday, last week, last month, last year
on time	tomorrow
late	

Practice: Identifying Time

DIRECTIONS: Listen to the questions, which are followed by three responses. They will not be written out for you. Choose the best response to each question.

1. (A) (B) (C)
2. (A) (B) (C)
3. (A) (B) (C)
4. (A) (B) (C)
5. (A) (B) (C)
6. (A) (B) (C)
7. (A) (B) (C)
8. (A) (B) (C)
9. (A) (B) (C)
10. (A) (B) (C)

IDENTIFYING PEOPLE

You will hear questions that ask about people. Some questions will begin with *Who* or *Whose*. Others will be *yes/no* questions. The answer to a *yes/no* question is sometimes a statement without *yes* or *no*.

Example 1

Who's responsible for making the bank deposits?
(A) Ms. Rotelli always makes the deposits.
(B) We'll send our response soon.
(C) We use the National Bank.

The correct answer is (A). Choice (B) tries to confuse you with the similar-sounding word *response* for *responsible.* Choice (C) tries to confuse you by repeating the word *bank*.

Example 2

Are you in charge of this project?
(A) No, they only charged us 100 dollars.
(B) No, Mrs. Ono is the supervisor.
(C) No, it's not very large.

The correct answer is (B). Choice (A) tries to confuse you by using *charged* but with a different meaning. Choice (C) tries to confuse you with the similar-sounding word *large* for *charge*.

Example 3

I called the contractor to repair the leak.
(A) You should have called a plumber.
(B) His contract is due next week.
(C) The telephone repair person contacted me.

The correct answer is (A). A plumber can repair a leaking pipe. Choice (B) tries to confuse you by using the word *contract* with a different meaning and using the similar-sounding word *week* for *leak*. Choice (C) tries to confuse you by using the associated word *telephone* for *called* and the similar-sounding word *contacted* for *contractor*. The word *repair* is repeated.

These are some words you might hear in questions about people:

who
whose
who's
name
an occupation title

Practice: Identifying People

DIRECTIONS: Listen to the following questions, which are followed by three responses. They will not be written out for you. Choose the best response to each question.

1. Ⓐ Ⓑ Ⓒ
2. Ⓐ Ⓑ Ⓒ
3. Ⓐ Ⓑ Ⓒ
4. Ⓐ Ⓑ Ⓒ
5. Ⓐ Ⓑ Ⓒ
6. Ⓐ Ⓑ Ⓒ
7. Ⓐ Ⓑ Ⓒ
8. Ⓐ Ⓑ Ⓒ
9. Ⓐ Ⓑ Ⓒ
10. Ⓐ Ⓑ Ⓒ

IDENTIFYING AN OPINION

You will hear questions that ask someone's opinion. Some questions will begin with *What* or *How*. Others will be *yes/no* questions. The answer to a *yes/no* question is sometimes a statement without *yes* or *no*.

Example 1

What did you think of the movie?
(A) I liked it a lot.
(B) I saw it yesterday.
(C) I moved the furniture myself.

The correct answer is (A). Choice (B) tries to confuse you by giving an inappropriate response to an opinion question. Choice (C) tries to confuse you with the similar-sounding word *moved* for *movie*.

Example 2

Do you think we need to hire more people?
(A) Yes, I'd like to hear more about it.
(B) Yes, we need a few more employees.
(C) Yes, prices are getting higher.

The correct answer is (B). Choice (A) tries to confuse you with the similar-sounding word *hear* for *hire*. Choice (C) tries to confuse you with *higher*, which sounds the same as *hire*.

Example 3

I loved this book.
(A) I like to cook, too.
(B) Book me a ticket, please.
(C) I didn't think it was so great.

The correct answer is (C). The listener does not agree with the speaker. Choice (A) uses the associated word *like* for *love* and the similar-sounding word *cook* for *book*. Choice (B) repeats the word *book* but with a different meaning and as a verb, not a noun.

These are some words you might hear in questions about an opinion:

what	believe
how	your opinion
why	like/didn't like
because	love
think	

DIRECTIONS: Listen to the questions, which are followed by three responses. They will not be written out for you. Choose the best response to each question.

1. Ⓐ Ⓑ Ⓒ
2. Ⓐ Ⓑ Ⓒ
3. Ⓐ Ⓑ Ⓒ
4. Ⓐ Ⓑ Ⓒ
5. Ⓐ Ⓑ Ⓒ
6. Ⓐ Ⓑ Ⓒ
7. Ⓐ Ⓑ Ⓒ
8. Ⓐ Ⓑ Ⓒ
9. Ⓐ Ⓑ Ⓒ
10. Ⓐ Ⓑ Ⓒ

IDENTIFYING A CHOICE

You will hear questions that give someone a choice. Some questions will begin with *What* or other *wh*-question words. Others will be *yes/no* questions. The answer to a *yes/no* question is sometimes a statement without *yes* or *no*. These questions usually will have two choices joined by *or*.

Example 1

Which does that author write more of, poems or essays?
(A) She almost always writes poems.
(B) I read those poems yesterday.
(C) She owns two homes.

The correct answer is (A). Choice (B) tries to confuse you by repeating the word *poems*. Choice (C) tries to confuse you with the similar-sounding word *homes* for *poems*.

Example 2

Do you prefer yellow or blue?
(A) Yes, I do.
(B) He's a very nice fellow.
(C) Blue's my favorite color.

The correct answer is (C). Choice (A) tries to confuse you by giving an inappropriate response to a choice question. Choice (C) tries to confuse you with the similar-sounding word *fellow* for *yellow*.

Example 3

I can't decide between the morning flight or the afternoon one.
(A) We took a ride yesterday afternoon.
(B) Go before noon. It's less crowded.
(C) There are more flies at noon.

The correct answer is (B). The listener gives the speaker a reason to choose the morning flight. Choice (A) tries to confuse you by using the similar-sounding word *ride* for *decide*. Choice (C) uses the similar-sounding words *more* for *morning*, *flies* for *flight*, and *noon* for *afternoon*.

These are some words you might hear in questions that give someone a choice:

what
which
or
prefer
rather

Practice: Identifying a Choice

 DIRECTIONS: Listen to the questions, which are followed by three responses. They will not be written out for you. Choose the best response to each question.

1. (A) (B) (C)
2. (A) (B) (C)
3. (A) (B) (C)
4. (A) (B) (C)
5. (A) (B) (C)
6. (A) (B) (C)
7. (A) (B) (C)
8. (A) (B) (C)
9. (A) (B) (C)
10. (A) (B) (C)

IDENTIFYING A SUGGESTION

You will hear questions that give a suggestion. Some questions will begin with *Why* or *Let's*. Others will be *yes/no* questions. The answer to a *yes/no* question is sometimes a statement without *yes* or *no*. Most of the questions that give a suggestion are *yes/no* questions.

Example 1

Why don't we take a break?
(A) That sounds like a good idea.
(B) It didn't break.
(C) This is very good cake.

The correct answer is (A). Choice (B) tries to confuse you by using the word *break* with a different meaning. Choice (C) tries to confuse you by using the similar-sounding word *cake* for *break*.

Example 2

Can I get you something to eat?
(A) Yes, I picked up something.
(B) Thank you. That's very kind of you.
(C) We ate everything on the table.

The correct answer is (B). Choices (A) and (C) try to confuse you by incorrectly answering a present tense question with a past tense answer.

Example 3

Let's not take a taxi.
(A) Yes, I'd rather walk.
(B) The tax is included.
(C) I wrote a note to Tashi.

The correct answer is (A). The speaker made the suggestion not to take a taxi and the listener agreed. Choice (B) tries to confuse you by using the similar-sounding word *tax* for *taxi*. Choice (C) tries to confuse you by using the similar-sounding phrase *note to* with *not take* and *taxi* with *Tashi*.

These are some words you might hear in questions giving a suggestion:

why don't we	how about
why don't you	should
let's	ought to
what about	

Practice: Identifying a Suggestion

 DIRECTIONS: Listen to the questions or statements, which are followed by three responses. They will not be written out for you. Choose the best response to each question or statement.

1. (A) (B) (C)
2. (A) (B) (C)
3. (A) (B) (C)
4. (A) (B) (C)
5. (A) (B) (C)
6. (A) (B) (C)
7. (A) (B) (C)
8. (A) (B) (C)
9. (A) (B) (C)
10. (A) (B) (C)

IDENTIFYING A REASON

You will hear questions that ask for a reason. Some questions will begin with *Why*. Others will be *yes/no* questions. The answer to a *yes/no* question is sometimes a statement without *yes* or *no*.

Example 1

Why didn't you make the dinner reservation?
(A) I reserved my hotel room.
(B) I eat dinner at six.
(C) I forgot the name of the restaurant.

The correct answer is (C). Choice (A) tries to confuse you by using the word *reserved* in a different context. Choice (B) tries to confuse you by repeating the word *dinner*.

Example 2

Aren't you working late again tonight?
(A) No, I have to go home early.
(B) I left at eight o'clock.
(C) Wait until tomorrow night.

The correct answer is (A). Choice (B) tries to confuse you by answering incorrectly with the past tense. Choice (C) tries to confuse you by using the similar-sounding words *wait* for *late* and *night* for *tonight*.

Example 3

I can't drive without my glasses.
(A) Can you dive, but not swim?
(B) The glasses are full of water.
(C) And I don't have a license.

The correct answer is (C). The reason the speaker can't drive is he doesn't have his eyeglasses. The listener can't drive because he doesn't have a driver's license. Choice (A) uses the similar-sounding word *dive* for *drive*. Choice (B) uses *water glasses* instead of *eyeglasses*.

These are some words you might hear in questions asking for a reason:

why
why didn't
excuse
reason

Practice: Identifying a Reason

DIRECTIONS: Listen to the questions, which are followed by three responses. They will not be written out for you. Choose the best response to each question.

1. Ⓐ Ⓑ Ⓒ
2. Ⓐ Ⓑ Ⓒ
3. Ⓐ Ⓑ Ⓒ
4. Ⓐ Ⓑ Ⓒ
5. Ⓐ Ⓑ Ⓒ
6. Ⓐ Ⓑ Ⓒ
7. Ⓐ Ⓑ Ⓒ
8. Ⓐ Ⓑ Ⓒ
9. Ⓐ Ⓑ Ⓒ
10. Ⓐ Ⓑ Ⓒ

You will hear questions that ask about a location. Some questions will begin with *What* or *Where*. Others will be *yes/no* questions. The answer to a *yes/no* question is sometimes a statement without *yes* or *no*.

Example 1

What about moving the desk next to the door?
(A) There isn't enough room.
(B) I didn't open the door.
(C) He's next in line.

The correct answer is (A). Choices (B) and (C) try to confuse you by repeating the words *door* and *next*.

Example 2

Can you tell me how to get to the post office?
(A) OK, I'll wait in your office.
(B) Yes, get me some stamps.
(C) Sure. Go to the corner and take a right.

The correct answer is (C). Choice (A) tries to confuse you by repeating the word *office*. Choice (B) tries to confuse you by using the word *get* but with a different meaning.

Example 3

I left my pen on your desk.
(A) My dogs are in the pen.
(B) I put it in the drawer.
(C) No, I left at eleven.

The correct answer is (B). The location of the pen moved from the desk to the desk drawer. Choice (A) repeats *pen* but with a different meaning. Choice (C) repeats the word *left* with a different meaning and uses the similar-sounding word *eleven* for *pen*.

These are some words you might hear in questions asking about a location.

what
where
how far
next to
beside
under
over
at
near
far
by
behind
right
left
names of places

Practice: Identifying a Location

DIRECTIONS: Listen to the questions, which are followed by three responses. They will not be written out for you. Choose the best response to each question.

1. Ⓐ Ⓑ Ⓒ
2. Ⓐ Ⓑ Ⓒ
3. Ⓐ Ⓑ Ⓒ
4. Ⓐ Ⓑ Ⓒ
5. Ⓐ Ⓑ Ⓒ
6. Ⓐ Ⓑ Ⓒ
7. Ⓐ Ⓑ Ⓒ
8. Ⓐ Ⓑ Ⓒ
9. Ⓐ Ⓑ Ⓒ
10. Ⓐ Ⓑ Ⓒ

STRATEGY REVIEW

In the exercises for Part 2, you learned how certain words would help you identify the purpose of a question. Knowing these words will help you choose the right answer. Listen for words that identify:

- time, such as *when, how long, what time*, etc.
- people, such as *who, whose, who's*, etc.
- an opinion, such as *what, how, why*, etc.
- a choice, such as *what, which, or*, etc.
- a suggestion, such as *why, let's, what about*, etc.
- a reason, such as *why, excuse, reason*, etc.
- a location, such as *what, where, how far*, etc.

In the exercises for Part 2, you saw how certain answer choices try to confuse you. Here are the ways that choices may seem correct to you.

- Some choices have words that sound similar.
- Some choices repeat words.
- Some choices have words used in a different context.
- Some choices use incorrect verb tense or person.
- Some choices are an inappropriate response to the type of question.

Look at these examples:

Example 1

Mary is never late for her meetings.
  (A) He is always on time.   (incorrect person)
  (B) Her meeting is running late.   (words used in a different context)
  (C) She's very punctual.   (correct answer)

Example 2

Are you hiring an assistant or a secretary?
  (A) I need both.   (correct answer)
  (B) Yes, I am.   (inappropriate response to choice question)
  (C) I was hired yesterday.   (incorrect verb tense and person)

Example 3

How can I get to the train station from here?
- (A) The radio station is a block away.   (word used in a different context)
- (B) You can take the A-4 bus.   (correct answer)
- (C) The plane leaves in ten minutes.   (words that sound similar)

STRATEGY PRACTICE

DIRECTIONS: Listen to the questions, which are followed by three responses. They will not be written out for you. Choose the best response to each question. Listen again and see if you can recognize how a choice tries to confuse you.

1. (A) (B) (C)
2. (A) (B) (C)
3. (A) (B) (C)
4. (A) (B) (C)
5. (A) (B) (C)
6. (A) (B) (C)
7. (A) (B) (C)
8. (A) (B) (C)
9. (A) (B) (C)
10. (A) (B) (C)
11. (A) (B) (C)
12. (A) (B) (C)
13. (A) (B) (C)
14. (A) (B) (C)
15. (A) (B) (C)
16. (A) (B) (C)
17. (A) (B) (C)
18. (A) (B) (C)
19. (A) (B) (C)
20. (A) (B) (C)

PART 3—CONVERSATIONS

These are the directions for Part 3 of the new TOEIC® test. Study them now. If you understand these directions now, you will not have to read them during the test.

PART 3

Directions: You will hear some conversations between two people. You will be asked to answer three questions about what the speakers say in each conversation. Select the best response to each question and mark the letter (A), (B), (C), or (D) on your answer sheet. The conversations will not be printed in your test book and will be spoken only one time.

IMPORTANT NOTE:
This chapter focuses on learning strategies for Part 3 of the new TOEIC. In this chapter there is only one question for each conversation. This one question focuses on a particular strategy. The Strategy Review at the end of this chapter has three questions for each conversation just like the new TOEIC.

In this chapter you will learn how certain words will help you identify the purpose of a question. These are the purposes you will learn about:

- identifying time
- identifying people
- identifying intent
- identifying the topic
- identifying a reason
- identifying a location
- identifying an opinion
- identifying stress and tone

IDENTIFYING TIME

On the new TOEIC test, one of the three questions for a conversation may ask about time. For example:

When will he go?
How often does she come?
How long will they stay?

Read the questions and the answer choices quickly before you listen to the conversation. When you listen to the conversation, listen for answers to the questions about time.

Example 1

SPEAKER A: You're expecting Jeff Tuesday morning, right?
SPEAKER B: No, he won't be here tomorrow. Not until the day after.
SPEAKER A: At least he'll be here for Wednesday night's reception.

When is Jeff coming to visit?   Ⓐ Ⓑ Ⓒ Ⓓ
(A) Today.
(B) Tomorrow.
(C) Tuesday.
(D) Wednesday.

The correct answer is (D). Tomorrow is Tuesday, and he is coming the day after on Wednesday. Choice (A) tries to confuse you with the similar sounding word *today* for *day*. Choice (B) is mentioned as the day he is NOT coming. Choice (C) is the original day he was to have come, but he is not coming on Tuesday.

Example 2

SPEAKER A: Is this a daily or a weekly newsletter?
SPEAKER B: Neither. It's a monthly.
SPEAKER A: Once every four weeks. That's enough time to read it.

How often does the magazine come out?   Ⓐ Ⓑ Ⓒ Ⓓ
(A) Every day.
(B) Once a week.
(C) Once every other week.
(D) Once a month.

The correct answer is (D). The magazine is a monthly. It is delivered once a month. Choice (A) means *daily*, which is mentioned, but Speaker B says it's not a daily. Choice (B) means *weekly*, which is mentioned, but Speaker B says it is not a weekly. Choice (C) is incorrect because it says *every other week*.

Look for these words in a question that asks about time:

when
how often
how soon
how long ago

Practice: Identifying Time

DIRECTIONS: Listen to the conversation and then choose the statement that best answers the question.

1. When did the package arrive?   Ⓐ Ⓑ Ⓒ Ⓓ
   (A) This morning.
   (B) Two days ago.
   (C) Last Tuesday.
   (D) On Friday.

2. How long ago did the speakers visit Paris?   Ⓐ Ⓑ Ⓒ Ⓓ
   (A) A month ago.
   (B) Two months ago.
   (C) A year ago.
   (D) Eight years ago.

3. When will Mark start his new job?   Ⓐ Ⓑ Ⓒ Ⓓ
   (A) This afternoon.
   (B) On Monday.
   (C) In eight days.
   (D) In two weeks.

4. How often does the woman travel to Tokyo?   Ⓐ Ⓑ Ⓒ Ⓓ
   (A) Once a month.
   (B) Four times a month.
   (C) Once a year.
   (D) Four times a year.

5. How soon will the contract be ready?   Ⓐ Ⓑ Ⓒ Ⓓ
   (A) By morning.
   (B) By this afternoon.
   (C) In three days.
   (D) In nine days.

6. How long ago did the man buy the telephone?   Ⓐ Ⓑ Ⓒ Ⓓ
   (A) A week ago.
   (B) Three weeks ago.
   (C) A year ago.
   (D) Five years ago.

7. When will the conference take place? Ⓐ Ⓑ Ⓒ Ⓓ
   (A) This afternoon.
   (B) Tomorrow.
   (C) On Friday.
   (D) Next month.

8. How often does Tim order office supplies? Ⓐ Ⓑ Ⓒ Ⓓ
   (A) Every two days.
   (B) Once a week.
   (C) Every ten days.
   (D) Once a month.

9. How soon will the car be ready? Ⓐ Ⓑ Ⓒ Ⓓ
   (A) This afternoon.
   (B) Tomorrow.
   (C) The day after tomorrow.
   (D) On Friday.

10. How long has the woman been waiting? Ⓐ Ⓑ Ⓒ Ⓓ
    (A) Ten minutes.
    (B) Fifteen minutes.
    (C) Thirty minutes.
    (D) Forty minutes.

IDENTIFYING PEOPLE

On the new TOEIC test, one of the three questions for a conversation may ask about people and their occupations. For example:

Who are the speakers?
What is his job?

Read the questions and the answer choices quickly before you listen to the conversation. When you listen to the conversation, listen for answers to the questions about people.

Example 1

SPEAKER A: I've made your hotel reservations and reconfirmed your flights.
SPEAKER B: What about transfers from the airport to the hotel?
SPEAKER A: I can get you a car and driver, or you could take a taxi.

What is the first speaker's occupation?   Ⓐ   Ⓑ   Ⓒ   Ⓓ
(A) A chauffer.
(B) A hotel clerk.
(C) A flight attendant.
(D) A travel agent.

The correct answer is (D). Choice (A) is associated with *car and driver*, which is mentioned in a different context in the conversation. Choice (B) is associated with *hotel reservations*. Choice (C) is associated with *flights*.

Example 2

SPEAKER A: Laura, can you help me figure out how many chairs we need for the seminar?
SPEAKER B: You should direct all your questions to John. He's the one in charge of this event.
SPEAKER A: Sorry. I just thought since you're the office manager, you would know.

Who is responsible for organizing the event?   Ⓐ   Ⓑ   Ⓒ   Ⓓ
(A) Laura.
(B) The director.
(C) John.
(D) The office manager.

The correct answer is (C). Choice (A) mentions *Laura*, but she says she is not in charge. Choice (B) tries to confuse you with the similar-sounding word *director* for *direct*. Choice (D) is Laura's occupation, and she has said she is not in charge.

Look for these words in a question that asks about people:

who

whom*

whose

job

name

*rarely used on the TOEIC test

Practice: Identifying People

DIRECTIONS: Listen to the conversation and then choose the statement that best answers the question.

1. Who received a promotion?   Ⓐ Ⓑ Ⓒ Ⓓ
   (A) Only Pat.
   (B) Only Sam.
   (C) Both Sam and Jim.
   (D) Sam, Jim, and Pat.

2. What is Ms. Fujita's job?   Ⓐ Ⓑ Ⓒ Ⓓ
   (A) She's the director.
   (B) She's the accountant.
   (C) She's the director's assistant.
   (D) She's the accountant's assistant.

3. Who is the man talking to?   Ⓐ Ⓑ Ⓒ Ⓓ
   (A) A waitress.
   (B) A grocery store clerk.
   (C) A friend.
   (D) A specialist.

4. Who left the telephone message?   Ⓐ Ⓑ Ⓒ Ⓓ
   (A) An accountant.
   (B) A painter.
   (C) A telephone operator.
   (D) An office manager.

5. Whose office is at the end of the hall?   Ⓐ Ⓑ Ⓒ Ⓓ
   (A) Cindy's boss's office.
   (B) Cindy's office.
   (C) John's boss's office.
   (D) John's office.

6. What is the new accountant's name? Ⓐ Ⓑ Ⓒ Ⓓ
   (A) Bill.
   (B) Bob.
   (C) Mr. Wilson.
   (D) Mrs. Ortega.

7. What is Frank's profession? Ⓐ Ⓑ Ⓒ Ⓓ
   (A) He's a lawyer.
   (B) He's an economist.
   (C) He's a student.
   (D) He's a professor.

8. Who is in the hospital? Ⓐ Ⓑ Ⓒ Ⓓ
   (A) Marsha.
   (B) Jim.
   (C) Linda.
   (D) Jim's wife.

9. Whose car is parked by the front door? Ⓐ Ⓑ Ⓒ Ⓓ
   (A) Martin's car.
   (B) Sandy's car.
   (C) The secretary's car.
   (D) The director's car.

10. What is the woman's job? Ⓐ Ⓑ Ⓒ Ⓓ
   (A) She's a bank teller.
   (B) She's a police officer.
   (C) She's a bus driver.
   (D) She's a mail carrier.

IDENTIFYING INTENT

On the new TOEIC® test, one of the three questions for a conversation may ask about a person's intent to do something. For example:

> What will she do?
> What does she plan on buying?

Read the questions and the answer choices quickly before you listen to the conversation. When you listen to the conversation, listen for answers to the questions about intent.

Example 1

> SPEAKER A: I'm going to the electronics store after lunch. Do you want to go?
> SPEAKER B: Sure. Are you getting something for your computer?
> SPEAKER A: No, I just need to pick up a new battery for my phone.

What does Speaker A want to purchase?
(A) Food.
(B) A computer.
(C) A battery.
(D) A phone.

The correct answer is (C). Choice (A) uses the word *food*, which is associated with *lunch* but isn't what she's going to buy. Choice (B), *computer,* is mentioned in *something for your computer,* but she says that's not what she will buy. Choice (D), *phone,* is mentioned, but it is the battery, not the phone itself, that she will buy.

Example 2

> SPEAKER A: Could you answer the phone for me this afternoon?
> SPEAKER B: Of course. Are you going to be in a meeting?
> SPEAKER A: No, I have to leave a little early to get to the bank before it closes.

What does she want to do?
(A) Buy clothes.
(B) Go to the bank.
(C) Go to a meeting.
(D) Answer the phones.

The correct answer is (B). Choice (A) tries to confuse you with the similar-sounding word *clothes* for *closes.* Choice (C), *go to a meeting,* is mentioned, but she says that she isn't going to do that. Choice (D) is what she asks her colleague to do.

Look for these words in a question that asks about intent:

plan
going to
will
probably

Practice: Identifying Intent

DIRECTIONS: Listen to the conversation and then choose the statement that best answers the question.

1. What do the speakers plan to do this Sunday?　　　Ⓐ　Ⓑ　Ⓒ　Ⓓ
   - (A) Watch a baseball game.
   - (B) See a movie.
   - (C) Go to a concert.
   - (D) Visit the capital.

2. What will the man probably do?　　　Ⓐ　Ⓑ　Ⓒ　Ⓓ
   - (A) Buy a new rug.
   - (B) Buy new furniture.
   - (C) Paint the old furniture.
   - (D) Get another office.

3. What is the woman going to do?　　　Ⓐ　Ⓑ　Ⓒ　Ⓓ
   - (A) Eat a pizza.
   - (B) Pick up her office.
   - (C) Put things in order.
   - (D) Make a delivery.

4. What will the man probably have?　　　Ⓐ　Ⓑ　Ⓒ　Ⓓ
   - (A) Some ice cream.
   - (B) Some hot tea.
   - (C) Some cold cuts.
   - (D) Some iced tea.

5. What form of transportation will the speakers use?　　　Ⓐ　Ⓑ　Ⓒ　Ⓓ
   - (A) Train.
   - (B) Walking.
   - (C) Bus.
   - (D) Cab.

6. How will the woman pay?　　　Ⓐ　Ⓑ　Ⓒ　Ⓓ
   - (A) With a money order.
   - (B) With a credit card.
   - (C) With cash.
   - (D) With a check.

7. What will the woman probably do?   Ⓐ Ⓑ Ⓒ Ⓓ
   (A) Turn off the air-conditioning.
   (B) Open the window.
   (C) Turn on the air-conditioning.
   (D) Close the window.

8. What will the man do?   Ⓐ Ⓑ Ⓒ Ⓓ
   (A) Buy a new machine.
   (B) Fix the old machine.
   (C) Plug the machine in.
   (D) Use his coworker's machine.

9. What does the woman want to do?   Ⓐ Ⓑ Ⓒ Ⓓ
   (A) Look at the movie schedule.
   (B) Borrow some paper.
   (C) Read the news.
   (D) Buy a newspaper.

10. What will the woman probably buy?   Ⓐ Ⓑ Ⓒ Ⓓ
   (A) A sweater.
   (B) A skirt.
   (C) A suit.
   (D) A dress.

IDENTIFYING THE TOPIC

On the new TOEIC® test, one of the three questions for a conversation may ask about the topic. For example:

What are they talking about?
What is the problem?

Read the questions and the answer choices quickly before you listen to the conversation. When you listen to the conversation, listen for answers to the questions about the topic.

Example 1

SPEAKER A: Would you like more coffee?
SPEAKER B: No! This coffee tastes terrible. Is the machine broken again?
SPEAKER A: No, I think it's just dirty. No one ever cleans it.

What is the problem?   Ⓐ   Ⓑ   Ⓒ   Ⓓ
(A) The coffee is cold.
(B) The machine is dirty.
(C) The machine is broken.
(D) There isn't any more coffee.

The correct answer is (B). Choice (A) repeats the word *coffee*, but the problem with the coffee is its taste, not its temperature. Choice (C) is mentioned as a possibility but is not the problem. Choice (D) tries to confuse you by repeating the word *more*.

Example 2

SPEAKER A: Give me your number and I'll call you later.
Speaker B: OK. It's 555-1331.
Speaker A: Is that home or office?

What are they discussing?   Ⓐ   Ⓑ   Ⓒ   Ⓓ
(A) A telephone number.
(B) An address.
(C) A letter.
(D) An office.

The correct answer is (A). Choice (B) uses *address*, which is associated with *home*. Choice (C) tries to confuse you with the similar-sounding word *letter* for *later*. Choice (D) tries to confuse you by repeating the word *office*.

Look for these words in a question that asks about the topic:

talking about
discussing
about

Practice: Identifying the Topic

DIRECTIONS: Listen to the conversation and then choose the statement that best answers the question.

1. What is wrong with the car?   (A) (B) (C) (D)
   (A) It has broken glass.
   (B) It has a flat tire.
   (C) It doesn't run fast.
   (D) It's out of gas.

2. What are the speakers talking about?   (A) (B) (C) (D)
   (A) A cake.
   (B) Some steak.
   (C) A diet.
   (D) The cook.

3. What is the problem with the restaurant? (A) (B) (C) (D)
   (A) It doesn't look nice.
   (B) It's too far away.
   (C) The service isn't good.
   (D) The food is bad.

4. What are the speakers discussing?   (A) (B) (C) (D)
   (A) Airplane tickets.
   (B) Movie tickets.
   (C) A hotel reservation.
   (D) Books.

5. What is the lecture about?   (A) (B) (C) (D)
   (A) How to speak in public.
   (B) How to save money.
   (C) How to buy a house.
   (D) How to live without a lot of money.

6. What are the speakers talking about?   (A) (B) (C) (D)
   (A) Going to the movies.
   (B) A TV show.
   (C) Eating dinner.
   (D) A snowstorm.

7. What is the problem with the hamburger?   (A) (B) (C) (D)
   (A) It doesn't taste good.
   (B) It's still in the kitchen.
   (C) It's undercooked.
   (D) It's burnt.

8. What are the speakers talking about? Ⓐ Ⓑ Ⓒ Ⓓ
   (A) Photocopy paper.
   (B) Money.
   (C) The newspaper.
   (D) Furniture.

9. What is the book about? Ⓐ Ⓑ Ⓒ Ⓓ
   (A) Earning money.
   (B) Managing your finances.
   (C) Finding a job.
   (D) Organizing your time.

10. What are the speakers discussing? Ⓐ Ⓑ Ⓒ Ⓓ
    (A) Going to work.
    (B) Going to a party.
    (C) Going out for dinner.
    (D) Going out for a drink.

IDENTIFYING A REASON

On the new TOEIC test, one of the three questions for a conversation may ask about a reason for doing something. For example:

Why is he going?
Why is she speaking softly?

Read the questions and the answer choices quickly before you listen to the conversation. When you listen to the conversation, listen for answers to the questions about the reason.

Example 1

SPEAKER A: Maria, I hear you're moving away. Did you get a new job?
SPEAKER B: No, I'm going back to school. I'm going to get a degree in economics.
SPEAKER A: Oh, yes. I hear the university in that city is very good.

Why is Maria moving to a new city? Ⓐ Ⓑ Ⓒ Ⓓ
(A) Because she got a new job.
(B) Because she wants to study at the university.
(C) Because the economy is bad.
(D) Because her old city isn't very good.

The correct answer is (B). Choice (A) repeats the words *a new job,* but Maria says that is not the reason she is moving. Choice (C) tries to confuse you by using the word *economy,* which is similar to *economics.* Choice (D) tries to confuse you by repeating the words *very good* in a different context.

Example 2

SPEAKER A: Look how late it is. I'll never get to the meeting on time.

SPEAKER B: Well, here comes the bus now, so you're on your way.

SPEAKER A: I'm still going to be late.

Why is Speaker A upset?   Ⓐ Ⓑ Ⓒ Ⓓ

(A) It's time to go home.

(B) He forgot to eat.

(C) He has to take the bus.

(D) He's going to arrive late.

The correct answer is (D). Choice (A) tries to confuse you by using the word *time* in a different context. Choice (B) tries to confuse you by using the similar-sounding word *eat* for *meeting*. Choice (C), *take the bus*, is mentioned, but it is not the reason that Speaker A is upset.

Look for this word in a question that asks about a reason:

why

Practice: Identifying a Reason

DIRECTIONS: Listen to the conversation and then choose the statement that best answers the question.

1. Why are there no chairs?   Ⓐ Ⓑ Ⓒ Ⓓ

   (A) The chairs haven't been ordered yet.

   (B) Nobody wants to sit down.

   (C) The chairs haven't arrived yet.

   (D) People prefer to sit on the floor.

2. Why will the man call the woman?   Ⓐ Ⓑ Ⓒ Ⓓ

   (A) Because he needs some help.

   (B) To invite her to dinner.

   (C) Because he's bored.

   (D) To arrange a meeting.

3. Why is the woman going to Hawaii?   Ⓐ Ⓑ Ⓒ Ⓓ

   (A) To spend her vacation.

   (B) To buy new clothes.

   (C) To attend a conference.

   (D) To visit friends.

4. Why did the woman arrive late?   Ⓐ Ⓑ Ⓒ Ⓓ

   (A) She was in an accident.

   (B) She had a flat tire.

   (C) She felt tired.

   (D) She was waiting for someone.

5. Why is the window closed? Ⓐ Ⓑ Ⓒ Ⓓ
   (A) It's cool outside.
   (B) The air-conditioning is on.
   (C) The room isn't warm enough.
   (D) The street is very noisy.

6. Why doesn't the man want to take the elevator? Ⓐ Ⓑ Ⓒ Ⓓ
   (A) The elevator is slow.
   (B) They're going down.
   (C) It's late.
   (D) He likes to walk.

7. Why is the man staying late at the office? Ⓐ Ⓑ Ⓒ Ⓓ
   (A) He has to finish his work.
   (B) He's expecting a phone call.
   (C) He has a day off tomorrow.
   (D) He isn't tired.

8. Why isn't the meeting in the conference room? Ⓐ Ⓑ Ⓒ Ⓓ
   (A) There aren't enough chairs.
   (B) It isn't big enough.
   (C) The office is more comfortable.
   (D) It's being painted.

9. Why does the woman suggest taking the subway? Ⓐ Ⓑ Ⓒ Ⓓ
   (A) The office is close.
   (B) A car is too fast.
   (C) Traffic is heavy.
   (D) It's late.

10. Why didn't the man eat lunch? Ⓐ Ⓑ Ⓒ Ⓓ
    (A) He forgot to eat.
    (B) He wasn't hungry.
    (C) He got to the cafeteria too late.
    (D) He didn't have time.

IDENTIFYING A LOCATION

On the new TOEIC test, one of the three questions for a conversation may ask about the location. For example:

Where are the speakers?
Where is the hotel?

Read the questions and the answer choices quickly before you listen to the conversation. When you listen to the conversation, listen for answers to the questions about the location.

Example 1

SPEAKER A: Are you going up?
SPEAKER B: Yes. Which floor do you want?
SPEAKER A: The fourth floor, please. I'm going to Dr. Roberts' office.

Where does this conversation take place? Ⓐ Ⓑ Ⓒ Ⓓ
(A) In an airplane.
(B) In an elevator.
(C) In a flower shop.
(D) In a doctor's office.

The correct answer is (B). Choice (A), *in an airplane*, is associated with *going up*. Choice (C) tries to confuse you by using the similar-sounding word *flower* for *floor*. Choice (D) repeats the words *doctor's office*, but that is where the speaker is going.

Example 2

SPEAKER A: Do you still have those books about art museums that I lent you?
SPEAKER B: Yes, but not here in the office. They're at home.
SPEAKER A: I really need them back soon. I have to return them to the library.

Where are the books now? Ⓐ Ⓑ Ⓒ Ⓓ
(A) At an art museum.
(B) In the office.
(C) At home.
(D) In the library.

The correct answer is (C). Choice (A) is mentioned as the topic of the books, not their location. Choice (B) is mentioned as a place where the books are not. Choice (C) is the place where the speaker will take the books.

Look for this word in a question that asks about location:

where

DIRECTIONS: Listen to the conversation and then choose the statement that best answers the question.

1. Where will the speakers get together?   (A) (B) (C) (D)
   (A) Downstairs.
   (B) At the park.
   (C) At the office.
   (D) At a café.

2. Where are the speakers?   (A) (B) (C) (D)
   (A) At a train station.
   (B) At a bus stop.
   (C) At a swimming pool.
   (D) At an airport.

3. Where does the conversation take place?   (A) (B) (C) (D)
   (A) In a hotel.
   (B) At an airport.
   (C) In a parking garage.
   (D) At a store.

4. Where did the man leave his phone?   (A) (B) (C) (D)
   (A) In the office.
   (B) At a restaurant.
   (C) In a cab.
   (D) On a bus.

5. Where will the man wait?   (A) (B) (C) (D)
   (A) Upstairs.
   (B) By the front door.
   (C) Outside.
   (D) Near the elevator.

6. Where does this conversation take place?   (A) (B) (C) (D)
   (A) On a bus.
   (B) In a cab.
   (C) At a fair.
   (D) In a store.

7. Where are the speakers?   (A) (B) (C) (D)
   (A) In a grocery store.
   (B) In a restaurant.
   (C) In a kitchen.
   (D) On an airplane.

8. Where are the speakers going? Ⓐ Ⓑ Ⓒ Ⓓ
   (A) To a bookstore.
   (B) To the library.
   (C) To school.
   (D) To the police station.

9. Where does this conversation take place? Ⓐ Ⓑ Ⓒ Ⓓ
   (A) In Los Angeles.
   (B) At an airport.
   (C) At a travel agency.
   (D) On an airplane.

10. Where are the speakers? Ⓐ Ⓑ Ⓒ Ⓓ
    (A) In an office.
    (B) In a gym.
    (C) In a garage.
    (D) In a park.

IDENTIFYING AN OPINION

On the new TOEIC test, one of the three questions for a conversation may ask about a speaker's opinion. For example:

What is her opinion about cooking?
What does the speaker think about soccer?

Read the questions and the answer choices quickly before you listen to the conversation. When you listen to the conversation, listen for answers to the questions about an opinion.

Example 1

SPEAKER A: I think I'll like working with the new manager. He's very efficient.
SPEAKER B: I agree with you, Max. And he's friendly, too.
SPEAKER A: I'm sure he's the most experienced person in this office.

What is Max's opinion of the manager? Ⓐ Ⓑ Ⓒ Ⓓ
(A) He's agreeable.
(B) He's friendly.
(C) He's efficient.
(D) He's inexperienced.

The correct answer is (C). Choice (A) tries to confuse you by using *agreeable*, related to but different in meaning from *agree*. Choice (B) is the opinion of Max's friend. Choice (D) sounds similar to what Max said but actually has the opposite meaning.

Example 2

SPEAKER A: What a movie. I've never laughed so hard.
SPEAKER B: It really was awfully funny.
SPEAKER A: I just love movies like that.

What is said about the movie?   (A) (B) (C) (D)
(A) It was hard to understand.
(B) It was funny.
(C) It was awful.
(D) It was about love.

The correct answer is (B). Choices (A), (C), and (D) try to confuse you by using the words *hard*, *awful*, and *love* but with different meanings.

Look for these words in a question that asks about an opinion:

think of
opinion
say about

Practice: Identifying an Opinion

DIRECTIONS: Listen to the conversation and then choose the statement that best answers the question.

1. What does the man think of the bus?   (A) (B) (C) (D)
   (A) It's inconvenient.
   (B) It's relaxing.
   (C) It's too expensive.
   (D) It's fast.

2. What do the speakers say about Bob?   (A) (B) (C) (D)
   (A) His work is good.
   (B) He's improving.
   (C) He talks too much.
   (D) He isn't doing a good job.

3. What is the speakers' opinion of the hotel?   (A) (B) (C) (D)
   (A) It's nice.
   (B) It isn't comfortable.
   (C) It's too big.
   (D) Its service could be better.

4. What do the speakers think of the weather?   (A) (B) (C) (D)
   (A) It's too warm.
   (B) There's too much snow.
   (C) It rains a lot.
   (D) It's too cold.

5. What do the speakers say about TV?   (A) (B) (C) (D)
   (A) It's boring.
   (B) There aren't many programs.
   (C) It's funny.
   (D) The programs are good.

6. What is the woman's opinion of the lecture?   (A) (B) (C) (D)
   (A) It wasn't enjoyable.
   (B) It was terrible.
   (C) It was interesting.
   (D) It wasn't long enough.

7. What does José say about his job?   (A) (B) (C) (D)
   (A) It's important.
   (B) It's too far away.
   (C) It's difficult.
   (D) It's like his old job.

8. What does Sally think of her Spanish class?   (A) (B) (C) (D)
   (A) She thinks it's too hard.
   (B) She likes it.
   (C) She thinks it's very easy.
   (D) She's having fun.

9. What do the speakers say about Bill?   (A) (B) (C) (D)
   (A) He's lazy.
   (B) He's sick today.
   (C) He's usually late.
   (D) He's usually right.

10. What does the man think of the pizza?   (A) (B) (C) (D)
    (A) It's not very good.
    (B) It's delicious.
    (C) It's terrible.
    (D) It's too greasy.

IDENTIFYING STRESS AND TONE

On the new TOEIC you will hear conversations where the speakers use tone or stress to indicate what they mean.

A statement can become a question if it is said with rising intonation.

Statement   You're going to work early.

Question   You're going to work early?

A statement spoken with rising intonation can mean (1) *Are you going to work early?* or (2) *Why are you going to work early?*

Intonation can be used to convey the speaker's feeling about something. *I love pizza* said with sarcastic intonation means *I hate pizza.*

Stress is used to emphasize the important part of a statement. In a sentence emphasized as: *I ate <u>ten</u> cookies,* the important information is the amount of cookies eaten (ten cookies, not five cookies). If the noun is emphasized as: *I ate ten <u>cookies</u>,* the important information is what was eaten (cookies, rather than sandwiches).

Read the question and the answer choices quickly before you listen to the conversation. When you listen to the conversation, listen for the meaning conveyed by the intonation and stress.

Example 1

SPEAKER A: You didn't like this movie?
SPEAKER B: I really like war movies (said with intonation of disgust).
SPEAKER A: I always thought you preferred them over comedies.

What does the second speaker think about war movies?
(A) She hasn't seen one.
(B) She likes them a lot.
(C) She prefers comedies.
(D) She hates them.

The correct answer is (D). *I really like war movies* said with an intonation of disgust really means that the speaker does not like war movies.

Example 2

> SPEAKER A: While you're out, will you get me a ten-cent stamp?
>
> SPEAKER B: Ten stamps. Sure. What denomination?
>
> SPEAKER A: No, <u>one</u> stamp, worth ten cents.

What does the first speaker want?   (A) (B) (C) (D)

(A) Ten cents.

(B) Ten stamps.

(C) One ten-cent stamp.

(D) A one-cent stamp.

The correct answer is (C). The stress on the word *one* in the last line makes it clear that that is the number of stamps she wants.

Practice: Identifying Stress and Tone

DIRECTIONS: Listen to the conversation and then choose the statement that best answers the question.

1. What is the problem?   (A) (B) (C) (D)

   (A) The repair person is tired.

   (B) The machine is broken.

   (C) They can't turn the machine on.

   (D) The machine is downstairs.

2. Why is the woman surprised?   (A) (B) (C) (D)

   (A) She's paying for dinner.

   (B) The man is offering to treat.

   (C) They're going out to eat.

   (D) The man is picking up the food.

3. What did the woman do last night?   (A) (B) (C) (D)

   (A) She went home.

   (B) She slept.

   (C) She stayed at the office.

   (D) She went to a restaurant.

4. What does the woman like to eat?   (A) (B) (C) (D)

   (A) Chicken.

   (B) Ham.

   (C) Fish.

   (D) Hamburgers.

5. What did the man think of the meeting? Ⓐ Ⓑ Ⓒ Ⓓ
   (A) It was informative.
   (B) It was a waste of time.
   (C) It was interesting.
   (D) It was useful.

6. What is the man going to do? Ⓐ Ⓑ Ⓒ Ⓓ
   (A) Cash a check.
   (B) Call the bank.
   (C) Count his money.
   (D) Go to the bank.

7. What does the man want to do? Ⓐ Ⓑ Ⓒ Ⓓ
   (A) Cook.
   (B) Stay inside.
   (C) Watch TV.
   (D) Go to a soccer game.

8. What does the woman think of the restaurant? Ⓐ Ⓑ Ⓒ Ⓓ
   (A) The food is delicious.
   (B) It's a popular place.
   (C) The food isn't good.
   (D) The prices aren't high.

9. What does the man think of the job? Ⓐ Ⓑ Ⓒ Ⓓ
   (A) It's a bad job.
   (B) It could be better.
   (C) It's a great job.
   (D) It could be more interesting.

10. What did the man do? Ⓐ Ⓑ Ⓒ Ⓓ
    (A) He left the office.
    (B) He finished his work.
    (C) He had some coffee.
    (D) He continued working.

STRATEGY REVIEW

In the exercises for Part 3, you learned how certain words would help you identify the purpose of a question. Knowing these words will help you choose the right answer. Listen for words that identify:

- time, such as *when, how long, what time,* etc.

- people, such as *who, whose, who's,* etc.

- intent, such as *plan, going to, will,* etc.

- the topic, such as *talking about, discussing, about,* etc.

- a reason, such as *why, what, or,* etc.

- a location, such as *where, what, how far,* etc.

- an opinion, such as *what, believe, think,* etc.

Remember to listen for tone and stress to identify meaning.

In the exercises for Part 3, you saw how certain answer choices try to confuse you. Here are the ways that choices may seem correct to you.

- words that sound like the correct answer

- words in a different context or with a different meaning

- incorrect details provided

- incorrect inferences made

- irrelevant details provided

Look at these examples:

Example 1

SPEAKER A: The prices at this restaurant are low, but the food's always cold.
SPEAKER B: I know, and the people who work here aren't very friendly.
SPEAKER A: Let's eat somewhere else.

What do they say about the restaurant?
(A)   The people are friendly.   (incorrect detail)
(B)   The prices are low.   (correct answer)
(C)   The food is old.   (sounds like correct answer)
(D)   The service is slow.   (sounds like correct answer)

Example 2

SPEAKER A: I'd like to book a flight to Santiago.
SPEAKER B: Certainly. When would you like to fly?
SPEAKER A: Next Monday. Can you make a hotel reservation for me, also?

What is Speaker B's occupation?
(A) Travel agent.   (correct answer)
(B) Pilot.   (incorrect inference)
(C) Hotel manager.   (incorrect detail)
(D) Librarian.   (incorrect inference)

Example 3

SPEAKER A: How's your accounting class, Marvin?

SPEAKER B: The teacher's interesting, but the work is really hard.

SPEAKER A: Well, at least you're not bored.

What does Marvin say about his class?
(A) It's boring.   (incorrect detail)
(B) The chairs are hard.   (word used in a different context)
(C) There's too much work. (incorrect detail)
(D) The teacher is interesting. (correct answer)

STRATEGY PRACTICE

DIRECTIONS: Listen to the conversations. You will answer three questions about each conversation. Choose the best answer to each question. Listen again and see if you can recognize how a choice tries to confuse you.

1. How long have the speakers been waiting?   Ⓐ Ⓑ Ⓒ Ⓓ
   (A) Two minutes.
   (B) Fifteen minutes.
   (C) Fifty minutes.
   (D) Sixty minutes.

2. What are they buying?   Ⓐ Ⓑ Ⓒ Ⓓ
   (A) Shirts.
   (B) Skirts.
   (C) Shorts.
   (D) Wallets.

3. What will they use to pay for their purchases?   Ⓐ Ⓑ Ⓒ Ⓓ
   (A) Money order.
   (B) Credit card.
   (C) Check.
   (D) Cash.

4. According to the man, where will the speakers spend their vacation? Ⓐ Ⓑ Ⓒ Ⓓ
  - (A) At a friend's house.
  - (B) At a beach.
  - (C) At a lake.
  - (D) At a club.

5. What does the man want to do during his vacation? Ⓐ Ⓑ Ⓒ Ⓓ
  - (A) Visit a club.
  - (B) Go fishing.
  - (C) Swim.
  - (D) Rest.

6. How will they get there? Ⓐ Ⓑ Ⓒ Ⓓ
  - (A) By car.
  - (B) By bus.
  - (C) By train.
  - (D) By plane.

7. Why did Tina miss the meeting? Ⓐ Ⓑ Ⓒ Ⓓ
  - (A) She was sick.
  - (B) She arrived too late.
  - (C) She had an accident.
  - (D) Her car wouldn't start.

8. What does the woman want to discuss with Tina? Ⓐ Ⓑ Ⓒ Ⓓ
  - (A) A news report.
  - (B) A budget report.
  - (C) A traffic report.
  - (D) A weather report.

9. What time does the woman want to see Tina? Ⓐ Ⓑ Ⓒ Ⓓ
  - (A) 2:00.
  - (B) 7:00.
  - (C) 8:00.
  - (D) 11:00.

10. Where is the woman's new job?

    (A) At a pool.

    (B) At a school.

    (C) At an office.

    (D) At a hospital.

Ⓐ   Ⓑ   Ⓒ   Ⓓ

11. How does the woman feel about her new job?

    (A) She likes it.

    (B) She's bored.

    (C) She feels terrible.

    (D) She's uncomfortable.

Ⓐ   Ⓑ   Ⓒ   Ⓓ

12. How often does the woman get a paycheck?

    (A) Once a week.

    (B) Once a month.

    (C) Every two weeks.

    (D) Every two months.

Ⓐ   Ⓑ   Ⓒ   Ⓓ

13. What color is the jacket?

    (A) White.

    (B) Green.

    (C) Blue.

    (D) Red.

Ⓐ   Ⓑ   Ⓒ   Ⓓ

14. Why is the man returning it to the store?

    (A) The woman dislikes it.

    (B) It doesn't look good.

    (C) It doesn't fit right.

    (D) It lost a button.

Ⓐ   Ⓑ   Ⓒ   Ⓓ

15. How much did the man pay for it?

    (A) $70.

    (B) $300.

    (C) $317.

    (D) $370.

Ⓐ   Ⓑ   Ⓒ   Ⓓ

PART 4—TALKS

These are the directions for Part 4 of the new TOEIC® test. Study them now. If you understand these directions now, you will not have to read them during the test.

PART 4

Directions: You will hear some talks given by a single speaker. You will be asked to answer three questions about what the speaker says in each talk. Select the best response to each question and mark the letter (A), (B), (C), or (D) on your answer sheet. The talks will not be printed in your test book and will be spoken only one time.

In this chapter you will learn how certain words will help you identify the purpose of a question. These are the purposes you will learn about:

- identifying the sequence
- identifying the audience
- identifying a situation
- identifying the topic
- identifying a request

IDENTIFYING THE SEQUENCE

You will read questions that ask about sequence. Read the question and the answer choices quickly before you listen to the talk. When you listen to the talk, listen for answers to questions about sequence.

Example

We have arrived at our final destination. Please wait for the plane to come to a complete stop and the doors to open before leaving your seat. On entering the airport, you will go through Immigration. Please have your passport ready to show to the Immigration officer.

When can you leave your seat?   Ⓐ   Ⓑ   Ⓒ   Ⓓ
(A) After the doors are opened.
(B) After you complete some forms.
(C) After your passport is ready.
(D) After you enter the airport.

The correct answer is (A). Choice (B) tries to confuse you by repeating the word *complete* in a different context. Choices (C) and (D) repeat details of the talk that are not related to the question.

Look for these words in a question that asks about sequence:

when
before
after
first
last

Practice: Identifying the Sequence

DIRECTIONS: Listen to the talk and then choose the statement that best answers the question.

1. What should you do before answering the questions?
   (A) Write carefully.
   (B) Check the answer sheet.
   (C) Turn the test over.
   (D) Read the directions.

   Ⓐ Ⓑ Ⓒ Ⓓ

2. What will happen after the concert?
   (A) Refreshments will be served.
   (B) A professor will give a talk.
   (C) The director will introduce someone.
   (D) People will discuss their hobbies.

   Ⓐ Ⓑ Ⓒ Ⓓ

3. What should you do when entering the building?
   (A) Read the signs.
   (B) Get a pass.
   (C) Go immediately to your destination.
   (D) Contact your company.

   Ⓐ Ⓑ Ⓒ Ⓓ

4. What should you do before you pay?
   (A) Check the size of your items.
   (B) Write a check.
   (C) Show your receipt.
   (D) Talk to a guard.

   Ⓐ Ⓑ Ⓒ Ⓓ

5. Which show will be first?
   (A) The stock market report.
   (B) The weather report.
   (C) The news.
   (D) The interview.

   Ⓐ Ⓑ Ⓒ Ⓓ

6. Which event will take place first?   (A) (B) (C) (D)
   - (A) A parade.
   - (B) Speeches.
   - (C) Fireworks.
   - (D) A soccer game.

7. What will happen after lunch?   (A) (B) (C) (D)
   - (A) Coffee will be served.
   - (B) Professor Jamison will speak.
   - (C) Schedule changes will be made.
   - (D) Ms. Carter will give a talk.

8. Which country will the president visit first?   (A) (B) (C) (D)
   - (A) Colombia.
   - (B) Mexico.
   - (C) Peru.
   - (D) Ecuador.

9. What is the first step when using the bread machine?   (A) (B) (C) (D)
   - (A) Assemble the machine.
   - (B) Choose a recipe.
   - (C) Measure the ingredients.
   - (D) Taste the bread.

10. What is the last piece of information you should enter?   (A) (B) (C) (D)
   - (A) A credit card number.
   - (B) The name of the class.
   - (C) Your address.
   - (D) Your Social Security number.

IDENTIFYING THE AUDIENCE

You will read questions that ask about audience. Read the question and the answer choices quickly before you listen to the talk. When you listen to the talk, listen for answers to questions about audience.

Example

Good service is the basis of good business and will earn you good tips. Make sure the food you serve is prepared just as the customer requested it. Keep water glasses filled and remove dirty dishes as soon as the customer has finished eating.

Who is this talk directed to?   Ⓐ Ⓑ Ⓒ Ⓓ
(A) Restaurant customers.
(B) Waiters.
(C) Business owners.
(D) Dishwashers.

The correct answer is (B). Choice (A) repeats a detail of the talk that is not related to the answer. Choices (C) and (D) make incorrect inferences about details of the talk.

Look for these words in a question that asks about audience:

> who
> directed to
> talking to

Practice: Identifying the Audience

 DIRECTIONS: Listen to the talk and then choose the statement that best answers the question.

1. Who is this talk directed to?   Ⓐ Ⓑ Ⓒ Ⓓ
    (A) Bookstore owners.
    (B) Professors.
    (C) Students.
    (D) Economists.

2. Who is the speaker talking to?   Ⓐ Ⓑ Ⓒ Ⓓ
    (A) Store employees.
    (B) Customers.
    (C) Police officers.
    (D) Bank tellers.

3. Who is this message for? ⒶⒷⒸⒹ
   (A) Ambulance drivers.
   (B) Patients.
   (C) Medical advisors.
   (D) Office workers.

4. Who is the speaker talking to? ⒶⒷⒸⒹ
   (A) Airline pilots.
   (B) Flight attendants.
   (C) Airplane passengers.
   (D) People with small children.

5. Who is this talk directed to? ⒶⒷⒸⒹ
   (A) Radio station employees.
   (B) Public servants.
   (C) Government officials.
   (D) All city residents.

6. Who would call this telephone number? ⒶⒷⒸⒹ
   (A) People who want information about entertainment.
   (B) People who want to hear a weather report.
   (C) People who need jobs.
   (D) People who need bus and train schedules.

7. Who is the speaker talking to? ⒶⒷⒸⒹ
   (A) Museum guards.
   (B) Bus drivers.
   (C) City bus passengers.
   (D) Tourists.

8. Who is this announcement for? ⒶⒷⒸⒹ
   (A) Auto mechanics.
   (B) Construction workers.
   (C) Commuters.
   (D) Airplane passengers.

9. Who is this advertisement directed to? ⒶⒷⒸⒹ
   (A) Employers.
   (B) Computer technicians.
   (C) Trainers.
   (D) Job seekers.

10. Who is this talk directed to? ⒶⒷⒸⒹ
   (A) People who want to become bankers.
   (B) People who want to buy a house.
   (C) People who want to work in an office.
   (D) People who want to go to the supermarket.

IDENTIFYING A SITUATION

You will read questions that ask about a situation. Read the question and the answer choices quickly before you listen to the short talk. When you listen to the talk, listen for answers to questions about situation.

Example

Thank you for calling Island Travel. If you'd like to book a place on our Hawaii tour, press 1. To make hotel or airplane reservations, press 2.

Where would you hear this message?　　　　Ⓐ　Ⓑ　Ⓒ　Ⓓ
(A)　At a bookstore.
(B)　At a hotel.
(C)　On an airplane.
(D)　At a travel agency.

The correct answer is (D). Choice (A) uses the word *book* with a different meaning. Choices (B) and (C) repeat details of the message that are not related to the correct answer.

Look for this word in a question that asks about a situation:

　　where

Practice: Identifying a Situation

 DIRECTIONS: Listen to the talk and then choose the statement that best answers the question.

　1.　Where would you hear this announcement?　　　　Ⓐ　Ⓑ　Ⓒ　Ⓓ
　　　(A)　At a coffee shop.
　　　(B)　At a grocery store.
　　　(C)　At an airport.
　　　(D)　At a factory.

　2.　Where is this announcement being made?　　　　Ⓐ　Ⓑ　Ⓒ　Ⓓ
　　　(A)　On a subway.
　　　(B)　At the airport.
　　　(C)　On a bus.
　　　(D)　In a taxi.

　3.　Where would you hear this announcement?　　　　Ⓐ　Ⓑ　Ⓒ　Ⓓ
　　　(A)　At a bus station.
　　　(B)　At a school.
　　　(C)　At a nightclub.
　　　(D)　At a soccer stadium.

4. Where is Martha going? (A) (B) (C) (D)
   (A) To the park.
   (B) To the gym.
   (C) Home.
   (D) To a restaurant.

5. Where would you hear this announcement? (A) (B) (C) (D)
   (A) On an elevator.
   (B) At a theater.
   (C) In a store.
   (D) On a bus.

6. Where can this talk be heard? (A) (B) (C) (D)
   (A) In a restaurant.
   (B) In a private home.
   (C) At a museum.
   (D) At a university.

7. Where is the speaker? (A) (B) (C) (D)
   (A) At a restaurant.
   (B) At a party.
   (C) At a theater.
   (D) At a hotel.

8. Where is this announcement being made? (A) (B) (C) (D)
   (A) At a school.
   (B) In a garden.
   (C) At a swimming pool.
   (D) On a farm.

9. Where can this announcement be heard? (A) (B) (C) (D)
   (A) At a bookstore.
   (B) At a hotel.
   (C) At a library.
   (D) At an accountant's office.

10. Where is Donna now? (A) (B) (C) (D)
    (A) At the office.
    (B) On the way to the office.
    (C) At the airport.
    (D) On the way to the airport.

IDENTIFYING THE TOPIC

You will read questions that ask about topics. Read the question and the answer choices quickly before you listen to the talk. When you listen to the talk, listen for answers to questions about the topic.

Example

Umbrella sales are sure to go up with all this rain we've been having. Rain continues all week. Saturday will be cloudy and breezy, and the rain returns on Sunday. This is the time to invest in an umbrella company!

What is this announcement about?
(A) A sale on umbrellas.
(B) The weather.
(C) Train schedules.
(D) Stock market investments.

The correct answer is (B). Choices (A) and (D) try to confuse you by repeating details that are not related to the question. Choice (C) uses the similar-sounding word *train* for *rain.*

Look for these words in a question that asks about the topic:

topic
purpose
about
talk about
discussing
kind

DIRECTIONS: Listen to the talk and then choose the statement that best answers the question.

1. What will Mr. Kim talk about?   Ⓐ Ⓑ Ⓒ Ⓓ
   (A) Law.
   (B) Retirement.
   (C) Photography.
   (D) Traveling.

2. What is the topic of the meeting?   Ⓐ Ⓑ Ⓒ Ⓓ
   (A) Office expenses.
   (B) Going out for lunch.
   (C) Riding in taxis.
   (D) Changes in the office.

3. What is the purpose of this announcement?   Ⓐ Ⓑ Ⓒ Ⓓ
   (A) To give the weather report.
   (B) To talk about traffic problems.
   (C) To announce that schools are closed.
   (D) To report the news.

4. What is the magazine about?   Ⓐ Ⓑ Ⓒ Ⓓ
   (A) Commercials.
   (B) Sports.
   (C) Television.
   (D) News.

5. What kind of business is advertised?   Ⓐ Ⓑ Ⓒ Ⓓ
   (A) A conference planning service.
   (B) A hotel.
   (C) A catering service.
   (D) An entertainment business.

6. What is this announcement about?   Ⓐ Ⓑ Ⓒ Ⓓ
   (A) Weather.
   (B) Vacations.
   (C) Books.
   (D) Mail.

7. What is the purpose of this talk?   Ⓐ Ⓑ Ⓒ Ⓓ
   (A) To explain why eating breakfast is important.
   (B) To explain what to eat for breakfast.
   (C) To explain when to eat breakfast.
   (D) To explain who should eat breakfast.

8. What kind of insurance is advertised?   (A) (B) (C) (D)
  (A) Health insurance.
  (B) Life insurance.
  (C) Car insurance.
  (D) Fire insurance.

9. What is the purpose of this announcement?   (A) (B) (C) (D)
  (A) To report the news.
  (B) To explain the new schedule.
  (C) To introduce musicians.
  (D) To discuss rock music.

10. What is the topic of this report?   (A) (B) (C) (D)
  (A) Business sales.
  (B) Taxi fares.
  (C) Elections.
  (D) A tax increase.

IDENTIFYING A REQUEST

You will read questions that ask about requests. Read the question and the answer choices quickly before you listen to the talk. When you listen to the talk, listen for answers to questions about requests.

Example

The ABC Supermarket has openings for managers. Interested applicants should apply in person at 24 Riverdale Avenue on Saturday at 9:00 A.M. Bring three copies of your résumé. Phone calls will not be accepted.

  How can you apply for this job?   (A) (B) (C) (D)
  (A) Call the supermarket.
  (B) Send in a résumé.
  (C) Go to 24 Riverdale Avenue.
  (D) Fill out an application.

The correct answer is (C). Choices (A) and (B) repeat details of the announcement that are not correct. Choice (D) tries to confuse you by using the similar-sounding and related word *application* for *applicant*.

Look for these words in a question that asks about a request:

  request
  ask
  how can

DIRECTIONS: Listen to the talk and then choose the statement that best answers the question.

1. What are passengers asked to do?   Ⓐ   Ⓑ   Ⓒ   Ⓓ
   (A) Stand up.
   (B) Stay seated.
   (C) Make a complete stop.
   (D) Remain on the train.

2. What are the members of the audience asked to do?   Ⓐ   Ⓑ   Ⓒ   Ⓓ
   (A) Record the show.
   (B) Take pictures of the actors.
   (C) Turn off their cell phones.
   (D) Wait in the lobby.

3. How can you make an appointment with Mr. Schwartz?   Ⓐ   Ⓑ   Ⓒ   Ⓓ
   (A) Wait for the beep.
   (B) Return the call.
   (C) Press one.
   (D) Send an e-mail message.

4. What are the passengers asked to do?   Ⓐ   Ⓑ   Ⓒ   Ⓓ
   (A) Stand in line.
   (B) Pay by check.
   (C) Show their passports.
   (D) Carry their own bags.

5. What are drivers asked to do?   Ⓐ   Ⓑ   Ⓒ   Ⓓ
   (A) Go downtown.
   (B) Drive north on State Street.
   (C) Use Constitution Avenue.
   (D) Avoid accidents.

6. How can callers speak to a customer service   Ⓐ   Ⓑ   Ⓒ   Ⓓ
   representative?
   (A) Call the business line.
   (B) Turn off the phone.
   (C) Leave a message on the answering machine.
   (D) Stay on the line.

7. What are people asked to do?   Ⓐ   Ⓑ   Ⓒ   Ⓓ
   (A) Send food and clothing.
   (B) Leave their homes.
   (C) Donate money.
   (D) Go to Springfield.

8. What are staff members asked to do?   Ⓐ   Ⓑ   Ⓒ   Ⓓ
   (A) Give Mrs. Jackson some help.
   (B) Ask the manager for assistance.
   (C) Introduce themselves to Mrs. Jackson.
   (D) Learn the office routine.

9. What are staff members asked to do?   Ⓐ   Ⓑ   Ⓒ   Ⓓ
   (A) Test the alarm.
   (B) Continue with their usual routine.
   (C) Leave the building.
   (D) Avoid the elevator.

10. What is the driver of the white car asked to do?   Ⓐ   Ⓑ   Ⓒ   Ⓓ
    (A) Make a delivery.
    (B) Visit the building.
    (C) Use the back entrance.
    (D) Move the car.

STRATEGY REVIEW

In the exercises for Part 4, you learned how certain words would help you identify the purpose of a question. Knowing these words will help you choose the right answer. Listen for words that identify:

- a sequence, such as *when*, *before*, *first*, etc.

- the audience, such as *who*, *directed to*, *talking to*, etc.

- the situation, such as *where*

- the topic, such as *talking about*, *discussing*, *about*, etc.

- a request, such as *request*, *ask*, *how can*, etc.

In the exercises for Part 4, you saw how certain answer choices try to confuse you. Here are the ways that choices may seem correct to you.

- words that sound like the correct answer

- words related to the correct answer

- words used in a different context or with a different meaning

- incorrect details provided

- incorrect inferences made

Look at these examples:

Example 1

You will hear:

> "Bilbo's Department Store has openings for
> cashiers, management trainees, and buyer's
> assistants. Call 555-2121 to apply or send
> your résumé to 152 South State Street."

For one of the three questions, you might hear:

Who is this advertisement for?
(A) Job seekers.   (correct answer)
(B) Shoppers.   (incorrect inference)
(C) Train passengers.   (word used with a different meaning)
(D) Employers.   (word related to correct answer)

Example 2

You will hear:

> "Next Tuesday is **Library Forgiveness Day.** All overdue books
> and late fines are forgiven. Return your overdue books to the
> library on Tuesday and you won't be charged a late fine."

For one of the three questions, you might hear:

What are library users asked to do next Tuesday?
(A) Pay a fine.   (incorrect detail)
(B) Return overdue books.   (correct answer)
(C) Give new books to the library.   (sounds like correct answer)
(D) Charge their fines to their credit card.   (incorrect detail)

STRATEGY PRACTICE

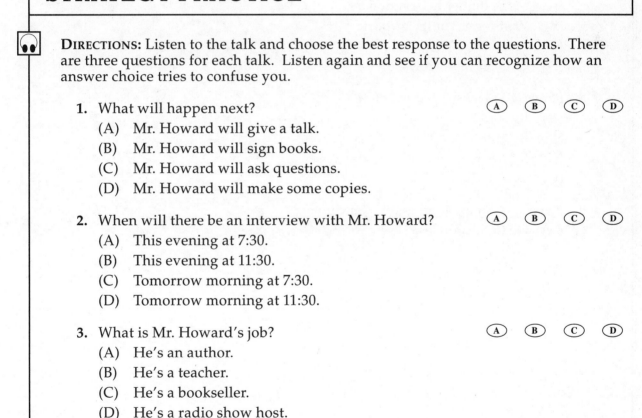

DIRECTIONS: Listen to the talk and choose the best response to the questions. There are three questions for each talk. Listen again and see if you can recognize how an answer choice tries to confuse you.

1. What will happen next?   Ⓐ Ⓑ Ⓒ Ⓓ
    (A) Mr. Howard will give a talk.
    (B) Mr. Howard will sign books.
    (C) Mr. Howard will ask questions.
    (D) Mr. Howard will make some copies.

2. When will there be an interview with Mr. Howard?   Ⓐ Ⓑ Ⓒ Ⓓ
    (A) This evening at 7:30.
    (B) This evening at 11:30.
    (C) Tomorrow morning at 7:30.
    (D) Tomorrow morning at 11:30.

3. What is Mr. Howard's job?   Ⓐ Ⓑ Ⓒ Ⓓ
    (A) He's an author.
    (B) He's a teacher.
    (C) He's a bookseller.
    (D) He's a radio show host.

4. How is the weather this morning?   Ⓐ Ⓑ Ⓒ Ⓓ
   (A) Rainy.
   (B) Icy.
   (C) Windy.
   (D) Warm.

5. When will it start to snow?   Ⓐ Ⓑ Ⓒ Ⓓ
   (A) This morning.
   (B) This afternoon.
   (C) This evening.
   (D) Tomorrow.

6. Why will schools be closed tomorrow?   Ⓐ Ⓑ Ⓒ Ⓓ
   (A) Because of traffic delays.
   (B) Because of bad weather.
   (C) Because of the weekend.
   (D) Because of a holiday.

7. What does Mary ask Charles to do?   Ⓐ Ⓑ Ⓒ Ⓓ
   (A) Make dinner reservations.
   (B) Wait for her at the airport.
   (C) Meet her at the hotel.
   (D) Call her tomorrow.

8. How will Mary get to the hotel?   Ⓐ Ⓑ Ⓒ Ⓓ
   (A) By car.
   (B) By taxi.
   (C) By train.
   (D) By walking.

9. What does Mary want to do after dinner?   Ⓐ Ⓑ Ⓒ Ⓓ
   (A) Go to the movies.
   (B) Sit and talk.
   (C) Take a walk.
   (D) Have a rest.

10. What will be the first item in the program?   Ⓐ Ⓑ Ⓒ Ⓓ
    (A) A question and answer session.
    (B) A musical performance.
    (C) A slide show.
    (D) A lecture.

11. Who will play music?   Ⓐ Ⓑ Ⓒ Ⓓ
    (A) An Italian artist.
    (B) Matilda Wimple.
    (C) Dr. James.
    (D) Students.

12. What refreshments will be served?   Ⓐ Ⓑ Ⓒ Ⓓ
    (A) Coffee.
    (B) Dinner.
    (C) Breakfast.
    (D) Wine and cheese.

13. What can be seen from the guest's room?   Ⓐ Ⓑ Ⓒ Ⓓ
    (A) The ocean.
    (B) The pool.
    (C) The park.
    (D) The parking lot.

14. Where does the speaker ask the guest to park?   Ⓐ Ⓑ Ⓒ Ⓓ
    (A) On the other side of the pool.
    (B) By the side of the building.
    (C) By the front door.
    (D) In the garage.

15. What is free for hotel guests?   Ⓐ Ⓑ Ⓒ Ⓓ
    (A) The fitness room.
    (B) The sauna.
    (C) Breakfast.
    (D) Dinner.

LISTENING COMPREHENSION REVIEW

Do this Listening Comprehension Review as if you were taking Parts 1, 2, 3, and 4 of the new TOEIC test. You should take no more than 45 minutes to do this review. Use the Listening Comprehension Review Answer Sheet on page 291.

LISTENING TEST

In the listening test, you will be asked to demonstrate how well you understand spoken English. The entire Listening test will last approximately 45 minutes. There are four parts, and directions are given for each part. You must mark your answers on the separate answer sheet. Do not write your answers in the test book.

PART 1

Directions: For each question in this part, you will hear four statements about a picture in your test book. When you hear the statements, you must select the one statement that best describes what you see in the picture. Then find the number of the question on your answer sheet and mark your answer. The statements will not be printed in your test book and will be spoken only one time.

Example   *Sample Answer*

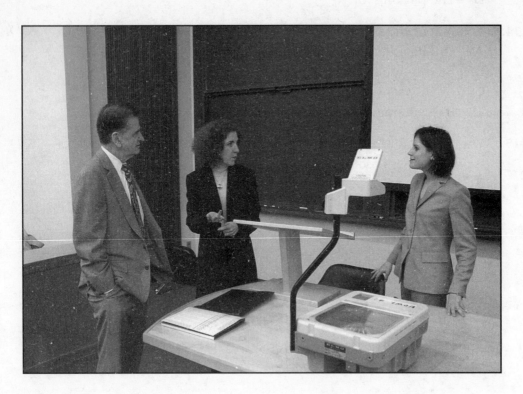

Statement (C), "They're standing near the table," is the best description of the picture, so you should select answer (C) and mark it on your answer sheet.

1.

2.

GO ON TO THE NEXT PAGE

3.

4.

5.

6.

GO ON TO THE NEXT PAGE ▶

LISTENING COMPREHENSION REVIEW

7.

8.

9.

10.

GO ON TO THE NEXT PAGE ▶

Directions: You will hear a question or statement and three responses spoken in English. They will not be printed in your test book and will be spoken only one time. Select the best response to the question or statement and mark the letter (A), (B), or (C) on your answer sheet.

Example

You will hear: Where is the meeting room?

Sample Answer

You will also hear: (A) To meet the new director.
　　　　　　　　　(B) It's the first room on the right.
　　　　　　　　　(C) Yes, at two o'clock.

Your best response to the question "Where is the meeting room?" is choice (B), "It's the first room on the right," so (B) is the correct answer. You should mark answer (B) on your answer sheet.

11. Mark your answer on your answer sheet.

12. Mark your answer on your answer sheet.

13. Mark your answer on your answer sheet.

14. Mark your answer on your answer sheet.

15. Mark your answer on your answer sheet.

16. Mark your answer on your answer sheet.

17. Mark your answer on your answer sheet.

18. Mark your answer on your answer sheet.

19. Mark your answer on your answer sheet.

20. Mark your answer on your answer sheet.

21. Mark your answer on your answer sheet.

22. Mark your answer on your answer sheet.

23. Mark your answer on your answer sheet.

24. Mark your answer on your answer sheet.

25. Mark your answer on your answer sheet.

26. Mark your answer on your answer sheet.

27. Mark your answer on your answer sheet.

28. Mark your answer on your answer sheet.

29. Mark your answer on your answer sheet.

30. Mark your answer on your answer sheet.

31. Mark your answer on your answer sheet.

32. Mark your answer on your answer sheet.

33. Mark your answer on your answer sheet.

34. Mark your answer on your answer sheet.

35. Mark your answer on your answer sheet.

36. Mark your answer on your answer sheet.

37. Mark your answer on your answer sheet.

38. Mark your answer on your answer sheet.

39. Mark your answer on your answer sheet.

40. Mark your answer on your answer sheet.

Directions: You will hear some conversations between two people. You will be asked to answer three questions about what the speakers say in each conversation. Select the best response to each question and mark the letter (A), (B), (C), or (D) on your answer sheet. The conversations will not be printed in your test book and will be spoken only one time.

41. What is the man doing?
   (A) Mailing a letter.
   (B) Replying to e-mail.
   (C) Answering the phone.
   (D) Repairing the computer.

42. What does the woman want to do?
   (A) Have lunch.
   (B) Drink coffee.
   (C) Go to bed.
   (D) Take a seat.

43. When will the man meet the woman?
   (A) At noon.
   (B) In ten minutes.
   (C) At 5:00.
   (D) In fifteen minutes.

44. Where does this conversation take place?
   (A) In an apartment.
   (B) In an office.
   (C) On a plane.
   (D) At a hotel.

45. What will the woman do?
   (A) Sleep.
   (B) Work.
   (C) Cook.
   (D) Read.

46. How does the man feel?
   (A) Bored.
   (B) Tired.
   (C) Angry.
   (D) Hungry.

47. What is the man's job?
   (A) Clock repair person.
   (B) Receptionist.
   (C) Telemarketer.
   (D) Usher.

48. What time is the woman's appointment?
   (A) 1:00.
   (B) 4:00.
   (C) 8:00.
   (D) 9:00.

49. What will the woman do?
   (A) Make a call.
   (B) Sit down.
   (C) Play ball.
   (D) Make a new appointment.

50. When does the woman plan to invite people for dinner?
   (A) Tuesday.
   (B) Thursday.
   (C) Friday.
   (D) Saturday.

51. Who will she invite?
   (A) Business associates.
   (B) School friends.
   (C) Neighbors.
   (D) Her sisters.

52. How many guests does she plan to have?
   (A) Two.
   (B) Four.
   (C) Six.
   (D) Ten.

GO ON TO THE NEXT PAGE

53. When will they go to the presentation?
   (A) 9:00.
   (B) 11:00.
   (C) 1:00.
   (D) 2:00.

54. What is the presentation about?
   (A) Cooking.
   (B) Books.
   (C) Trains.
   (D) Games.

55. What does the man want to do after the presentation?
   (A) Go home.
   (B) Have lunch.
   (C) Buy a watch.
   (D) Look around.

56. When is the report due?
   (A) Monday.
   (B) Tuesday.
   (C) Wednesday.
   (D) Thursday.

57. What kind of report is it?
   (A) A news report.
   (B) A management report.
   (C) An expense report.
   (D) A meeting report.

58. How does the man feel about the situation?
   (A) Sad.
   (B) Frightened.
   (C) Ill.
   (D) Mad.

59. Where does this conversation take place?
   (A) In a hotel.
   (B) At a restaurant.
   (C) At the beach.
   (D) In an apartment building.

60. What is the woman's favorite thing about the place?
   (A) The restaurants.
   (B) The pool.
   (C) The beds.
   (D) The fitness room.

61. What will the man do all day?
   (A) Sleep.
   (B) Eat.
   (C) Swim.
   (D) Exercise.

62. Where does the conversation take place?
   (A) In a waiting room.
   (B) In a store.
   (C) In a post office.
   (D) In a library.

63. What does the woman want?
   (A) A book.
   (B) Adhesive tape.
   (C) Envelopes.
   (D) Letter paper.

64. What does the man suggest doing?
   (A) Placing an order.
   (B) Using the smaller size.
   (C) Looking somewhere else.
   (D) Getting a bigger box.

65. How many phone calls did they
answer?
(A) Two.
(B) Four.
(C) Nine.
(D) Ten.

66. What is the woman waiting for?
(A) An e-mail message.
(B) A phone call.
(C) A package.
(D) A letter.

67. What does the man want help with?
(A) Writing a report.
(B) Sending mail.
(C) Cleaning his office.
(D) Fixing his computer.

68. How will the woman pay?
(A) By check.
(B) With a credit card.
(C) In cash.
(D) With a money order.

69. What is the woman buying?
(A) Cards.
(B) Shoes.
(C) A book.
(D) A purse.

70. How much does her purchase cost?
(A) $17.50.
(B) $25.
(C) $75.
(D) $100.

GO ON TO THE NEXT PAGE

Directions: You will hear some talks given by a single speaker. You will be asked to answer three questions about what the speaker says in each talk. Select the best response to each question and mark the letter (A), (B), (C), or (D) on your answer sheet. The talks will not be printed in your test book and will be spoken only one time.

71. Where would this announcement be heard?
    (A) On a train.
    (B) At an airport.
    (C) In an airplane.
    (D) On a bus.

72. Who is speaking?
    (A) A pilot.
    (B) A tour guide.
    (C) A weather forecaster.
    (D) A passenger.

73. What can be seen from the window?
    (A) A cemetery.
    (B) Radar screens.
    (C) Some woods.
    (D) A mountain.

74. Where is the tour?
    (A) In a garden.
    (B) In a forest.
    (C) In a museum.
    (D) In a flower shop.

75. What does the tour guide ask the participants to do?
    (A) Pick some flowers.
    (B) Wear warm clothes.
    (C) Stay in their seats.
    (D) Clean the windows.

76. Where is the first stop?
    (A) Under the trees.
    (B) On the left.
    (C) By a river branch.
    (D) To the rear.

77. Who is the message intended for?
    (A) City garbage collectors.
    (B) Community bus drivers.
    (C) Kids with school on Saturdays.
    (D) Members of the community.

78. What was the clean-up drive like last year?
    (A) There were free refreshments.
    (B) Fifty people showed up.
    (C) It wasn't successful.
    (D) There were no participants.

79. What time will the clean-up drive begin?
    (A) 10:00 A.M.
    (B) 1:00 P.M.
    (C) 3:00 P.M.
    (D) 3:15 P.M.

80. What is Dr. Quimby Jones's profession?
    (A) Radio show host.
    (B) Medical doctor.
    (C) Professor.
    (D) Farmer.

81. What is the last item on the radio program?
    (A) A talk about economics.
    (B) Reading letters and e-mails from listeners.
    (C) A discussion about agriculture.
    (D) Answering telephone calls.

82. How long does the entire radio show last?
    (A) Ten minutes.
    (B) Thirty minutes.
    (C) One hour.
    (D) One hour and ten minutes.

83. Who is the speaker?
    (A) A university president.
    (B) A special guest.
    (C) A professor.
    (D) A student.

84. What is the subject of the class?
    (A) Chinese History.
    (B) Art History.
    (C) Writing.
    (D) Travel.

85. What will the class do today?
    (A) Read books.
    (B) Look at slides.
    (C) Watch a video.
    (D) Visit an art museum.

86. According to the weather report, what is the weather like now?
    (A) There are floods.
    (B) There is heavy rain.
    (C) There is a hailstorm.
    (D) There are strong winds.

87. How long will this weather condition last?
    (A) Two to four hours.
    (B) Four more hours.
    (C) Twenty-four hours.
    (D) Thirty-four hours.

88. What should people near the Green River listen for tomorrow?
    (A) Vacation orders.
    (B) The train schedule.
    (C) Orders to evacuate.
    (D) A new weather report.

89. What helped pay for the food at the luncheon?
    (A) Employee contributions.
    (B) Last year's revenue.
    (C) The generosity of the speaker.
    (D) Donations from local restaurants.

90. What is the main purpose of the speech?
    (A) To discuss future sales plans.
    (B) To analyze last year's meeting.
    (C) To improve customer service.
    (D) To describe the luncheon.

91. What will the meeting participants do this afternoon?
    (A) Write new ads.
    (B) Meet in groups.
    (C) Visit customers' homes.
    (D) Plan next year's luncheon.

92. What has been the major complaint about the parking lot?
    (A) There hasn't been enough security.
    (B) There are never enough parking spaces.
    (C) Cars get too hot or people get too wet.
    (D) People are charged too much to park there.

93. When will the parking garage probably be finished?
    (A) In December.
    (B) In January.
    (C) In six months.
    (D) In one year.

94. Where should people park until the garage is completed?
    (A) On the street.
    (B) Around the corner.
    (C) In another parking garage.
    (D) In a shopping center parking lot.

95. What is the telephone number that people should call?
    (A) 703-555-8000.
    (B) 603-555-6069.
    (C) 603-555-9000.
    (D) 212-555-5394.

96. Who created this advertisement?
    (A) Investment bankers.
    (B) A real estate company.
    (C) A group of realtors.
    (D) Real estate investors.

97. Who is likely to call the phone number?
    (A) A person who wants to get rid of a house.
    (B) A person who would rather rent a house.
    (C) A person who needs a house immediately.
    (D) A person who is thinking about buying a house.

98. Where would this announcement be heard?
    (A) At a farm.
    (B) At a theater.
    (C) At a grocery store.
    (D) At a cell phone store.

99. Where can the lost cell phone be claimed?
    (A) In aisle 10.
    (B) In the produce section.
    (C) In the frozen food section.
    (D) In the customer service office.

100. Who can take advantage of the sale?
    (A) People with a Shoppers' Club card.
    (B) All customers.
    (C) Children.
    (D) Parents.

READING

In the second section of the new TOEIC® test, you will be tested on how well you understand written English. There are three parts to this section with special directions for each part:

Part 5   Incomplete Sentences

Part 6   Text Completion

Part 7   Reading Comprehension

Each part contains activities to help you practice these strategies. Each part ends with a Strategy Review consisting of questions similar to those on the new TOEIC test. In this part of the Introductory Course for the new TOEIC test, you will learn strategies to help you on the Reading section.

PART 5—INCOMPLETE SENTENCES

These are the directions for Part 5 of the new TOEIC® test. Study them now. If you understand these directions now, you will not have to read them during the test.

READING TEST

In the Reading test, you will read a variety of texts and answer several different types of reading comprehension questions. The entire Reading test will last 75 minutes. There are three parts, and directions are given for each part. You are encouraged to answer as many questions as possible within the time allowed.

You must mark your answers on the separate answer sheet. Do not write your answers in the test book.

PART 5

Directions: A word or phrase is missing in each of the sentences below. Four answer choices are given below each sentence. Select the best answer to complete the sentence. Then mark the letter (A), (B), (C), or (D) on your answer sheet.

In this section, you will learn the most common types of items found on Part 5:

- word families
- similar words
- prepositions
- conjunctions
- adverbs of frequency
- causative verbs
- conditional sentences
- verb tense
- two-word verbs

WORD FAMILIES

Word families are words that look alike but have different endings.

ROOT WORD:	nation			
ENDINGS:	*-al*	*-ize*	*-ly*	*-ity*
WORDS:	national	nationalize	nationally	nationality

These endings (*-al, -ize, -ly, -ity, -ful, -sion,* etc.) change the original word to either a noun, verb, adjective, or adverb. For example, the word *care* can be made into an adjective (*careful*) or an adverb (*carefully*).

STRATEGIES FOR WORD FAMILY ITEMS

ASK YOURSELF THESE QUESTIONS:

■ Do you need a noun? If so, does the ending make the word a noun?

Noun endings: *-ance, -ancy, -ence, -ation, -dom, -ism, -ment, -ness, -ship, -or, -er, -ion*

INCORRECT	[I was sorry to hear about his <u>ill</u>.]
CORRECT	I was sorry to hear about his <u>illness</u>.

■ Do you need an adjective? If so, does the ending make the word an adjective?

Adjective endings: *-able, -ible, -al, -ful, -ish, -ive*

INCORRECT	[This is a <u>wonder</u> report!]
CORRECT	This is a <u>wonderful</u> report!

■ Do you need an adverb? If so, does the ending make the word an adverb?

Adverb endings: *-ly, -ward, -wise*

INCORRECT	[She entered the data very <u>careful</u>.]
CORRECT	She entered the data very <u>carefully</u>.

■ Do you need a verb? If so, does the ending make the word a verb?

Verb endings: *-en, -ify, -ize*

INCORRECT	[We are going to <u>wide</u> the parking lot.]
CORRECT	We are going to <u>widen</u> the parking lot.

Practice

▷ Mark the choice that best completes the sentence.

1. We need to _____ the language in this report;
    it is too complex.
    (A) simplify   (C) simply
    (B) simple   (D) simplistic
    ⒜ ⒝ ⒞ ⒟

2. In my opinion, her leaving early was a very _____
    thing to do.
    (A) children   (C) childishly
    (B) childish   (D) child
    ⒜ ⒝ ⒞ ⒟

3. We could call the TV stations and _____ the opening
    of our new store.
    (A) publicity   (C) publicize
    (B) public   (D) publisher
    ⒜ ⒝ ⒞ ⒟

4. I like my work because I have the _____ to make my
    own decisions.
    (A) freed   (C) freedom
    (B) freely   (D) free
    ⒜ ⒝ ⒞ ⒟

5. Our company believes it is the best _____ to handle
    the account.
    (A) organizing   (C) organizational
    (B) organization (D) organize
    ⒜ ⒝ ⒞ ⒟

6. Most meetings are not as _____ as this one was.
    (A) interested   (C) interest
    (B) interestingly (D) interesting
    ⒜ ⒝ ⒞ ⒟

7. A doctor's _____ manner makes patients feel comfortable.
    (A) friendship   (C) friendly
    (B) friend   (D) friendliness
    ⒜ ⒝ ⒞ ⒟

8. It was very _____ of the boss to buy us those nice gifts.
    (A) thoughtless   (C) thought
    (B) thoughtful   (D) thoughtfully
    ⒜ ⒝ ⒞ ⒟

9. One of your duties will be some _____ typing.
    (A) light   (C) lighten
    (B) lightened   (D) lightness
    ⒜ ⒝ ⒞ ⒟

10. She would like a _____ raise, not just a few dollars.
    (A) really   (C) real
    (B) realist   (D) reality
    ⒜ ⒝ ⒞ ⒟

SIMILAR WORDS

Similar words are often confusing if they have similar meanings but cannot be interchanged. Sometimes they have the same root, prefix, or suffix. Sometimes they have similar spelling. The grammatical structure and the meaning of the sentence will help you determine which is correct.

STRATEGIES FOR SIMILAR WORD ITEMS

ASK YOURSELF THESE QUESTIONS:

■ Many words seem similar because they contain similar letters. Do the other words in the sentence help you understand the meaning of the word?

INCORRECT	[The manager will <u>except</u> the gift.]
CORRECT	The manager will <u>accept</u> the gift.

■ Some words can refer to the same topic but have different meanings. Do you know the different meanings of a word?

INCORRECT	[Do you have change for a ten-dollar <u>currency</u>?]
CORRECT	Do you have change for a ten-dollar <u>bill</u>?

■ Some words have similar spellings, but they have very different meanings or are different parts of speech. Can you tell the difference?

INCORRECT	[The athlete does not want to <u>loose</u> the race.]
CORRECT	The athlete does not want to <u>lose</u> the race.

▶ Mark the choice that best completes the sentence.

1. The task was divided into _____ parts.   (A) (B) (C) (D)
   (A) like   (C) equal
   (B) same   (D) even

2. We were _____ impressed with the recommendations   (A) (B) (C) (D)
   at the end of the report.
   (A) specially   (C) especial
   (B) special   (D) especially

3. Your _____ during our visit has been greatly appreciated.   (A) (B) (C) (D)
   (A) hospice   (C) hospitality
   (B) hospital   (D) hospitable

4. With prices _____ at such a rapid rate, buyers should   (A) (B) (C) (D)
   compare prices.
   (A) ascending   (C) enlarging
   (B) increasing   (D) expanding

5. No one is at fault, according to the company _____.   (A) (B) (C) (D)
   (A) speaker   (C) teller
   (B) man   (D) spokesperson

6. Your advice was very _____.   (A) (B) (C) (D)
   (A) cooperating   (C) helpful
   (B) contributive (D) improving

7. I think the _____ for his services is high.   (A) (B) (C) (D)
   (A) duty   (C) fine
   (B) fee   (D) tariff

8. We've decided to _____ the company Macrodisk, Inc.   (A) (B) (C) (D)
   (A) name   (C) nominate
   (B) identify   (D) denominate

9. Have you checked out the _____ of that contract?   (A) (B) (C) (D)
   (A) rightfulness (C) legality
   (B) lawfulness   (D) authority

10. The experience I received being an apprentice was _____.   (A) (B) (C) (D)
    (A) costly   (C) expensive
    (B) pricey   (D) invaluable

PREPOSITIONS

Small words that introduce phrases are **prepositions.** Prepositional phrases show time, placement, direction, cause, and location.

STRATEGIES FOR PREPOSITION ITEMS

ASK YOURSELF THESE QUESTIONS:

■ Do you need to refer to a specific time? If so, is the preposition *at*?

INCORRECT	[The morning shift starts on 9:00.]
CORRECT	The morning shift starts at 9:00.

■ Do you need to refer to a specific day? If so, is the preposition *on*?

INCORRECT	[The conference will be held at Friday.]
CORRECT	The conference will be held on Friday.

■ Do you need to refer to a specific date? If so, is the preposition *on*?

INCORRECT	[The contract deadline is in February 10.]
CORRECT	The contract deadline is on February 10

■ Do you need to talk about a specific city? If so, is the preposition *in*?

INCORRECT	[Our headquarters are at Baltimore.]
CORRECT	Our headquarters are in Baltimore.

■ Do you know the meaning of the preposition? Is the preposition logical?

INCORRECT	[The letter was written from his secretary.]
CORRECT	The letter was written by his secretary.

Practice

> Mark the choice that best completes the sentence.

1. The mail carrier left the mail _____ the secretary's desk.
   (A) to
   (B) on
   (C) at
   (D) above

   (A) (B) (C) (D)

2. The software company offers training _____ Atlanta.
   (A) at
   (B) on
   (C) by
   (D) in

   (A) (B) (C) (D)

3. There will be a holiday _____ Monday.
   (A) on
   (B) from
   (C) at
   (D) in

   (A) (B) (C) (D)

4. The presentation starts _____ 9:30 A.M. in the conference room.
   (A) on
   (B) at
   (C) in
   (D) for

   (A) (B) (C) (D)

5. The doctor will not give the patient the test results _____ tomorrow.
   (A) on
   (B) until
   (C) from
   (D) at

   (A) (B) (C) (D)

6. That clerk stands _____ a counter all day.
   (A) on
   (B) in
   (C) behind
   (D) above

   (A) (B) (C) (D)

7. Please hand in that report _____ Friday afternoon.
   (A) by
   (B) at
   (C) in
   (D) over

   (A) (B) (C) (D)

8. Have you read this article _____ our competitors?
   (A) over
   (B) above
   (C) for
   (D) about

   (A) (B) (C) (D)

9. We do almost all our corresponding _____ e-mail.
   (A) in
   (B) by
   (C) on
   (D) with

   (A) (B) (C) (D)

10. The sale goes on _____ the 16th.
    (A) through
    (B) into
    (C) towards
    (D) for

    (A) (B) (C) (D)

CONJUNCTIONS

Words, phrases, and clauses are joined by words called **conjunctions.**

Coordinate conjunctions join two equal terms: *and, or, nor, but.*

Subordinate conjunctions join two clauses: *although, since, because, when, before,* etc.

STRATEGIES FOR CONJUNCTION ITEMS

ASK YOURSELF THESE QUESTIONS:

■ Do you need to join two nouns, two adjectives, two prepositional phrases, or any equal terms? If so, is there a coordinate conjunction joining them?

INCORRECT	[The president <u>also</u> his assistant are coming.]
CORRECT	The president <u>and</u> his assistant are coming.

■ Do you need to join two sentences? If so, is there a coordinate conjunction joining them?

INCORRECT	[I can make the copies <u>too</u> John can collate the pages.]
CORRECT	I can make the copies, <u>and</u> John can collate the pages.

■ Do you need to join a dependent clause with an independent clause? If so, is there a subordinate conjunction joining them?

INCORRECT	[<u>But</u> he had a suggestion, he didn't raise his hand.]
CORRECT	<u>Although</u> he had a suggestion, he didn't raise his hand.

■ Do you understand the meanings of the conjunctions and of the other words in the sentence? Is the sentence logical? Does it make sense?

INCORRECT	[I know him <u>but</u> his wife.]
CORRECT	I know him <u>and</u> his wife.

Practice

▶ Mark the choice that best completes the sentence.

1. _____ they were tired, they worked overtime.   (A) (B) (C) (D)
   (A) Because   (C) Since
   (B) In spite   (D) Although

2. Neither Ms. Chen _____ Mr. Martinez was able to   (A) (B) (C) (D)
   attend the seminar.
   (A) nor   (C) neither
   (B) and   (D) or

3. _____ Mr. Park worked for us, he had received   (A) (B) (C) (D)
   training abroad.
   (A) Before   (C) While
   (B) After   (D) When

4. Please answer the phone _____ it rings.   (A) (B) (C) (D)
   (A) during   (C) because
   (B) when   (D) and

5. You can look at the clothes in the shop windows,   (A) (B) (C) (D)
   _____ you can't go in and buy them.
   (A) but   (C) after
   (B) or   (D) while

6. The soccer game won't be postponed _____ it   (A) (B) (C) (D)
   looks like rain.
   (A) because   (C) since
   (B) even though   (D) as

7. _____ profits have improved, we're all getting bonuses.   (A) (B) (C) (D)
   (A) Since   (C) Although
   (B) Before   (D) During

8. Ms. Adams refused the promotion _____ the large raise.   (A) (B) (C) (D)
   (A) because   (C) despite
   (B) but   (D) neither

9. The hotel will accept no guests _____ it's being renovated.   (A) (B) (C) (D)
   (A) and   (C) because of
   (B) while   (D) after

10. Restaurant food handlers must wear latex gloves   (A) (B) (C) (D)
    _____ health regulations.
    (A) because of   (C) since
    (B) because   (D) though

ADVERBS OF FREQUENCY

Adverbs of frequency can be divided into two groups: **adverbs of definite frequency** such as *every day, annually, twice a week* and **adverbs of indefinite frequency** such as *always, rarely, never.*

STRATEGIES FOR ADVERB OF FREQUENCY ITEMS

ASK YOURSELF THESE QUESTIONS:

- Are you sure of the position of the adverb? Is there a definite frequency adverb? If so, remember that a definite frequency adverb usually goes at the beginning or the end of the sentence.

INCORRECT	[Mr. Escobar walks every day to work.]
CORRECT	Mr. Escobar walks <u>to work</u> every day.

- Are you sure of the position of the adverb? Is there an indefinite frequency adverb? If so, there are three possibilities to remember: the adverb goes <u>after</u> *be* (He **is always** busy.); the adverb goes <u>before</u> all other simple verbs (He **always eats** lunch.); the adverb goes between the first auxiliary and the main verb in a complex verb form (He **has always liked** you.).

INCORRECT	[He <u>always</u> is working late.]
CORRECT	He is <u>always</u> working late.

- Do you understand the finer meanings of the adverb? Is the sentence logical?

INCORRECT	[There is <u>yet</u> time before the seminar begins.]
CORRECT	There is <u>still</u> time before the seminar begins.

➤ Mark the choice that best completes the sentence.

1. Mr. Lee is never sick and comes in on time _____.
   (A) never   (C) sometimes
   (B) rarely   (D) every day

   Ⓐ Ⓑ Ⓒ Ⓓ

2. The supervisor _____ tries to be fair.
   (A) always   (C) every day
   (B) usual   (D) ever

   Ⓐ Ⓑ Ⓒ Ⓓ

3. Our department has _____ been this productive before.
   (A) still   (C) yet
   (B) never   (D) lately

   Ⓐ Ⓑ Ⓒ Ⓓ

4. Ms. Carver _____ late since she was promoted.
   (A) has been rarely   (C) rarely has been
   (B) has rarely been   (D) rarely been

   Ⓐ Ⓑ Ⓒ Ⓓ

5. Our boss gives all of the management team bonuses _____.
   (A) never   (C) still
   (B) always   (D) annually

   Ⓐ Ⓑ Ⓒ Ⓓ

6. We have _____ pre-registered for the conference.
   (A) yet   (C) already
   (B) still   (D) ever

   Ⓐ Ⓑ Ⓒ Ⓓ

7. Mr. Kim _____ calls in the auditors.
   (A) frequently   (C) timely
   (B) yet   (D) already

   Ⓐ Ⓑ Ⓒ Ⓓ

8. The boss treats everybody to lunch _____.
   (A) never   (C) rarely
   (B) on occasion   (D) normally

   Ⓐ Ⓑ Ⓒ Ⓓ

9. We're _____ waiting for a fax from the head office.
   (A) already   (C) every day
   (B) yet   (D) still

   Ⓐ Ⓑ Ⓒ Ⓓ

10. The Sales Department holds a meeting _____.
    (A) usually   (C) weekly
    (B) already   (D) always

    Ⓐ Ⓑ Ⓒ Ⓓ

CAUSATIVE VERBS

When someone makes something happen, you use a **causative verb** to show this. Look carefully at the form of the verb in the clause that follows the causative verb. Some causative verbs are *get, make, have, order, want.*

STRATEGIES FOR CAUSATIVE VERB ITEMS

ASK YOURSELF THESE QUESTIONS:

- Does the subject of the noun clause that follows the causative verb perform the action? If so, is the verb after that noun clause the simple form, the infinitive form, or the present participle form of the verb?

INCORRECT	[I had my coworker <u>helped</u> me.]
CORRECT	I had my coworker <u>help</u> me.
INCORRECT	[I got my coworker <u>help</u> me.]
CORRECT	I got my coworker <u>to help</u> me.
INCORRECT	[The supervisor had him <u>stocked</u> shelves all day.]
CORRECT	The supervisor had him <u>stocking</u> shelves all day.

- Does the subject of the noun clause that follows the causative verb receive the action? If so, is the verb after that noun clause the past participle (*-ed/-en*) form of the verb?

INCORRECT	[Mr. Watson wants the report <u>rewrote</u> soon.]
CORRECT	Mr. Watson wants the report <u>rewritten</u> soon.

Practice

⟶ Mark the choice that best completes the sentence.

1. The guard made the visitors _____ at the gate.   Ⓐ Ⓑ Ⓒ Ⓓ
   (A) waiting   (C) to wait
   (B) waited   (D) wait

2. My assistant wasn't able to get his check _____ because   Ⓐ Ⓑ Ⓒ Ⓓ
   the bank was closed.
   (A) cash   (C) cashing
   (B) cashed   (D) cashes

3. Our company wants its customers _____.   Ⓐ Ⓑ Ⓒ Ⓓ
   (A) satisfies   (C) satisfied
   (B) satisfying   (D) satisfy

4. I'll have my secretary _____ for the package.   Ⓐ Ⓑ Ⓒ Ⓓ
   (A) will sign   (C) sign
   (B) signs   (D) to sign

5. Before the prime minister arrived, the police ordered   Ⓐ Ⓑ Ⓒ Ⓓ
   the area _____.
   (A) clear   (C) clearing
   (B) cleared   (D) be clear

6. We forced our competitors _____ their prices.   Ⓐ Ⓑ Ⓒ Ⓓ
   (A) to lower   (C) lowered
   (B) lower   (D) lowering

7. With some effort, Ms. Manson got her schedule _____.   Ⓐ Ⓑ Ⓒ Ⓓ
   (A) to change   (C) change
   (B) changed   (D) changing

8. The boss had me _____ all of last month's sales figures.   Ⓐ Ⓑ Ⓒ Ⓓ
   (A) to check   (C) checking
   (B) checked   (D) checks

9. The airport guard made us _____ our pockets at the   Ⓐ Ⓑ Ⓒ Ⓓ
   security gate.
   (A) to empty   (C) emptying
   (B) empty   (D) emptied

10. The architects want all the hallways _____.   Ⓐ Ⓑ Ⓒ Ⓓ
    (A) widen   (C) widening
    (B) widened   (D) to widen

CONDITIONAL SENTENCES

There are two parts to a **conditional sentence: the condition** (*if*) and **the result**. There are also two types of conditional sentences: **real** and **unreal** (contrary-to-fact).

REAL CONDITION   RESULT

If you come before the meeting, we'll have time to talk.

UNREAL CONDITION   RESULT

If my windows were larger, I would get more light.

STRATEGIES FOR CONDITIONAL SENTENCE ITEMS

ASK YOURSELF THESE QUESTIONS:

■ Is it a real condition? If so, is the verb in the *if* clause in the simple present or present progressive form? Is the verb in the result in the present, future, or imperative form?

> **INCORRECT**   [If Gianni will be there, we'll give him the message.]
>
> **CORRECT**   If Gianni is there, we'll give him the message.

■ Is it an unreal condition in the present using the verb *be*? If so, is *was* or *were* the form of *be* that is used?

> **INCORRECT**   [If she is the boss, she would hire him.]
>
> **CORRECT**   If she was/were the boss, she would hire him.

■ Is it an unreal condition in the present or future tense? If so, is the verb in the condition in the present subjunctive form? Does the verb in the result contain *would* or *could* + the simple (base) form?

> **INCORRECT**   [If humans have two heads, they couldn't make decisions easily.]
>
> **CORRECT**   If humans had two heads, they couldn't make decisions easily.

⟶ Mark the choice that best completes the sentence.

1. If the student _____ for tomorrow's exam, she'll
   be more confident.
   (A) prepares   (C) prepare
   (B) prepared   (D) would prepare

   Ⓐ   Ⓑ   Ⓒ   Ⓓ

2. If Mr. Kennedy _____ the information, he would
   put it in the report.
   (A) has   (C) will have
   (B) would have   (D) had

   Ⓐ   Ⓑ   Ⓒ   Ⓓ

3. If you _____ how to use the word processor, ask any
   one of us.
   (A) won't understand (C) understood
   (B) don't understand (D) not understand

   Ⓐ   Ⓑ   Ⓒ   Ⓓ

4. If you aren't able to finish the letter now, _____ it later.
   (A) you could have done (C) you can do
   (B) you have done   (D) you will can do

   Ⓐ   Ⓑ   Ⓒ   Ⓓ

5. If I _____ you, I would take the job and then ask for
   more money.
   (A) had been   (C) were
   (B) am   (D) will be

   Ⓐ   Ⓑ   Ⓒ   Ⓓ

6. If you _____ to cancel your reservation, please do so
   forty-eight hours before that date.
   (A) needed   (C) need
   (B) will need   (D) had needed

   Ⓐ   Ⓑ   Ⓒ   Ⓓ

7. Their marriage wouldn't be so good if they _____ so well
   with each other.
   (A) communicated   (C) don't communicate
   (B) didn't communicate (D) communicate

   Ⓐ   Ⓑ   Ⓒ   Ⓓ

8. If we don't entertain our out-of-town buyers, they _____
   such big orders.
   (A) will place   (C) would place
   (B) might not place   (D) wouldn't place

   Ⓐ   Ⓑ   Ⓒ   Ⓓ

9. Come to our next picnic if you _____ the chance.
   (A) have   (C) had
   (B) will have   (D) don't have

   Ⓐ   Ⓑ   Ⓒ   Ⓓ

10. If I didn't think the gym was helping me feel better,
    I _____ my membership.
    (A) would be renewing   (C) will be renewing
    (B) wouldn't be renewing (D) can't renew

   Ⓐ   Ⓑ   Ⓒ   Ⓓ

VERB TENSE

Look for time expressions in the sentence to help you decide on the verb tense: *every day, last week, tomorrow,* etc. Another clue is to look at the tense of other verbs in the sentence. Remember that some verbs can only be used in certain tenses.

STRATEGIES FOR VERB TENSE ITEMS

ASK YOURSELF THESE QUESTIONS:

■ Is there a time expression in the sentence? If so, does the verb tense agree with the meaning of the time expression?

      INCORRECT   [I work in this department since 1994.]

      CORRECT   I've worked in this department since 1994.

■ Does the sentence have two clauses (an independent clause and a dependent clause)? If so, is the tense of the verb in the dependent clause correct?

      INCORRECT   [Ms. Martin tested the copying machine before she buys it.]

      CORRECT   Ms. Martin tested the copying machine before she bought it.

■ Is the verb being used as a *stative* verb? That is, does it describe a *state* rather than an action? If so, check to make sure the verb is not a progressive form (*-ing*). Note: *Seem, know,* and other verbs are always stative. *Become, be,* and other verbs can describe a state or an action.

      INCORRECT   [I am understanding what he's saying.]

      CORRECT   I understand what he's saying.

Practice

▶ Mark the choice that best completes the sentence.

1. When the messenger _____ , will you please give him this package?   Ⓐ Ⓑ Ⓒ Ⓓ
   (A) will arrive   (C) arriving
   (B) arrives   (D) would arrive

2. The assistant to Ms. Brigham _____ more responsible in the last year.   Ⓐ Ⓑ Ⓒ Ⓓ
   (A) is becoming   (C) has become
   (B) has been becoming   (D) becomes

3. The Paris branch of our bank _____ five years ago today.   Ⓐ Ⓑ Ⓒ Ⓓ
   (A) opens   (C) opened
   (B) has opened   (D) was opening

4. The consultant _____ the results of his recommendations by the end of the month.   Ⓐ Ⓑ Ⓒ Ⓓ
   (A) knows   (C) has known
   (B) does know   (D) will know

5. My supervisor promises that I _____ a raise next year.   Ⓐ Ⓑ Ⓒ Ⓓ
   (A) would get   (C) will get
   (B) should get   (D) get

6. After you _____ enough practice, it will be easy for you to do.   Ⓐ Ⓑ Ⓒ Ⓓ
   (A) have had   (C) had
   (B) will have   (D) are having

7. The boss _____ for those reports all morning.   Ⓐ Ⓑ Ⓒ Ⓓ
   (A) is waiting   (C) has been waiting
   (B) waits   (D) will waiting

8. I _____ something very strange, like burning wires.   Ⓐ Ⓑ Ⓒ Ⓓ
   (A) am smelling   (C) smelling
   (B) smell   (D) had smelled

9. You can take those files to the records room unless Kim _____ it first.   Ⓐ Ⓑ Ⓒ Ⓓ
   (A) does   (C) is doing
   (B) will do   (D) had done

10. We _____ at that restaurant in a few months.   Ⓐ Ⓑ Ⓒ Ⓓ
    (A) don't eat   (C) haven't eaten
    (B) won't eat   (D) didn't eat

TWO-WORD VERBS

Two-word verbs such as *look at, get by, take in* are usually common verbs (*look, get, take,* etc.) combined with other words that are often prepositions (*at, by, in, from, out,* etc.).

STRATEGIES FOR TWO-WORD VERB ITEMS

ASK YOURSELF THESE QUESTIONS:

▪ Are you unsure about the meaning? If so, check your dictionary. There are no rules about two-word verbs that will help you predict their meaning.

Mark the choice that best completes the sentence.

1. The new lawyer has gone to _____ the file.   Ⓐ Ⓑ Ⓒ Ⓓ
   (A) look away   (C) look into
   (B) look for   (D) look out

2. Who will _____ the advertising manager's projects   Ⓐ Ⓑ Ⓒ Ⓓ
   while she is on vacation?
   (A) take away   (C) take over
   (B) take up   (D) take off

3. The personnel officer believes that we can _____ with   Ⓐ Ⓑ Ⓒ Ⓓ
   our present staff.
   (A) get off   (C) get up
   (B) get by   (D) get on

4. The chairwoman decided to _____ sending the letter   Ⓐ Ⓑ Ⓒ Ⓓ
   until Monday.
   (A) take on   (C) put off
   (B) keep up   (D) pick up

5. Could you show me how to _____ the copy machine?   Ⓐ Ⓑ Ⓒ Ⓓ
   (A) take hold   (C) find out
   (B) turn on   (D) leave off

6. Please _____ this article for any typos or other errors.   Ⓐ Ⓑ Ⓒ Ⓓ
   (A) check into   (C) look over
   (B) look for   (D) check up

7. Did I tell you? I _____ Ms. Flynn at the conference.   Ⓐ Ⓑ Ⓒ Ⓓ
   (A) ran over   (C) found out
   (B) ran into   (D) brought up

8. I can't find the Simpson will anywhere. I _____!   Ⓐ Ⓑ Ⓒ Ⓓ
   (A) give up   (C) give over
   (B) give out   (D) give back

9. You don't need to give me your decision right now. _____.   Ⓐ Ⓑ Ⓒ Ⓓ
   (A) Check it over.   (C) Think it over.
   (B) Look it over.   (D) Turn it over.

10. When you get to Hong Kong, are you going to _____   Ⓐ Ⓑ Ⓒ Ⓓ
    Mr. Cao?
    (A) call on   (C) call off
    (B) look through (D) pick off

STRATEGY REVIEW

Review these strategies for Part 5 of the new TOEIC test.

■ For word family items, ask yourself:

    Do you need a noun, adjective, adverb, or verb?

■ For similar word items, ask yourself:

    Do answer options contain similar letters or spellings?

    Do options refer to the same topic, but with different meanings?

■ For preposition items, ask yourself:

    Do you need to refer to a specific time, day, date, or city?

    Are the preposition choices logical?

■ For conjunction items, ask yourself:

    What do you need to join and what conjunction is needed?

    Are the conjunction choices logical?

■ For adverb of frequency items, ask yourself:

    Is the position of the adverb correct?

    Are the adverb choices logical?

■ For causative verb items, ask yourself:

    What is the form of the verb in the noun clause?

    Who performs the action?

■ For conditional sentence items, ask yourself:

    Is the condition real or unreal?

    Is the condition in the present, past, or future?

■ For verb tense items, ask yourself:

    What time expressions are in the sentence?

    If there are two clauses in the sentence, are the verb tenses appropriate?

    Is there a stative verb?

■ For two-word verb items, ask yourself:

    Is the meaning of the two-word verb logical?

STRATEGY PRACTICE

DIRECTIONS: Read the following statements and choose the word or phrase that best completes the sentence. Use the strategies you have learned.

1. The office manager prefers her coffee with cream
   _____ sugar.
   (A) but   (C) and
   (B) nor   (D) plus

   (A) (B) (C) (D)

2. Office hours will be from 8:30 _____ 5:00.
   (A) at   (C) by
   (B) to   (D) toward

   (A) (B) (C) (D)

3. If the secretary _____ where the missing files are,
   we can stop looking for them.
   (A) knew   (C) had known
   (B) would know   (D) knows

   (A) (B) (C) (D)

4. The cashier has to turn the key _____ to open the safe.
   (A) clocked   (C) clockwise
   (B) clock   (D) clocking

   (A) (B) (C) (D)

5. The chairman of the board is not _____; he has been
   married for two years.
   (A) singular   (C) only
   (B) single   (D) sole

   (A) (B) (C) (D)

6. When the president arrived, everyone _____.
   (A) has left already   (C) already left
   (B) had already left   (D) left already

   (A) (B) (C) (D)

7. Mr. Hao was able to get the envelopes _____ before
   the mail carrier arrived.
   (A) addressed   (C) were addressing
   (B) were addressed (D) being addressed

   (A) (B) (C) (D)

8. Since many of our clients insist on French food, we
   _____ make reservations for lunch at the restaurant
   Lion d'Or.
   (A) often have   (C) have often to
   (B) have to often (D) often have to

   (A) (B) (C) (D)

9. _____ you finish typing that report, make five copies
   of it and give it to all of the officers.
   (A) While   (C) But
   (B) When   (D) Although

   (A) (B) (C) (D)

10. Let's have this letter _____ by express mail.
    (A) sends   (C) sent
    (B) send   (D) being sent

    (A) (B) (C) (D)

11. Since we need to know who belongs to this organization, could you have the computer do a printout of the entire _____?
    (A) membership   (C) members
    (B) remembrances   (D) memories

    Ⓐ Ⓑ Ⓒ Ⓓ

12. Ms. Parker was very _____ with the answers the job applicant gave during the interview.
    (A) impress   (C) impression
    (B) impressionable   (D) impressed

    Ⓐ Ⓑ Ⓒ Ⓓ

13. I'll stay late tonight if we _____ by 5:00.
    (A) did not finish   (C) had not finished
    (B) do not finish   (D) will not finish

    Ⓐ Ⓑ Ⓒ Ⓓ

14. The final draft will be completed _____ Wednesday.
    (A) to   (C) on
    (B) at   (D) from

    Ⓐ Ⓑ Ⓒ Ⓓ

15. The benefits program _____ in the next few months.
    (A) had changed   (C) changed
    (B) were changed   (D) will be changed

    Ⓐ Ⓑ Ⓒ Ⓓ

16. Mr. Honda is a terrific worker. He _____ two promotions this year.
    (A) has been giving   (C) was given
    (B) gave   (D) giving

    Ⓐ Ⓑ Ⓒ Ⓓ

17. If we keep _____ like this, we should be done before the deadline.
    (A) working   (C) to work
    (B) worked   (D) work

    Ⓐ Ⓑ Ⓒ Ⓓ

18. I don't need those statistics right now, but please have them ready _____ five o'clock.
    (A) on   (C) in
    (B) by   (D) since

    Ⓐ Ⓑ Ⓒ Ⓓ

19. I'll be home for dinner unless the boss _____ me to work overtime.
    (A) will ask   (C) asks
    (B) is asking   (D) asked

    Ⓐ Ⓑ Ⓒ Ⓓ

20. Make sure you get these contracts _____ before you meet with the lawyer.
    (A) signed   (C) signing
    (B) to sign   (D) sign

    Ⓐ Ⓑ Ⓒ Ⓓ

PART 6—TEXT COMPLETION

These are the directions for Part 6 of the new TOEIC® test. Study them now. If you understand these directions now, you will not have to read them on the test.

PART 6

Directions: Read the texts that follow. A word or phrase is missing in some of the sentences. Four answer choices are given below each of the sentences. Select the best answer to complete the text. Then mark the letter (A), (B), (C), or (D) on your answer sheet.

In this section, you will learn the most common types of items in the text completion passages in Part 6. A text completion passage is a passage with words deleted. You will need to understand the whole passage to choose the correct word to complete the blank.

You will find the items you studied in Part 5 useful for Part 6. In this section, you will study other common types of items found on Part 6.

- words in context
- pronouns
- subject-verb agreement
- modal auxiliaries
- adjective comparisons
- gerunds or infinitives

WORDS IN CONTEXT

In Part 6 in the new TOEIC, you will have to choose a word that is the correct word in the context of the passage. You will have to be able to recognize words that carry the meaning in both a positive and a negative context.

STRATEGIES FOR WORDS IN CONTEXT

ASK YOURSELF THESE QUESTIONS:

- Should the missing word carry a meaning similar to the positive context?

    We worked all last night to finish the project on time.

    INCORRECT [Our *clock* was this morning.]

    CORRECT Our *deadline* was this morning.

- Should the missing word carry a meaning similar to the negative context?

    She never gave her friends anything.

    INCORRECT [She wasn't very *loyal*.]

    CORRECT She wasn't very *generous*.

Practice

▶ Mark the choice that best completes the sentence.

1. You have not paid your invoices in three months.   Ⓐ Ⓑ Ⓒ Ⓓ
   Interest of 16.8% is being applied to your _____ balance.
   (A) upstanding
   (B) remunerated
   (C) remainder
   (D) overdue

2. Members must be single and earn at least $2 million   Ⓐ Ⓑ Ⓒ Ⓓ
   a year. If you meet these qualifications, you are
   _____ for membership.
   (A) eligible
   (B) titled
   (C) inadequate
   (D) financed

3. Ms. Jones worked for the company for just two weeks before she unexpectedly left. We will never know whether she was terminated or whether she _____.   Ⓐ Ⓑ Ⓒ Ⓓ
   (A) fired
   (B) resigned
   (C) hired
   (D) applied

4. Some people don't know how to eat properly. Their table manners are _____.   Ⓐ Ⓑ Ⓒ Ⓓ
   (A) attractive
   (B) shameful
   (C) appealing
   (D) edifying

5. We are unable to respond to your request at this time. We will try to _____ you within the week.   Ⓐ Ⓑ Ⓒ Ⓓ
   (A) ignore
   (B) get back to
   (C) delay
   (D) turn around

6. If you have any comments or suggestions, do not hesitate to let us know. We look forward to hearing your _____.   Ⓐ Ⓑ Ⓒ Ⓓ
   (A) feedback
   (B) talk
   (C) complaints
   (D) problems

7. The highway is under repair, and traffic is often at a standstill. You might find it _____ to take the underground train.   Ⓐ Ⓑ Ⓒ Ⓓ
   (A) inconvenient
   (B) faster
   (C) inadvisable
   (D) idle

8. We never thought the meeting would be so long and boring. Next time let's make it shorter and more _____.   Ⓐ Ⓑ Ⓒ Ⓓ
   (A) dull
   (B) interesting
   (C) curious
   (D) lengthy

9. At our new headquarters, we finally have more than enough room for everyone. Our offices are modern and _____ .   Ⓐ Ⓑ Ⓒ Ⓓ
   (A) traditional
   (B) undersized
   (C) overcrowded
   (D) spacious

10. The way you do business is hardly effective or efficient. In fact, you are the most _____ manager in our company.   Ⓐ Ⓑ Ⓒ Ⓓ
    (A) capable
    (B) talented
    (C) incompetent
    (D) accomplished

PRONOUNS

Words that take the place of nouns or noun phrases are **pronouns.**

SUBJECT PRONOUNS	*I, you, she, he, it, we, they*
OBJECT PRONOUNS	*me, you, her, him, it, us, them*
POSSESSIVE ADJECTIVES	*my, your, her, his, its, our, their*
POSSESSIVE PRONOUNS	*mine, yours, hers, his, its, ours, theirs*
REFLEXIVE PRONOUNS	*myself, yourself, herself, himself, itself, ourselves, yourselves, themselves*

STRATEGIES FOR PRONOUN ITEMS

ASK YOURSELF THESE QUESTIONS:

■ Does the pronoun agree with the noun it replaces in number (singular or plural)?

| **INCORRECT** | [I made the mistake, so I will correct *them*.] |
| **CORRECT** | I made the mistake, so I will correct *it*. |

■ Does the pronoun agree with the noun it replaces in gender (*he, she,* or *it*)?

| **INCORRECT** | [We waited for Mrs. Baxter, but *he* was late.] |
| **CORRECT** | We waited for Mrs. Baxter, but *she* was late. |

■ Does the pronoun agree with the noun it replaces grammatically (subject, object, possessive, or reflexive)?

| **INCORRECT** | [My boss asked *myself* to work late.] |
| **CORRECT** | My boss asked *me* to work late. |

➤ Mark the choice that best completes the sentence.

1. The doors and windows are open. Shut _____ if you want.
   (A) it
   (B) her
   (C) their
   (D) them

   Ⓐ Ⓑ Ⓒ Ⓓ

2. I finished the job alone. I worked all night by _____.
   (A) it
   (B) its
   (C) me
   (D) myself

   Ⓐ Ⓑ Ⓒ Ⓓ

3. These books are _____, and the ones on the desk are mine.
   (A) you
   (B) your
   (C) yours
   (D) yourself

   Ⓐ Ⓑ Ⓒ Ⓓ

4. My sister's husband is an architect. _____ designed my house.
   (A) He
   (B) She
   (C) You
   (D) It

   Ⓐ Ⓑ Ⓒ Ⓓ

5. My mother talked to me yesterday, but I didn't tell _____ I was sick.
   (A) him
   (B) she
   (C) her
   (D) it

   Ⓐ Ⓑ Ⓒ Ⓓ

6. I get too many e-mails. I can't read _____ all.
   (A) them
   (B) myself
   (C) mine
   (D) its

   Ⓐ Ⓑ Ⓒ Ⓓ

7. We wanted to arrive before dinner, but _____ flight   Ⓐ Ⓑ Ⓒ Ⓓ
   was delayed.
   (A) it
   (B) its
   (C) our
   (D) ours

8. Read these papers, sign your name on the bottom of   Ⓐ Ⓑ Ⓒ Ⓓ
   each page, and then fax _____ to the lawyer.
   (A) her
   (B) it
   (C) his
   (D) them

9. You should have gone to the airport _____ to meet the   Ⓐ Ⓑ Ⓒ Ⓓ
   client. She didn't know where to go.
   (A) herself
   (B) her
   (C) yourself
   (D) you

10. If the weather is nice, we'll have the meeting outdoors.   Ⓐ Ⓑ Ⓒ Ⓓ
    If _____ isn't, we won't.
    (A) our
    (B) ourselves
    (C) it
    (D) its

SUBJECT-VERB AGREEMENT

The subject and verb of a sentence or clause must agree in number (singular, plural) and person (first, second, third).

STRATEGIES FOR SUBJECT-VERB AGREEMENT ITEMS

ASK YOURSELF THESE QUESTIONS:

▪ Is the noun a collective noun? Is it considered a unit? If so, is the verb singular?

INCORRECT	[The committee <u>are</u> meeting again on Monday morning.]
CORRECT	The committee <u>is</u> meeting again on Monday morning.

▪ Is the noun a collective noun that refers to single, separate elements? Is it considered plural? If so, is the verb plural?

INCORRECT	[The police <u>is</u> currently investigating the situation.]
CORRECT	The police <u>are</u> currently investigating the situation.

▪ Is the noun ending in –s considered singular? If so, is the verb singular?

INCORRECT	[The news <u>have</u> not been good lately.]
CORRECT	The news <u>has</u> not been good lately.

▪ Is there a phrase that separates the subject from the verb? If so, have you found the verb? Have you found the subject of that verb? Do they agree?

INCORRECT	[The price of our goods <u>are</u> lower than that of our competitors.]
CORRECT	The price of our goods <u>is</u> lower than that of our competitors.

Mark the choice that best completes the sentence.

1. We are interviewing everyone who _____ interest in the job.
   (A) express
   (B) expresses
   (C) expressing
   (D) to express

   Ⓐ Ⓑ Ⓒ Ⓓ

2. This group of doctors _____ in important research.
   (A) is involved
   (B) are involved
   (C) be involving
   (D) been involving

   Ⓐ Ⓑ Ⓒ Ⓓ

3. Mathematics _____ not easy for my brother.
   (A) was
   (B) were
   (C) are
   (D) be

   Ⓐ Ⓑ Ⓒ Ⓓ

4. The results of our efforts to get more business _____ been successful.
   (A) is
   (B) are
   (C) has
   (D) have

   Ⓐ Ⓑ Ⓒ Ⓓ

5. The computers that were ordered last week _____ on solar power.
   (A) run
   (B) runs
   (C) running
   (D) to run

   Ⓐ Ⓑ Ⓒ Ⓓ

6. The trade newsletter where we advertise _____ widely distributed.
   (A) has
   (B) have
   (C) is
   (D) are

   Ⓐ Ⓑ Ⓒ Ⓓ

7. My family _____ to open a restaurant soon.   Ⓐ Ⓑ Ⓒ Ⓓ
   (A) plans
   (B) plan
   (C) planning
   (D) planner

8. The United States _____ taxes to develop the   Ⓐ Ⓑ Ⓒ Ⓓ
   infrastructure for commerce.
   (A) raise
   (B) raises
   (C) rise
   (D) risen

9. The accountant determined how much money   Ⓐ Ⓑ Ⓒ Ⓓ
   _____ spent on this project.
   (A) was
   (B) were
   (C) is
   (D) be

10. The government _____ to send a team of consultants Ⓐ Ⓑ Ⓒ Ⓓ
    to work with the farmers.
    (A) want
    (B) wants
    (C) wanting
    (D) to want

MODAL AUXILIARIES

Modal auxiliaries are "helping" words that give specific meaning to and indicate the tense of the verb. Examples of modal auxiliaries are:

PRESENT/FUTURE	PAST/INDIRECT SPEECH	MODAL PERFECTS
shall*/will	*would*	*will/would have*
can	*could*	*could have*
may/might	*might*	*may/might have*
should	*should*	*should have*
ought to	*ought to*	*ought to have*
must	*had to*	*must have*

*Shall was traditionally used for the future in British English in the first and third persons. Today, *will* is more common. *Shall* is used in both British and American English in formal speech to make an offer or a suggestion in the form of a question: *Shall I answer the phone for you? Shall we take another look at the budget?* It is generally not tested on the new TOEIC.

STRATEGIES FOR MODAL AUXILIARY ITEMS

ASK YOURSELF THESE QUESTIONS:

■ Is the main verb of the sentence in the present tense? If so, is there a modal in a present form in the subordinate clause?

INCORRECT	[He is sure he <u>could</u> meet us there.]
CORRECT	He is sure he <u>can</u> meet us there.

■ Is the main verb of the sentence in the past tense? If so, is there a modal in a past form in the subordinate clause?

INCORRECT	[He thought he <u>will</u> retire soon.]
CORRECT	He thought he <u>would</u> retire soon.

■ Has the action of the verb in the subordinate clause occurred before the action of the main verb? If so, is there a modal perfect in the subordinate clause?

INCORRECT	[I think that I <u>might make</u> a mistake yesterday.]
CORRECT	I think that I <u>might have made</u> a mistake yesterday.

Mark the choice that best completes the sentence.

1. The company hired a public relations firm which
   _____ improve their image.   Ⓐ Ⓑ Ⓒ Ⓓ
   (A) will have
   (B) ought to have
   (C) may have
   (D) could

2. The management is meeting to determine who
   _____ promoted.   Ⓐ Ⓑ Ⓒ Ⓓ
   (A) must
   (B) will be
   (C) could have been
   (D) might have

3. She was told she would have seniority and _____ ask   Ⓐ Ⓑ Ⓒ Ⓓ
   for more vacation time.
   (A) could
   (B) could have
   (C) can
   (D) will

4. The committee could not agree on what action
   _____ taken.   Ⓐ Ⓑ Ⓒ Ⓓ
   (A) would have been
   (B) ought to have
   (C) should be
   (D) had to

5. We _____ follow these steps to use the new   Ⓐ Ⓑ Ⓒ Ⓓ
   photocopier.
   (A) could have
   (B) would
   (C) ought to have
   (D) must

6. I would do it if I could, but I can't, so I _____ even try.   Ⓐ Ⓑ Ⓒ Ⓓ
   (A) had not to
   (B) won't
   (C) ought to
   (D) must have

7. Our ancestors _____ remarkable people to have Ⓐ Ⓑ Ⓒ Ⓓ
   lived with such hardships.
   (A) could have been
   (B) must have been
   (C) should be
   (D) will be

8. You should have told me sooner so that I _____ Ⓐ Ⓑ Ⓒ Ⓓ
   helped you.
   (A) could have
   (B) ought to
   (C) can
   (D) must

9. Once you eat here, you _____ pleased with the service Ⓐ Ⓑ Ⓒ Ⓓ
   and the food.
   (A) had to be
   (B) might have been
   (C) could have been
   (D) will be

10. The new software we plan to install _____ make our Ⓐ Ⓑ Ⓒ Ⓓ
    department more productive.
    (A) will
    (B) would have
    (C) might have
    (D) had to

ADJECTIVE COMPARISONS

Comparisons are used to compare only two things. There are three different structures to use for comparisons:

1. If the adjective is one syllable (*tall*), add *–er* (*taller*).

2. If the adjective is two syllables and ends with *–y* (*busy*), change the *y* to *i* and then add *–er* (*busier*).

3. If the adjective is two syllables or more (*handsome/expensive*), put *more* before it (*more handsome/more expensive*).

If the people or things being compared are used in the sentence, put *than* after the comparative form (*taller than/busier than/more expensive than*).

Superlatives are used to compare three or more things:

1. If the adjective is one syllable (*tall*), add *–est* (*tallest*). Also put *the* before it (*the tallest*).

2. If the adjective is two syllables and ends with *–y* (*busy*), change the *y* to *i* and then add *–est* (*busiest*). Also put *the* before it (*the busiest*).

3. If the adjective is two syllables or more (*handsome/expensive*), put *the most* before it (*the most handsome/the most expensive*).

STRATEGIES FOR ADJECTIVE COMPARISON ITEMS

ASK YOURSELF THESE QUESTIONS:

▪ Is it a comparison of two things? If so, is *than* used?

INCORRECT	[He seems more qualified <u>then</u> he is.]
CORRECT	He seems more qualified <u>than</u> he is.

▪ Is it a comparison of more than two things? If so, does *the* precede the adjective?

INCORRECT	[Our company submitted highest bid.]
CORRECT	Our company submitted <u>the</u> highest bid.

▪ Are two equal things being compared? If so, is *as* + adjective + *as* being used?

INCORRECT	[They are not <u>experienced as</u> they could be.]
CORRECT	They are not <u>as experienced as</u> they could be.

▪ Is there an irregular adjective form? If so, be sure to memorize it.

IRREGULAR ADJECTIVES	COMPARATIVE FORMS	SUPERLATIVE FORMS
good	*better*	*best*
bad	*worse*	*worst*
far	*farther, further*	*farthest, furthest*
little	*less*	*least*
many, much	*more*	*most*

INCORRECT	[This is the <u>good</u> evaluation I've ever gotten.]
CORRECT	This is the <u>best</u> evaluation I've ever gotten.

> Mark the choice that best completes the sentence.

1. He was _____ qualified of all the applicants.   Ⓐ Ⓑ Ⓒ Ⓓ
   (A) less
   (B) the least
   (C) least
   (D) the less

2. Stock prices are _____ they were last week.   Ⓐ Ⓑ Ⓒ Ⓓ
   (A) the highest
   (B) high
   (C) higher
   (D) higher than

3. _____ person in our community is the mayor.   Ⓐ Ⓑ Ⓒ Ⓓ
   (A) The most famous
   (B) The more famous
   (C) Famous
   (D) More famous

4. The benefits are _____ now than last year.   Ⓐ Ⓑ Ⓒ Ⓓ
   (A) good
   (B) better
   (C) best
   (D) the best

5. This restaurant serves _____ food that I've ever eaten.   Ⓐ Ⓑ Ⓒ Ⓓ
   (A) the bad
   (B) worse
   (C) the worst
   (D) worst

6. The proposal wasn't _____ ours.   Ⓐ Ⓑ Ⓒ Ⓓ
   (A) as
   (B) as complete
   (C) complete as
   (D) as complete as

7. When she was _____ than I am now, she started her   Ⓐ Ⓑ Ⓒ Ⓓ
   own company.
   (A) young
   (B) younger
   (C) youngest
   (D) the most young

8. Mr. Nakamura, _____ addition to our company, is a great golfer. ⒶⒷⒸⒹ
   (A) a newest
   (B) the newest
   (C) new
   (D) newer

9. _____ late than never. ⒶⒷⒸⒹ
   (A) Good
   (B) Better
   (C) Best
   (D) The best

10. Press _____ button to call the nurse. ⒶⒷⒸⒹ
    (A) topmore
    (B) topmost
    (C) the topmore
    (D) the topmost

GERUNDS OR INFINITIVES

Gerunds (*–ing* words) and **infinitives** (*to* + verb) are verb forms that can be used as nouns. They can be used as subjects, objects, or objects of prepositions. When they are used as direct objects, you have to look at the main verb to decide whether to use the gerund or infinitive form. You can find lists of these special verbs in most grammar reference books.

STRATEGIES FOR GERUND OR INFINITIVE ITEMS

ASK YOURSELF THESE QUESTIONS:

▪ Is the main verb one that can only be followed by a gerund (*admit, consider, enjoy, regret,* etc.)? If so, is the direct object in the gerund (*–ing*) form?

    INCORRECT   [Charlie regrets to take that extra piece of pie.]

    CORRECT   Charlie regrets taking that extra piece of pie.

▪ Is the main verb one that can only be followed by an infinitive (*afford, ask, decide, expect,* etc.)? If so, is the direct object in the infinitive (*to . . .*) form?

    INCORRECT   [We expect finishing before the deadline.]

    CORRECT   We expect to finish before the deadline.

Mark the choice that best completes the sentence.

1. The new accountant is considering _____ to
    another department.   Ⓐ Ⓑ Ⓒ Ⓓ
    (A) to transfer
    (B) transferring
    (C) transferred
    (D) transfer

2. Mr. Smith wanted _____ his coworkers.   Ⓐ Ⓑ Ⓒ Ⓓ
    (A) to meet
    (B) meeting
    (C) met
    (D) meet

3. We forgot _____ the door when we left.   Ⓐ Ⓑ Ⓒ Ⓓ
    (A) locked
    (B) locking
    (C) lock
    (D) to lock

4. They had _____ lunch until tomorrow.   Ⓐ Ⓑ Ⓒ Ⓓ
    (A) postpone
    (B) to postpone
    (C) postponing
    (D) to be postponed

5. The doctor told him to avoid _____ meat.   Ⓐ Ⓑ Ⓒ Ⓓ
    (A) eating
    (B) eat
    (C) eaten
    (D) to eat

6. We offered _____ for coffee during the break. Ⓐ Ⓑ Ⓒ Ⓓ
    (A) to go
    (B) going
    (C) gone
    (D) went

7. Jack admitted _____ home office equipment for his   Ⓐ   Ⓑ   Ⓒ   Ⓓ
   personal use.
   (A) to take
   (B) taking
   (C) take
   (D) took

8. The new employee promised not _____ late again.   Ⓐ   Ⓑ   Ⓒ   Ⓓ
   (A) to be
   (B) being
   (C) be
   (D) been

9. I hope _____ the MBA program at Harvard.   Ⓐ   Ⓑ   Ⓒ   Ⓓ
   (A) entered
   (B) enter
   (C) entering
   (D) to enter

10. Stop _____ your money.   Ⓐ   Ⓑ   Ⓒ   Ⓓ
    (A) to waste
    (B) wasted
    (C) wasting
    (D) waste

STRATEGY REVIEW

Review these strategies for Part 6 of the new TOEIC test.

■ For words-in-context items, ask yourself:

Should the missing word carry a meaning similar to the positive context?

Should the missing word carry a meaning similar to the negative context?

■ For pronoun items, ask yourself:

Does the pronoun agree with the noun it replaces in number (singular or plural)?

Does the pronoun agree with the noun it replaces in gender (*he, she,* or *it*)?

Does the pronoun agree with the noun it replaces grammatically (subject, object, possessive, or reflexive)?

■ For subject-verb items, ask yourself:

Is the noun a collective noun and considered a unit with a singular verb?

Is the noun a collective noun and considered singular with a plural verb?

Is the noun ending in –*s* considered singular with a singular verb?

Is there a phrase that separates the verb from the subject?

■ For modal auxiliary items, ask yourself:

If the main verb of the sentence is in the present tense, is there a modal in a present form in the subordinate clause?

If the main verb of the sentence is in the past tense, is there a modal in a past form in the subordinate clause?

If the action of the verb in the subordinate clause occurred before the action of the main verb, is there a modal perfect in the subordinate clause?

■ For adjective comparison items, ask yourself:

Are two things compared using *than*?

Are more than two things compared, and does *the* precede the adjective?

Are all things being compared, and is the superlative being used?

Are two things being compared equally with *as* + adjective + *as*?

Is there an irregular adjective form?

■ For gerund or infinitive items, ask yourself:

Can the main verb only be followed by a gerund?

Can the main verb only be followed by an infinitive?

DIRECTIONS: Read the following passages and choose the word or phrase that best completes the blanks. Use the strategies you have learned.

Questions 1–4 refer to the following letter.

624 South Wells Street
Reno, Nevada 89400

Mr. Norm Thompson
97 Vine Circle
Reno, Nevada 89400

Dear Mr. Thompson:

I want to rent an apartment. My friend says that you are a good _____

1. (A) landlord
    (B) occupant
    (C) tenant
    (D) painter

and that you own apartments in different parts of the city. Can I rent an apartment from you?

My family needs a new place to live. We love our _____. It's quiet, and

2. (A) neighbor
    (B) neighborly
    (C) neighboring
    (D) neighborhood

it's close to my job. However, our apartment is _____ small for us. There

3. (A) too
    (B) a lot
    (C) some
    (D) enough

are four of us: my wife, our two children, and me. We need a larger apartment. We are looking for one with three bedrooms and a large kitchen.

We live near Plumas Pass, and we would like to stay in this area. If you have an apartment in Plumas Pass that is _____ now, please let me know. Thank you for your help.

4. (A) distant
    (B) occupied
    (C) available
    (D) expensive

Sincerely,

Fabian Ricardo

Fabian Ricardo

Montalvo Industries announced Friday that it take on 100 new _____ over the next 6 months.

5. (A) employees
   (B) merchants
   (C) customers
   (D) products

"Our market is expanding," said company CEO Shirley Henrico, "so we need to _____ our production. That's why we need to hire more workers." The

6. (A) grow
   (B) more
   (C) bigger
   (D) increase

company plans _____ a new, larger factory on the outskirts of the city,

7. (A) build
   (B) builds
   (C) to build
   (D) building

which will be equipped with all the latest technology. "We are building a very modern factory," said Ms. Henrico. "We are very proud of _____."

8. (A) us
   (B) it
   (C) me
   (D) him

The Stardust Cinema announces the third annual

Festival of _____ Films

9. (A) Classic
    (B) National
    (C) Cartoon
    (D) International

September 20–27

We will show the best films of this year
from all around the world.

See your favorite foreign actors perform
in our comfortable, modern theater.
_____ will be four different shows every day.

10. (A) There
    (B) They
    (C) We
    (D) It

Tickets are $10 a show, or $35 for four shows.

Children 12–17 years old
must be accompanied _____ an adult.

11. (A) to
    (B) by
    (C) for
    (D) with

Children under 12 will not be _____.

12. (A) treated
    (B) educated
    (C) admitted
    (D) employed

PART 7—
READING COMPREHENSION

These are the general directions for Part 7 of the new TOEIC® test. Study them now. If you understand these general directions now, you will not have to read them during the test.

PART 7

Directions: In this part you will read a selection of texts, such as magazine and newspaper articles, letters, and advertisements. Each text is followed by several questions. Select the best answer for each question and mark the letter (A), (B), (C), or (D) on your answer sheet.

It is important to read the specific directions carefully. The specific directions tell you what passage to read and which questions to answer.

In the first section of Part 7, there are 28 questions. You will read seven to ten reading passages and answer two to four questions for each passage. You will see directions like this:

Questions 153–155 refer to the following e-mail.
Questions 156–159 refer to the following announcement.

In the second section of Part 7, there are 20 questions. You will read 4 pairs of reading passages. Each pair of passages will have 5 questions. You will see directions like this:

Questions 181–185 refer to the following invoice and letter.
Questions 186–190 refer to the following advertisement and e-mail.

Part 7 Sections	Number of Questions	Number of Passages	Questions	Question Numbers
Single passages	28	7 to 10	2 to 4 per passage	153–180
Double passages	20	4 pairs	5 per pair of passages	181–200

In this section, you will read the most common types of passages found on the new TOEIC test:

- advertisements

- business correspondence

- forms, charts, and graphs

- articles and reports

- announcements and paragraphs

READING STRATEGIES

■ Read the questions BEFORE you read the passage.

> If you know what a question asks, you will have a specific purpose when you read. Look for the answer to the question as you read.

■ Do not read the answers before you read the passage.

> Save yourself some time. You will probably find the answer to the question yourself.

■ If you cannot answer a question, scan the passage and look for the answer options.

> If you cannot answer a question, read the four answer options. Scan the passage, looking for these four options. Be careful. The option may be a synonym or paraphrase of the correct answer.

■ Be prepared for four question types on the new TOEIC test: main idea questions, detail questions, inference questions, and vocabulary questions. You will find these questions in both the single passage and double passage sections of part 7. Samples of each question type are below.

MAIN IDEA QUESTIONS

What is being advertised?
What is the purpose of the letter?
What is the main idea of this article?
What is this announcement about?
What is the purpose of this graph?
What is the reason for this correspondence?
What is the topic of the meeting?
What is being discussed?

DETAIL QUESTIONS

How much is a (product)?
When was the e-mail sent?
What percentage of users are over 30?
Who is (name or title)?
What dates are critical?
Who has to attend the meeting?
How much time does the graph cover?
Where is Mr. Brown working now?

INFERENCE QUESTIONS

Who might use the product?
What is the tone of the memo?
Who would use the information?
Who would most likely read this report?

What is the writer's opinion?

Where would you find these instructions?

Why did Ms. Jones write this letter?

What will the employee do next?

VOCABULARY QUESTIONS

The word "promotion" in paragraph 1, line 3, is closest in meaning to . . .

The word "automated" in paragraph 5, line 2 is closest in meaning to . . .

The word "competent" in line 2 is closest in meaning to . . .

The word "produce" in line 1 of the ad is closest in meaning to . . .

The word "data" below the graph is closest in meaning to . . .

Advertisements

How much is (a product)?	*detail*
What is being advertised?	*main idea*
Who might use the product?	*inference*

Business correspondence

When was the fax sent?	*detail*
What is the purpose of the letter?	*main idea*
What is the tone of the memo?	*inference*

Forms, charts, and graphs

What percentage of users are over 30?	*detail*
What is the purpose of the circle graph?	*main idea*
Who would use this information?	*inference*

Articles and reports

What dates are critical?	*detail*
What is the main idea of this article?	*main idea*
Who would most likely read this report?	*inference*

Announcements and paragraphs

Who is (name or title)?	*detail*
What is the announcement about?	*main idea*
What is the writer's opinion?	*inference*

PRACTICE: READING COMPREHENSION

Advertisement 1

> Small computer software company is looking for an office manager. College degree not required, but applicant must have at least two years experience at a similar job. Call Ms. Chang (director) at 348-555-0987.

1. What kind of job is advertised?
   (A) Director of a computer company
   (B) Office manager
   (C) Computer programmer
   (D) College professor

   (A) (B) (C) (D)

2. What is a requirement for this job?
   (A) A college degree
   (B) Less than two years experience
   (C) Telephone skills
   (D) Two or more years experience

   (A) (B) (C) (D)

READING FAST

Read the ad as fast as you can. How long did it take?

_____ minutes _____ seconds

OFFICE SUPPLY SALE

This week only

- Computer paper (white only)   25% off
- Envelopes (all colors, including pink, purple, and gold)   50% off
- Notebooks—buy five, get one free
- Pens (blue, black, and red ink)   12 for $1

Sale ends Saturday
Store closed Sunday

3. What kind of computer paper is on sale?   (A) (B) (C) (D)
   - (A) White
   - (B) All colors
   - (C) Pink, purple, and gold
   - (D) Red, blue, and black

4. How can you get a free notebook?   (A) (B) (C) (D)
   - (A) Pay one dollar
   - (B) Spend $25 on computer paper
   - (C) Buy colored envelopes
   - (D) Buy five notebooks

5. When is the sale?   (A) (B) (C) (D)
   - (A) All weekend
   - (B) On Sunday only
   - (C) All week
   - (D) On Saturday only

READING FAST

Read the ad as fast as you can. How long did it take?

_____ minutes _____ seconds

Sea Island Resort

Spend your next vacation with us.

Enjoy our:
- private beach
- two swimming pools
- four tennis courts
- five restaurants
- beautiful weather all year

It's easy to get here.
We're just eight kilometers from the airport.

Call your travel agent to make reservations.

6. What is this ad for? Ⓐ Ⓑ Ⓒ Ⓓ
- (A) An airline
- (B) A travel agency
- (C) A vacation place
- (D) A sports club

7. What is one thing you cannot do at Sea Island Resort? Ⓐ Ⓑ Ⓒ Ⓓ
- (A) Swim
- (B) Play tennis
- (C) Eat
- (D) Play golf

8. The word "private" in line 5 is closest in meaning to Ⓐ Ⓑ Ⓒ Ⓓ
- (A) not public
- (B) large
- (C) sandy
- (D) personal

9. How can you make reservations for Sea Island Resort? Ⓐ Ⓑ Ⓒ Ⓓ
- (A) Call a travel agent
- (B) Write a letter to the resort owner
- (C) Call the airport
- (D) Send an e-mail

READING FAST

Read the ad as fast as you can. How long did it take?

_____ minutes _____ seconds

Market Products, Inc.
830 2nd Ave. Suite 20B
New York, NY 10015

June 7, 20___

Ms. Lucy Harper
2091 W 4th Avenue
Apartment 101
Buffalo, NY 12345

Dear Ms. Harper:

Thank you for your letter of April 15 looking for a job at Market Products. You have good experience and an excellent education. I am sorry to tell you, however, that we don't have any job openings at this time. We will keep your résumé and contact you if we have any job openings in the future. Good luck.

Best regards,

Joan Rogers

Joan Rogers
Human Resources Director

---

10. Why did Joan Rogers write this letter?　　　(A)　(B)　(C)　(D)
    - (A) To offer Ms. Harper a job
    - (B) To sell products to Ms. Harper
    - (C) To reply to Ms. Harper's letter
    - (D) To explain the work of Market Products

11. When did she write the letter?　　　(A)　(B)　(C)　(D)
    - (A) On April 5
    - (B) On April 15
    - (C) On June 7
    - (D) On June 17

READING FAST

Read the letter as fast as you can. How long did it take?

_____ minutes _____ seconds

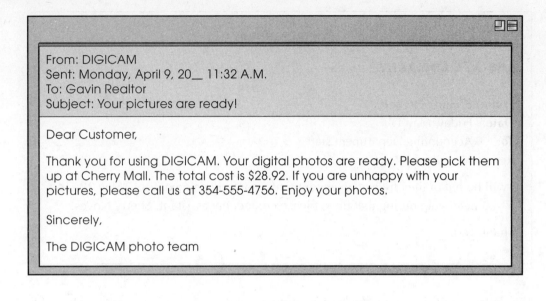

From: DIGICAM
Sent: Monday, April 9, 20__ 11:32 A.M.
To: Gavin Realtor
Subject: Your pictures are ready!

Dear Customer,

Thank you for using DIGICAM. Your digital photos are ready. Please pick them up at Cherry Mall. The total cost is $28.92. If you are unhappy with your pictures, please call us at 354-555-4756. Enjoy your photos.

Sincerely,

The DIGICAM photo team

12. What type of correspondence is this? (A) (B) (C) (D)
    (A) A cover letter
    (B) An e-mail
    (C) A memo
    (D) A fax

13. What is the reason for this correspondence? (A) (B) (C) (D)
    (A) There is a job opening at Digicam.
    (B) Some photos are ready.
    (C) The client forgot to pay.
    (D) The customer was unhappy.

14. What should customers who do not like their photos do? (A) (B) (C) (D)
    (A) Call Cherry Mall
    (B) Return their photos
    (C) Ask for a refund
    (D) Call Digicam

READING FAST

Read the e-mail as fast as you can. How long did it take?

_____ minutes _____ seconds

Memorandum

The XYZ Company

From: Brianna Herbert
Date: Friday, May 17
To: Accounting Department staff
Re: Next week

I will be out of the office at an accountants' conference next week, May 20–24. If you need help during that time, please contact my assistant, Sherry Noyes.

Thank you.

---

15. Where will Brianna Herbert be next week? Ⓐ Ⓑ Ⓒ Ⓓ
    (A) In the office
    (B) At a conference
    (C) On vacation
    (D) At the XYZ Company

16. Who is Sherry Noyes? Ⓐ Ⓑ Ⓒ Ⓓ
    (A) An accountant
    (B) The writer of the memo
    (C) The owner of the XYZ Company
    (D) Brianna Herbert's assistant

17. The word "contact" in line 8 is closest in meaning to Ⓐ Ⓑ Ⓒ Ⓓ
    (A) work with
    (B) call
    (C) touch
    (D) look at

18. Who should read the memo? Ⓐ Ⓑ Ⓒ Ⓓ
    (A) All staff at the XYZ company
    (B) Brianna Herbert
    (C) People who work in the accounting department
    (D) Conference planners

READING FAST

Read the memo as fast as you can. How long did it take?

_____ minutes _____ seconds

ROSIE'S STEAKHOUSE
We care about your service.

Date: *Feb 17, 20___*
Server's Name: *Julie*
Number of guests: *2*

The server was: (Excellent)   Good   Fair   Poor
The food was: Excellent   Good   Fair   (Poor)

Other comments: *Our server was very friendly and polite. She brought our drinks on time. However, we waited a long time for our food. Also, my husband was angry because his fish was not well-cooked. We will not return.*

---

19. How did the customers rate the food?   (A) (B) (C) (D)
    (A) Excellent
    (B) Good
    (C) Fair
    (D) Poor

20. Which of the following describes Julie?   (A) (B) (C) (D)
    (A) Slow
    (B) Friendly
    (C) Fair
    (D) Angry

READING FAST

Read the chart as fast as you can. How long did it take?

_____ minutes _____ seconds

CITY ZOO

Month	Number of visitors
January	5,000
February	4,500
March	4,675
April	4,980
May	5,950
June	5,897

21. How many people visited the zoo in February? Ⓐ Ⓑ Ⓒ Ⓓ
    (A) 4,000
    (B) 4,500
    (C) 4,675
    (D) 5,000

22. When did 4,980 people visit the zoo? Ⓐ Ⓑ Ⓒ Ⓓ
    (A) March
    (B) April
    (C) May
    (D) June

23. Which was the most popular month to visit the zoo? Ⓐ Ⓑ Ⓒ Ⓓ
    (A) March
    (B) April
    (C) May
    (D) June

READING FAST

Read the form as fast as you can. How long did it take?

_____ minutes _____ seconds

MT TELEPHONES
Best Sales of the Year
(Sales in thousands)

(Each quarter represents 3 months in the year)

24. The word "represents" is closest in meaning to
    (A) costs
    (B) stands for
    (C) means
    (D) takes on

    Ⓐ Ⓑ Ⓒ Ⓓ

25. Who had the highest sales in the first quarter?
    (A) B. Jones
    (B) C. Smith
    (C) A. Rayne
    (D) There was a tie.

    Ⓐ Ⓑ Ⓒ Ⓓ

26. How much money in sales did C. Smith have in
    the third quarter?
    (A) $60
    (B) $30,000
    (C) $40,000
    (D) $60,000

    Ⓐ Ⓑ Ⓒ Ⓓ

27. How many months does this graph represent?
    (A) 1
    (B) 3
    (C) 4
    (D) 12

    Ⓐ Ⓑ Ⓒ Ⓓ

READING FAST

Read the graph as fast as you can. How long did it take?

_____ minutes _____ seconds

Maple Plaza, our city's newest mall, will open on October 25. The new mall will have 31 stores and 8 restaurants. It will also have a movie theater, which will open in November. The biggest store at the mall will be McGruder's Department Store. There will be a party to celebrate the new mall on October 26 from noon to 5:00 PM. All members of the public are invited.

28. What will happen on October 25?　　Ⓐ　Ⓑ　Ⓒ　Ⓓ
    (A) A movie theater will open.
    (B) McGruder's will have a sale.
    (C) There will be a party.
    (D) A new mall will open.

29. How many stores will Maple Plaza have?　　Ⓐ　Ⓑ　Ⓒ　Ⓓ
    (A) 8
    (B) 26
    (C) 31
    (D) 34

READING FAST

Read the article as fast as you can. How long did it take?

_____ minutes _____ seconds

Do you know that computers can cause headaches? According to a recent report, many computer workers have this problem. If you work at a computer more than six hours a day, you might get headaches. To avoid this problem, take a break once every hour. Get up and walk around for a few minutes. Let your eyes and mind rest. This is a good way to stop headaches without taking aspirin.

30. What type of reading is this?   Ⓐ   Ⓑ   Ⓒ   Ⓓ
    (A)   A memo
    (B)   An article
    (C)   An advertisement
    (D)   An e-mail

31. According to the report, who gets headaches?   Ⓐ   Ⓑ   Ⓒ   Ⓓ
    (A)   People who use computers more than
          six hours a day
    (B)   All computer workers
    (C)   Everybody who works more than six hours a day
    (D)   Computer programmers

32. How can you avoid headaches?   Ⓐ   Ⓑ   Ⓒ   Ⓓ
    (A)   Walk every six hours
    (B)   Take aspirin
    (C)   Get a better computer
    (D)   Take a break once an hour

READING FAST

Read the report as fast as you can. How long did it take?

_____ minutes _____ seconds

> People are buying more cell phones. The country's largest cell phone company, Phonecom, reported its sales numbers yesterday. This year it has sold 38% more cell phones than it did last year. It has sold 25% of its phones to government offices, 40% to private companies, and 35% to individuals for personal use.

33. What does this report tell us?　　Ⓐ　Ⓑ　Ⓒ　Ⓓ
   (A)　Government offices bought fewer cell phones last year.
   (B)　Cell phones are more expensive this year than last year.
   (C)　A phone company has sold 38,000 phones this year.
   (D)　This year people bought more cell phones than last year.

34. What is Phonecom?　　Ⓐ　Ⓑ　Ⓒ　Ⓓ
   (A)　A large cell phone company
   (B)　A government office
   (C)　A marketing company
   (D)　A telephone store

35. Which group has bought the most cell phones?　　Ⓐ　Ⓑ　Ⓒ　Ⓓ
   (A)　Government offices
   (B)　Private companies
   (C)　Individuals
   (D)　Phone companies

36. The word "reported" in line 2 is closest in meaning to　　Ⓐ　Ⓑ　Ⓒ　Ⓓ
   (A)　stood by
   (B)　increased
   (C)　denied
   (D)　announced

READING FAST

Read the report as fast as you can. How long did it take?

_____ minutes _____ seconds

ATTENTION ALL
EMPLOYEES

We have 20 free tickets for the National Championship tennis match next Friday evening. If you are interested in these tickets, please contact Mr. Green in the accounting office before 5:00 PM on Wednesday. We can allow up to 4 tickets per employee.

37. When can the tickets be used?   Ⓐ   Ⓑ   Ⓒ   Ⓓ
    (A) Before Wednesday
    (B) Wednesday at 5:00 PM
    (C) Friday at 5:00 PM
    (D) Next Friday evening

38. How many tickets can one employee get?   Ⓐ   Ⓑ   Ⓒ   Ⓓ
    (A) 1
    (B) 4
    (C) 5
    (D) 20

READING FAST

Read the announcement as fast as you can.
How long did it take?

_____ minutes _____ seconds

Come and say good-bye!

Please join Murray Jones
in a celebration of his retirement
after 40 years with the GY Camera Company

Place: Castle Restaurant
Date: March 10
Time: 6:00 PM

Kindly RSVP
(Lynn Mickleson, Office Manager, 555-7643)
by March 1.

We hope to see you there!

39. Who is Murray Jones? (A) (B) (C) (D)
   (A) The office manager
   (B) A company employee
   (C) A restaurant owner
   (D) A photographer

40. What is the party for? (A) (B) (C) (D)
   (A) A birthday
   (B) A retirement
   (C) An anniversary
   (D) A new employee

41. When is the event? (A) (B) (C) (D)
   (A) Tomorrow
   (B) On March 1
   (C) On March 10
   (D) In 40 years

READING FAST

Read the announcement as fast as you can.
How long did it take?

_____ minutes _____ seconds

Do you drink too much coffee?

How much coffee is too much? Most doctors say one cup a day is more than enough. However, most people who work in offices drink two or more cups a day. Many drink coffee during breaks, at lunch, and on their way to and from work. On the other hand, most people don't drink enough water. This is especially a problem for coffee drinkers. When people drink coffee, they don't drink water. Most doctors agree that everyone should drink at least eight glasses of water a day.

42. What type of reading is this?   (A) (B) (C) (D)
    (A) A letter
    (B) A table
    (C) An article
    (D) A memo

43. How much coffee should people drink a day?   (A) (B) (C) (D)
    (A) One cup or less
    (B) More than one cup
    (C) Two or more cups
    (D) At least three cups

44. The word "especially" in line 2, second column, is closest in meaning to   (A) (B) (C) (D)
    (A) only
    (B) never
    (C) hardly
    (D) particularly

45. How much water should people drink every day?   (A) (B) (C) (D)
    (A) Less than four glasses
    (B) Eight or more glasses
    (C) One glass for every cup of coffee
    (D) No more than two glasses

READING FAST

Read the report as fast as you can. How long did it take?

_____ minutes   _____ seconds

STRATEGY REVIEW

Review these strategies for Part 7 of the new TOEIC test.

- ▓ Read the specific directions before you read the passage(s).

- ▓ Read the questions BEFORE you read the passage(s).

- ▓ Do not read the answers before you read the passage(s).

- ▓ If you cannot answer a question, scan the passage(s) and look for the answer options.

- ▓ Be prepared for four common question types on the new TOEIC exam: main idea questions, detail questions, inference questions, and vocabulary questions.

STRATEGY PRACTICE

Single Passages

DIRECTIONS: Read the following passages and answer the questions. Use the reading strategies you have learned. Once you are finished, go over the questions again and identify the question type. Write whether they are detail questions, main idea questions, or inference questions.

Questions 1–2 refer to the following advertisement.

Glenville
7400 sq. ft. residential lot for sale.

The city of Glenville is selling houses, buildings, and lots seized by the city for nonpayment of taxes. These properties will be sold by local real estate brokers. The first such property to be sold, a residential lot, will be offered by John Michaels of the Glenville Leasing and Land Sales Company. 478-555-1253, ext. 5

---

1. What is the advertisement offering?   (A) (B) (C) (D)
   - (A) A house for sale
   - (B) An apartment building for rent
   - (C) An office for lease
   - (D) A piece of land for sale

2. Who is John Michaels?   (A) (B) (C) (D)
   - (A) The owner of the property
   - (B) A real estate agent
   - (C) A stockbroker
   - (D) The city comptroller

> ## Notice of Fare Increase and Bus Schedule Changes
>
> Due to city budget cuts, the following changes will be made to the city bus service, effective April 1.
>
> Fares on all city buses will be increased from $1.25 to $1.50.
>
> Bus schedule changes will be made as follows:
>
> ➡ The #36 bus route from downtown to the airport will run every thirty minutes instead of every 20 minutes.
>
> ➡ The #5 bus route from downtown to City Park will run every 35 minutes instead of every 25 minutes.
>
> ➡ The #16 bus route from the university to the Outer City Shopping Mall will run once every hour instead of every 40 minutes.
>
> There will be no bus service after 10:00 P.M. on weeknights and after 11:30 P.M. on Friday and Saturday nights.

3. Why will the bus schedules change?   Ⓐ Ⓑ Ⓒ Ⓓ
   (A) The city does not have enough money.
   (B) There are not enough people to ride the buses.
   (C) People don't like to take the bus at night.
   (D) The buses are too slow.

4. The word "budget" in paragraph 1, line 1,   Ⓐ Ⓑ Ⓒ Ⓓ
   is closest in meaning to
   (A) rental
   (B) transportation
   (C) financial plan
   (D) route

5. After April 1, how often will the bus to City Park run?   Ⓐ Ⓑ Ⓒ Ⓓ
   (A) Every 5 minutes
   (B) Every 25 minutes
   (C) Every 35 minutes
   (D) Every hour

6. What will happen to bus fares?   Ⓐ Ⓑ Ⓒ Ⓓ
   (A) They will be higher on all buses.
   (B) They will be lower on all buses.
   (C) They will stay the same on some buses.
   (D) They will be higher on some buses.

Educational Opportunities
Scholarship Fund

1701 University Circle
Orford, NY 12184

Your gift will make it possible for needy young people to get a college degree. We rely on gifts from people like you. Please be as generous as possible.

☐ $25   ☐ $75   ☐ $100   ☐ $250

Thank you!

Name _____

Street _____

City/State/ Zip _____

Check one:

___ Check enclosed

___ Money order enclosed

___ Charge my credit card: No. _____ Expiration date _____

Signature (required for credit card charges) _____

---

7. What is this form for?   Ⓐ Ⓑ Ⓒ Ⓓ
    (A) Ordering holiday gifts
    (B) Contributing to a scholarship fund
    (C) Paying college tuition
    (D) Requesting information on educational opportunities

8. What possible form of payment is not listed?   Ⓐ Ⓑ Ⓒ Ⓓ
    (A) Cash
    (B) Check
    (C) Money order
    (D) Credit card

9. Who should sign this form?   Ⓐ Ⓑ Ⓒ Ⓓ
    (A) Anybody who sends in a payment
    (B) Anybody who has a credit card
    (C) Anybody who needs a scholarship
    (D) Anybody who pays by credit card

Questions 10–12 refer to the following paragraph.

Thank you for becoming a National Bank credit card customer. Your new credit card is enclosed. Before using your card, please read the enclosed material describing your rights and responsibilities as a National Bank credit card user. If you have any questions, call 800-555-0998. To activate your card, call 800-555-4557 to confirm that you have received your card. Your card will not be valid for use until you call this number.

10. Who is this notice for?   Ⓐ   Ⓑ   Ⓒ   Ⓓ
    (A) A person who has an account at the
         National Bank
    (B) A person who has a new credit card
         from the National Bank
    (C) A person who wants to work at the National
         Bank
    (D) A person who wants to find out about services
         at the National Bank

11. Why would a bank customer call 800-555-0998?   Ⓐ   Ⓑ   Ⓒ   Ⓓ
    (A) To ask questions about credit cards
    (B) To order a new credit card
    (C) To make the new credit card valid
    (D) To order materials about credit cards

12. What must the customer do to receive his new card?   Ⓐ   Ⓑ   Ⓒ   Ⓓ
    (A) Call 800-555-4557
    (B) Answer some questions
    (C) It is enclosed with this notice.
    (D) Go to the bank

Memorandum

TO: All Staff Members
FROM: Eric Sato, Office Manager
RE: New Photocopy Machine
DATE: October 18

I know you will all be pleased to learn that the new photocopy machine has finally arrived. The new machine has more features and performs more functions than the old one. While this will make things more convenient for us in the long run, it can make it more complicated to learn how to run the machine initially. In addition, we all want to avoid the problem of constant breakdowns that we had with the old machine. Therefore, I ask that if you have any questions or problems with the machine, please ask my assistant, Ms. Ono, to help you. Similarly, please do not attempt to remove paper jams, add toner, or refill the paper bin until Ms. Ono has shown you how to do this. Ms. Ono has received training from the manufacturer of the machine and is fully knowledgeable about how to run it and how to troubleshoot it. Thank you for your cooperation, and enjoy the new machine.

13. What is the purpose of this memo?   Ⓐ Ⓑ Ⓒ Ⓓ
    (A) To explain to the staff how to run photocopy machines
    (B) To inform the staff that the old machine is broken
    (C) To tell the staff about the new photocopy machine
    (D) To let the staff know that Ms. Ono will receive training

14. What should staff members do if they have a   Ⓐ Ⓑ Ⓒ Ⓓ
    problem with the machine?
    (A) Speak to Ms. Ono
    (B) Ask the Office Manager for assistance
    (C) Call the manufacturer
    (D) Read the training manual

15. Why is the new machine complicated?   Ⓐ Ⓑ Ⓒ Ⓓ
    (A) It needs toner.
    (B) It's new.
    (C) It breaks down a lot.
    (D) It has many features and functions.

Questions 16–18 refer to the following advertisement.

Attention Sales and Marketing Professionals

CAREER FAIR

Thursday, May 25
9:30–3:30
Hoover Hotel
1007 Elm Street

If you are looking for a position as a:

- Store Manager
- Sales Associate
- Sales Representative
- Marketing Executive
- Executive Assistant

or other position in the Sales and Marketing field, then don't miss this event!

Free registration!

Register online at *www.salesmkting.com*.

Onsite registration begins at 8:30. Doors open at 9:30.

Complimentary lunch buffet from 12:00–1:00 for all registered participants.

All day parking in the hotel garage half-price for registered participants.

Call 633-555–9730 for more information.

Don't miss our special Career Fair seminars:

How to Write a Winning Résumé   10:30–11:30
Preparing for the Job Interview   1:00–2:00

Seminars are $12 each or $20 for both, payable at the door.

16. Who is this advertisement for?   Ⓐ Ⓑ Ⓒ Ⓓ
    (A) Hotel managers
    (B) Job seekers
    (C) Hotel guests
    (D) Employers

17. How can you register for the career fair?   Ⓐ Ⓑ Ⓒ Ⓓ
    (A) Call 633-555-9730
    (B) Send a registration form by mail
    (C) Pay at the door
    (D) Arrive at the hotel at 8:30

18. How much does the lunch cost?   Ⓐ Ⓑ Ⓒ Ⓓ
    (A) $12
    (B) $20
    (C) It's free.
    (D) It's half the usual price.

The Jolly Hamburger restaurant chain reported that, because of cost cutting, it was able to double its profits this year to $52 million. Jolly Hamburger is the second largest fast-food company in the country, after Big Burgers, which reported profits this year of $60 million, up from $48 million last year. Jolly Hamburger plans to broaden its customer base by introducing a special low-fat, low-sodium menu geared toward senior citizens.

19. How was Jolly Hamburger able to increase its profits?   Ⓐ   Ⓑ   Ⓒ   Ⓓ
   (A) By lowering its prices
   (B) By introducing a new menu
   (C) By getting more customers
   (D) By decreasing its expenses

20. What were Jolly Hamburger's profits last year?   Ⓐ   Ⓑ   Ⓒ   Ⓓ
   (A) $26 million
   (B) $48 million
   (C) $52 million
   (D) $104 million

Questions 21–25 refer to the following advertisement and letter.

WORLD WIDE SCHOOL OF LANGUAGES

Classes in French, English, Spanish, Japanese, Korean, and Arabic

Beginning, Intermediate, Advanced, and Professional level classes

Small group classes

Tutoring available for French, Spanish, and Japanese only

Morning (three hours/day) and evening (two hours/week)

Weekend schedule also available

All our teachers are native speakers and are professionally trained in the latest methodologies.

Traveling? We also have locations in several other cities.
Call our office to find out where.
888-555-4761

October 2

Dear Yoko,

I have exciting news for you. Do you remember how I've always wanted to learn Korean? Well now I'm finally doing it. I've found a fantastic language school not far from my apartment, and I'm taking classes there. Of course, I'm really busy at work all day, so I'm studying in the evening. The classes are really interesting and the homework load is not so bad. I'm really learning a lot. The best part of all is that my company is paying 100% of the class tuition.

You know you've been saying that you want to improve your English. You're in luck! I checked and found out that the World Wide School of Languages has a branch in your city. I really recommend their classes. I think their highest-level English class would be just right for you. Your company would probably pay for the classes because you use English a lot at work. You can also arrange to get university credit. I think it's a great deal.

The other good news is that my company is sending me on a trip next month to your city. So I'll see you soon.

Love,

Maki

21. Which language is NOT taught at the World Wide School of Languages?
   (A) French
   (B) English
   (C) German
   (D) Japanese

   Ⓐ Ⓑ Ⓒ Ⓓ

22. Where do Maki's Korean classes take place?
   (A) Near her work
   (B) At the university
   (C) Near her home
   (D) In Yoko's city

   Ⓐ Ⓑ Ⓒ Ⓓ

23. How many hours a week is Maki studying Korean?
   (A) Two
   (B) Three
   (C) Ten
   (D) Fifteen

   Ⓐ Ⓑ Ⓒ Ⓓ

24. What level class does Maki recommend for Yoko?
   (A) Beginning
   (B) Intermediate
   (C) Advanced
   (D) Professional

   Ⓐ Ⓑ Ⓒ Ⓓ

25. What will Maki do next month?
   (A) Take a business trip
   (B) Study English
   (C) Work at the university
   (D) Go on vacation

   Ⓐ Ⓑ Ⓒ Ⓓ

SUPPLY STATION

YOUR OFFICE SUPPLY COMPANY

Sale!   Sale!   Sale!

Don't miss this unique opportunity.
Printers, ink, and paper are discounted 15% or more.

BMX all-in-one printer, scanner, copier, fax
prints up to 30 pages/minute
prints top-quality color photos
was $325 now only **$250**

Maxi Systems printer
prints up to 25 pages/minute
scans and copies too
was $299 now only **$215**

Printer Ink
Type C ink cartridges, compatible with all BMX and Maxi Systems printers
1-cartridge pack: $30   sale price: **$24**
2-cartridge pack: $54   sale price: **$43**

Buy now. Sale lasts Monday–Friday only

To: Lucy Johnson, Assistant Office Manager
From: Mary Choi, Office Manager
Re: Office supply sale

Lucy,

Have you seen this ad? I think we should take advantage of it. Look at how fast that BMX printer prints. It's twice as fast our old printer. I think that would make a big difference. And there's a big savings on printer ink, too. Let's get ten of the two-cartridge packs. While you're at the store, see what the sale prices are on paper. Have them charge it to our office account and check to see if we have a credit. I think we do from the cell phone I returned last month. The sale ends tomorrow, so you'd better get down there as soon as possible. Thanks.

Mary

26. What is on sale this week?   Ⓐ   Ⓑ   Ⓒ   Ⓓ
   (A) Only printing supplies
   (B) All office supplies
   (C) Cameras
   (D) Ink pens

27. How fast does the old printer print?   Ⓐ   Ⓑ   Ⓒ   Ⓓ
   (A) 15 pages/minute
   (B) 20 pages/minute
   (C) 25 pages/minute
   (D) 30 pages/minute

28. How much will Lucy spend on ink cartridges?   Ⓐ   Ⓑ   Ⓒ   Ⓓ
   (A) $240
   (B) $300
   (C) $430
   (D) $540

29. How will Lucy pay for her purchases?   Ⓐ   Ⓑ   Ⓒ   Ⓓ
   (A) By cash
   (B) With a credit card
   (C) With a business check
   (D) By charging it to an account

30. What day was the memo written?   Ⓐ   Ⓑ   Ⓒ   Ⓓ
   (A) Monday
   (B) Tuesday
   (C) Thursday
   (D) Friday

READING REVIEW

Do this Reading Review as if you were taking Parts 5, 6, and 7 of the new TOEIC® test. You should take no more than 75 minutes to do this review. Use the Reading Review Answer Sheet on page 291.

READING TEST

In the Reading test, you will read a variety of texts and answer several different types of reading comprehension questions. The entire Reading test will last 75 minutes. There are three parts, and directions are given for each part. You are encouraged to answer as many questions as possible within the time allowed.

You must mark your answers on the separate answer sheet. Do not write your answers in the test book.

PART 5

Directions: A word or phrase is missing in each of the sentences below. Four answer choices are given below each sentence. Select the best answer to complete the sentence. Then mark the letter (A), (B), (C), or (D) on your answer sheet.

---

101. The files were _____ alphabetically.
    (A) organization
    (B) organizer
    (C) organize
    (D) organized

102. The business consultant suggested a _____ sales plan.
    (A) modify
    (B) modifies
    (C) modified
    (D) modifying

103. _____ there were so many customer complaints, we withdrew the item from the market.
    (A) Therefore
    (B) Because
    (C) Although
    (D) However

104. The contractor is _____ for his quality workmanship.
    (A) respected
    (B) respects
    (C) respect
    (D) respecting

105. Employees' work hours are _____ before the holidays.
    (A) insisted
    (B) installed
    (C) increased
    (D) intruded

106. The _____ report will be published next Monday.
    (A) selling
    (B) sales
    (C) sell
    (D) sells

107. The architect must consider every detail of a floor _____.
    (A) planning
    (B) plan
    (C) plans
    (D) planned

108. Mr. Lafferty wants to meet _____ six o'clock sharp.
    (A) on
    (B) upon
    (C) at
    (D) during

109. The sales personnel were given specific _____ about how to market the new product.
    (A) instructions
    (B) delays
    (C) reservations
    (D) adjustments

110. This construction project is as important as any other project _____ this year.
    (A) undertaking
    (B) undertook
    (C) undertaken
    (D) undertake

111. The supervisor talked about _____ changing patterns in consumer habits.
    (A) slowly
    (B) slowing
    (C) slows
    (D) slowed

112. This year tourism is growing _____ last year's predictions.
    (A) outside
    (B) inside
    (C) beyond
    (D) before

113. The grievance committee made _____ demands on management.
    (A) reasonable
    (B) reasonably
    (C) reason
    (D) reasoning

114. The _____ of the office party must take responsibility for the cleanup.
    (A) plans
    (B) planning
    (C) planned
    (D) planners

115. Mr. Shultz has _____ own plan for reorganizing the accounting department.
    (A) him
    (B) his
    (C) he
    (D) himself

116. There are early _____ that the market is beginning to recover.
    (A) indications
    (B) solutions
    (C) proposals
    (D) revisions

117. Before you leave, please _____ the data in the database.
    (A) submerge
    (B) propose
    (C) admit
    (D) enter

118. _____ the new product didn't sell well, it's still on the market.
    (A) However
    (B) So that
    (C) Although
    (D) Nevertheless

119. _____ have the employees complained so much about working conditions in the factory.
    (A) Never
    (B) Ever
    (C) Soon
    (D) Forever

120. Staff _____ an environmental group will be here to check for evidence of pollution.
    (A) of
    (B) by
    (C) about
    (D) from

121. The crew worked _____ to avoid problems in the future.
    (A) careful
    (B) carefully
    (C) care
    (D) more careful

122. _____ job performance is awarded with a salary bonus.
    (A) Except
    (B) Exception
    (C) Exceptional
    (D) Exceptionally

GO ON TO THE NEXT PAGE

123. The _____ on the merger lasted until midnight.
- (A) negotiated
- (B) negotiations
- (C) negotiator
- (D) negotiates

124. When it came to solving a mechanical problem, he did not have a _____.
- (A) clue
- (B) sense
- (C) hint
- (D) thought

125. _____ a good credit history, don't expect to get a loan easily.
- (A) From
- (B) Unless
- (C) Without
- (D) Since

126. The company managers _____ the union about any changes in employee vacation allowances.
- (A) advice
- (B) advising
- (C) advised
- (D) advisor

127. The president answers all his calls _____.
- (A) himself
- (B) he
- (C) him
- (D) his

128. To _____ disruption during the day, construction is done at night.
- (A) criticize
- (B) localize
- (C) sanitize
- (D) minimize

129. Mr. Nigel becomes _____ when he has to wait too long.
- (A) evident
- (B) extraordinary
- (C) impatient
- (D) inconclusive

130. The negotiations failed because _____ broke down.
- (A) communicative
- (B) communicated
- (C) communications
- (D) communicate

131. _____ amazes Ms. Fifel is the speed of her new computer.
- (A) That
- (B) Which
- (C) Who
- (D) What

132. Any changes to the employee handbook must be _____ in writing.
- (A) proposed
- (B) propelled
- (C) preferred
- (D) preordained

133. _____ to the directory will be published every month.
- (A) Additional
- (B) Additions
- (C) Added
- (D) Adding

134. The audience was asked to _____ from talking during announcements.
- (A) refrain
- (B) respect
- (C) reserve
- (D) restore

135. The news was so _____ that the company invested even more money in the project.
- (A) encourage
- (B) encouraged
- (C) encouraging
- (D) encourages

136. The job couldn't be finished because of an _____ supply of essential materials.
- (A) improper
- (B) unlikely
- (C) unlucky
- (D) inadequate

137. A positive _____ helps everyone be productive.
  (A) alteration
  (B) attitude
  (C) anxiety
  (D) ambivalence

138. Mr. Logan's instructions were _____ clear that no one had any questions.
  (A) such
  (B) ever
  (C) so
  (D) too

139. The _____ to the training has been very positive.
  (A) respondent
  (B) respond
  (C) responsible
  (D) response

140. Demand for the new line of cars is up; _____, production will increase.
  (A) however
  (B) despite
  (C) therefore
  (D) regardless

GO ON TO THE NEXT PAGE

Directions: Read the texts that follow. A word or phrase is missing in some of the sentences. Four answer choices are given below each of the sentences. Select the best answer to complete the text. Then mark the letter (A), (B), (C), or (D) on your answer sheet.

Questions 141–144 refer to the following e-mail.

To: Naser Abdul
From: Nicholas Reed
Subject: Request for office equipment

Dear Naser,
My first week working for the Citron Company has been very good. I
_____ my new job. Now I need some things for my office. Can you help me?

141.   (A) enjoyed
       (B) will enjoy
       (C) am enjoying
       (D) was enjoying

_____, there is a problem with the computer. It works very

142.   (A) First
       (B) Also
       (C) Then
       (D) Finally

_____, and it is difficult to get on the Internet. I think the computer

143.   (A) slow
       (B) slowly
       (C) slower
       (D) slowness

doesn't have enough memory.

There is also a problem with the heating system in my office. The office is very cold
early in the day, but _____ the afternoon it is too hot. One last

144.   (A) at
       (B) in
       (C) of
       (D) on

thing, my desk is very small. I need a bigger desk. Can you get me one?

Everything else is okay. Thank you for your help, Naser.

Sincerely,
Nicholas Reed, Office Specialist

ATTENTION
ALL EMPLOYEES

Our office is collecting money for
the _____ of last week's
145. (A) observers
      (B) victims
      (C) planners
      (D) reporters

terrible floods. Many people in our
city lost their homes and all their
_____ in the floods. We
146. (A) possesses
      (B) possessed
      (C) possessing
      (D) possessions

would like to send money to help
them. If you wish to make a
_____, please bring a
147. (A) cake
      (B) friend
      (C) salary
      (D) donation

check or cash to Mr. Kim in Human
Resources before 5:00 on Friday. We
_____ a check
148. (A) send
      (B) sent
      (C) will send
      (D) might send

in the name of everyone in the office
to the Flood Fund.

GO ON TO THE NEXT PAGE

Are you looking for an economical car to rent?

Look no more.

Come to

Mr. Miser's Car Rental Agency

Why pay more than you have to?

At Mr. Miser's, we have _____ prices in town.

149. (A) low
     (B) lower
     (C) lowers
     (D) the lowest

Why travel farther than you have to?

Mr. Miser's has three convenient _____.

150. (A) cars
     (B) prices
     (C) locations
     (D) schedules

We have offices at the airport, at the train station,
and downtown on Main Street.

At Mr. Miser's we _____ to serve you with a friendly smile.

151. (A) always ready are
     (B) always are ready
     (C) are always ready
     (D) are ready always

Next time, _____ your car from Mr. Miser's.

152. (A) rent
     (B) rents
     (C) renting
     (D) will rent

Directions: In this part you will read a selection of texts, such as magazine and newspaper articles, letters, and advertisements. Each text is followed by several questions. Select the best answer for each question and mark the letter (A), (B), (C), or (D) on your answer sheet.

Questions 153–155 refer to the following announcement.

According to a new report, people now work more hours than before. Ten years ago, most professional people worked 40 hours a week or less. Now, 75% of professionals work 50 hours a week or more, and 15% of professionals work 55 hours a week or more. Researchers in the Labor Department released these numbers last week.

153. Who is the report about?
(A) Laborers
(B) Professionals
(C) All workers
(D) Researchers

154. Ten years ago, how many hours a week did most professional people work?
(A) 40 or less
(B) 50 or more
(C) 55 or more
(D) 75 or less

155. When did researchers report these figures?
(A) Yesterday
(B) 7 days ago
(C) 15 days ago
(D) 10 years ago

Ike's Ice Cream Shop
Liters of Ice Cream Sold

156. How many liters of ice cream did Ike sell in January?
(A) 90
(B) 95
(C) 100
(D) 110

157. When did Ike sell 135 liters of ice cream?
(A) March
(B) April
(C) May
(D) June

158. When did Ike sell the least amount of ice cream?
(A) January
(B) February
(C) March
(D) April

159. How much time does this graph cover?
(A) One month
(B) Six weeks
(C) Half a year
(D) One year

GO ON TO THE NEXT PAGE

Questions 160–161 refer to the following letter.

March 21, 20___

Amelia Greene
Director
Worldwide Travel Agency
78 North Street
Mayfield, TX 23450

Dear Ms. Greene:

I am interested in working at the Worldwide Travel Agency. I have five years' experience as a travel agent. I also have a lot of experience working with computers, and I can use different kinds of software.

I am enclosing my résumé. I hope to hear from you soon.

Sincerely,

Charles Chung

Charles Chung

160. Why did Charles Chung write this letter?
(A) He wants a job.
(B) He wants to buy a computer.
(C) He wants to take a trip.
(D) He wants help writing his résumé.

161. What did Charles Chung do for five years?
(A) He studied computers.
(B) He worked for Ms. Greene.
(C) He traveled around the world.
(D) He worked as a travel agent.

> **The Law Office of Murphy & Mann is moving.**
>
> *Our new address, starting April 12, is:*
> 45 Oakland Avenue
> Suite 10
>
> (near the corner of Oakland Avenue and Broadwood Road,
> across the street from the National State Bank)
>
> Our new office hours are M–F 8:30–6:00
> Sat. 9–12:30
>
> Our phone number will stay the same:
> 301-555-7140

162. When will the new office open?
   (A) April 1
   (B) April 2
   (C) April 12
   (D) April 21

163. Where is the new office?
   (A) On Oakland Avenue
   (B) In Suite 45
   (C) On Broadwood Road
   (D) Next to a bank

164. What will NOT change?
   (A) The suite number
   (B) The office hours
   (C) The telephone number
   (D) The location

GO ON TO THE NEXT PAGE

The new express train will begin service between Riverdale and Mayfield on October 24. The trip takes five hours on the older, slower train. On the express train it will take only three hours. The express train will have larger, more comfortable seats, and there will be free food for the passengers. There will be two express trains a day between Riverdale and Mayfield. There will also be four regular trains. Many people will prefer the regular trains because the tickets are cheaper.

165. How long is the trip on the express train?
   (A) Two hours
   (B) Three hours
   (C) Four hours
   (D) Five hours

166. How many regular trains will there be a day?
   (A) Two
   (B) Three
   (C) Four
   (D) Five

167. Why would people prefer the regular trains?
   (A) The seats are larger.
   (B) The tickets are less expensive.
   (C) The food tastes better.
   (D) They are more comfortable.

168. The word "service" in line 1 is closest in meaning to
   (A) commuting
   (B) setting up
   (C) operation
   (D) making do

Questions 169–172 refer to the following advertisement.

ABC Market
Sale—this weekend only

Fresh Oranges—$1.50/kilo
Fresh Apples—$1.75/kilo
Beef—$1.25/2 kilos
Chicken—$1.25/kilo

Cookies—$2.50/bag OR *buy 2 bags,*
get the third bag free!

Store hours:
M–F 8:30–6:30   Sat. & Sun. 12–5

169. What kind of business is advertised?
 (A) A grocery store
 (B) A school supply store
 (C) A restaurant
 (D) A bakery

170. When is the sale?
 (A) Today
 (B) Monday through Friday
 (C) Saturday and Sunday
 (D) All week

171. The word "Fresh" in line 3 is closest in meaning to
 (A) Inexpensive
 (B) Colorful
 (C) Newly picked
 (D) Special

172. How much do cookies cost?
 (A) $2 a bag
 (B) $2.50 a bag
 (C) $3 a bag
 (D) They're free.

GO ON TO THE NEXT PAGE

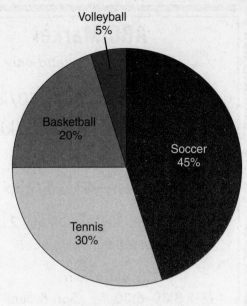

Favorite Sports

173. Which is the most popular
sport?
(A) Volleyball
(B) Basketball
(C) Tennis
(D) Soccer

174. What percent of people prefer
basketball?
(A) 5%
(B) 20%
(C) 30%
(D) 45%

Subscribe now!

Receive *Business Times* in your home every month!

Six months — pay only $26
One year — pay only $45
Two years — pay only $75

Name: *Helena Bishop*

Address: *1776 Washington Street*

Eugene, OR 42308

check one: __ 6 months **X** one year __ two years

Payment method: __ check __ money order **X** credit card

---

175. What is *Business Times*?
   (A) A TV show
   (B) A book
   (C) A magazine
   (D) A radio program

176. How much will Helena Bishop pay?
   (A) $26
   (B) $45
   (C) $75
   (D) $90

177. How will she pay?
   (A) Check
   (B) Money order
   (C) Credit card
   (D) Cash

GO ON TO THE NEXT PAGE

Questions 178–180 refer to the following letter.

Mill Workers' Union, Local 806
3660 South River Trail
Two Rivers, ME 05601
March 19, 20___

Ms. Samantha Fagan, President & CEO
Lumber Yard Industries
9871 Kennewick Drive
Grove Isle, ME 05603

Dear Ms. Fagan:

As a union arbitrator, I have been asked by a number of your employees to write to you. It is in regard to your decision to make the mill off-limits to smokers. That means from now on, all employees who wish to smoke must go outdoors, but not near the main entrance.

Many of your employees who smoke consider this a very harsh decision. They appreciate that nonsmokers do not wish to be exposed to cigarette smoke, but they cannot understand why they are being treated as second-class citizens. They feel it is unfair to force them to have to go outdoors in order to smoke. You know that we get a lot of rain and cold temperatures in this area for a good part of the year. Should they go outside in the rain? Should they be out in freezing weather?

Your employees who smoke would like a meeting with you. They would like to offer suggestions that would be acceptable to both sides. For example, perhaps a separate employee lounge for smokers could be created within the mill. In that way, both parties would feel satisfied. A meeting between you and your employees who smoke would be most advantageous.

I hope you will consider this request and agree to meet with those employees. Thank you in advance for your time and consideration.

Sincerely yours,

Faith Dunnaway
Faith Dunnaway

178. What outdoor area is currently off-limits to employees who smoke?
- (A) The picnic area
- (B) The parking lot
- (C) The recycling area
- (D) The main entrance

179. What is the primary issue?
- (A) Some employees can smoke, while others can't.
- (B) Employees who smoke don't think they're being treated fairly.
- (C) The employee lounge needs to be enlarged.
- (D) Weather conditions are making it hard for employees to work.

180. What is the request that Faith Dunnaway is making in the letter?
- (A) Ms. Fagan should allow smoking in the mill.
- (B) Ms. Fagan should meet with employees who smoke.
- (C) Two employee lounges should be built.
- (D) Ms. Fagan should come to the union offices.

GO ON TO THE NEXT PAGE

Questions 181–185 refer to the following agenda and e-mail.

**Multiple Marketing, Inc.
Department Heads Meeting
Monday, April 15 4:00 p.m.
Place: Company Cafeteria**

A G E N D A

1. Budget report
Marguerite Rodin

2. Fall conference plans
Cindy Lee

3. New hiring policy
Yasser Ahmed

4. Office supplies issues
Jan Petersen

To: Sam Blair
From: Rose Daniels
Subject: Yesterday's Meeting

Mr. Blair,
The meeting yesterday went as planned, for the most part. It started on time and everyone was there, except you, of course. We rearranged the order of the agenda a bit. We talked about the third item first because it's such a pressing issue for all of us. We were able to get to all the items on the agenda because we agreed to stay until everything was finished. The meeting lasted two and a half hours. Also, we changed the location. The cafeteria was being cleaned, so we moved the meeting to the lounge. It worked out fine. We set the date for next month's meeting. It will be on the 18th.
Rose

181. Where was the meeting held?
    (A) In the cafeteria
    (B) In the director's office
    (C) In the conference room
    (D) In the lounge

182. What item was discussed first?
    (A) The budget report
    (B) The fall conference plans
    (C) The new hiring policy
    (D) The office supplies issues

183. Who did NOT attend the meeting?
    (A) Sam Blair
    (B) Rose Daniels
    (C) Jan Petersen
    (D) Marguerite Rodin

184. What time did the meeting end?
    (A) 4:00
    (B) 4:15
    (C) 6:00
    (D) 6:30

185. When will the next meeting be held?
    (A) April 15
    (B) April 18
    (C) May 15
    (D) May 18

GO ON TO THE NEXT PAGE

COMPUTER INSTITUTE OF TECHNOLOGY

FALL SCHEDULE

Keyboarding

Beginning	Mon. and Wed.	5:30–6:30
Intermediate	Mon. and Wed.	6:30–7:30
Advanced	Tue. and Thur.	5:30–6:30

Word Processing

Level I	Mon. and Wed.	6:00–7:30
Level II	Mon. and Wed.	7:30–9:00
Level III	Tue. and Thur.	6:00–7:30
Level IV	Tue. and Thur.	7:30–9:00

Web Page Design

Basic	Mon., Tue., and Thur.	6:00–7:00
Advanced	Tue. and Wed.	7:00–8:00
All levels	Sat.	9:00–1:00

*Classes begin on the first Monday of every month.
Each class lasts one month. Tuition is $275 per class.
To register for classes, download a registration form from our
website. Mail the completed form with your check or
credit card information to:*

COMPUTER INSTITUTE OF TECHNOLOGY
811 Horseshoe Boulevard • Hilltown, MI 02046

To: G. Y. Kim
From: Elizabeth Jones
Re: Computer training

Mr. Kim,

I am interested in taking some computer classes that I think would give me some useful skills for my work. I hope the company can pay the tuition for these classes. I am most interested in learning web page design. Then I could develop and maintain our company's web page, and we wouldn't have to pay an outside consultant to do it. The Computer Institute of Technology offers a Beginning web page design class. It starts at 6:00, which would give me half an hour to get there after I leave work. It's not far from the office, so that's plenty of time. That class ends at 7:00, so I could also take a word processing class that begins at 7:30 on Tuesdays and Thursdays. I like this school because the schedule and the location are both very convenient. I know this training would really improve the work I do for you, so I hope you can help me with the tuition. I have attached the class schedule for you to see. Thank you.

Elizabeth Jones

186. How many days a week are classes offered at the Computer Institute of Technology?
   (A) Two
   (B) Three
   (C) Four
   (D) Five

187. How can a student register for classes?
   (A) Call the school
   (B) Mail a form
   (C) Visit the school
   (D) Send an e-mail

188. What time does Elizabeth leave work?
   (A) 5:30
   (B) 6:00
   (C) 7:00
   (D) 7:30

189. Which word processing class does Elizabeth want to take?
   (A) Level I
   (B) Level II
   (C) Level III
   (D) Level IV

190. How much money will Elizabeth need to pay for her classes?
   (A) $275
   (B) $475
   (C) $500
   (D) $550

GO ON TO THE NEXT PAGE

To: All personnel
From: Luis Mora, Office Manager
Re: Conference room painting

We all know that the painting of both conference rooms is long overdue. We've been waiting months for this to happen, and now it will. Painting of Conference Room 1 will begin next Tuesday and should take no more than two days. Meetings that you have scheduled for next week can be held in the cafeteria. The painting of Conference Room 2 will be scheduled for a later date. If you have any questions, don't hesitate to contact me. Thank you for your cooperation.

To: Luis Mora
From: George Werner
Subject: Conference room

Luis,
I know we've all been waiting for the conference rooms to be painted, but it couldn't be more inconvenient for me. I have an important meeting planned for the day the painting begins. I can't have it in my office because only four or five people can sit there comfortably, and I need room for ten people. Conference Room 2 is already booked through Friday. The meeting place you suggest is too informal for an important meeting. Would it be possible to schedule the painting so that it begins on Wednesday or Thursday? Please let me know.
George

191. What will be painted next week?
    (A) One conference room
    (B) Two conference rooms
    (C) The cafeteria
    (D) Some offices

192. How long will the painting probably take?
    (A) Two days
    (B) A week
    (C) A month
    (D) Several months

193. Why did George write the e-mail?
    (A) To invite Luis to a meeting
    (B) To ask for his office to be painted
    (C) To find a different room for his meeting
    (D) To ask for the painting schedule to be changed

194. What day will George's meeting be?
    (A) Tuesday
    (B) Wednesday
    (C) Thursday
    (D) Friday

195. According to George, which place is too informal for his meeting?
    (A) His office
    (B) Luis's office
    (C) The cafeteria
    (D) Conference Room 2

GO ON TO THE NEXT PAGE

Questions 196–200 refer to the following advertisement and letter.

RESEARCH ASSOCIATE

Top advertising firm seeks research associate to join our team of market researchers. Seeking creative, energetic team worker to work with a group of four other researchers. Must have a Master's in Business Administration and three to five years' experience in market research. Send résumé and cover letter to: Priscilla Kovacs, Director of Human Resources, Avid Advertising Associates, 1456 State Street, Suite 101, Springfield, OH 48804.

Jung Choi
25 Water Street, Apt. 10
Springfield, OH 48804

Dear Ms. Choi:

Thank you for your interest in our company. Unfortunately, the research associate position that we advertised has already been filled. However, you have a strong background, and we might be interested in considering you for a position in the future. Your résumé shows that you have the educational level we require, and your Bachelor's degree in Psychology strengthens your qualifications as a market researcher. You also have more years of experience in the field than we asked for. I would like to keep your résumé on file and contact you when we have another position available. If you don't hear from me in six months' time, please give me a call.

Sincerely,

Priscilla Kovacs

Priscilla Kovacs

196. What is Priscilla Kovacs job?
    (A) Research associate
    (B) Director of Human Resources
    (C) Head researcher
    (D) Psychologist

197. Why wasn't Choi hired for the position?
    (A) Her résumé was lost.
    (B) She decided she didn't want it.
    (C) She didn't have the qualifications.
    (D) The position had already been filled.

198. What degree does Choi have?
    (A) Master of Psychology
    (B) Associate of Business
    (C) Master of Business Administration
    (D) Bachelor of Business Administration

199. How many years' experience does Choi have as a market researcher?
    (A) Less than 3 years
    (B) Three years
    (C) Five years
    (D) More than five years

200. What suggestion does Ms. Kovacs make to Ms. Choi?
    (A) Write a new résumé
    (B) Call her in six months
    (C) Get a job as a psychologist
    (D) Get more experience in the field

PRACTICE TEST ONE

Practice Test One is similar to an actual new TOEIC test. You can take this test before you study this book. Then, after you finish studying this book, take Practice Test Two and compare your score on Practice Test One with Practice Test Two in order to measure your improvement.

Read all directions carefully. This will help you become familiar with the new TOEIC test directions and item types.

Use the Practice Test One Answer Sheet on page 293.

LISTENING TEST

In the listening test, you will be asked to demonstrate how well you understand spoken English. The entire Listening test will last approximately 45 minutes. There are four parts, and directions are given for each part. You must mark your answers on the separate answer sheet. Do not write your answers in the test book.

PART 1

Directions: For each question in this part, you will hear four statements about a picture in your test book. When you hear the statements, you must select the one statement that best describes what you see in the picture. Then find the number of the question on your answer sheet and mark your answer. The statements will not be printed in your test book and will be spoken only one time.

Example

Sample Answer

  ⬤

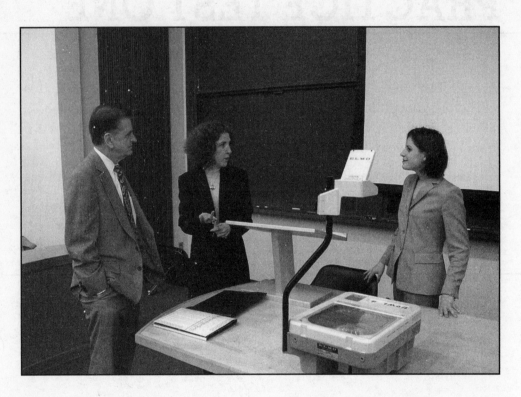

Statement (C), "They're standing near the table," is the best description of the picture, so you should select answer (C) and mark it on your answer sheet.

1.

2.

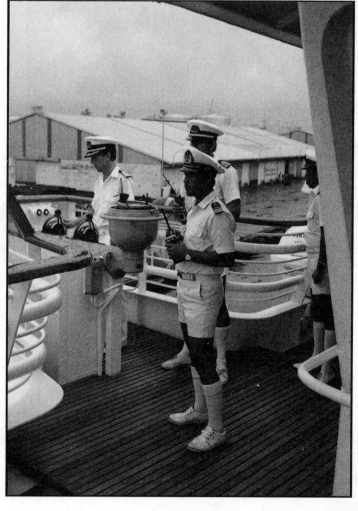

GO ON TO THE NEXT PAGE

3.

4.

5.

6.

GO ON TO THE NEXT PAGE

7.

8.

9.

10.

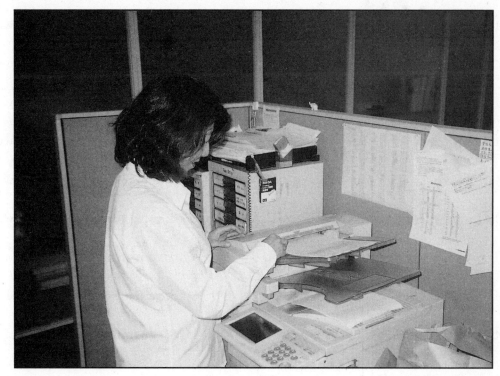

GO ON TO THE NEXT PAGE ▶

Directions: You will hear a question or statement and three responses spoken in English. They will not be printed in your test book and will be spoken only one time. Select the best response to the question or statement and mark the letter (A), (B), or (C) on your answer sheet.

Example

Sample Answer

Ⓐ ● Ⓒ

You will hear: Where is the meeting room?

You will also hear: (A) To meet the new director.
(B) It's the first room on the right.
(C) Yes, at two o'clock.

Your best response to the question "Where is the meeting room?" is choice (B), "It's the first room on the right," so (B) is the correct answer. You should mark answer (B) on your answer sheet.

11. Mark your answer on your answer sheet.

12. Mark your answer on your answer sheet.

13. Mark your answer on your answer sheet.

14. Mark your answer on your answer sheet.

15. Mark your answer on your answer sheet.

16. Mark your answer on your answer sheet.

17. Mark your answer on your answer sheet.

18. Mark your answer on your answer sheet.

19. Mark your answer on your answer sheet.

20. Mark your answer on your answer sheet.

21. Mark your answer on your answer sheet.

22. Mark your answer on your answer sheet.

23. Mark your answer on your answer sheet.

24. Mark your answer on your answer sheet.

25. Mark your answer on your answer sheet.

26. Mark your answer on your answer sheet.

27. Mark your answer on your answer sheet.

28. Mark your answer on your answer sheet.

29. Mark your answer on your answer sheet.

30. Mark your answer on your answer sheet.

31. Mark your answer on your answer sheet.

32. Mark your answer on your answer sheet.

33. Mark your answer on your answer sheet.

34. Mark your answer on your answer sheet.

35. Mark your answer on your answer sheet.

36. Mark your answer on your answer sheet.

37. Mark your answer on your answer sheet.

38. Mark your answer on your answer sheet.

39. Mark your answer on your answer sheet.

40. Mark your answer on your answer sheet.

Directions: You will hear some conversations between two people. You will be asked to answer three questions about what the speakers say in each conversation. Select the best response to each question and mark the letter (A), (B), (C), or (D) on your answer sheet. The conversations will not be printed in your test book and will be spoken only one time.

41. Where does the conversation take place?
    (A) At a post office.
    (B) At a park.
    (C) At a business office.
    (D) At an airport.

42. When were the contracts mailed?
    (A) Earlier in the week.
    (B) Yesterday morning.
    (C) Last night.
    (D) This morning.

43. What time is it now?
    (A) 7:00.
    (B) 7:45.
    (C) 11:00.
    (D) 11:45.

44. What level class does the man want to take?
    (A) Basic.
    (B) Beginning.
    (C) Intermediate.
    (D) Advanced.

45. How much will the class cost?
    (A) $90.
    (B) $400.
    (C) $500.
    (D) $600.

46. What time of day does the man want to study?
    (A) Morning.
    (B) Noon.
    (C) Afternoon.
    (D) Night.

47. When will Mr. Katz arrive?
    (A) Today.
    (B) Tonight.
    (C) Tomorrow morning.
    (D) Tomorrow night.

48. How is the weather in New York?
    (A) It's raining.
    (B) It's snowing.
    (C) It's icy.
    (D) It's nice.

49. How did the woman hear about the weather?
    (A) Mr. Katz told her.
    (B) On the radio.
    (C) In the newspaper.
    (D) On TV.

50. Where will they have the retirement party?
    (A) In the conference room.
    (B) In Mr. Lee's office.
    (C) In the party room.
    (D) In a restaurant.

51. How many guests will there be?
    (A) 15.
    (B) 16.
    (C) 50.
    (D) 60.

52. When will the party be?
    (A) Tuesday.
    (B) Wednesday.
    (C) Thursday.
    (D) Friday.

GO ON TO THE NEXT PAGE

53. Where does the conversation take place?
    (A) In a restaurant.
    (B) In a stadium.
    (C) In a theater.
    (D) In a train station.

54. How long will the woman have to wait?
    (A) Four or five minutes.
    (B) Ten minutes.
    (C) Forty minutes.
    (D) Forty-five minutes.

55. What does the man suggest doing?
    (A) Making reservations.
    (B) Waiting.
    (C) Trying another place.
    (D) Returning later.

56. Why can't the woman speak with Mr. Curtis right now?
    (A) He's too busy.
    (B) He's on a business trip.
    (C) He went downtown.
    (D) He's talking on the phone.

57. What will the woman do?
    (A) Leave a message.
    (B) Return later.
    (C) Make an appointment.
    (D) Call back.

58. Why does the woman want to see Mr. Curtis?
    (A) To show him some contracts.
    (B) To give him a book.
    (C) To open a bank account.
    (D) To sell him a boat.

59. Why did Mr. Cho stop work?
    (A) He's been feeling tired.
    (B) He's on vacation.
    (C) He was fired.
    (D) He retired.

60. When did Mr. Cho stop work?
    (A) Two days ago.
    (B) On Tuesday.
    (C) Last week.
    (D) Last month.

61. Why did the speakers like Mr. Cho?
    (A) He told jokes.
    (B) He worked hard.
    (C) He cleaned the office.
    (D) He brought them cookies.

62. How long have the speakers been waiting for Janet?
    (A) Thirty minutes.
    (B) One hour.
    (C) Since 8:00.
    (D) Since 9:00.

63. Why is Janet late this time?
    (A) She had a dentist appointment.
    (B) She had to work late.
    (C) She had to stop at the store.
    (D) She had to exercise.

64. How does the man feel?
    (A) Happy.
    (B) Annoyed.
    (C) Sad.
    (D) Relaxed.

65. What is the man's problem?
    (A) The hotel lost his reservation.
    (B) The room is too expensive.
    (C) He doesn't like the room.
    (D) He lost his key.

66. How long will the man stay at the hotel?
    (A) One day.
    (B) Two days.
    (C) Three days.
    (D) Four days.

67. How much does the room cost?
    (A) $65.
    (B) $155.
    (C) $160.
    (D) $165.

68. What happened to Carl?
    (A) He got a promotion.
    (B) He bought a new house.
    (C) He got married.
    (D) He painted his office.

69. How does the man feel about Carl's situation?
    (A) He's unhappy.
    (B) He's glad.
    (C) He's fearful.
    (D) He's mad.

70. What does the man want to do?
    (A) Meet Carl's wife.
    (B) Leave the office.
    (C) Visit Carl's house.
    (D) Give a party.

GO ON TO THE NEXT PAGE

Directions: You will hear some talks given by a single speaker. You will be asked to answer three questions about what the speaker says in each talk. Select the best response to each question and mark the letter (A), (B), (C), or (D) on your answer sheet. The talks will not be printed in your test book and will be spoken only one time.

71. Who was responsible for the problem?
    (A) A park ranger.
    (B) A boy scout.
    (C) A spokesperson.
    (D) A smoker.

72. What was destroyed?
    (A) Campgrounds.
    (B) Houses.
    (C) A car.
    (D) A town.

73. When do authorities expect the fire to be put out?
    (A) On Monday.
    (B) On Wednesday.
    (C) By today.
    (D) In two days.

74. What type of place is the announcement about?
    (A) A school.
    (B) A church.
    (C) A village.
    (D) A hospital.

75. Who receives services at this place?
    (A) Poor people.
    (B) Middle-income people.
    (C) Rich people.
    (D) Retired people.

76. Why are they changing the name of the place?
    (A) The old name was too long.
    (B) Dr. Schweitzer was a popular physician.
    (C) They would like to have a separate identity.
    (D) Villa Hospitalis has moved to another city.

77. What is the specialty of Fuji House?
    (A) Seafood.
    (B) Chicken.
    (C) Tempura.
    (D) Pork.

78. What describes the food at Fuji House?
    (A) It's very expensive.
    (B) It's vegetarian only.
    (C) It smells and tastes delicious.
    (D) It comes from all over the world.

79. When is Fuji House open?
    (A) Every day.
    (B) Monday and Friday only.
    (C) Saturday and Sunday only.
    (D) Monday through Friday only.

80. Why are these people meeting?
    (A) To discuss employee concerns.
    (B) To elect the Manager of the Year.
    (C) To choose the Employee of the Year.
    (D) To vote for a new contract.

81. How will the employees vote?
    (A) By using a ballot.
    (B) By raising their hands.
    (C) By calling out people's names.
    (D) By registering a name electronically.

82. How many prizes will the winner get?
    (A) One.
    (B) Two.
    (C) Three.
    (D) Four.

83. When does this tour take place?
    (A) In the morning.
    (B) In the afternoon.
    (C) In the evening.
    (D) At night.

84. Where will the tour end?
    (A) At the main gate.
    (B) At Machu Picchu.
    (C) At the main plaza.
    (D) At the Temple of the Sun.

85. What does the tour guide request of the tourists?
    (A) To use the litter cans.
    (B) Not to wander away.
    (C) Not to touch the monuments.
    (D) Not to ask questions until he has finished.

---

86. Why is the woman calling?
    (A) To return a phone call.
    (B) To ask for Max's address.
    (C) To verify her phone number.
    (D) To make an appointment with Max.

87. What is she confused about?
    (A) The reason for Max's phone call.
    (B) The time she should call back.
    (C) The name of her street.
    (D) Max's last name.

88. When can Max call her back?
    (A) Before noon.
    (B) At noon.
    (C) This afternoon.
    (D) After three days.

---

89. Why did county residents lose electric power?
    (A) There was a big storm.
    (B) There are too many residents in the county.
    (C) Work crews are installing a new system.
    (D) Power Company employees are on strike.

90. How many residents don't have power?
    (A) 15,000.
    (B) 50,000.
    (C) 100,000.
    (D) 150,000.

91. Who will have power this evening?
    (A) Power Company employees.
    (B) The western part of the county.
    (C) Just a few lucky residents.
    (D) The entire county.

---

92. What is being announced?
    (A) A golf tournament.
    (B) The opening of a sports facility.
    (C) The start of a renovation project.
    (D) Reduced-price orientation sessions.

93. When will the event take place?
    (A) November 1.
    (B) November 21.
    (C) December 1.
    (D) December 21.

94. What special offer is being announced?
    (A) Free golf clubs.
    (B) Private swim lessons.
    (C) Two-for-one memberships.
    (D) Overnight rooms for guests.

GO ON TO THE NEXT PAGE

95. When will the train for Springdale leave?
    (A) In five minutes.
    (B) In fifteen minutes.
    (C) At 7:30.
    (D) At 10:30.

96. Who will be allowed to get on the train first?
    (A) Passengers with reservations.
    (B) Passengers with children.
    (C) Passengers with no bags.
    (D) Passengers with pets.

97. What are passengers allowed to take on the train?
    (A) Nothing.
    (B) Small bags.
    (C) Large suitcases.
    (D) Musical instruments.

98. How many lectures are there in the series?
    (A) Seven.
    (B) Ten.
    (C) Eleven.
    (D) Seventeen.

99. What is the topic of tonight's lecture?
    (A) Butterflies.
    (B) Deserts.
    (C) Oceans.
    (D) Plants.

100. What will happen after the talk?
    (A) A trip to Central America will be organized.
    (B) There will be a display of butterflies.
    (C) The speaker will show a video.
    (D) There will be a sale of photos.

This is the end of the Listening test. Turn to Part 5 in your test book.

101. Can you explain all the _____ I see on my pay statement?
(A) deduct
(B) deductions
(C) deductibles
(D) deducting

102. I'm sorry, but this area is _____ to bank personnel only.
(A) restricted
(B) restriction
(C) restrict
(D) restricts

103. The human resources manager hasn't arrived _____, so please have a seat.
(A) already
(B) still
(C) soon
(D) yet

104. Management has _____ to make a reasonable offer at the next contract bargaining session.
(A) promises
(B) promise
(C) promised
(D) promising

105. Employees are _____ to put in for vacation time at least two months in advance.
(A) requested
(B) referred
(C) rejected
(D) reported

106. The sales manager didn't care for our _____ about last quarter's sales slump.
(A) remarking
(B) remarkable
(C) remarked
(D) remarks

107. My cousin's _____ advice about selling our stock saved us thousands.
(A) amazingly
(B) amazed
(C) amazing
(D) amazement

108. I'm surprised _____ how fast customers get served in this restaurant.
(A) on
(B) at
(C) in
(D) for

109. In order to get a _____, you must bring in the defective product with a valid receipt.
(A) reimbursement
(B) premium
(C) duplication
(D) refund

110. Ms. Kim is learning Russian _____ she can communicate with her new father-in-law.
(A) so that
(B) because
(C) although
(D) then

GO ON TO THE NEXT PAGE

111. The CFO believes that a _____ large volume of sales is the reason we are out of the red.
    (A) surprised
    (B) surprising
    (C) surprisingly
    (D) surprise

112. Making decisions about layoffs isn't _____ our supervisor's job description.
    (A) within
    (B) into
    (C) about
    (D) inside

113. When starting a new business, it isn't _____ to expect profits during the first year.
    (A) real
    (B) realistic
    (C) realistically
    (D) really

114. It is only through a _____ effort on the part of all employees that a company will prosper.
    (A) collaboration
    (B) collaborative
    (C) collaborator
    (D) collaboratively

115. That decision of _____ to repaint the house now was a very smart one.
    (A) your
    (B) you
    (C) yourself
    (D) yours

116. Before investing in a new drug, we carry out extensive _____ to see if there is a need for one.
    (A) investigation
    (B) investing
    (C) planning
    (D) research

117. All branch managers must _____ a semi-annual report for the main office by the end of May.
    (A) compensate
    (B) deliver
    (C) apply
    (D) prepare

118. Doing business in 2010 will be extremely _____ what it was like in 1910.
    (A) different from
    (B) different to
    (C) different
    (D) different then

119. _____ has there been more of a demand for e-business courses at universities than there is now.
    (A) Always
    (B) Never
    (C) Rare
    (D) Often

120. The company's new database system will be installed and running _____ the end of the year.
    (A) in
    (B) from
    (C) by
    (D) on

121. The head of the space program will not be satisfied unless all work is done with the utmost _____.
    (A) accurate
    (B) accurately
    (C) accuracy
    (D) more accuracy

122. Clients will receive _____ questionnaires to see if they are satisfied with our gym equipment.
    (A) periodical
    (B) periodic
    (C) periodically
    (D) period

123. With the approach of the holiday season, employees are _____ awaiting their bonuses.
    (A) anxiety
    (B) anxious
    (C) anxiousness
    (D) anxiously

124. We have just received a troubling _____ on the expected rise in health care costs.
(A) accounting
(B) documentation
(C) report
(D) observance

125. Could you please elaborate _____ your claim that housekeeping didn't keep your room clean?
(A) on
(B) over
(C) for
(D) into

126. It is recommended that potential investors _____ the help of financial advisors before investing.
(A) are seeking out
(B) seek out
(C) to seek out
(D) sought out

127. With globalization now a part of our lives, it is impossible for a country to do business by _____.
(A) itself
(B) it
(C) its own
(D) it's self

128. The government's decision to lower tariffs will allow the volume of imports to _____ tremendously.
(A) extrapolate
(B) exhibit
(C) expand
(D) exhale

129. Our _____ cost-cutting measures will ensure greater profits for the company in the next fiscal year.
(A) outrageous
(B) lucrative
(C) aggressive
(D) astounding

130. Our hotel has every _____ of making your annual convention the most memorable one ever.
(A) intent
(B) intently
(C) intend
(D) intention

131. Shopping on the Internet is for those consumers for _____ going to malls has become a nightmare.
(A) who
(B) whom
(C) which
(D) that

132. Because of security concerns, all job applicants are _____ carefully before interviews are granted.
(A) screamed
(B) screened
(C) scrawled
(D) scraped

133. Mr. Hansen's _____ from his position as chief comptroller has been a shock to all of us.
(A) resigning
(B) resigned
(C) resigns
(D) resign

134. Investors are relieved that all _____ say the stock market will bounce back in the next six months.
(A) predicaments
(B) predilections
(C) predictions
(D) predicates

135. This new trade agreement has created all kinds of _____ possibilities for both our countries.
(A) excited
(B) exciting
(C) excitement
(D) excitable

136. The use of e-mail has caused an _____ leap in business communications throughout the world.
(A) unacceptable
(B) implacable
(C) inadvertent
(D) unimaginable

137. Because of renovations to our offices, future social _____ will be held in the company cafeteria.
(A) events
(B) reunions
(C) councils
(D) invocations

GO ON TO THE NEXT PAGE

138. The last company blood drive was _____ a success that we plan on having one every two months.
- (A) such
- (B) so
- (C) too
- (D) much

139. The staff breathed a _____ sigh of relief when it was announced that there would be no layoffs.
- (A) collected
- (B) collective
- (C) collecting
- (D) collectible

140. Consumers are spending less these days _____ reports that the economy is steadily improving.
- (A) in spite
- (B) because of
- (C) although
- (D) despite

Directions: Read the texts that follow. A word or phrase is missing in some of the sentences. Four answer choices are given below each sentence. Select the best answer to complete the text. Then mark the letter (A), (B), (C), or (D) on your answer sheet.

GO ON TO THE NEXT PAGE

Bournesville Bank

is pleased to announce the opening of a new branch at
1109 South Boulevard in the Green Lake section of town.

This _____ a full-service branch

141. (A) has been
(B) will be
(C) being
(D) was

Where you can be sure of receiving the professional, prompt,
and friendly service that you are accustomed to
at all Bournesville Bank branches.

Please join us for the grand opening
of our new branch on
Monday, May 22
during our regular business hours
9:00 A.M. to 3:00 P.M.

There will be refreshments, live _____, and prizes.

142. (A) entertain
(B) entertainer
(C) entertaining
(D) entertainment

Bank staff will be on hand to explain all the services available to our
customers. Everyone who opens a new _____ during the

143. (A) vault
(B) ledger
(C) account
(D) entrance

Grand Opening will receive a special bonus gift.
This gift is our way of saying "Thank you" for doing business with us.

Bournesville Bank, your partner in all your business and personal _____ needs.

144. (A) psychological
(B) professional
(C) educational
(D) financial

Profits Up In _____ Sector

145. (A) Transportation
(B) Agriculture
(C) Technology
(D) Finance

Galaxy Systems reported a fourth quarter profit of $250,000, compared _____ a loss of nearly $2

146. (A) to
(B) of
(C) by
(D) at

million during the same period last year. This was the first quarter with a profit for the computer company, which began operations five years ago.

According to the year-end report from Goldsboro, Inc., the company's profits rose 20%, or $2.5 million since the end of last year. This is good news for the financial software company, which had been suffering losses during the past several years. The rise in profits is attributed to the introduction of a new software system for personal finance accounting. The company hopes to further increase its _____ next year by

147. (A) debts
(B) products
(C) factories
(D) earnings

expanding its markets overseas.

Profits for Providence Communications Company were up only 5% at the end of the fourth quarter. This is a much smaller increase than the company has reported for several years running. Providence has been losing a significant portion of its market share to competitors, but the company is optimistic about the future. "We're confident that our plans for bringing more efficient and less _____ wireless service to our

148. (A) cost
(B) costly
(C) coasted
(D) costing

customers will result in increased market share and greater profits than the company has ever enjoyed in the past," said Thomas P. Witherspoon, CEO.

GO ON TO THE NEXT PAGE

Questions 149–152 refer to the following letter.

Rita Harwood
Manager
Tinkum Square Hotel
Portsmouth, NJ 14689

Dear Ms. Harwood:

I am writing to let you know of the exemplary care and service I received from

_____ staff during my stay at the Tinkum Square Hotel last July. From the

149. (A) my
     (B) our
     (C) your
     (D) their

moment of my arrival until the day I _____, I received nothing but courteous

                     150. (A) retired
                               (B) resigned
                               (C) departed
                               (D) graduated

and efficient service from all members of the hotel staff.

I especially want to bring to your attention two staff members who provided me with
assistance above and beyond the call of duty. On my way to the airport after a pleasant week
at Tinkum Square, I discovered that I had left my computer behind. I immediately called the
manager on duty, Robert Dunstan, who supervised an emergency search for my computer.
After it was discovered in the hotel restaurant, Mr. Dunstan's assistant, Martha Jones, got
into a taxi and personally delivered the computer to me at the airport. It was all done so

_____ that I had my computer in hand well before I had to board the plane.

151. (A) speedy
     (B) speeded
     (C) speeding
     (D) speedily

I know that you would want to hear about this example of the loyalty and professionalism of
Mr. Dunstan and Ms. Jones. I look forward to _____ at Tinkum Square during

                           152. (A) staying
                                   (B) working
                                   (C) looking
                                   (D) existing

my next business trip to Portsmouth.

Sincerely,
James L. Keenan
James L. Keenan

Directions: In this part you will read a selection of texts, such as magazine and newspaper articles, letters, and advertisements. Each text is followed by several questions. Select the best answer for each question and mark the letter (A), (B), (C), or (D) on your answer sheet.

GO ON TO THE NEXT PAGE

FEELING STRESSED?

Need a *real* break during working hours?
Having trouble relaxing after work?

Human Resources is bringing you
"The Stress Buster"

❧ 15 minutes of total relaxation free of charge
❧ Choose the table for full bodywork.
❧ Choose the chair for neck, shoulders, and back.

Where: Employee Lounge
When: Mondays, Wednesdays, Fridays
Times: During breaks, lunchtime, after work

---

153. What is this announcement about?
 (A) Length of breaks
 (B) Massages
 (C) Furniture sales
 (D) Language classes

154. How much will this service cost the employees?
 (A) Fifteen dollars for fifteen minutes
 (B) They pay nothing.
 (C) It depends on the service.
 (D) Human Resources has the rate.

MEMORANDUM

TO: All Atlantis Corporation Employees
FROM: Myrtle Sternbridge, Chief Financial Officer   *MS*
RE: Two-day unpaid leave
DATE: June 3

It is my unhappy duty to inform you that the Board of Directors has voted to impose a two-day layoff for all employees in order to avoid an operating budget shortfall. The company is facing a serious crisis due to poor profits over the past two quarters. The budget is short by about $13 million and, according to our bylaws, the budget must be balanced by June 30, the end of this fiscal year.

It is necessary for all employees to give up two days' pay in order to put an end to the budget crisis. Employees are to speak to their supervisors regarding scheduling the two days that they are not to report to work.

According to the agreement reached between Atlantis Corp. and the union, employees will be reimbursed for the days they lose during the first six months of the next fiscal year if profits improve.

I sincerely regret the need to take such drastic measures to end the current budget crisis, but with your cooperation, we can see this through.

---

155. Why must employees give up two days'
     pay at this time?
     (A) To pay back money they were
          overpaid
     (B) To contribute to a company charity
     (C) To end a budget crisis in this fiscal
          year
     (D) The bylaws state they have to.

156. What is causing this budget crisis?
     (A) There is a surplus of $13 million.
     (B) There is a shortage of $13 million.
     (C) The CFO did not plan out the
          operating budget properly.
     (D) Nobody can pinpoint the reasons
          for this budget crisis.

157. How will the days be taken off?
     (A) Employees will arrange days off
          with their supervisors.
     (B) All employees are to stay home
          starting June 30.
     (C) A specific plan has not been worked
          out yet.
     (D) Employees can arrange to take two
          days off this or next fiscal year.

GO ON TO THE NEXT PAGE

Questions 158–160 refer to the following notice.

Miami-Dade County Transit Authority

LANE CLOSURES

Due to continued construction on Interstate 95, the two left lanes on the north side will be closed from NE 79th St. to NE 135th St. between the hours of midnight and 6:00 A.M., Monday to Friday, and 10:00 P.M. to 7 A.M. weekends.

Lane closures are scheduled to begin on October 16 and continue until November 6.

We regret any inconvenience to motorists.

158. Which part of the highway will have lane closures?
(A) All north side lanes
(B) One lane on each side
(C) The two left lanes on each side
(D) The two left lanes on the north side

159. Who is authorizing the lane closures?
(A) The city
(B) The county
(C) The state
(D) The district

160. Which of the following exits will NOT be in the affected area?
(A) NE 125th Street
(B) NE 95th Street
(C) NE 151st Street
(D) NE 82nd Street

Those old *Movie Goer* magazines in the basement may be worth more than you would imagine. A 1952 copy featuring Clark Gable can be worth over $750, and an old Lucille Ball is valued at $900. But it's not just the oldies that are worth so much money. A collection of twenty-five *Lost in Space* covers from June, 2001 sells for more than $450 online. "The Internet has been great for collecting and has made it a lot easier to find things," says George Boulis, 58, a Boston-based collector who has all the *Movie Goer Magazine* covers. They're worth about $28,000. And what do you think is the most valuable issue? The first one, of course: A mint-condition copy goes for more than $1,850.

161. What is this article about?
(A) The literary value of *Movie Goer Magazine*
(B) How George Boulis became a very rich man
(C) The monetary value of old issues of *Movie Goer Magazine*
(D) The monetary value of old covers of *Movie Goer Magazine*

162. Where does the writer assume the readers may have old issues of this magazine?
(A) In the attic
(B) In the basement
(C) Under their beds
(D) In their garages

163. Which is the most valuable issue of this magazine?
(A) The premier issue
(B) The ultimate issue
(C) The one with Lucille Ball
(D) The one with Clark Gable

BCAST	8:00	8:30	9:00	9:30	10:00	10:30
2	Washington Week	Wall Street Week Ⓑ	McLaughlin Report		Hurricane Watch	
4	48 Hours		Diagnosis Murder: Town Without Pity (2006) Ⓜ			
5	Dateline NBC				Law and Order: Special Victims Unit	
6	Dateline NBC				Law and Order: Special Victims Unit	
7	Sports Extra		X-Files		News	
10	Financial Success with Sonya Ozman Ⓑ		Lilo & Stitch: Aloha from Hollywood		20/20	

CABLE						
A&E	Biography		Tea with Mussolini (1999) Ⓜ			
AMC	Working Girl (1988) Ⓜ				Working Girl (1988) Ⓜ	
BPL	Business Week in Review Ⓑ		Business Week in Review Ⓑ		It's Your Money Ⓑ	
CNN	Live from . . .		Larry King Live		NewsNight with Aaron Brown	
DSC	U.S. Mint Ⓑ		Inside the World's Mightiest Bank Ⓑ		Three Gorges	
MTV	To Be Announced					

Ⓑ = Business   Ⓜ = Movies

164. How long is *Financial Success with Sonya Ozman* on the air?
   (A) Thirty minutes
   (B) One hour
   (C) Two hours
   (D) Three hours

165. How many different shows about business are being televised in this schedule?
   (A) Two
   (B) Four
   (C) Six
   (D) Eight

166. Which financial show is repeated on the same station?
   (A) *Business Week in Review*
   (B) *Law and Order: Special Victims Unit*
   (C) *Working Girl*
   (D) *Dateline NBC*

167. Which station shows only business programs?
   (A) DSC
   (B) BPL
   (C) 2
   (D) AMC

168. The word "Unit" in line 3 of the first box is closest in meaning to
   (A) Apartment
   (B) Individual
   (C) Department
   (D) Investigation

LONDON—In May, Great Britain's Home Office, deciding on compensation for a man who served four years in prison for industrial espionage that he did not commit, ruled that he was entitled to about $1.1 million. They said, however, that he would have to reimburse the prison about $23,000 for four years' room and board. The outraged Michael O'Brien, age 34, was freed by a Court of Appeal. He said, "They don't charge guilty people for bed and board. They only charge innocent people!"

169. Who decided that Michael O'Brien should be released from prison?
- (A) The Queen
- (B) A group of judges
- (C) A government agency
- (D) Popular opinion

170. What had Mr. O'Brien been convicted of?
- (A) Robbing a bank
- (B) Forging documents
- (C) Spying on other companies
- (D) Embezzling thousands from his company

171. The word "commit" in line 5 is closest in meaning to
- (A) believe in
- (B) profit from
- (C) condone
- (D) carry out

172. What is upsetting Mr. O'Brien?
- (A) He has to pay back money to the prison.
- (B) He has to pay money to the Home Office.
- (C) He will have more money than he ever dreamed of.
- (D) The authorities never caught the real spy.

GO ON TO THE NEXT PAGE

Questions 173–175 refer to the following advertisement.

easy ways to
shop

shop over 350 stores
call 1.800.GOTRENDY

shop by mail
call 1.800.555.8183

shop online
trendymale.com

3181 River Road
Rockville, NM 13579
909–555–5208

buy one sale or
clearance item, **get one**
50% off*

*2nd item must be of equal or lesser value. Applies to
sale and clearance merchandise only. May not be
combined with any other coupon offer, promotion, or
previous purchases. Excludes fragrance, gift certificate,
catalogue, or online purchases. Not valid on designer
merchandise. Not valid on Trendy Male Outlets.
Sale Monday, June 17 through Sunday, July 7.

Trendy Male

save
up to 60%
or more off
original
prices

173. How many ways can you buy
merchandise at "Trendy Male"?
(A) One
(B) Two
(C) Three
(D) Four

174. If you buy a shirt on sale for $46.00, how
much will you pay for another, similar
shirt?
(A) $15.00
(B) $23.00
(C) $27.60
(D) $46.00

175. How long will this offer last?
(A) Eleven days
(B) Sixteen days
(C) Twenty-one days
(D) Twenty-six days

Questions 176–178 refer to the following instructions.

Connect the lead from the charger to the bottom of your cellular phone or to a charging stand. Then plug the charger into a standard wall outlet. When the battery is charging, the battery strength indicator on the right side of the display scrolls.
Note: When you charge the battery for the first time, the battery strength indicator will not scroll the entire time; this is normal.

If your phone displays **Not charging,** charging is suspended. Check that the battery is connected to an approved charging device. If the battery is very hot or cold, wait for a while; charging will automatically resume after the battery is restored to its normal operating state. If charging still fails, contact your dealer.

176. What device are these instructions for?
(A) A portable phone
(B) A palm pilot
(C) A cell phone
(D) A laptop computer

177. What should you do if the battery is not charging?
(A) Check that the battery is connected to the charger
(B) Call the factory
(C) Call your dealer immediately
(D) Check the normal operating time

178. What should you do if the device fails to charge properly?
(A) Return it to the company
(B) Get in touch with the place you bought it from
(C) Send it back to the factory
(D) Throw it away and buy another one

GO ON TO THE NEXT PAGE

Prepare for a New Career
Or get your H.S. Diploma at home.

You've always wanted to start a new career, but could never find the time to get the training you need. Until now. The Learning Center can help you study at home in your spare time to get the skills you need to succeed!

Get your career diploma as a private investigator or medical transcriptionist in as little as six months! Earn your high school diploma in as little as nine months. In as little as two years, you could even have your degree in accounting!

Join the 8 million men and women who enrolled with The Learning Center to change their lives for the better. Call, write, or visit our website today for FREE information!

For fastest service, call toll free:
1-800-555-9878 ext. 834
Visit our website **www.thelearningcenter.com**

Choose ONE of the programs below:
06 High School   57 Private Investigator
86 Accounting   21 Medical Transcriptionist

Dept. LV168R
456 Elm Road
Boynton Cove, FL 31245

---

179. When does the ad say you would be able to study for a career?
(A) In the mornings
(B) In the evenings
(C) On the weekends
(D) Whenever you had free time

180. How long would it take you to get a degree in accounting?
(A) Six months
(B) Nine months
(C) Eighteen months
(D) Two years

To: Ronald Richards, Peter Kim, Hiro Sachimoto, Giovanna Bertini
From: Isabelle Santelli
Subject: Meeting reminder

This is a reminder that this month's department meeting will take place this Thursday at 12:00 in Conference Room 2. Please note location change. The meeting will NOT take place in my office. We will review progress on the Lockerman project and look at the budget for the rest of the year. This is a lunchtime meeting and sandwiches and coffee will be served. Please let me know by Wednesday if you won't be able to make the meeting. Thank you.

Isabelle Santelli

To: I. Santelli
From: R. Richards
Subject: Re: Meeting reminder

Isabelle,

 I'm sorry I won't be able to make the meeting. I'm leaving for Sydney that morning and can't get a later flight. Before I go, I'll put on your desk the figures you'll need for the second item on the meeting agenda. I've prepared a thorough report, so you'll be able to have that part of the discussion without me. Also, Peter worked with me on this and can probably answer any questions.

 I'll be meeting with Mr. Lockerman first thing Friday and will send you the particulars later that day, or by Saturday morning at the latest.

Ronald

---

181. Who should attend the meeting on Thursday?
(A) Conference committee members
(B) All company personnel
(C) Department members
(D) Mr. Lockerman

182. Where will the meeting take place?
(A) In a conference room
(B) In a sandwich shop
(C) In a cafeteria
(D) In an office

183. When will Mr. Richards go to Sydney?
(A) Wednesday
(B) Thursday
(C) Friday
(D) Saturday

184. Who worked on a report with Mr. Richards?
(A) Mr. Sachimoto
(B) Ms. Santelli
(C) Ms. Bertini
(D) Mr. Kim

185. What will Mr. Richards leave for Ms. Santelli?
(A) Information about the budget
(B) Mr. Lockerman's address
(C) The meeting agenda
(D) His Sydney itinerary

GO ON TO THE NEXT PAGE

Peninsula Office Supplies and Equipment
105978 Rutherford Drive • Suite 110
Greensboro, RI 45790

Invoice No. 1078
Date: November 10
Ship Date: November 15

Item	Price
1 computer stand—model B	$150
2 desk chairs model ZY	$225
1 large watercooler	$ 85
3 paper cutters	$180
subtotal	$640
shipping & handling	$ 75
amount due	$715

The above amount has been charged to your credit card.
Thank you for doing business with us.

November 21

Customer Service Department
Peninsula Office Supplies and Equipment
105978 Rutherford Drive, Suite 110
Greensboro, RI 45790

Dear Customer Service:

On November 18, we received a shipment of office furniture and equipment from your company. Unfortunately, the items we received were not the same as the items we ordered. I am enclosing a copy of the bill so that you can see exactly what was delivered to us. We did order a computer stand, but requested model D, which is half the price of model B. We also asked for only one desk chair, and we didn't order any paper cutters at all. At least the watercooler was correct.

I have tried calling your Customer Service number repeatedly, but the line is always busy. Several attempts at e-mailing have also resulted in no response. Please let me know how we can return the office furniture which was erroneously delivered and receive instead the furniture that we actually ordered. I would like to resolve this matter as quickly as possible.

Sincerely yours,

H. J. Simpson

H. J. Simpson
Office Manager

186. How long was the shipment in transit?
    (A) 3 days
    (B) 5 days
    (C) 8 days
    (D) 11 days

187. Why did Mr. Simpson write the letter?
    (A) Because he received the wrong order
    (B) Because the furniture arrived damaged
    (C) Because he didn't like what he ordered
    (D) Because the furniture was too expensive

188. How much does a model D computer stand cost?
    (A) $50
    (B) $75
    (C) $150
    (D) $300

189. How many watercoolers did Mr. Simpson order?
    (A) None
    (B) One
    (C) Two
    (D) Three

190. What happened when Mr. Simpson called the Customer Service number?
    (A) He was asked to send an e-mail.
    (B) His order was reshipped.
    (C) He received a refund.
    (D) He got a busy signal.

GO ON TO THE NEXT PAGE

High-Speed Train Service
Mitteldorf-Kohlberg Line

LV MITTELDORF	ARR KOHLBERG
5:45*	10:30
7:30**	11:50
8:15	**12:35**
11:00**	**3:20**
12:20*	**5:05**
4:35	**8:55**

Times listed in bold are P.M.
* Makes intermediate stops at Badstein and Grauling
** Monday, Wednesday, and Friday only

Reservations are required on all trains.

One-way ticket prices as of April 1:
Business Class: $175
Tourist Class: $135

Round-trip fares are double the one-way fare.

To: Park Travel Agency
From: Hilda Heinz
Subject: Train ticket

Dear Mr. Park,

Thank you for forwarding the train schedule to me. I'm not an early riser, but I need to be in Kohlberg by the early afternoon, so I'll take the second train in the morning next Tuesday the 22nd. I'll return the following Friday. I haven't seen the return schedule, but time is not so important for my return. Would you please make me a reservation that would have me back in Mitteldorf by about 5 or 6 in the afternoon? I prefer to travel business class, of course. Please bill my account and have the ticket sent to my office.

Thank you, as always, for your kind and efficient service.
Hilda Heinz

191. What time does the earliest train arrive in Kohlberg?
   (A) 3:20
   (B) 5:05
   (C) 8:55
   (D) 10:30

192. How long is a nonstop trip between Mitteldorf and Kohlberg?
   (A) Three and a half hours
   (B) Four hours and twenty minutes
   (C) Four hours and forty-five minutes
   (D) Five and a half hours

193. Which train does Ms. Heinz plan to take on Tuesday?
   (A) 5:45
   (B) 7:30
   (C) 8:15
   (D) 11:00

194. How much will Ms. Heinz pay for her round-trip ticket?
   (A) $135
   (B) $175
   (C) $270
   (D) $350

195. When does Ms. Heinz want to arrive in Mitteldorf on her return?
   (A) As early as possible
   (B) Before noon
   (C) In the early afternoon
   (D) In the late afternoon

GO ON TO THE NEXT PAGE

Have your next company banquet at the

Hotel Grandiflor

WE OFFER:

- Table seating for up to 250 guests
- A choice of catered meals prepared by our European-trained chefs
- Two world-class dance floors

We also provide on request professional assistance in selecting decorations, music, and seating arrangements.
Rooms are available for both midday and evening banquets.
Meal options include buffet, 3-course, and 5-course meals.

Impress your clients and reward your employees by inviting them to lunch or dinner at the Hotel Grandiflor.

Contact Cathy Chang, Events Manager, or Lois Street, Head Manager

---

To: Cathy Chang
From: Georgette Blanc
Subject: Banquet plans

Dear Ms. Chang:

I saw your hotel's ad in the May 23 issue of the *Business Gazette*. I am planning the annual employee appreciation banquet for my company, Agrix International, and am interested in the possibility of hosting it at the Hotel Grandiflor.

Our banquet is scheduled for the evening of July 15. We only plan to have half the number of guests mentioned in your ad, so I am sure you can accommodate our numbers. I think a five-course dinner would be too much, but I am interested in discussing with you the other two meal options. Mostly I am concerned about having both vegetarian and meat choices available for our guests.

I am also interested in your professional assistance in planning other aspects of the evening. We would need seating arrangements that are conducive to conversation but that will also accommodate the awards ceremony that is the main focus of the evening. We also would like to have dancing after the meal and would appreciate your assistance in selecting a suitable and affordable band.

Please call me or my assistant, Robert de Luc, at 656-555-0987 to discuss arrangements and costs.

Georgette Blanc

196. What is the name of the hotel's events manager?
- (A) Cathy Chang
- (B) Lois Street
- (C) Georgette Blanc
- (D) Robert de Luc

197. What is the main purpose of the banquet mentioned in the e-mail?
- (A) To celebrate an anniversary
- (B) To honor employees
- (C) To discuss business
- (D) To impress clients

198. When will the banquet take place?
- (A) May 3
- (B) May 23
- (C) July 5
- (D) July 15

199. How many guests will be invited to the banquet?
- (A) 15
- (B) 125
- (C) 250
- (D) 500

200. Which type of meal would be of interest to the banquet planner?
- (A) Meat-only three-course meal
- (B) Five-course meal
- (C) Light lunch
- (D) Vegetarian and meat buffet

Stop! This is the end of the test. If you finish before time is called, you may go back to Parts 5, 6, and 7 and check your work.

PRACTICE TEST TWO

Practice Test Two is similar to an actual new TOEIC test. You can take this test after you finish studying this book in order to measure your improvement.

Read all directions carefully. This will help you become familiar with the new TOEIC test directions and item types.

Use the Practice Test Two Answer Sheet on page 295.

LISTENING TEST

In the Listening test, you will be asked to demonstrate how well you understand spoken English. The entire Listening test will last approximately 45 minutes. There are four parts, and directions are given for each part. You must mark your answers on the separate answer sheet. Do not write your answers in the test book.

PART I

Directions: For each question in this part, you will hear four statements about a picture in your test book. When you hear the statements, you must select the one statement that best describes what you see in the picture. Then find the number of the question on your answer sheet and mark your answer. The statements will not be printed in your test book and will be spoken only one time.

Example

Sample Answer

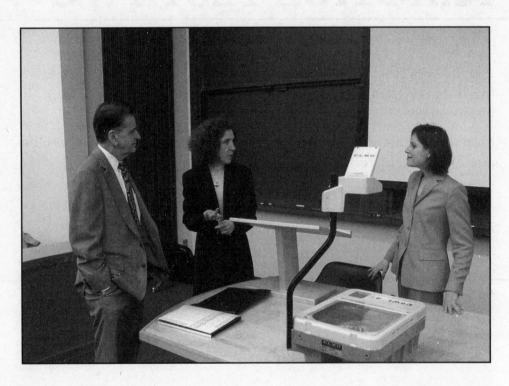

Statement (C), "They're standing near the table," is the best description of the picture, so you should select answer (C) and mark it on your answer sheet.

1.

2.

GO ON TO THE NEXT PAGE

3.

4.

5.

6.

GO ON TO THE NEXT PAGE

7.

8.

9.

10.

GO ON TO THE NEXT PAGE

PART 2

Directions: You will hear a question or statement and three responses spoken in English. They will not be printed in your test book and will be spoken only one time. Select the best response to the question or statement and mark the letter (A), (B), or (C) on your answer sheet.

Example

You will hear: Where is the meeting room?

You will also hear: (A)   To meet the new director.
                      (B)   It's the first room on the right.
                      (C)   Yes, at two o'clock.

Your best response to the question "Where is the meeting room?" is choice (B), "It's the first room on the right," so (B) is the correct answer. You should mark answer (B) on your answer sheet.

---

11.   Mark your answer on your answer sheet.   26.   Mark your answer on your answer sheet.

12.   Mark your answer on your answer sheet.   27.   Mark your answer on your answer sheet.

13.   Mark your answer on your answer sheet.   28.   Mark your answer on your answer sheet.

14.   Mark your answer on your answer sheet.   29.   Mark your answer on your answer sheet.

15.   Mark your answer on your answer sheet.   30.   Mark your answer on your answer sheet.

16.   Mark your answer on your answer sheet.   31.   Mark your answer on your answer sheet.

17.   Mark your answer on your answer sheet.   32.   Mark your answer on your answer sheet.

18.   Mark your answer on your answer sheet.   33.   Mark your answer on your answer sheet.

19.   Mark your answer on your answer sheet.   34.   Mark your answer on your answer sheet.

20.   Mark your answer on your answer sheet.   35.   Mark your answer on your answer sheet.

21.   Mark your answer on your answer sheet.   36.   Mark your answer on your answer sheet.

22.   Mark your answer on your answer sheet.   37.   Mark your answer on your answer sheet.

23.   Mark your answer on your answer sheet.   38.   Mark your answer on your answer sheet.

24.   Mark your answer on your answer sheet.   39.   Mark your answer on your answer sheet.

25.   Mark your answer on your answer sheet.   40.   Mark your answer on your answer sheet.

Directions: You will hear some conversations between two people. You will be asked to answer three questions about what the speakers say in each conversation. Select the best response to each question and mark the letter (A), (B), (C), or (D) on your answer sheet. The conversations will not be printed in your test book and will be spoken only one time.

41. Who sent the package?
(A) Mr. Ozawa.
(B) Ms. Jones.
(C) Mr. Ozawa's boss.
(D) Mr. Ozawa's secretary.

42. When is the meeting with Ms. Jones?
(A) Right now.
(B) This morning.
(C) Tonight.
(D) Tomorrow.

43. Where is Mr. Ozawa now?
(A) At lunch.
(B) At his desk.
(C) In a meeting.
(D) In the mailroom.

44. Where are the speakers?
(A) At home.
(B) At a bank.
(C) At the office.
(D) At a restaurant.

45. What will the woman do?
(A) Buy a card.
(B) Pay the bill.
(C) Play a game.
(D) Cook a meal.

46. What will the man give the woman?
(A) Some money.
(B) Some letters.
(C) A wallet.
(D) A meal.

47. How many people will eat dinner?
(A) Two.
(B) Three.
(C) Eight.
(D) Nine.

48. What time will they eat dinner?
(A) 8:30.
(B) 8:45.
(C) 9:00.
(D) 10:00.

49. What will they do before dinner?
(A) Visit the kitchen.
(B) Look for a table.
(C) Sit in the bar.
(D) Fix the car.

50. What are the speakers discussing?
(A) Washing the windows.
(B) Buying new chairs.
(C) Painting the room.
(D) Cleaning the rug.

51. What color is the rug?
(A) Green.
(B) White.
(C) Yellow.
(D) Blue.

52. When will they start work on the project?
(A) Tonight.
(B) Tomorrow.
(C) On Friday.
(D) Next week.

GO ON TO THE NEXT PAGE

53. Why did Jim miss the meeting?
    (A) He was feeling sick.
    (B) He had to type a memo.
    (C) He left his watch at home.
    (D) The copy machine didn't work.

54. What time was the meeting?
    (A) 3:00.
    (B) 4:00.
    (C) 6:00.
    (D) 8:00.

55. Why does the man have to hurry?
    (A) The meeting starts soon.
    (B) He has to mail a letter.
    (C) It's starting to rain.
    (D) He has to catch a train.

56. Where will the speakers go to work?
    (A) The conference room.
    (B) The business office.
    (C) The elevator.
    (D) Their desks.

57. What will they take with them?
    (A) Pens.
    (B) Notepads.
    (C) A computer.
    (D) Computer paper.

58. What kind of work are they doing?
    (A) Ordering office supplies.
    (B) Planning a conference.
    (C) Fixing a computer.
    (D) Writing a report.

59. Who will be in the office tomorrow?
    (A) Sam.
    (B) Sam's boss.
    (C) Sam's friend.
    (D) Sam's assistant.

60. What does the woman want help with?
    (A) Cooking lunch.
    (B) Finding a book.
    (C) Going over accounts.
    (D) Planning a conference.

61. When will the woman go to the office?
    (A) After work.
    (B) After lunch.
    (C) Before lunch.
    (D) At dinnertime.

62. What does the man want to buy?
    (A) A fax machine.
    (B) A newspaper.
    (C) A telephone.
    (D) A briefcase.

63. How much is the sale?
    (A) 10 percent off.
    (B) 15 percent off.
    (C) 20 percent off.
    (D) 50 percent off.

64. When does the sale end?
    (A) Today.
    (B) Tomorrow.
    (C) On Saturday.
    (D) Next week.

65. What is broken?
    (A) The air conditioner.
    (B) The photocopier.
    (C) The telephone.
    (D) The light.

66. When will the repair person arrive?
    (A) At noon.
    (B) Next week.
    (C) Right away.
    (D) This afternoon.

67. What will the man do while he is waiting?
    (A) Eat a meal.
    (B) Read e-mail.
    (C) Write a report.
    (D) Make a phone call.

68. Why can't the man meet with the woman this week?
    (A) He has to meet with another person.
    (B) He needs to rest this week.
    (C) He'll be away on a trip.
    (D) His office won't be open.

69. What does the woman want to discuss?
    (A) Conference plans.
    (B) A letter.
    (C) Money.
    (D) A class.

70. What time will the woman be at the man's office?
    (A) 9:00.
    (B) 10:00.
    (C) 11:00.
    (D) 1:00.

GO ON TO THE NEXT PAGE

Directions: You will hear some talks given by a single speaker. You will be asked to answer three questions about what the speaker says in each talk. Select the best response to each question and mark the letter (A), (B), (C), or (D) on your answer sheet. The talks will not be printed in your test book and will be spoken only one time.

71. What time will the train leave?
    (A) 10:10.
    (B) 10:15.
    (C) 10:30.
    (D) 10:40.

72. Who should arrive at the gate early?
    (A) Passengers who can offer help.
    (B) Passengers with luggage.
    (C) Passengers who have questions.
    (D) Passengers who have children.

73. What form of payment is accepted for tickets on the train?
    (A) Cash.
    (B) Check.
    (C) Credit card.
    (D) Money order.

74. Who is talking?
    (A) A news reporter.
    (B) A weather forecaster.
    (C) A pilot.
    (D) A travel agent.

75. When is the speaker talking?
    (A) In the early morning.
    (B) At noon.
    (C) In the evening.
    (D) Late at night.

76. How will the weather be tomorrow?
    (A) Rainy.
    (B) Cloudy.
    (C) Sunny.
    (D) Cold.

77. Where would you hear this announcement?
    (A) At a grocery store.
    (B) At a department store.
    (C) At a restaurant.
    (D) At a library.

78. What is on sale?
    (A) Beef.
    (B) Vegetables.
    (C) Fruit.
    (D) Suits.

79. Who can use the express check-out lanes?
    (A) People buying ground beef.
    (B) People buying sale items.
    (C) People buying vegetables.
    (D) People buying only 15 items.

80. Who is talking?
    (A) A student.
    (B) A professor.
    (C) An author.
    (D) A medical doctor.

81. What is the subject of the class?
    (A) Math.
    (B) Computers.
    (C) Finance.
    (D) Health.

82. How many tests will there be?
    (A) One.
    (B) Two.
    (C) Seven.
    (D) Ten.

83. Who was Bob Wilson?
   (A) A mayor.
   (B) A bus driver.
   (C) A war hero.
   (D) An artist.

84. How long will they stay at the Wilson House?
   (A) Half an hour.
   (B) One hour.
   (C) One hour and ten minutes.
   (D) Two hours.

85. Where will they go after visiting the Wilson House?
   (A) To a restaurant.
   (B) To a bus station.
   (C) To a monument.
   (D) To a museum.

86. What are the tickets for?
   (A) A city bus tour.
   (B) A theater.
   (C) A sports event.
   (D) An awards ceremony.

87. Where can you get tickets?
   (A) At the stadium.
   (B) At the front desk.
   (C) At the bus station.
   (D) At the ticket counter.

88. What time will the bus leave?
   (A) 3:00 in the morning.
   (B) 6:00 in the morning.
   (C) 3:00 in the afternoon.
   (D) 6:00 in the evening.

89. What is Ms. Park's book about?
   (A) Public speaking.
   (B) Sports.
   (C) Making money.
   (D) Retail business.

90. What will Ms. Park do?
   (A) Introduce someone.
   (B) Receive an award.
   (C) Read from her book.
   (D) Make copies of the book.

91. What can you do at the back of the auditorium?
   (A) Buy a book.
   (B) Read some signs.
   (C) Play a game.
   (D) Answer questions.

92. Who is Pamela Jones?
   (A) A telephone operator.
   (B) A scientist.
   (C) An assistant.
   (D) A newspaper reporter.

93. Why can't she answer the telephone right now?
   (A) She's at a conference.
   (B) She's talking to someone else.
   (C) She's reading the newspaper.
   (D) She's working on a story.

94. What should you do if you want to leave a message?
   (A) Talk to Ms. Jones's assistant.
   (B) Call the main switchboard.
   (C) Stay on the line.
   (D) Send a message by e-mail.

95. Which flight will arrive on time?
    (A) The flight from Hong Kong.
    (B) The flight from Sydney.
    (C) The flight from London.
    (D) The flight from Paris.

96. Why was a flight canceled?
    (A) Because of rain in London.
    (B) Because of a blizzard in Paris.
    (C) Because no tickets were sold.
    (D) Because the schedule changed.

97. When does the special sale end?
    (A) This evening.
    (B) On the weekend.
    (C) Next week.
    (D) Next month.

98. How many shows will the theater have today?
    (A) One.
    (B) Two.
    (C) Three.
    (D) Five.

99. What is half price?
    (A) The midnight show.
    (B) Tickets for people younger than 18.
    (C) Shows before five o'clock.
    (D) Snacks sold in the lobby.

100. What is not allowed inside the theater?
    (A) Popcorn.
    (B) Drinks.
    (C) Any snack.
    (D) Outside food.

This is the end of the Listening test. Turn to Part 5 in your test book.

In the Reading test, you will read a variety of texts and answer several different types of reading comprehension questions. The entire Reading test will last 75 minutes. There are three parts, and directions are given for each part. You are encouraged to answer as many questions as possible within the time allowed.

You must mark your answers on the separate answer sheet. Do not write your answers in the test book.

PART 5

Directions: A word or phrase is missing in each of the sentences below. Four answer choices are given below each sentence. Select the best answer to complete the sentence. Then mark the letter (A), (B), (C), or (D) on your answer sheet.

101. Customer _____ is one of the top priorities of this company.
   (A) satisfied
   (B) satisfying
   (C) satisfy
   (D) satisfaction

102. Remember that feeling confident and _____ is an important part of giving a presentation.
   (A) relaxing
   (B) relaxes
   (C) relaxed
   (D) relax

103. Final arrangements for the board of directors' meeting haven't _____ been made.
   (A) already
   (B) still
   (C) while
   (D) yet

104. We have _____ all project managers to turn in their reports by the end of the week.
   (A) asking
   (B) asked
   (C) ask
   (D) asks

105. Nobody will be _____ to the room after the meeting has started.
   (A) admitted
   (B) omitted
   (C) permitted
   (D) submitted

106. Customer _____ representatives are available to answer your questions twenty-four hours a day.
   (A) servants
   (B) serving
   (C) serve
   (D) service

107. While some people enjoy receiving calls from telemarketers, other people find such calls _____.
   (A) annoys
   (B) annoying
   (C) annoyingly
   (D) annoyed

108. If you are interested _____ receiving free samples of our product, simply fill out the enclosed card.
   (A) to
   (B) in
   (C) of
   (D) about

109. Because of the mild climate and rich soil, a wide variety of crops can be _____ in this region.
   (A) grown up
   (B) increased
   (C) raised
   (D) enlarged

GO ON TO THE NEXT PAGE

110. _____ she has worked very hard during the past year, Ms. Gomez has still failed to get a promotion.
(A) Although
(B) Because
(C) So
(D) In spite of

111. The new advertising campaign resulted in a _____ large increase in sales.
(A) surprised
(B) surprisingly
(C) surprise
(D) surprises

112. A fine will be charged for all materials that are returned to the library _____ the due date.
(A) past
(B) over
(C) later
(D) above

113. We felt that the recent reports were not particularly _____.
(A) informs
(B) information
(C) informative
(D) inform

114. The slow _____ on this project has been a cause for concern.
(A) progress
(B) progressed
(C) progressive
(D) progresses

115. After you have had a chance to look over the enclosed documents, please return _____ to the front office.
(A) they
(B) them
(C) their
(D) theirs

116. Due to the _____ weather conditions, all flights have been postponed until further notice.
(A) current
(B) abundant
(C) actual
(D) eventual

117. We need all the help we can get and would like everyone in the office to _____ us in getting this job completed on time.
(A) resist
(B) desist
(C) insist
(D) assist

118. The new computer does not seem to work _____ the old one did.
(A) as well
(B) as well than
(C) as good as
(D) as well as

119. _____ have market conditions been as favorable as they are now.
(A) Reliably
(B) Fortunately
(C) Never
(D) Usually

120. Most _____ the people who responded to the survey were pleased with the new product.
(A) of
(B) for
(C) to
(D) from

121. Fill out this form _____ before turning it in to your supervisor.
(A) completed
(B) complete
(C) completion
(D) completely

122. All new staff members should become _____ with the standard office procedures.
(A) family
(B) familiar
(C) familiarly
(D) familiarize

123. The recent changes in the economy have led to greater _____ in our company's products.
(A) interest
(B) interesting
(C) interested
(D) interestingly

124. Weather conditions _____ the region have had a negative impact on agricultural production.
(A) whole
(B) during
(C) throughout
(D) entire

125. While we understand the desire to save money, we usually advise _____ choosing an insurance plan merely because it has the lowest price.
(A) for
(B) from
(C) against
(D) over

126. Please call the travel agent this afternoon to _____ your travel plans.
(A) confirmation
(B) confirm
(C) confirmed
(D) confirming

127. The manager has asked that all vacation requests be handed in to _____ office by 9:00 on Monday morning.
(A) she's
(B) her
(C) she
(D) hers

128. _____ for improvements in current economic conditions have been met with nothing but disappointment.
(A) Expectations
(B) Experiences
(C) Experiments
(D) Expressions

129. Any personal items left in the lockers will be _____ at the end of the month.
(A) reminded
(B) remarked
(C) remodeled
(D) removed

130. The director would like to express his appreciation for the _____ efforts made by all members of the staff during this time of crisis.
(A) admirable
(B) admired
(C) admirably
(D) admiral

131. The person to _____ you submitted your request is no longer in charge of this section.
(A) whom
(B) which
(C) who
(D) where

132. We would be very interested in hearing your _____ of the current political crisis.
(A) reaction
(B) mind
(C) reason
(D) opinion

133. While negative criticism is rarely appreciated, _____ advice is always welcome.
(A) constructive
(B) construction
(C) construct
(D) constructing

134. We hope that you will _____ all of the evidence before making your final decision in this matter.
(A) confuse
(B) convince
(C) consider
(D) concur

135. Mr. Chang will serve as _____ director until a permanent director can be found.
(A) act
(B) acting
(C) actor
(D) acted

GO ON TO THE NEXT PAGE

136. It is important to respond to customer complaints with as pleasant an _____ as possible.
(A) assertion
(B) attitude
(C) assignment
(D) attendant

137. While it is _____ to know the final results this soon, we have received some preliminary information.
(A) impossible
(B) impatient
(C) improper
(D) impolite

138. Our team worked _____ hard on that project that we finished it two days before the deadline.
(A) too
(B) so
(C) such
(D) a lot

139. _____ can be the cause of many work delays.
(A) Careless
(B) Cared
(C) Carelessness
(D) Carelessly

140. _____ the growing demand for our product, we are making plans to increase production.
(A) Although
(B) In spite of
(C) Because of
(D) Consequently

Directions: Read the texts that follow. A word or phrase is missing in some of the sentences. Four answer choices are given below each of the sentences. Select the best answer to complete the text. Then mark the letter (A), (B), (C), or (D) on your answer sheet.

Questions 141–144 refer to the following announcement.

The National Museum of Art

is proud to announce the upcoming _____ of

141. (A) exhibit
     (B) lecture
     (C) auction
     (D) purchase

European Expressionist paintings and prints,
from January 15 through March 15.

We are very fortunate to be able to bring this opportunity to area residents and visitors.
This show includes works on loan from museums and collectors all around the world.
It is the first time this area has seen _____ wide representation of

142. (A) very
     (B) such a
     (C) so that
     (D) enough

Expressionist works together in one place.

_____ for the show are available by calling

143. (A) Guides
     (B) Tickets
     (C) Brochures
     (D) Schedules

the museum's Special Events office at
342-555-0980, or by visiting our website: www.artmuseum.org.
Prices are $25 general admission and $20 for senior citizens and students
with a valid ID. Children under 12 will be charged half price.
Entrance prices also include admission to the museum's permanent collection.
A recorded tour and headphones will be available at the exhibit for $6.

During the show, the Museum Gift Store _____ on sale catalogues,

144. (A) has had
     (B) had
     (C) has
     (D) will have

art reproductions, calendars, coffee mugs, and other souvenirs of the show.

April 17

To whom it may concern:

This letter is _____ for Mr. Young Kim, who has worked for this company as an administrative

145. (A) a background
(B) an instruction
(C) a reference
(D) an acceptance

assistant for the past three years.

During most of his time here, Mr. Kim has worked directly under _____ supervision. He has

146. (A) your
(B) his
(C) her
(D) my

served as an assistant to a busy accounting office with a staff of five. He _____ himself to be

147. (A) always has shown
(B) always has shows
(C) has always shown
(D) has shown always

reliable and hardworking. He has never shirked his duties, even when the office workload has required him to work late into the evening or on a weekend. I always feel sure that whatever task I may give him, it will be done promptly and with a smile. Mr. Kim's friendliness and upbeat attitude have been a real contribution to the office environment.

We will miss Mr. Kim, but we understand that he is ready to move on to a _____ that will make

148. (A) position
(B) degree
(C) residence
(D) professor

better use of his skills and provide him with more opportunities for his future. I can recommend him without reservation and know he will make a great contribution to any work environment.

Sincerely,

Ivan Sokolow

Ivan Sokolow

GO ON TO THE NEXT PAGE

Questions 149–152 refer to the following memo.

To: All personnel
From: Marina Petrowski, Director
Re: Travel expenses

We are all aware that the procedures for charging and reporting expenses for business trips taken on behalf of the company have long been out of hand. As a result _____ recommendations from the Budget Office, the following procedures

149. (A) of
 (B) as
 (C) for
 (D) if

will be adopted.

Company personnel will no longer be given company credit cards to cover expenses while on out of town trips. Instead, all travel expenses, with the _____ of

150. (A) excepts
 (B) excepted
 (C) exception
 (D) excepting

airline tickets which will continue to be charged directly to the company, will be paid for out of pocket. In order to receive _____, an expense report must be

151. (A) bonuses
 (B) assistance
 (C) supervisors
 (D) reimbursement

submitted to your department head within ten days of returning from a trip. All charges must be itemized on the report and accompanied by receipts. Approval of each item will be made at the discretion of each department head, following, of course, the company expense guidelines (see attached). Generally, charges for hotels, meals, and transportation will be _____. Non-work related items such as

152. (A) reported
 (B) expensive
 (C) authorized
 (D) unallowable

entertainment, excessive taxi rides, and bar bills will not. I am sure you will all understand the necessity of this strict attitude toward expense reporting. I am counting on everyone's cooperation.

Directions: In this part you will read a selection of texts, such as magazine and newspaper articles, letters, and advertisements. Each text is followed by several questions. Select the best answer for each question and mark the letter (A), (B), (C), or (D) on your answer sheet.

GO ON TO THE NEXT PAGE

JOB FAIR

A job fair will be held at the Downtown Convention Center
on Saturday, April 15th, from 9:00 A.M. to 5:00 P.M.

If you are interested in a career in:

- Computer Programming
- Hotel Management
- Marketing
- Business Administration
- Journalism

. . . then this is your opportunity to meet people who are currently working in these and other fields and who have job openings for you. The job fair will be held in Conference Room 1 and doors open at 9:00 A.M. Bring ten copies of your résumé and a list of references.

The Downtown Convention Center is located at 125 South State Street, across from the Seward Hotel. It can be reached by the Main Street and Cross City bus lines. The job fair is sponsored by the City Chamber of Commerce.

153. What can you do at the job fair?
   (A) Learn how to write a résumé
   (B) Meet potential employers
   (C) Attend a conference
   (D) Buy things on sale

154. Where will the job fair be held?
   (A) In the convention center
   (B) On Main Street
   (C) On South State Street
   (D) At the Chamber of Commerce

Capital Motel
Telephone Instructions

This telephone has been provided for your convenience.

- To reach the front desk, dial 1.
- To reach room service, dial 2.
- To reach maid service, dial 3.
- To make a local call, dial 9 and then the number.
- To make a long distance call, dial 1 to ask for assistance.

Local Numbers of Interest

Movie Hotline 567-555-2113
Tourist Information. 567-555-3456
Airport Shuttle 567-555-5525
City Public Transportation 567-555-1014

155. What should you do to call someone in another city?
(A) Call Tourist Information
(B) Call room service
(C) Call City Public Transportation
(D) Call the front desk

156. If you dial 9-567-555-1014, what information can you find out?
(A) Which bus to take downtown
(B) Which movies are showing tonight
(C) Where to eat dinner
(D) How to make a local call

157. How can you ask someone to clean your room?
(A) Make a long distance call
(B) Dial 3
(C) Call room service
(D) Ask for Tourist Information

GO ON TO THE NEXT PAGE

Questions 158–160 refer to the following letter.

New World Computers, Inc.

Sept. 12, 20___

Mary Matta
27 High Road
Ipswich, MA 01801

Dear Ms. Matta:

   According to our records, you recently contacted the New World Computers Technical Support Service and spoke with our representative, Joan Kim. We hope your experience was pleasant and effective. We would appreciate your giving us feedback on your experience with Technical Support by taking a few minutes to fill out the enclosed Customer Survey form. By letting us know about the quality of the support you received, you will help us ensure that we continue to provide you and all our customers with the excellent service that you deserve.

   Please return the form in the enclosed envelope, or you can complete it online by going to our website at www.nwc.com/customersurvey. If you have any questions, please contact the Customer Support Office at 800-555-8978. Thank you for being a New World Computers' customer.

Sincerely,

Samuel Lee

Samuel Lee, Support Service Manager

---

158. What is the purpose of this letter?
(A) To ask for the customer's opinion
(B) To offer technical support
(C) To sell a new computer
(D) To advertise a website

159. How can the customer complete the form?
(A) By calling the Customer Support Office
(B) By going online
(C) By contacting Ms. Kim
(D) By writing to Mr. Lee

160. Who did the customer speak with?
(A) The Support Service Manager
(B) A Technical Support representative
(C) Someone in the Customer Support Office
(D) A New World Computers customer

Office Center Towers

This is to inform all tenants that tomorrow morning, October 10th, service work will be performed on the building fire alarm system between the hours of 8:30 and 10:00. As part of this procedure, it will be necessary to test the alarm and you may hear it go off three or four times in the course of the morning. Do not be concerned when you hear the alarm go off. It is part of the normal service routine. If you have any questions, please contact the building superintendent's office. Thank you for your patience.

161. What is the purpose of this notice?
- (A) To let tenants know that the fire alarm system will be repaired
- (B) To tell tenants about a fire that occurred in the building
- (C) To warn tenants about the danger of fires
- (D) To inform tenants about what to do in case of fire

162. What should tenants do if they hear the fire alarm during 8:30 and 10:00?
- (A) Leave the building immediately
- (B) Contact the building superintendent
- (C) Continue with their usual activities
- (D) Wait patiently for the fire department to arrive

GO ON TO THE NEXT PAGE

Are you getting ready to put your house on the market?
Are you thinking of selling it yourself?
Don't do it on your own!

Research has shown that on the average real estate agents
get a 30% higher sales price on single-family homes than
owners who try to do the selling themselves.

Come learn the ins and outs of the real estate market and
how to get the best possible price for your house.
On Friday, January 20th at 7:30 P.M., Ms. Miranda Ortiz,
a real estate agent with over twenty years' experience in
the field, will talk about the current competitive real estate
market and strategies for pricing and selling your single-
family home or apartment. A question and answer session
will follow the talk and refreshments will be served.
Admission to this event is free, but because of the high
level of interest, reservations are required.

Please call Mr. Jones at
676-555-0944 to reserve your space.

163. Who is this notice aimed at?
(A) Real estate agents
(B) Home owners
(C) Researchers
(D) Marketing experts

164. What kind of event does it advertise?
(A) An estate sale
(B) A party
(C) A lecture
(D) A competition

165. What should you do if you want to attend the event?
(A) Put your house on the market
(B) Send in some money
(C) Call Ms. Ortiz
(D) Make a reservation

Thank you for buying a product from the Office Ware mail-order catalog. We hope you are satisfied with your purchase of our quality merchandise. Please examine the contents of this package immediately to make sure that your order has arrived complete and in undamaged condition. In the event that you are not totally satisfied with your purchase for any reason, you can return it to us within thirty days for a full refund, no questions asked. Just repack it in the same box you received it in, and apply the enclosed return shipping label to the outside of the box. Return postage will be paid by the customer. If you wish to return a product after thirty days from the purchase date, please call the customer service office at 800-555-1002 and ask to speak with a purchase order representative.

166. Where would you find these instructions?
(A) In a catalog
(B) Enclosed in a package
(C) Hanging up in a post office
(D) At a store

167. The word "condition" in line 6 is closest in meaning to
(A) fitness
(B) appearance
(C) state
(D) shipment

168. What should you do to return a product the day after receiving it?
(A) Repack it and mail it back
(B) Wait for thirty days
(C) Call the customer service office
(D) Order a new catalog

169. What will happen if you return a product before thirty days have passed?
(A) The company will ask you some questions.
(B) A customer service representative will call you.
(C) You will get all your money back.
(D) You will have to send in a new purchase order.

GO ON TO THE NEXT PAGE

World Travel Tours
32 Palm Tree Boulevard
Playa del Coco, Florida, 39539

Mr. and Mrs. Ivan Thomas
78 Putnam Street
River City, New York, 10131

Dear Mr. and Mrs. Thomas,

Thank you for joining the World Travel tour to Emerald Island. We look forward to seeing you at the Ocean Breezes Hotel on April 2nd. At your request we have reserved for you an ocean view room with twin beds. Please notify hotel staff in advance of your arrival if you wish to make any changes in this room arrangement.

When you check in at the hotel, mention that you are a participant in the World Travel tour, and the staff will inform the tour leader of your arrival. Tour participants will gather in the Ocean Breezes restaurant at 6:30 for dinner and a chance to meet each other. A complete itinerary for the tour will be distributed at that time. The tour leader will explain the tour activities and you will have the opportunity to ask questions.

Your hotel room and three meals a day at the hotel restaurant are included in the price of the tour. The cost of transportation between the airport and the hotel will be paid by the individual participants. I have enclosed some informational brochures that may be of interest to you. Please don't hesitate to contact me if you have any questions.

Sincerely,

George Harris

George Harris
Assistant Director of Tours

encl. Emerald Island Airport Shuttle Schedule
       Your Guide to Emerald Island

170. When should Mr. and Mrs. Thomas tell the hotel if they want to change their room reservation?
    (A) As soon as they arrive at the hotel
    (B) When the tour leader arrives at the hotel
    (C) Before they arrive at the hotel
    (D) After all the tour participants have arrived at the hotel

171. When will Mr. and Mrs. Thomas find out the complete tour schedule?
    (A) It is enclosed with the letter.
    (B) During dinner at the hotel restaurant.
    (C) When they check in at the hotel.
    (D) They already know it.

172. The word "distributed" in paragraph 2, line 4, is closest in meaning to
    (A) disturbed
    (B) revised
    (C) itemized
    (D) sent around

173. Who wrote the letter?
    (A) A tour participant
    (B) A travel agency employee
    (C) A hotel employee
    (D) The tour leader

To: All personnel
From: Joseph Oh
Re: Training seminar
Date: July 15

This is a reminder that a training seminar in the use of the new software package we have adopted will take place next Monday, Tuesday, and Wednesday from 9:30 to 3:00. All seminar participants should be seated in Conference Room B by 9:30. Participation in this training seminar is mandatory for all staff of the Finance Office. Any other staff members who wish to participate should contact Mr. Oh in the Human Resources Office before Friday.

We are pleased to have Patricia Rossi of Intelligent Software Design, Inc., as our trainer. Ms. Rossi brings to this seminar years of experience as a computer consultant, and her previous seminars at our company have been well-received.

174. Who must attend the seminar?
(A) All personnel
(B) Everybody in the Finance Office
(C) Anybody who wants to
(D) People contacted by Mr. Oh

175. Where will the seminar take place?
(A) At the Intelligent Software Design Company
(B) In the Human Resources Office
(C) In Conference Room B
(D) In the Finance Office

GO ON TO THE NEXT PAGE

NOTICE!!!

We regret that due to problems with the heating system in the auditorium, tonight's talk by Edward James entitled "My Thirty Years as a Career Diplomat" has been canceled. We are sorry for any inconvenience this may cause.

The auditorium should reopen by Friday and our weekly lecture series will resume next Monday at 8:00 P.M. with what promises to be an exciting talk by Sharon Rockford about her canoe trip down the Amazon River.

Don't miss it!

176. Why won't Mr. James speak tonight?
(A) He's busy working.
(B) It's inconvenient for him.
(C) The auditorium is closed for repairs.
(D) The weather is too hot.

177. What will happen next Monday?
(A) The auditorium will close at 8:00 P.M.
(B) There will be a new talk.
(C) Mr. James will return to the auditorium.
(D) There will be a class about writing résumés.

Travelers' Guide to Greenville International Airport

Airport Services

- Business Centers can be found in Terminals 1, 4, and 7. Postage and mailboxes, photocopy machines, Internet access, conference rooms, pay phones, and a hotel hotline are available in all centers.

- A variety of food stands can be found in every terminal but Terminal 5. In addition, you can enjoy fine dining at the Runway View Restaurant in Terminal 3. The Worldwide Cafe in Terminal 6 serves sandwiches, desserts, and coffee, and provides Internet connection for your laptop computer.

- The Travelers Help Center, located in Terminal 2, can provide you with city maps and public transportation information. Taxi stands and bus stops are located in the front of each terminal.

---

178. Where can you go to send e-mail?
(A) Terminal 2
(B) Terminal 3
(C) Terminal 5
(D) Terminal 6

179. What is one thing you cannot do at a Business Center?
(A) Buy stamps
(B) Send a fax
(C) Make hotel reservations
(D) Have a meeting

180. What is available in all the terminals?
(A) Business Centers
(B) Food
(C) Transportation
(D) Maps

GO ON TO THE NEXT PAGE

OFFICE ASSISTANT
Busy architectural firm seeks independent hard worker to be our office assistant. Responsible for answering phones, making appointments and schedules, maintaining database, typing letters and documents, and other tasks as needed. High school diploma required, some college desirable. Must have knowledge of word processing and database software. Send résumé to Mr. J. Woo, Architect, Modern Designs, Inc., 51 River Street, Middletown, California 94945

Mr. J. Woo
Modern Designs, Inc.
51 River Street
Middletown, California 94945

Dear Mr. Woo:
I saw your ad in last Sunday's *City Times* looking for an office assistant. I am well-qualified for the position you offer. I am very organized and hardworking. I have the computer skills and educational level you require. I am particularly interested in this position since in the future I would like to enter your profession. In fact, I am taking a night class at the university now, and hope to enter as a full-time student after I gain a few years of work experience. I am enclosing my résumé, and you may call my high school if you would like to see a copy of my high school record. I hope to hear from you soon.

Sincerely,
Lu Wang
Lu Wang

181. According to the ad, what will the new office assistant have to do?
    (A) Photocopy documents
    (B) Make phone calls
    (C) Maintain computers
    (D) Make appointments

182. What kind of computer program does Lu Wang know how to use?
    (A) E-mail
    (B) Web browser
    (C) Word processing
    (D) Architectural software

183. What kind of job does Lu Wang want in the future?
    (A) Architect
    (B) High school teacher
    (C) University professor
    (D) Computer programmer

184. What is Lu Wang doing now?
    (A) Studying in high school
    (B) Taking a university class
    (C) Seeking a job as an architect
    (D) Working as an office assistant

185. What has Lu Wang enclosed with her letter?
    (A) Her résumé
    (B) Her schedule
    (C) Her high school record
    (D) Her university's catalog

GO ON TO THE NEXT PAGE

You're invited!

What: Farewell party
Where: Conference Room 2
When: Thursday, 4:30 P.M.

As you all know, Martha Cunningham and her family are moving to another city. Let's show her how much we appreciate all the hard work she's done for us.

Please bring a refreshment to share. Call Ted Jones in the accounting office by Tuesday to let him know if you'll attend and what food you'll bring. Also, we're taking up a collection to buy a gift for Martha. If everyone contributes just $15, we'll have $300 to buy her something really special.

Thanks, Susan Billings

To:	Susan Billings
From:	Tom Williamson
Subject:	Farewell Party

Hi Susan,
I'm sorry I couldn't attend the party yesterday, as I'd planned, but I had a family emergency. Everything is OK now. I heard that everyone had a great time at the party and that you were able to raise $75 more than you expected. Fantastic. I'm sure Martha loved her gift. I did get a chance to sign the card before I left the office. Did you get the cake I sent over? It was a chocolate one from the Paris Bakery, so I hope it arrived on time for everyone to enjoy.
See you at the meeting this afternoon.
Tom

186. Who was the party for?
   (A) Tom
   (B) Ted
   (C) Susan
   (D) Martha

187. When did Tom write the e-mail?
   (A) Tuesday
   (B) Wednesday
   (C) Thursday
   (D) Friday

188. Why couldn't Tom attend the party?
   (A) He had an emergency.
   (B) He had made other plans.
   (C) He had to attend a meeting.
   (D) He had to work on the accounts.

189. How much money was raised for the gift?
   (A) $15
   (B) $75
   (C) $300
   (D) $375

190. What did Tom send to the party?
   (A) Money
   (B) A card
   (C) Food
   (D) A gift

GO ON TO THE NEXT PAGE

The Dental Office of
Dr. Lilia Molari, DDS
Notice to all patients

OUR POLICY
We are here to serve you. In order to do so,
the following policies are in effect.

Cancellation Policy
When you make an appointment, we
reserve that time for you. Cancellations
must be made 24 hours in advance or a
$40 cancellation fee will be charged.

Payment Policy
We expect payment in full upon receipt of
services. Payment may be made by check,
credit card, or money order only.

Office Hours: Mon.–Thurs. 9–5, Fri. 12–8
Emergency phone: 555-9754
when the office is closed.

During normal office hours,
call us at 555-4825.

To: Dental Office
From: Jim Wilson
Subject: my appointment

I'm sorry I can't make my appointment this morning. I have to attend an emergency meeting in the afternoon and will have to spend the morning preparing for it. I know this is less than 24 hours notice so I'll be charged the cancellation fee. I'll have my assistant write and send a check today.

I'd like to reschedule my appointment, but my days are really full for the next several weeks. You have evening hours don't you? Please give me the next available appointment you have after 5:30 in the evening. Let me know by e-mail or phone. My office phone: 555-8977, and cell phone: 555-6295.
Jim Wilson

191. What form of payment is NOT accepted by the dental office?
    (A) Cash
    (B) Check
    (C) Credit Card
    (D) Money Order

192. If a patient has an emergency on Saturday morning, what number should he call?
    (A) 555-9754
    (B) 555-4825
    (C) 555-8977
    (D) 555-6295

193. What will Jim Wilson do this afternoon?
    (A) Go to the dentist
    (B) Attend a meeting
    (C) Call for an appointment
    (D) Send a check to his assistant

194. How much will Jim Wilson pay for his appointment today?
    (A) $24
    (B) $40
    (C) $240
    (D) $400

195. What day of the week will Jim Wilson's next appointment be?
    (A) Monday
    (B) Tuesday
    (C) Thursday
    (D) Friday

While you were out . . .

To: Harry Pak
Pamela Lopez of One World called.
Time: 11:15 A.M.
About: Your upcoming trip.

She can't get you a flight on Tuesday morning. There is a flight late Tuesday afternoon and one on Wednesday morning. Which do you prefer? Also, she can get you a room at the Grand Hotel, as you requested, but she can get you a better deal at the Marionette Hotel or the Riverside Hotel. Which hotel do you prefer? What day do you want to return? Please let her know before 3:00 this afternoon.

While you were out . . .

To: Pamela Lopez
Harry Pak of Pak and Associates called.
Time: 12:30 P.M.
About: Flights and hotels.

About the flight, he'll take the second option, but he'll stay with his first choice for his hotel. He plans to stay the weekend and would like a flight back on Monday evening, arriving no later than 8:30, if possible. Also, he has a vacation next month and would like to go to the beach. Can you look into travel arrangements for him?

196. What is Pamela Lopez's job?
- (A) Secretary
- (B) Hotel clerk
- (C) Travel agent
- (D) Airline ticket agent

197. What time did Pamela Lopez call Harry Pak?
- (A) 3:00
- (B) 8:30
- (C) 11:15
- (D) 12:30

198. When does Harry Pak want to start his trip?
- (A) Monday evening
- (B) Tuesday morning
- (C) Tuesday afternoon
- (D) Wednesday morning

199. Which hotel does Harry Pak want to stay at?
- (A) The Grand Hotel
- (B) The Marionette Hotel
- (C) The Riverside Hotel
- (D) The One World Hotel

200. When will Mr. Pak take a vacation at the beach?
- (A) Next weekend
- (B) Next week
- (C) Next month
- (D) Next year

Stop! This is the end of the test. If you finish before time is called, you may go back to Parts 5, 6, and 7 and check your work.

ANSWER SHEETS

ANSWER SHEET: Listening Comprehension Review

Name _____

Listening Comprehension

Part 1 | **Part 2** | **Part 3** | **Part 4**

Part 1

	Answer A B C D
1	Ⓐ Ⓑ Ⓒ Ⓓ
2	Ⓐ Ⓑ Ⓒ Ⓓ
3	Ⓐ Ⓑ Ⓒ Ⓓ
4	Ⓐ Ⓑ Ⓒ Ⓓ
5	Ⓐ Ⓑ Ⓒ Ⓓ
6	Ⓐ Ⓑ Ⓒ Ⓓ
7	Ⓐ Ⓑ Ⓒ Ⓓ
8	Ⓐ Ⓑ Ⓒ Ⓓ
9	Ⓐ Ⓑ Ⓒ Ⓓ
10	Ⓐ Ⓑ Ⓒ Ⓓ

Part 2

	Answer A B C
11	Ⓐ Ⓑ Ⓒ
12	Ⓐ Ⓑ Ⓒ
13	Ⓐ Ⓑ Ⓒ
14	Ⓐ Ⓑ Ⓒ
15	Ⓐ Ⓑ Ⓒ
16	Ⓐ Ⓑ Ⓒ
17	Ⓐ Ⓑ Ⓒ
18	Ⓐ Ⓑ Ⓒ
19	Ⓐ Ⓑ Ⓒ
20	Ⓐ Ⓑ Ⓒ
21	Ⓐ Ⓑ Ⓒ
22	Ⓐ Ⓑ Ⓒ
23	Ⓐ Ⓑ Ⓒ
24	Ⓐ Ⓑ Ⓒ
25	Ⓐ Ⓑ Ⓒ
26	Ⓐ Ⓑ Ⓒ
27	Ⓐ Ⓑ Ⓒ
28	Ⓐ Ⓑ Ⓒ
29	Ⓐ Ⓑ Ⓒ
30	Ⓐ Ⓑ Ⓒ

Part 3

	Answer A B C
31	Ⓐ Ⓑ Ⓒ
32	Ⓐ Ⓑ Ⓒ
33	Ⓐ Ⓑ Ⓒ
34	Ⓐ Ⓑ Ⓒ
35	Ⓐ Ⓑ Ⓒ
36	Ⓐ Ⓑ Ⓒ
37	Ⓐ Ⓑ Ⓒ
38	Ⓐ Ⓑ Ⓒ
39	Ⓐ Ⓑ Ⓒ
40	Ⓐ Ⓑ Ⓒ
41	Ⓐ Ⓑ Ⓒ Ⓓ
42	Ⓐ Ⓑ Ⓒ Ⓓ
43	Ⓐ Ⓑ Ⓒ Ⓓ
44	Ⓐ Ⓑ Ⓒ Ⓓ
45	Ⓐ Ⓑ Ⓒ Ⓓ
46	Ⓐ Ⓑ Ⓒ Ⓓ
47	Ⓐ Ⓑ Ⓒ Ⓓ
48	Ⓐ Ⓑ Ⓒ Ⓓ
49	Ⓐ Ⓑ Ⓒ Ⓓ
50	Ⓐ Ⓑ Ⓒ Ⓓ
51	Ⓐ Ⓑ Ⓒ Ⓓ
52	Ⓐ Ⓑ Ⓒ Ⓓ
53	Ⓐ Ⓑ Ⓒ Ⓓ
54	Ⓐ Ⓑ Ⓒ Ⓓ
55	Ⓐ Ⓑ Ⓒ Ⓓ
56	Ⓐ Ⓑ Ⓒ Ⓓ
57	Ⓐ Ⓑ Ⓒ Ⓓ
58	Ⓐ Ⓑ Ⓒ Ⓓ
59	Ⓐ Ⓑ Ⓒ Ⓓ
60	Ⓐ Ⓑ Ⓒ Ⓓ
61	Ⓐ Ⓑ Ⓒ Ⓓ
62	Ⓐ Ⓑ Ⓒ Ⓓ
63	Ⓐ Ⓑ Ⓒ Ⓓ
64	Ⓐ Ⓑ Ⓒ Ⓓ
65	Ⓐ Ⓑ Ⓒ Ⓓ
66	Ⓐ Ⓑ Ⓒ Ⓓ
67	Ⓐ Ⓑ Ⓒ Ⓓ
68	Ⓐ Ⓑ Ⓒ Ⓓ
69	Ⓐ Ⓑ Ⓒ Ⓓ
70	Ⓐ Ⓑ Ⓒ Ⓓ

Part 4

	Answer A B C D
71	Ⓐ Ⓑ Ⓒ Ⓓ
72	Ⓐ Ⓑ Ⓒ Ⓓ
73	Ⓐ Ⓑ Ⓒ Ⓓ
74	Ⓐ Ⓑ Ⓒ Ⓓ
75	Ⓐ Ⓑ Ⓒ Ⓓ
76	Ⓐ Ⓑ Ⓒ Ⓓ
77	Ⓐ Ⓑ Ⓒ Ⓓ
78	Ⓐ Ⓑ Ⓒ Ⓓ
79	Ⓐ Ⓑ Ⓒ Ⓓ
80	Ⓐ Ⓑ Ⓒ Ⓓ
81	Ⓐ Ⓑ Ⓒ Ⓓ
82	Ⓐ Ⓑ Ⓒ Ⓓ
83	Ⓐ Ⓑ Ⓒ Ⓓ
84	Ⓐ Ⓑ Ⓒ Ⓓ
85	Ⓐ Ⓑ Ⓒ Ⓓ
86	Ⓐ Ⓑ Ⓒ Ⓓ
87	Ⓐ Ⓑ Ⓒ Ⓓ
88	Ⓐ Ⓑ Ⓒ Ⓓ
89	Ⓐ Ⓑ Ⓒ Ⓓ
90	Ⓐ Ⓑ Ⓒ Ⓓ
91	Ⓐ Ⓑ Ⓒ Ⓓ
92	Ⓐ Ⓑ Ⓒ Ⓓ
93	Ⓐ Ⓑ Ⓒ Ⓓ
94	Ⓐ Ⓑ Ⓒ Ⓓ
95	Ⓐ Ⓑ Ⓒ Ⓓ
96	Ⓐ Ⓑ Ⓒ Ⓓ
97	Ⓐ Ⓑ Ⓒ Ⓓ
98	Ⓐ Ⓑ Ⓒ Ⓓ
99	Ⓐ Ⓑ Ⓒ Ⓓ
100	Ⓐ Ⓑ Ⓒ Ⓓ

Reading

Part 5 | **Part 6** | **Part 7**

Part 5

	Answer A B C D
101	Ⓐ Ⓑ Ⓒ Ⓓ
102	Ⓐ Ⓑ Ⓒ Ⓓ
103	Ⓐ Ⓑ Ⓒ Ⓓ
104	Ⓐ Ⓑ Ⓒ Ⓓ
105	Ⓐ Ⓑ Ⓒ Ⓓ
106	Ⓐ Ⓑ Ⓒ Ⓓ
107	Ⓐ Ⓑ Ⓒ Ⓓ
108	Ⓐ Ⓑ Ⓒ Ⓓ
109	Ⓐ Ⓑ Ⓒ Ⓓ
110	Ⓐ Ⓑ Ⓒ Ⓓ
111	Ⓐ Ⓑ Ⓒ Ⓓ
112	Ⓐ Ⓑ Ⓒ Ⓓ
113	Ⓐ Ⓑ Ⓒ Ⓓ
114	Ⓐ Ⓑ Ⓒ Ⓓ
115	Ⓐ Ⓑ Ⓒ Ⓓ
116	Ⓐ Ⓑ Ⓒ Ⓓ
117	Ⓐ Ⓑ Ⓒ Ⓓ
118	Ⓐ Ⓑ Ⓒ Ⓓ
119	Ⓐ Ⓑ Ⓒ Ⓓ
120	Ⓐ Ⓑ Ⓒ Ⓓ
121	Ⓐ Ⓑ Ⓒ Ⓓ
122	Ⓐ Ⓑ Ⓒ Ⓓ
123	Ⓐ Ⓑ Ⓒ Ⓓ
124	Ⓐ Ⓑ Ⓒ Ⓓ
125	Ⓐ Ⓑ Ⓒ Ⓓ
126	Ⓐ Ⓑ Ⓒ Ⓓ
127	Ⓐ Ⓑ Ⓒ Ⓓ
128	Ⓐ Ⓑ Ⓒ Ⓓ
129	Ⓐ Ⓑ Ⓒ Ⓓ
130	Ⓐ Ⓑ Ⓒ Ⓓ
131	Ⓐ Ⓑ Ⓒ Ⓓ
132	Ⓐ Ⓑ Ⓒ Ⓓ
133	Ⓐ Ⓑ Ⓒ Ⓓ
134	Ⓐ Ⓑ Ⓒ Ⓓ
135	Ⓐ Ⓑ Ⓒ Ⓓ
136	Ⓐ Ⓑ Ⓒ Ⓓ
137	Ⓐ Ⓑ Ⓒ Ⓓ
138	Ⓐ Ⓑ Ⓒ Ⓓ
139	Ⓐ Ⓑ Ⓒ Ⓓ
140	Ⓐ Ⓑ Ⓒ Ⓓ

Part 6

	Answer A B C D
141	Ⓐ Ⓑ Ⓒ Ⓓ
142	Ⓐ Ⓑ Ⓒ Ⓓ
143	Ⓐ Ⓑ Ⓒ Ⓓ
144	Ⓐ Ⓑ Ⓒ Ⓓ
145	Ⓐ Ⓑ Ⓒ Ⓓ
146	Ⓐ Ⓑ Ⓒ Ⓓ
147	Ⓐ Ⓑ Ⓒ Ⓓ
148	Ⓐ Ⓑ Ⓒ Ⓓ
149	Ⓐ Ⓑ Ⓒ Ⓓ
150	Ⓐ Ⓑ Ⓒ Ⓓ
151	Ⓐ Ⓑ Ⓒ Ⓓ
152	Ⓐ Ⓑ Ⓒ Ⓓ
153	Ⓐ Ⓑ Ⓒ Ⓓ
154	Ⓐ Ⓑ Ⓒ Ⓓ
155	Ⓐ Ⓑ Ⓒ Ⓓ
156	Ⓐ Ⓑ Ⓒ Ⓓ
157	Ⓐ Ⓑ Ⓒ Ⓓ
158	Ⓐ Ⓑ Ⓒ Ⓓ
159	Ⓐ Ⓑ Ⓒ Ⓓ
160	Ⓐ Ⓑ Ⓒ Ⓓ

Part 7

	Answer A B C D
161	Ⓐ Ⓑ Ⓒ Ⓓ
162	Ⓐ Ⓑ Ⓒ Ⓓ
163	Ⓐ Ⓑ Ⓒ Ⓓ
164	Ⓐ Ⓑ Ⓒ Ⓓ
165	Ⓐ Ⓑ Ⓒ Ⓓ
166	Ⓐ Ⓑ Ⓒ Ⓓ
167	Ⓐ Ⓑ Ⓒ Ⓓ
168	Ⓐ Ⓑ Ⓒ Ⓓ
169	Ⓐ Ⓑ Ⓒ Ⓓ
170	Ⓐ Ⓑ Ⓒ Ⓓ
171	Ⓐ Ⓑ Ⓒ Ⓓ
172	Ⓐ Ⓑ Ⓒ Ⓓ
173	Ⓐ Ⓑ Ⓒ Ⓓ
174	Ⓐ Ⓑ Ⓒ Ⓓ
175	Ⓐ Ⓑ Ⓒ Ⓓ
176	Ⓐ Ⓑ Ⓒ Ⓓ
177	Ⓐ Ⓑ Ⓒ Ⓓ
178	Ⓐ Ⓑ Ⓒ Ⓓ
179	Ⓐ Ⓑ Ⓒ Ⓓ
180	Ⓐ Ⓑ Ⓒ Ⓓ
181	Ⓐ Ⓑ Ⓒ Ⓓ
182	Ⓐ Ⓑ Ⓒ Ⓓ
183	Ⓐ Ⓑ Ⓒ Ⓓ
184	Ⓐ Ⓑ Ⓒ Ⓓ
185	Ⓐ Ⓑ Ⓒ Ⓓ
186	Ⓐ Ⓑ Ⓒ Ⓓ
187	Ⓐ Ⓑ Ⓒ Ⓓ
188	Ⓐ Ⓑ Ⓒ Ⓓ
189	Ⓐ Ⓑ Ⓒ Ⓓ
190	Ⓐ Ⓑ Ⓒ Ⓓ
191	Ⓐ Ⓑ Ⓒ Ⓓ
192	Ⓐ Ⓑ Ⓒ Ⓓ
193	Ⓐ Ⓑ Ⓒ Ⓓ
194	Ⓐ Ⓑ Ⓒ Ⓓ
195	Ⓐ Ⓑ Ⓒ Ⓓ
196	Ⓐ Ⓑ Ⓒ Ⓓ
197	Ⓐ Ⓑ Ⓒ Ⓓ
198	Ⓐ Ⓑ Ⓒ Ⓓ
199	Ⓐ Ⓑ Ⓒ Ⓓ
200	Ⓐ Ⓑ Ⓒ Ⓓ

ANSWER SHEET: Practice Test One

Name _____

Listening Comprehension

Part 1

	Answer
	A B C D
1	Ⓐ Ⓑ Ⓒ Ⓓ
2	Ⓐ Ⓑ Ⓒ Ⓓ
3	Ⓐ Ⓑ Ⓒ Ⓓ
4	Ⓐ Ⓑ Ⓒ Ⓓ
5	Ⓐ Ⓑ Ⓒ Ⓓ
6	Ⓐ Ⓑ Ⓒ Ⓓ
7	Ⓐ Ⓑ Ⓒ Ⓓ
8	Ⓐ Ⓑ Ⓒ Ⓓ
9	Ⓐ Ⓑ Ⓒ Ⓓ
10	Ⓐ Ⓑ Ⓒ Ⓓ

Part 2

	Answer
	A B C
11	Ⓐ Ⓑ Ⓒ
12	Ⓐ Ⓑ Ⓒ
13	Ⓐ Ⓑ Ⓒ
14	Ⓐ Ⓑ Ⓒ
15	Ⓐ Ⓑ Ⓒ
16	Ⓐ Ⓑ Ⓒ
17	Ⓐ Ⓑ Ⓒ
18	Ⓐ Ⓑ Ⓒ
19	Ⓐ Ⓑ Ⓒ
20	Ⓐ Ⓑ Ⓒ

	Answer
	A B C
21	Ⓐ Ⓑ Ⓒ
22	Ⓐ Ⓑ Ⓒ
23	Ⓐ Ⓑ Ⓒ
24	Ⓐ Ⓑ Ⓒ
25	Ⓐ Ⓑ Ⓒ
26	Ⓐ Ⓑ Ⓒ
27	Ⓐ Ⓑ Ⓒ
28	Ⓐ Ⓑ Ⓒ
29	Ⓐ Ⓑ Ⓒ
30	Ⓐ Ⓑ Ⓒ

Part 3

	Answer
	A B C
31	Ⓐ Ⓑ Ⓒ
32	Ⓐ Ⓑ Ⓒ
33	Ⓐ Ⓑ Ⓒ
34	Ⓐ Ⓑ Ⓒ
35	Ⓐ Ⓑ Ⓒ
36	Ⓐ Ⓑ Ⓒ
37	Ⓐ Ⓑ Ⓒ
38	Ⓐ Ⓑ Ⓒ
39	Ⓐ Ⓑ Ⓒ
40	Ⓐ Ⓑ Ⓒ

	Answer
	A B C D
41	Ⓐ Ⓑ Ⓒ Ⓓ
42	Ⓐ Ⓑ Ⓒ Ⓓ
43	Ⓐ Ⓑ Ⓒ Ⓓ
44	Ⓐ Ⓑ Ⓒ Ⓓ
45	Ⓐ Ⓑ Ⓒ Ⓓ
46	Ⓐ Ⓑ Ⓒ Ⓓ
47	Ⓐ Ⓑ Ⓒ Ⓓ
48	Ⓐ Ⓑ Ⓒ Ⓓ
49	Ⓐ Ⓑ Ⓒ Ⓓ
50	Ⓐ Ⓑ Ⓒ Ⓓ

	Answer
	A B C D
51	Ⓐ Ⓑ Ⓒ Ⓓ
52	Ⓐ Ⓑ Ⓒ Ⓓ
53	Ⓐ Ⓑ Ⓒ Ⓓ
54	Ⓐ Ⓑ Ⓒ Ⓓ
55	Ⓐ Ⓑ Ⓒ Ⓓ
56	Ⓐ Ⓑ Ⓒ Ⓓ
57	Ⓐ Ⓑ Ⓒ Ⓓ
58	Ⓐ Ⓑ Ⓒ Ⓓ
59	Ⓐ Ⓑ Ⓒ Ⓓ
60	Ⓐ Ⓑ Ⓒ Ⓓ

	Answer
	A B C D
61	Ⓐ Ⓑ Ⓒ Ⓓ
62	Ⓐ Ⓑ Ⓒ Ⓓ
63	Ⓐ Ⓑ Ⓒ Ⓓ
64	Ⓐ Ⓑ Ⓒ Ⓓ
65	Ⓐ Ⓑ Ⓒ Ⓓ
66	Ⓐ Ⓑ Ⓒ Ⓓ
67	Ⓐ Ⓑ Ⓒ Ⓓ
68	Ⓐ Ⓑ Ⓒ Ⓓ
69	Ⓐ Ⓑ Ⓒ Ⓓ
70	Ⓐ Ⓑ Ⓒ Ⓓ

Part 4

	Answer
	A B C D
71	Ⓐ Ⓑ Ⓒ Ⓓ
72	Ⓐ Ⓑ Ⓒ Ⓓ
73	Ⓐ Ⓑ Ⓒ Ⓓ
74	Ⓐ Ⓑ Ⓒ Ⓓ
75	Ⓐ Ⓑ Ⓒ Ⓓ
76	Ⓐ Ⓑ Ⓒ Ⓓ
77	Ⓐ Ⓑ Ⓒ Ⓓ
78	Ⓐ Ⓑ Ⓒ Ⓓ
79	Ⓐ Ⓑ Ⓒ Ⓓ
80	Ⓐ Ⓑ Ⓒ Ⓓ

	Answer
	A B C D
81	Ⓐ Ⓑ Ⓒ Ⓓ
82	Ⓐ Ⓑ Ⓒ Ⓓ
83	Ⓐ Ⓑ Ⓒ Ⓓ
84	Ⓐ Ⓑ Ⓒ Ⓓ
85	Ⓐ Ⓑ Ⓒ Ⓓ
86	Ⓐ Ⓑ Ⓒ Ⓓ
87	Ⓐ Ⓑ Ⓒ Ⓓ
88	Ⓐ Ⓑ Ⓒ Ⓓ
89	Ⓐ Ⓑ Ⓒ Ⓓ
90	Ⓐ Ⓑ Ⓒ Ⓓ

	Answer
	A B C D
91	Ⓐ Ⓑ Ⓒ Ⓓ
92	Ⓐ Ⓑ Ⓒ Ⓓ
93	Ⓐ Ⓑ Ⓒ Ⓓ
94	Ⓐ Ⓑ Ⓒ Ⓓ
95	Ⓐ Ⓑ Ⓒ Ⓓ
96	Ⓐ Ⓑ Ⓒ Ⓓ
97	Ⓐ Ⓑ Ⓒ Ⓓ
98	Ⓐ Ⓑ Ⓒ Ⓓ
99	Ⓐ Ⓑ Ⓒ Ⓓ
100	Ⓐ Ⓑ Ⓒ Ⓓ

Reading

Part 5

	Answer
	A B C D
101	Ⓐ Ⓑ Ⓒ Ⓓ
102	Ⓐ Ⓑ Ⓒ Ⓓ
103	Ⓐ Ⓑ Ⓒ Ⓓ
104	Ⓐ Ⓑ Ⓒ Ⓓ
105	Ⓐ Ⓑ Ⓒ Ⓓ
106	Ⓐ Ⓑ Ⓒ Ⓓ
107	Ⓐ Ⓑ Ⓒ Ⓓ
108	Ⓐ Ⓑ Ⓒ Ⓓ
109	Ⓐ Ⓑ Ⓒ Ⓓ
110	Ⓐ Ⓑ Ⓒ Ⓓ

	Answer
	A B C D
111	Ⓐ Ⓑ Ⓒ Ⓓ
112	Ⓐ Ⓑ Ⓒ Ⓓ
113	Ⓐ Ⓑ Ⓒ Ⓓ
114	Ⓐ Ⓑ Ⓒ Ⓓ
115	Ⓐ Ⓑ Ⓒ Ⓓ
116	Ⓐ Ⓑ Ⓒ Ⓓ
117	Ⓐ Ⓑ Ⓒ Ⓓ
118	Ⓐ Ⓑ Ⓒ Ⓓ
119	Ⓐ Ⓑ Ⓒ Ⓓ
120	Ⓐ Ⓑ Ⓒ Ⓓ

	Answer
	A B C D
121	Ⓐ Ⓑ Ⓒ Ⓓ
122	Ⓐ Ⓑ Ⓒ Ⓓ
123	Ⓐ Ⓑ Ⓒ Ⓓ
124	Ⓐ Ⓑ Ⓒ Ⓓ
125	Ⓐ Ⓑ Ⓒ Ⓓ
126	Ⓐ Ⓑ Ⓒ Ⓓ
127	Ⓐ Ⓑ Ⓒ Ⓓ
128	Ⓐ Ⓑ Ⓒ Ⓓ
129	Ⓐ Ⓑ Ⓒ Ⓓ
130	Ⓐ Ⓑ Ⓒ Ⓓ

Part 6

	Answer
	A B C D
131	Ⓐ Ⓑ Ⓒ Ⓓ
132	Ⓐ Ⓑ Ⓒ Ⓓ
133	Ⓐ Ⓑ Ⓒ Ⓓ
134	Ⓐ Ⓑ Ⓒ Ⓓ
135	Ⓐ Ⓑ Ⓒ Ⓓ
136	Ⓐ Ⓑ Ⓒ Ⓓ
137	Ⓐ Ⓑ Ⓒ Ⓓ
138	Ⓐ Ⓑ Ⓒ Ⓓ
139	Ⓐ Ⓑ Ⓒ Ⓓ
140	Ⓐ Ⓑ Ⓒ Ⓓ

	Answer
	A B C D
141	Ⓐ Ⓑ Ⓒ Ⓓ
142	Ⓐ Ⓑ Ⓒ Ⓓ
143	Ⓐ Ⓑ Ⓒ Ⓓ
144	Ⓐ Ⓑ Ⓒ Ⓓ
145	Ⓐ Ⓑ Ⓒ Ⓓ
146	Ⓐ Ⓑ Ⓒ Ⓓ
147	Ⓐ Ⓑ Ⓒ Ⓓ
148	Ⓐ Ⓑ Ⓒ Ⓓ
149	Ⓐ Ⓑ Ⓒ Ⓓ
150	Ⓐ Ⓑ Ⓒ Ⓓ

	Answer
	A B C D
151	Ⓐ Ⓑ Ⓒ Ⓓ
152	Ⓐ Ⓑ Ⓒ Ⓓ
153	Ⓐ Ⓑ Ⓒ Ⓓ
154	Ⓐ Ⓑ Ⓒ Ⓓ
155	Ⓐ Ⓑ Ⓒ Ⓓ
156	Ⓐ Ⓑ Ⓒ Ⓓ
157	Ⓐ Ⓑ Ⓒ Ⓓ
158	Ⓐ Ⓑ Ⓒ Ⓓ
159	Ⓐ Ⓑ Ⓒ Ⓓ
160	Ⓐ Ⓑ Ⓒ Ⓓ

Part 7

	Answer
	A B C D
161	Ⓐ Ⓑ Ⓒ Ⓓ
162	Ⓐ Ⓑ Ⓒ Ⓓ
163	Ⓐ Ⓑ Ⓒ Ⓓ
164	Ⓐ Ⓑ Ⓒ Ⓓ
165	Ⓐ Ⓑ Ⓒ Ⓓ
166	Ⓐ Ⓑ Ⓒ Ⓓ
167	Ⓐ Ⓑ Ⓒ Ⓓ
168	Ⓐ Ⓑ Ⓒ Ⓓ
169	Ⓐ Ⓑ Ⓒ Ⓓ
170	Ⓐ Ⓑ Ⓒ Ⓓ

	Answer
	A B C D
171	Ⓐ Ⓑ Ⓒ Ⓓ
172	Ⓐ Ⓑ Ⓒ Ⓓ
173	Ⓐ Ⓑ Ⓒ Ⓓ
174	Ⓐ Ⓑ Ⓒ Ⓓ
175	Ⓐ Ⓑ Ⓒ Ⓓ
176	Ⓐ Ⓑ Ⓒ Ⓓ
177	Ⓐ Ⓑ Ⓒ Ⓓ
178	Ⓐ Ⓑ Ⓒ Ⓓ
179	Ⓐ Ⓑ Ⓒ Ⓓ
180	Ⓐ Ⓑ Ⓒ Ⓓ

	Answer
	A B C D
181	Ⓐ Ⓑ Ⓒ Ⓓ
182	Ⓐ Ⓑ Ⓒ Ⓓ
183	Ⓐ Ⓑ Ⓒ Ⓓ
184	Ⓐ Ⓑ Ⓒ Ⓓ
185	Ⓐ Ⓑ Ⓒ Ⓓ
186	Ⓐ Ⓑ Ⓒ Ⓓ
187	Ⓐ Ⓑ Ⓒ Ⓓ
188	Ⓐ Ⓑ Ⓒ Ⓓ
189	Ⓐ Ⓑ Ⓒ Ⓓ
190	Ⓐ Ⓑ Ⓒ Ⓓ

	Answer
	A B C D
191	Ⓐ Ⓑ Ⓒ Ⓓ
192	Ⓐ Ⓑ Ⓒ Ⓓ
193	Ⓐ Ⓑ Ⓒ Ⓓ
194	Ⓐ Ⓑ Ⓒ Ⓓ
195	Ⓐ Ⓑ Ⓒ Ⓓ
196	Ⓐ Ⓑ Ⓒ Ⓓ
197	Ⓐ Ⓑ Ⓒ Ⓓ
198	Ⓐ Ⓑ Ⓒ Ⓓ
199	Ⓐ Ⓑ Ⓒ Ⓓ
200	Ⓐ Ⓑ Ⓒ Ⓓ

ANSWER SHEET: Practice Test Two

Name _____

Listening Comprehension

Part 1

	Answer			
	A	B	C	D
1	Ⓐ	Ⓑ	Ⓒ	Ⓓ
2	Ⓐ	Ⓑ	Ⓒ	Ⓓ
3	Ⓐ	Ⓑ	Ⓒ	Ⓓ
4	Ⓐ	Ⓑ	Ⓒ	Ⓓ
5	Ⓐ	Ⓑ	Ⓒ	Ⓓ
6	Ⓐ	Ⓑ	Ⓒ	Ⓓ
7	Ⓐ	Ⓑ	Ⓒ	Ⓓ
8	Ⓐ	Ⓑ	Ⓒ	Ⓓ
9	Ⓐ	Ⓑ	Ⓒ	Ⓓ
10	Ⓐ	Ⓑ	Ⓒ	Ⓓ

Part 2

	Answer		
	A	B	C
11	Ⓐ	Ⓑ	Ⓒ
12	Ⓐ	Ⓑ	Ⓒ
13	Ⓐ	Ⓑ	Ⓒ
14	Ⓐ	Ⓑ	Ⓒ
15	Ⓐ	Ⓑ	Ⓒ
16	Ⓐ	Ⓑ	Ⓒ
17	Ⓐ	Ⓑ	Ⓒ
18	Ⓐ	Ⓑ	Ⓒ
19	Ⓐ	Ⓑ	Ⓒ
20	Ⓐ	Ⓑ	Ⓒ

	Answer		
	A	B	C
21	Ⓐ	Ⓑ	Ⓒ
22	Ⓐ	Ⓑ	Ⓒ
23	Ⓐ	Ⓑ	Ⓒ
24	Ⓐ	Ⓑ	Ⓒ
25	Ⓐ	Ⓑ	Ⓒ
26	Ⓐ	Ⓑ	Ⓒ
27	Ⓐ	Ⓑ	Ⓒ
28	Ⓐ	Ⓑ	Ⓒ
29	Ⓐ	Ⓑ	Ⓒ
30	Ⓐ	Ⓑ	Ⓒ

Part 3

	Answer		
	A	B	C
31	Ⓐ	Ⓑ	Ⓒ
32	Ⓐ	Ⓑ	Ⓒ
33	Ⓐ	Ⓑ	Ⓒ
34	Ⓐ	Ⓑ	Ⓒ
35	Ⓐ	Ⓑ	Ⓒ
36	Ⓐ	Ⓑ	Ⓒ
37	Ⓐ	Ⓑ	Ⓒ
38	Ⓐ	Ⓑ	Ⓒ
39	Ⓐ	Ⓑ	Ⓒ
40	Ⓐ	Ⓑ	Ⓒ

	Answer			
	A	B	C	D
41	Ⓐ	Ⓑ	Ⓒ	Ⓓ
42	Ⓐ	Ⓑ	Ⓒ	Ⓓ
43	Ⓐ	Ⓑ	Ⓒ	Ⓓ
44	Ⓐ	Ⓑ	Ⓒ	Ⓓ
45	Ⓐ	Ⓑ	Ⓒ	Ⓓ
46	Ⓐ	Ⓑ	Ⓒ	Ⓓ
47	Ⓐ	Ⓑ	Ⓒ	Ⓓ
48	Ⓐ	Ⓑ	Ⓒ	Ⓓ
49	Ⓐ	Ⓑ	Ⓒ	Ⓓ
50	Ⓐ	Ⓑ	Ⓒ	Ⓓ

	Answer			
	A	B	C	D
51	Ⓐ	Ⓑ	Ⓒ	Ⓓ
52	Ⓐ	Ⓑ	Ⓒ	Ⓓ
53	Ⓐ	Ⓑ	Ⓒ	Ⓓ
54	Ⓐ	Ⓑ	Ⓒ	Ⓓ
55	Ⓐ	Ⓑ	Ⓒ	Ⓓ
56	Ⓐ	Ⓑ	Ⓒ	Ⓓ
57	Ⓐ	Ⓑ	Ⓒ	Ⓓ
58	Ⓐ	Ⓑ	Ⓒ	Ⓓ
59	Ⓐ	Ⓑ	Ⓒ	Ⓓ
60	Ⓐ	Ⓑ	Ⓒ	Ⓓ

	Answer			
	A	B	C	D
61	Ⓐ	Ⓑ	Ⓒ	Ⓓ
62	Ⓐ	Ⓑ	Ⓒ	Ⓓ
63	Ⓐ	Ⓑ	Ⓒ	Ⓓ
64	Ⓐ	Ⓑ	Ⓒ	Ⓓ
65	Ⓐ	Ⓑ	Ⓒ	Ⓓ
66	Ⓐ	Ⓑ	Ⓒ	Ⓓ
67	Ⓐ	Ⓑ	Ⓒ	Ⓓ
68	Ⓐ	Ⓑ	Ⓒ	Ⓓ
69	Ⓐ	Ⓑ	Ⓒ	Ⓓ
70	Ⓐ	Ⓑ	Ⓒ	Ⓓ

Part 4

	Answer			
	A	B	C	D
71	Ⓐ	Ⓑ	Ⓒ	Ⓓ
72	Ⓐ	Ⓑ	Ⓒ	Ⓓ
73	Ⓐ	Ⓑ	Ⓒ	Ⓓ
74	Ⓐ	Ⓑ	Ⓒ	Ⓓ
75	Ⓐ	Ⓑ	Ⓒ	Ⓓ
76	Ⓐ	Ⓑ	Ⓒ	Ⓓ
77	Ⓐ	Ⓑ	Ⓒ	Ⓓ
78	Ⓐ	Ⓑ	Ⓒ	Ⓓ
79	Ⓐ	Ⓑ	Ⓒ	Ⓓ
80	Ⓐ	Ⓑ	Ⓒ	Ⓓ

	Answer			
	A	B	C	D
81	Ⓐ	Ⓑ	Ⓒ	Ⓓ
82	Ⓐ	Ⓑ	Ⓒ	Ⓓ
83	Ⓐ	Ⓑ	Ⓒ	Ⓓ
84	Ⓐ	Ⓑ	Ⓒ	Ⓓ
85	Ⓐ	Ⓑ	Ⓒ	Ⓓ
86	Ⓐ	Ⓑ	Ⓒ	Ⓓ
87	Ⓐ	Ⓑ	Ⓒ	Ⓓ
88	Ⓐ	Ⓑ	Ⓒ	Ⓓ
89	Ⓐ	Ⓑ	Ⓒ	Ⓓ
90	Ⓐ	Ⓑ	Ⓒ	Ⓓ

	Answer			
	A	B	C	D
91	Ⓐ	Ⓑ	Ⓒ	Ⓓ
92	Ⓐ	Ⓑ	Ⓒ	Ⓓ
93	Ⓐ	Ⓑ	Ⓒ	Ⓓ
94	Ⓐ	Ⓑ	Ⓒ	Ⓓ
95	Ⓐ	Ⓑ	Ⓒ	Ⓓ
96	Ⓐ	Ⓑ	Ⓒ	Ⓓ
97	Ⓐ	Ⓑ	Ⓒ	Ⓓ
98	Ⓐ	Ⓑ	Ⓒ	Ⓓ
99	Ⓐ	Ⓑ	Ⓒ	Ⓓ
100	Ⓐ	Ⓑ	Ⓒ	Ⓓ

Reading

Part 5

	Answer			
	A	B	C	D
101	Ⓐ	Ⓑ	Ⓒ	Ⓓ
102	Ⓐ	Ⓑ	Ⓒ	Ⓓ
103	Ⓐ	Ⓑ	Ⓒ	Ⓓ
104	Ⓐ	Ⓑ	Ⓒ	Ⓓ
105	Ⓐ	Ⓑ	Ⓒ	Ⓓ
106	Ⓐ	Ⓑ	Ⓒ	Ⓓ
107	Ⓐ	Ⓑ	Ⓒ	Ⓓ
108	Ⓐ	Ⓑ	Ⓒ	Ⓓ
109	Ⓐ	Ⓑ	Ⓒ	Ⓓ
110	Ⓐ	Ⓑ	Ⓒ	Ⓓ

	Answer			
	A	B	C	D
111	Ⓐ	Ⓑ	Ⓒ	Ⓓ
112	Ⓐ	Ⓑ	Ⓒ	Ⓓ
113	Ⓐ	Ⓑ	Ⓒ	Ⓓ
114	Ⓐ	Ⓑ	Ⓒ	Ⓓ
115	Ⓐ	Ⓑ	Ⓒ	Ⓓ
116	Ⓐ	Ⓑ	Ⓒ	Ⓓ
117	Ⓐ	Ⓑ	Ⓒ	Ⓓ
118	Ⓐ	Ⓑ	Ⓒ	Ⓓ
119	Ⓐ	Ⓑ	Ⓒ	Ⓓ
120	Ⓐ	Ⓑ	Ⓒ	Ⓓ

	Answer			
	A	B	C	D
121	Ⓐ	Ⓑ	Ⓒ	Ⓓ
122	Ⓐ	Ⓑ	Ⓒ	Ⓓ
123	Ⓐ	Ⓑ	Ⓒ	Ⓓ
124	Ⓐ	Ⓑ	Ⓒ	Ⓓ
125	Ⓐ	Ⓑ	Ⓒ	Ⓓ
126	Ⓐ	Ⓑ	Ⓒ	Ⓓ
127	Ⓐ	Ⓑ	Ⓒ	Ⓓ
128	Ⓐ	Ⓑ	Ⓒ	Ⓓ
129	Ⓐ	Ⓑ	Ⓒ	Ⓓ
130	Ⓐ	Ⓑ	Ⓒ	Ⓓ

	Answer			
	A	B	C	D
131	Ⓐ	Ⓑ	Ⓒ	Ⓓ
132	Ⓐ	Ⓑ	Ⓒ	Ⓓ
133	Ⓐ	Ⓑ	Ⓒ	Ⓓ
134	Ⓐ	Ⓑ	Ⓒ	Ⓓ
135	Ⓐ	Ⓑ	Ⓒ	Ⓓ
136	Ⓐ	Ⓑ	Ⓒ	Ⓓ
137	Ⓐ	Ⓑ	Ⓒ	Ⓓ
138	Ⓐ	Ⓑ	Ⓒ	Ⓓ
139	Ⓐ	Ⓑ	Ⓒ	Ⓓ
140	Ⓐ	Ⓑ	Ⓒ	Ⓓ

Part 6

	Answer			
	A	B	C	D
141	Ⓐ	Ⓑ	Ⓒ	Ⓓ
142	Ⓐ	Ⓑ	Ⓒ	Ⓓ
143	Ⓐ	Ⓑ	Ⓒ	Ⓓ
144	Ⓐ	Ⓑ	Ⓒ	Ⓓ
145	Ⓐ	Ⓑ	Ⓒ	Ⓓ
146	Ⓐ	Ⓑ	Ⓒ	Ⓓ
147	Ⓐ	Ⓑ	Ⓒ	Ⓓ
148	Ⓐ	Ⓑ	Ⓒ	Ⓓ
149	Ⓐ	Ⓑ	Ⓒ	Ⓓ
150	Ⓐ	Ⓑ	Ⓒ	Ⓓ

	Answer			
	A	B	C	D
151	Ⓐ	Ⓑ	Ⓒ	Ⓓ
152	Ⓐ	Ⓑ	Ⓒ	Ⓓ
153	Ⓐ	Ⓑ	Ⓒ	Ⓓ
154	Ⓐ	Ⓑ	Ⓒ	Ⓓ
155	Ⓐ	Ⓑ	Ⓒ	Ⓓ
156	Ⓐ	Ⓑ	Ⓒ	Ⓓ
157	Ⓐ	Ⓑ	Ⓒ	Ⓓ
158	Ⓐ	Ⓑ	Ⓒ	Ⓓ
159	Ⓐ	Ⓑ	Ⓒ	Ⓓ
160	Ⓐ	Ⓑ	Ⓒ	Ⓓ

Part 7

	Answer			
	A	B	C	D
161	Ⓐ	Ⓑ	Ⓒ	Ⓓ
162	Ⓐ	Ⓑ	Ⓒ	Ⓓ
163	Ⓐ	Ⓑ	Ⓒ	Ⓓ
164	Ⓐ	Ⓑ	Ⓒ	Ⓓ
165	Ⓐ	Ⓑ	Ⓒ	Ⓓ
166	Ⓐ	Ⓑ	Ⓒ	Ⓓ
167	Ⓐ	Ⓑ	Ⓒ	Ⓓ
168	Ⓐ	Ⓑ	Ⓒ	Ⓓ
169	Ⓐ	Ⓑ	Ⓒ	Ⓓ
170	Ⓐ	Ⓑ	Ⓒ	Ⓓ

	Answer			
	A	B	C	D
171	Ⓐ	Ⓑ	Ⓒ	Ⓓ
172	Ⓐ	Ⓑ	Ⓒ	Ⓓ
173	Ⓐ	Ⓑ	Ⓒ	Ⓓ
174	Ⓐ	Ⓑ	Ⓒ	Ⓓ
175	Ⓐ	Ⓑ	Ⓒ	Ⓓ
176	Ⓐ	Ⓑ	Ⓒ	Ⓓ
177	Ⓐ	Ⓑ	Ⓒ	Ⓓ
178	Ⓐ	Ⓑ	Ⓒ	Ⓓ
179	Ⓐ	Ⓑ	Ⓒ	Ⓓ
180	Ⓐ	Ⓑ	Ⓒ	Ⓓ

	Answer			
	A	B	C	D
181	Ⓐ	Ⓑ	Ⓒ	Ⓓ
182	Ⓐ	Ⓑ	Ⓒ	Ⓓ
183	Ⓐ	Ⓑ	Ⓒ	Ⓓ
184	Ⓐ	Ⓑ	Ⓒ	Ⓓ
185	Ⓐ	Ⓑ	Ⓒ	Ⓓ
186	Ⓐ	Ⓑ	Ⓒ	Ⓓ
187	Ⓐ	Ⓑ	Ⓒ	Ⓓ
188	Ⓐ	Ⓑ	Ⓒ	Ⓓ
189	Ⓐ	Ⓑ	Ⓒ	Ⓓ
190	Ⓐ	Ⓑ	Ⓒ	Ⓓ

	Answer			
	A	B	C	D
191	Ⓐ	Ⓑ	Ⓒ	Ⓓ
192	Ⓐ	Ⓑ	Ⓒ	Ⓓ
193	Ⓐ	Ⓑ	Ⓒ	Ⓓ
194	Ⓐ	Ⓑ	Ⓒ	Ⓓ
195	Ⓐ	Ⓑ	Ⓒ	Ⓓ
196	Ⓐ	Ⓑ	Ⓒ	Ⓓ
197	Ⓐ	Ⓑ	Ⓒ	Ⓓ
198	Ⓐ	Ⓑ	Ⓒ	Ⓓ
199	Ⓐ	Ⓑ	Ⓒ	Ⓓ
200	Ⓐ	Ⓑ	Ⓒ	Ⓓ

AUDIOSCRIPTS

AUDIOSCRIPT
LISTENING COMPREHENSION

PART 1—PHOTOS

Strategy Practice (page 32)

1. Look at the picture marked number 1 in your book.
   (A) The motorcycle is running down the road.
   (B) The windows are sitting against the wall.
   (C) The signs are hanging between the windows.
   (D) The bike is leaning against the wall.

2. Look at the picture marked number 2 in your book.
   (A) The man at the podium is making a speech.
   (B) The accountant is sitting at his desk.
   (C) The waiter is pouring water.
   (D) The speaker is pointing at the microphone.

3. Look at the picture marked number 3 in your book.
   (A) The newspaper is on the stand.
   (B) The table is set for breakfast.
   (C) The coffee cups are on the shelf.
   (D) The pots are in the basket.

4. Look at the picture marked number 4 in your book.
   (A) The plumbers are repairing the pipes.
   (B) The architects are designing a building.
   (C) The construction workers are walking across the beam.
   (D) The children are playing with building blocks.

5. Look at the picture marked number 5 in your book.
   (A) He's hammering a nail into the wall.
   (B) He's measuring the height of the tool.
   (C) He's mailing the card in his hands.
   (D) He's putting a note in his wallet.

6. Look at the picture marked number 6 in your book.
   (A) She's putting the hares in a cage.
   (B) She's hearing it again.
   (C) She's sleeping in the chair.
   (D) She's getting her hair done.

7. Look at the picture marked number 7 in your book.
   (A) The television is in the middle of the room.
   (B) The hotel room is ready for occupancy.
   (C) Dirty clothes are piled on the floor.
   (D) Room service trays are on the bed.

8. Look at the picture marked number 8 in your book.
   (A) The shopping bags are empty.
   (B) The passenger is checking his luggage.
   (C) The tourist is pulling his suitcase behind him.
   (D) The sidewalk is long and narrow.

9. Look at the picture marked number 9 in your book.
   (A) A small bridge passes over the canal.
   (B) The ice forms ridges on the water.
   (C) The TV channel is on all day.
   (D) A short boat crosses the river.

10. Look at the picture marked number 10 in your book.
    (A) They're changing the locks.
    (B) They're holding a box.
    (C) They're opening a package.
    (D) They're sealing an envelope.

PART 2—QUESTION-RESPONSE

Identifying Time (page 39)

1. You were here this morning, weren't you?
   (A) The sky was very clear this morning.
   (B) No, I had a meeting at the hotel.
   (C) He wasn't here.

2. When will you move your office?
   (A) At the end of the month, I hope.
   (B) It's my office.
   (C) I don't go to the movies often.

3. Mark is always on time for dinner, isn't he?
   (A) Yes, he's never late for anything.
   (B) Yes, he looks a lot thinner.
   (C) Yes, it takes a long time.

4. Has everyone shown up for the meeting yet?
   (A) I really enjoyed meeting everyone.
   (B) Yes, he is.
   (C) We're still waiting for Mr. Roberts.

5. When is the new manager going to start work?
   (A) Next Monday will be his first day.
   (B) I knew him in high school.
   (C) She goes to work by bus.

6. How much longer should we wait for them to arrive?
   (A) He'll be here soon.
   (B) This room is longer than the other one.
   (C) Let's just wait another few minutes.

7. How long is the movie?
   (A) About two and a half hours.
   (B) About five miles.
   (C) About two people falling in love.

8. Your meeting was shorter than expected, wasn't it?
   (A) Yes, it's too small for me.
   (B) Yes, it was over in less than an hour.
   (C) Yes, he's shorter than I am.

9. What time does the plane take off?
   (A) It leaves for New York.
   (B) It leaves from Gate 15.
   (C) It leaves at 5:45.

10. When is your appointment with Dr. Kovacs?
    (A) It's tomorrow afternoon.
    (B) It's in his office.
    (C) It's a doctor's appointment.

Identifying People (page 40)

1. Is the new secretary's name Bill or John?
   (A) He paid those bills yesterday.
   (B) I think he's called Bill.
   (C) He'll fill those orders for you.

2. Whose name is the reservation under?
   (A) It's under the table.
   (B) It's under my name.
   (C) It's the same.

3. Who didn't go to the meeting yesterday?
   (A) Martha wasn't there.
   (B) Yes, he did, and he told me all about it.
   (C) It was a very informative meeting.

4. Who's helping you with that report?
   (A) It's Susan's.
   (B) Eric's working on it with me.
   (C) Yes, it's very important.

5. What's the director's name?
   (A) Let me give you the directions.
   (B) We have the same one.
   (C) It's Mrs. Sullivan.

6. Who did you invite to the picnic?
   (A) No, the picnic's not at night.
   (B) Everybody in the office.
   (C) We'll go inside if it rains.

7. Is that man your new assistant?
   (A) Yes, he started working for me yesterday.
   (B) No, he doesn't need any assistance.
   (C) I love my new apartment.

8. Whose computer needs repairs?
   (A) George is an excellent repairman.
   (B) John's hasn't been working since yesterday.
   (C) Judy is our computer expert.

9. Who has copies of the report?
   (A) I copied it last night.
   (B) Sam can make copies for us.
   (C) I sent copies to everyone in our department.

10. Who's the new manager?
    (A) Her name is Samantha.
    (B) It belongs to Silvia.
    (C) I can manage it alone.

Identifying an Opinion (page 42)

1. How is the new technician doing?
   (A) He's doing a great job.
   (B) He's repairing the fax machine.
   (C) His name is Bob.

2. What's your opinion of the plans for the new office?
   - (A) We'll have a planning meeting next week.
   - (B) We don't have any openings right now.
   - (C) I think they're wonderful.

3. Do you think Sara will finish that report on time?
   - (A) Not unless she works faster.
   - (B) It's time to go to work.
   - (C) I heard the news report on the radio last night.

4. How does Bob like his new job?
   - (A) He's about thirty-five years old.
   - (B) I don't think he's very happy there.
   - (C) It's a new job.

5. What do you think of this weather?
   - (A) I'm not sure whether I'll go.
   - (B) Yes, let's get together.
   - (C) I love a rainy day.

6. Do you think John will be at the party?
   - (A) No, he wasn't there.
   - (B) No, I don't really enjoy parties.
   - (C) No, he's too busy this week.

7. How was the conference?
   - (A) It lasted several days.
   - (B) I thought it was boring.
   - (C) She's doing very well, thank you.

8. What's Nina's opinion of the change in plans?
   - (A) She says it's a good idea.
   - (B) She's all out of change.
   - (C) No, she didn't have to change planes.

9. What do you think of this color for my office?
   - (A) You should fill out the blue form.
   - (B) It's a bit cooler in here.
   - (C) I really don't like it at all.

10. What's your opinion of Albert's work?
    - (A) Yes, he works here.
    - (B) He always does an excellent job.
    - (C) He walks fast.

Identifying a Choice (page 43)

1. Should I fax my reply or send it by e-mail?
   - (A) Please fax it.
   - (B) Yes, you should try.
   - (C) I think you should relax.

2. Should we take a taxi or the bus?
   - (A) A taxi would be faster.
   - (B) Yes, I think we should.
   - (C) Pay your taxes on time.

3. Would you rather see a movie or watch TV?
   - (A) I need a new watch.
   - (B) That TV show was very moving.
   - (C) Let's go to a movie.

4. Should we eat at home or go to a restaurant?
   - (A) I'd rather stay home.
   - (B) You can eat the rest.
   - (C) I don't think they're home yet.

5. Which do you prefer, an aisle seat or a window seat?
   - (A) I'll sit down.
   - (B) I always sit by the window.
   - (C) Have a seat, please.

6. Which is better, the brown suit or the gray one?
   - (A) Fruit is better for you.
   - (B) The gray suit looks more professional.
   - (C) It's an old suit.

7. Would you prefer coffee or a cup of hot tea?
   - (A) Cold weather always makes me cough.
   - (B) Yes, it's very hot up here.
   - (C) Coffee with a little sugar would be nice.

8. Should I call you tonight or tomorrow?
   - (A) Tomorrow would be better.
   - (B) I'll stay two nights.
   - (C) Yes, I'll call you.

9. Would you rather take a plane or a train?
   - (A) Please take your time.
   - (B) Yes, I think it might rain.
   - (C) I'd feel more comfortable on a train.

10. Which do you like better, Italian food or Chinese?
    (A) I really enjoyed my trip to Italy.
    (B) I almost never eat Chinese food.
    (C) I'm learning to speak Chinese.

Identifying a Suggestion (page 45)

1. Don't leave the office without telling me.
   (A) Don't worry, I won't.
   (B) Yes, you can telephone me at my office.
   (C) No, he didn't leave the office.

2. Can't you figure out a cheaper way to get there?
   (A) You can sleep when we get there.
   (B) It wasn't too far away.
   (C) These are the cheapest tickets I could find.

3. Isn't it time to sign the contract?
   (A) Yes, we'll sign it tomorrow.
   (B) Yes, I saw the sign.
   (C) Yes, the train is on Track 9.

4. Would you like me to fax this for you?
   (A) Yes, I have all the facts.
   (B) No, don't bother.
   (C) I haven't faxed it.

5. Shouldn't we leave for the airport soon?
   (A) I don't think we need to hurry.
   (B) That report will be finished soon.
   (C) Yes, I left it at the airport.

6. Why don't we have lunch at the coffee shop?
   (A) The coffee shop is downstairs.
   (B) I don't drink much coffee.
   (C) That's a good idea.

7. Let's spend our vacation at the beach.
   (A) We had a great vacation.
   (B) That sounds like fun.
   (C) No, we didn't spend a lot of money there.

8. Wouldn't you like me to help you carry those packages?
   (A) Thank you, but they're not very heavy.
   (B) You can check your baggage over there.
   (C) Yes, these packages are for me.

9. Why don't you wait for me downstairs?
   (A) We waited for hours.
   (B) OK, look for me by the front door.
   (C) Yes, my weight has gone down.

10. Why don't you paint your office a different color?
    (A) Your office is cooler.
    (B) My collar is too tight.
    (C) I like the color it is now.

Identifying a Reason (page 46)

1. Why didn't you make those photocopies?
   (A) Yes, I made the copies.
   (B) The copy machine is broken again.
   (C) They're very nice photographs.

2. Why is Boris always late for meetings?
   (A) He's never on time for anything.
   (B) Let's wait for him here.
   (C) The meeting starts at eight.

3. Did you take the bus to work again?
   (A) Yes, I'm tired of driving all the time.
   (B) The buses are all working.
   (C) Let's take a walk in the rain.

4. Why isn't Yoko in her office?
   (A) The inner office is Yoko's.
   (B) Yes, this is her office.
   (C) She had to go to a conference downtown.

5. Why don't you ever answer your phone?
   (A) You can cancel it by phone.
   (B) I'm always too busy to talk on the phone.
   (C) I don't know the answer.

6. Will Irene be at the meeting?
   (A) Yes, she was there.
   (B) Yes, I enjoyed meeting her.
   (C) Yes, because she has to give the budget report.

7. Did Joe have an excuse for missing work yesterday?
   (A) Yes, he had a doctor's appointment.
   (B) Yes, I miss him very much.
   (C) Yes, it was yesterday.

8. Why did you lock your office?
   (A) I need a new clock in my office.
   (B) There were some robberies around here recently.
   (C) It's about a block from the office.

9. Why are you using my computer?
   (A) My computer is broken.
   (B) Yes, you can borrow my computer.
   (C) A computer is a useful machine.

10. Do you have a reason for leaving early?
    (A) She left early.
    (B) Spring is my favorite season.
    (C) Yes, I have to catch a plane.

Identifying a Location (page 48)

1. Where will you spend your vacation?
   (A) Perhaps I'll take the bus.
   (B) I'm going skiing in the mountains.
   (C) I won't spend much time there.

2. He's not from Tokyo, is he?
   (A) No, but he travels there often.
   (B) That plane isn't going to Tokyo.
   (C) Yes, he took yours.

3. Is there a bank near here?
   (A) Yes, I drank some, too.
   (B) Yes, there's one right next door.
   (C) Yes, Frank is here.

4. How far is it to the water fountain?
   (A) The mountains aren't far from the city.
   (B) It's just at the end of the hall.
   (C) The weather will be fair tomorrow.

5. Where do you keep the paper?
   (A) There's some on that shelf behind the desk.
   (B) I left the key in the door.
   (C) I usually buy the morning paper at the corner store.

6. What's behind that door?
   (A) Sam works right next door.
   (B) I'll get you some more.
   (C) It's the supply closet.

7. Is the restaurant far from here?
   (A) It's all the way downtown.
   (B) You can rest here.
   (C) It's a fantastic restaurant.

8. Do you know where Janet is this week?
   (A) Yes, it's this week.
   (B) She's at a conference.
   (C) She doesn't know what to wear.

9. Are there any good hotels downtown?
   (A) It's an excellent hotel.
   (B) Yes, there's one right near my office.
   (C) OK, I won't tell anyone.

10. Where did you put my messages?
    (A) I'll leave you a message.
    (B) Yes, you got several messages.
    (C) They're on your desk.

Strategy Practice (page 50)

1. When do you plan to retire?
   (A) I had a flat tire.
   (B) By the end of next year.
   (C) They aren't required.

2. I can't understand this new computer program.
   (A) Lee can show you how to use it.
   (B) It's Lee's computer.
   (C) Yes, I do.

3. What do you think of the job applicants?
   (A) This appliance will do the job.
   (B) That's Bob's application.
   (C) Not one of them is qualified for the job.

4. Do you want that sent to your home or office?
   (A) Yes, please.
   (B) I'll be home afterwards.
   (C) Please send it to my office.

5. Shouldn't we send this by registered mail?
   (A) Yes, that's a good idea.
   (B) The mail hasn't arrived yet.
   (C) I registered yesterday.

6. Why does this photocopy machine keep breaking down?
   (A) I'm making copies now.
   (B) It's time for a coffee break.
   (C) It's a very old machine.

7. I'm in the mood for a chicken sandwich.
   (A) There's sand in my food.
   (B) Which chickens are yours?
   (C) Me, too. Let's go eat lunch.

8. The bus will be here soon, won't it?
   (A) He'll be here shortly.
   (B) It should be here in five minutes.
   (C) It's almost noon.

9. Is Mr. Kim the new director?
   (A) No, Mrs. Cho is.
   (B) He's a very direct person.
   (C) Yes, I know the director.

10. How's that book you're reading?
    (A) I'm really enjoying it.
    (B) Writing takes a long time.
    (C) No, it isn't.

11. Oh, no. I forgot to order all the supplies.
    (A) The supplies are all in order.
    (B) Don't worry. Lucy did it for you.
    (C) I'm sorry, it's out of order.

12. Would you like me to help you finish that assignment?
    (A) I like this assignment.
    (B) No, you don't have to sign it.
    (C) Yes, I could really use some help.

13. Why didn't your wife come to the office party?
    (A) The party was last night.
    (B) She was busy at her job.
    (C) Yes, she'll come to the party.

14. Where can I find the manager?
    (A) Her office is upstairs.
    (B) She's a very kind manager.
    (C) I can manage her.

15. How long does it take to get downtown?
    (A) I usually take the bus.
    (B) He took it there.
    (C) About twenty minutes.

16. Whose signature do we need on this document?
    (A) I'll read it.
    (B) Mary did.
    (C) The director has to sign it.

17. That's the last time I'm staying at some convention hotel.
    (A) I thought it was very pleasant.
    (B) Yes, I would like some.
    (C) We stayed three nights.

18. Would you prefer to eat in the office or should we go out?
    (A) Yes, I would, thank you.
    (B) Let's go out to eat.
    (C) We should meet in the office.

19. Where should I put these letters?
    (A) Just leave them on my desk.
    (B) You can do it later.
    (C) Mail the letters today, please.

20. When is your next dentist appointment?
    (A) It was a real disappointment.
    (B) It's a week from tomorrow.
    (C) I think John will be appointed.

PART 3—CONVERSATIONS

Identifying Time (page 53)

1. Woman: I ordered that software last Tuesday. It should have arrived by now.
   Man: This package came for you this morning. Maybe it's your new software.
   Woman: It is. Finally it's here.
   Man: Good. Now maybe you can help me with my computer.

2. Man: What a great time we had in Paris. Let's go back soon.
   Woman: Oh, I'd love to, but don't you think we should wait until next year?
   Man: Maybe you're right. It was only last month that we were there.

3. Woman: Hey, Mark. I hear you got a new job. Congratulations!
   Man: Isn't it great? But they want me to start this Monday. That's so soon.
   Woman: That is a little odd. Usually they give you two weeks.

4. Man: You travel a lot for your job, don't you?
   Woman: Yes, I go to Tokyo at least once a month.
   Man: I suffer from jet lag. Once a year would be enough for me.
   Woman: You get used to it when you fly all the time.

5. Woman: Isn't the contract ready yet? We're all ready to sign it.
   Man: I called the office this morning. They said we'd have it by this afternoon.
   Woman: This afternoon? I guess that's OK, as long as it's here before three.

6. Man: I bought this cell phone just last week and already it's stopped working.
   Woman: It has a one-year guarantee, so I'd be happy to give you a new one for free.
   Man: Could you give me a better one this time? How about one with a five-year guarantee?
   Woman: Sorry. I don't make the rules.

7. **Woman:** Did you sign up for next month's business conference?

   Man: Not yet. I plan to send in my registration tomorrow.

   Woman: You'd better do it soon. Friday is the last day for registration.

8. **Man:** I can't give you any copier paper today. I'm all out. You'll have to wait until next week.

   Woman: Next week? Why? Can't you get any before then, Tim?

   Man: I only order office supplies once a month. Sorry.

9. **Woman:** I'm calling to find out when the repairs on my car will be finished.

   Man: We're working on it now, and your car should be ready the day after tomorrow.

   Woman: That soon? Great! I thought I'd have to leave it there until Friday at least.

10. **Man:** Am I very late? Have you been waiting for me long?

    Woman: Not really. My train arrived just fifteen minutes ago.

    Man: I'm sorry. I thought it wasn't supposed to arrive until 10:30.

    Woman: It did, but you didn't. Don't worry about it.

Identifying People (page 56)

1. **Woman:** Did you hear that Sam got a promotion?

   Man: Yeah, Jim told me. Isn't it great?

   Woman: Yes, but I wish Pat had gotten one too. She really deserves it.

   Man: Why? For taking every sick day she can?

2. **Woman:** This is Ms. Fujita. May I help you?

   Man: Yes, I'm calling from the accounting office. May I speak with the director?

   Woman: I'm sorry, she's not in. I'm her assistant. Perhaps I can help you.

3. **Man:** What are your specials tonight?

   Woman: We have fresh shrimp and roast beef.

   Man: Hmm. I think I'll just order something from the regular menu.

   Woman: Here's your menu. Let me know when you're ready to order.

4. **Man:** Did anyone call while I was out?

   Woman: You have a message from Mr. Peters. He says he's finished painting the new office.

   Man: Great. Please call him back and ask him to send the bill to the accounting office.

5. **Woman:** Is this your office, John?

   Man: No, it's Cindy's. Mine's the one at the end of the hall.

   Woman: How did you get such a nice office? Your boss must really like you.

   Man: He respects my opinion . . . and I was here first.

6. **Man:** I just received a bill from Mrs. Ortega.

   Woman: Mrs. Ortega is your accountant? I thought Mr. Wilson was.

   Man: He was. But then Bob recommended Mrs. Ortega. She does a much better job.

7. **Woman:** What's your daughter doing these days, Frank?

   Man: She's at the university now. She's studying economics.

   Woman: Economics? I thought she would become a lawyer like you.

8. **Man:** Oh, Marsha, have you seen Jim since his surgery?

   Woman: No, but . . . uh . . . Linda and I plan to visit him in the hospital this afternoon.

   Man: Good, because his wife says he really wants visitors.

9. **Woman:** Martin, isn't that Sandy's car parked by the front door?

   Man: No, it's Tom's. You know, the new secretary.

   Woman: Well, he'd better move it. He parked in the director's space.

10. **Man:** How much is the bus fare?

    Woman: It's $1.50. Do you want a transfer?

    Man: No, but please tell me when we get to my stop. I'm going to the central post office.

    Woman: It's the third stop after this.

Identifying Intent (page 59)

1. **Woman:** Well, I made the call, and I got the tickets for Sunday evening.

   Man: Great. I'm so looking forward to this. They're my favorite band.

   Woman: Mine too. It's at the Capital Theater. That's the best place for a concert.

2. **Man:** I'm so tired of this office. It's so ugly.

   Woman: Why don't you buy some new furniture? Or at least get a new rug.

   Man: Hmmm. New things are so expensive. But I could paint the furniture I have now.

3. **Woman:** I'd like to order a small plain pizza.

   Man: Would you like that delivered, or will you pick it up?

   Woman: I'll pick it up.

   Man: I'll send you a text message on your cell when it's ready to be picked up.

4. **Man:** I'm freezing cold.

   Woman: Then you probably don't want any ice cream.

   Man: No. I need something to warm me up, like a cup of tea.

   Woman: Well, maybe you should put on a sweater, and then we can have ice cream.

5. **Woman:** Let's take a cab. It's raining.

   Man: But just a little, and I have an umbrella. Let's walk.

   Woman: No, it's starting to rain harder. And here's a cab. Get in.

6. **Man:** Here's your order, ma'am. That'll be twenty-five dollars.

   Woman: Let me check my wallet. No, I don't have cash. Will a credit card do?

   Man: That will be fine.

7. **Woman:** It's really cold in here. Why don't you turn off the air-conditioning?

   Man: Why would the air-conditioning be on? It's winter.

   Woman: Oh, I see the problem. Someone left the window open.

8. **Man:** This old fax machine never works. It's time to get a new one.

   Woman: Are you sure? Maybe it's not plugged in.

   Man: Oh, you're right. How embarrassing.

9. **Woman:** Is that today's paper? Would you lend it to me a minute?

   Man: Sure. Do you want to see today's headlines?

   Woman: No, I just want to check the movie schedule.

   Man: There isn't any movie worth seeing. Trust me.

10. **Man:** Buy this sweater. It looks good on you.

    Woman: Yes, and it goes well with my skirt. But for the party I need a dress.

    Man: You're right. It's a formal party, and a long dress is more suitable than a skirt.

Identifying the Topic (page 62)

1. **Woman:** I'm so tired of having car problems.
   Man: What, your car broke down again?
   Woman: You won't believe this, but I ran out of gas.
   Man: You should start taking the bus.

2. **Man:** This steak is delicious. You should try it.
   Woman: Oh, no thanks. I don't like steak.
   Man: You'll like this. It's the cook's specialty.
   Woman: Perhaps, but I still don't eat meat.

3. **Woman:** I saw a nice-looking restaurant not far from here.
   Man: Yes, but I never go there. The service is terrible.
   Woman: That's too bad.
   Man: It doesn't matter how good the food is, the service is what's important.

4. **Man:** I've booked you on the 4:30 flight.
   Woman: Wonderful. Where can I pick up the tickets?
   Man: You can get them at the airport when you check in.
   Woman: Oh, then I had better leave early to have enough time at check in.

5. **Woman:** Are you interested in that lecture called "Buying your first home"?
   Man: No. I'd love to buy my own place to live, but I just don't have enough money.
   Woman: Maybe the speaker has some ideas about how to do it without a lot of money.

6. **Man:** The show starts at 5:15, so I'll meet you in front of the theater at 5:00.
   Woman: OK. I can't wait to see this one. All my favorite actors are in it.
   Man: I'll bring some snacks in case we get hungry during the show.

7. **Woman:** I'm sending this hamburger back to the kitchen.
   Man: Why? It looks nice and tasty to me. Is it undercooked?
   Woman: It's overcooked. Look how burnt it is.
   Man: That's the way I like it.

8. **Man:** Did you see the headlines this morning?
   Woman: No. I didn't buy the paper because I was out of cash.
   Man: You can read my copy. It's over there on my desk.
   Woman: That saves me 35 cents.

9. **Woman:** If you want to learn how to manage your finances, you should read this book.
   Man: I don't have time for books like that. What I need is to earn more money.
   Woman: Maybe you should look for a new job then.

10. **Man:** Can you come to my party? It's on Friday after work.
    Woman: I'd love to. Can I bring something to eat?
    Man: There'll be plenty of food there, but you could bring something to drink.
    Woman: I'd rather bring food.

Identifying a Reason (page 64)

1. **Woman:** This new conference room is nice, but where will everybody sit down?
   Man: We ordered the new chairs last week, but they haven't arrived yet.
   Woman: Well, I don't know what to do for now. We can't ask people to sit on the floor.

2. **Man:** I really need some help with this report I'm preparing for the board meeting.
   Woman: Why don't you call me at home this evening and we can talk it over.
   Man: Thank you. I'll call you after dinner.

3. **Woman:** Well, see you later. I'm off to buy some clothes for my trip to Hawaii.
   Man: Hawaii? I'd love to visit there. That's a great place for a vacation.
   Woman: It is, but I'm going there for a conference.

4. **Man:** You got here so late. We thought you had an accident.
   Woman: Not exactly. I had a flat tire.
   Man: I'm sorry. Well, come on in. Everybody's waiting for you.
   Woman: I'm sorry to be so late.

5. **Woman:** Do you mind if I open the window? It's so warm in here.
   Man: Please don't. The street noise really bothers me.
   Woman: I'll turn on the air-conditioning then. I need some cool air.
   Man: I like it warm. Why don't you just take off your coat?

6. **Man:** This elevator is so slow. Let's take the stairs.
   Woman: I can't walk down all those stairs.
   Man: Sure you can. Come on, I'm tired of waiting for this elevator.
   Woman: You go ahead. I'll wait for the elevator.

7. **Woman:** You're still here? I thought you'd finished all your work for today.
   Man: I have, but I'm waiting for an important phone call.
   Woman: Well, don't stay too late or you'll be tired all day tomorrow.

8. **Man:** Why are we meeting in this uncomfortable office?
   Woman: They're still painting the big conference room.
   Man: Well, I don't see how we can fit enough chairs in this small room.
   Woman: It will be tight, but it's a short meeting.

9. **Woman:** You should take the subway to the office today.
   Man: Why? Driving's faster and I'm already late.
   Woman: Traffic's really heavy today because several streets are closed for construction.

10. **Man:** I didn't get any lunch, and now I'm really hungry.
    Woman: I thought you went to the cafeteria.
    Man: Yes, but it was late and by the time I got there, there was nothing good left.
    Woman: You should have told me. I would have brought you something.

Identifying a Location (page 67)

1. **Man:** I'm getting together later with some friends from the office.
   Woman: Will you be at that café downstairs?
   Man: No, we're going to that other café, the one next to the park.
   Woman: Oh, I love that place. A great view of the park.

2. **Man:** Are you waiting for the number four? I think the rain is making it late.
   Woman: Probably, but I wish it would get here soon. I hate standing out here in the rain.
   Man: Me too. I can't wait to get home and take off these wet clothes.

3. **Woman:** I have a reservation for tonight and tomorrow night.
   Man: Yes, you're in room twenty-three on the second floor. Here's the key.
   Woman: Thank you. Can somebody help me with my bags?
   Man: I'm sorry, we don't have any porters to help you at this time of night, and the elevator is out of order. I'd help you, but I can't leave the front desk.

4. **Man:** I've looked all over the office, but I can't find my cell phone.

   Woman: Hmmm. Did you take a cab? Maybe you left it in the cab.

   Man: No, I took a bus. I know, I left it at the restaurant where I had lunch.

   Woman: Let's go back to the restaurant or at least call them.

5. **Woman:** Wait for me downstairs.

   Man: OK. Should I wait out by the front door?

   Woman: No, don't go outside. Just stand near the elevator.

   Man: OK. I'll see you downstairs in a few minutes.

6. **Man:** You can leave me on the next block. It's that blue house.

   Woman: All right. The fare's seven dollars and fifty cents.

   Man: Here you are. Keep the change.

7. **Woman:** Can you tell me where the frozen dinners are?

   Man: They're in the frozen food section, aisle five.

   Woman: Aisle five. They're on sale this week, right?

   Man: Yes. But the sale ends tomorrow.

8. **Man:** Are you ready to go? Do you have all your books?

   Woman: Yes. Some of these books I'm returning are overdue, you know.

   Man: Then you'll have to pay a late fine.

9. **Woman:** We'll be landing in Los Angeles soon.

   Man: I have to catch the connecting flight to Hawaii as soon as we land.

   Woman: I believe that flight is leaving from gate fifty-four. We're on time, so you'll be able to make your connection.

10. **Man:** This is a nice park. I should come here more often.

    Woman: It's really close to the office, and it's a good place to take a walk.

    Man: Yes, it's good to get a little exercise.

    Woman: You should take more walks in the park.

Identifying an Opinion (page 69)

1. **Woman:** I never take the bus. It's so inconvenient.

   Man: Really? I think it's relaxing. And it's inexpensive, too.

   Woman: Maybe, but the subway is faster.

   Man: Who likes to be underground? Not me.

2. **Man:** I don't know what to do about Bob.

   Woman: Yes, his work isn't very good. We'll have to talk to him.

   Man: He might lose his job if he doesn't improve.

   Woman: He has to learn to fit into the company.

3. **Woman:** This is a nice hotel, don't you think?

   Man: Yes. It isn't very big, but I like it.

   Woman: The beds are so comfortable, and I've never had better service.

   Man: I hope the restaurant is as good.

4. **Man:** This is a nice city, except for the cold weather.

   Woman: I know. The snow is pretty, but I prefer a warmer climate.

   Man: At least it isn't raining.

5. **Woman:** Have you seen any good TV programs lately?

   Man: I never watch TV. It's boring.

   Woman: Maybe you're right. There really aren't many interesting or funny programs.

   Man: Let's get some DVDs.

6. **Man:** What did you think of last night's lecture?

   Woman: I thought it was terribly interesting.

   Man: I enjoyed it, too, though it was a bit too long.

7. **Woman:** How do you like your new job, José?

   Man: It's difficult so far, but I like it.

   Woman: That's good. It's important to like your job.

   Man: It'd be better to like it <u>and</u> have it be easy.

8. **Man:** Are you having fun in your Spanish class, Sally?

   Woman: No, I don't really like it. It's too easy.

   Man: Maybe you can sign up for a harder class next semester.

   Woman: I like a challenge.

9. **Woman:** Have you seen Bill lately?

   Man: No, he's almost never here, and he doesn't do any work when he is.

   Woman: You're right. He always takes sick days. What a lazy guy.

10. **Man:** This pizza is delicious.

   Woman: You think it's good? It's terrible.

   Man: Why? Is it too greasy for you?

   Woman: Greasy, cold, the tomato sauce is runny and the cheese tastes old.

Identifying Stress and Tone (page 72)

1. **Man:** The copy machine isn't broken again?

   Woman: Yep. The repair person must be getting really tired of trying to fix this thing.

   Man: It seems like every time we turn this machine on it breaks down.

   Woman: Maybe the solution is to not turn it on.

2. **Woman:** You're picking up the check?

   Man: I thought I should pay for tonight's meal.

   Woman: You've never paid for dinner before.

   Man: Don't you remember that time in 1996?

3. **Man:** You didn't stay at the office all night?

   Woman: I did. I had a lot of work to do.

   Man: You must be really sleepy. Why don't you go home and get some rest?

   Woman: No, I still have more to do.

4. **Woman:** I'm starving. Is the chicken ready yet?

   Man: Chicken? You said you didn't like chicken, or fish. You said you wanted hamburgers.

   Woman: I didn't say I <u>didn't</u> like chicken. I <u>love</u> chicken. It's <u>hamburgers</u> I don't like.

   Man: Well, tonight it's hamburgers… or we go out.

5. **Man:** That meeting was really useful.

   Woman: Didn't you think it was informative? I thought it was very interesting.

   Man: No, it was a real waste of time.

   Woman: Maybe that's why you fell asleep.

6. **Woman:** When you go to the bank, could you cash this check for me?

   Man: I'm not <u>going</u> to the bank. I'm just going to <u>call</u> the bank.

   Woman: Oh. I thought you said you were going to put money into your account.

7. **Man:** It's so hot outside you could cook on the sidewalk.

   Woman: Then you don't want to go to that soccer game?

   Man: Of course I do. Do you think I just want to stay inside all day watching TV?

8. **Woman:** This is really delicious food.

   Man: I thought you would like this restaurant. It's the most popular one in town.

   Woman: Really? Then people must not care about bad food and high prices.

9. **Man:** This job is the worst, isn't it?

   Woman: I know I shouldn't complain, but things could be better.

   Man: I don't think so. I've never had a more interesting job than this one.

10. **Woman:** You finished all that work already?

Man: No, but I was tired, so I left the office early.

Woman: That wasn't a good idea. You should've just had some coffee and continued working.

Man: I don't see you volunteering to work all night.

Strategy Practice (page 75)

Questions 1 through 3 refer to the following conversation.

Woman: This line is too long. We've already been waiting 15 minutes.

Man: We're only buying these two shirts. Let's go to the express checkout lane. It's a lot shorter. Do you have your credit card ready?

Woman: The express lane is cash only, but I have enough cash.

Questions 4 through 6 refer to the following conversation.

Man: I'm tired of spending vacations at the beach. Let's go to the lake this year.

Woman: It always rains at the lake. And it's far away. And none of our friends go there.

Man: I know, but the fishing there is the best, and you enjoy the swimming.

Woman: I prefer swimming at the beach, and they have a better tennis club.

Man: We go there every year. This year we're flying to the lake.

Questions 7 through 9 refer to the following conversation.

Woman Tina missed the staff meeting yesterday. Was she sick?

Man: No, she got here too late because she was stuck in traffic.

Woman Oh, right. That accident downtown caused a big traffic jam, didn't it? Well, Tina missed some important information at the meeting, and I have to review the new budget report with her. Please tell her to see me in my office at 11.

Questions 10 through 12 refer to the following conversation.

Man: How's your new job at the hospital?

Woman: It's great. So much better than my old office job. And my co-workers are so nice.

Man: Good. That's important, to feel comfortable with your co-workers.

Woman: There's just one tiny problem. I only get paid once a month.

Man: That's terrible. You should work in a school like I do. I get my paycheck every two weeks.

Questions 13 through 15 refer to the following conversation.

Man: I'm taking this jacket right back to the store.

Woman: Why? It looks so good on you. Green is your color.

Man: It's brand new, and already it's lost a button. And it was expensive! $370!

PART 4—TALKS

Identifying the Sequence (page 79)

1. When you get your test, please write your name at the top. Write your name in capital letters before you do anything else. Be sure to read the directions carefully before you answer the questions. Make sure you mark your answers on the answer sheet. If you don't have a pencil, let me know. When you have finished, turn in your test and then you may go home.

2. Welcome to Philharmonic Hall. We are pleased to present Ms. Sue Kim playing a violin concerto. The concert this evening will be preceded by a brief talk by Professor Robert Simon on the history of the violin. Mr. Simon has lectured on the violin all around the world. Following the performance, we will all go to the lobby to enjoy refreshments. Now, here is our director, who will introduce Professor Simon.

3. When entering the building, please sign in at the desk and get a visitor's pass. Do not lose this pass. You will need to wear it at all times when you are in the building. Then wait for an escort to accompany you to your destination. You must also be escorted back to the reception desk. Please don't forget to sign out and return your pass when leaving. Thank you for your cooperation.

4. Attention customers. The store will close in fifteen minutes. Take all your purchases to the cashier now. If you are buying five or fewer items and are paying with cash, you can use the express checkout lane. Please have your receipt ready to show the guard when leaving the store. Check to make sure all your items are the right size and color before you pay, as we don't accept returns.

5. Coming up after the news is our weekend weather report. Then reporter Tom Tales will interview Susan Gilbert about her new book, *How to Get Rich in the Stock Market*. Ms. Gilbert is a renowned expert on investing and finances and writes the weekly newspaper column "You and Your Money." That should be a very informative show. Now, here's Peter Cook with the news.

6. There should be a large turnout for tomorrow afternoon's National Day parade. It will be preceded by speeches by the mayor and the chief of police. Then everyone is invited to enjoy a barbecue and fireworks at City Park in the evening. These are free events. And don't forget to attend the morning soccer game at National Stadium. Attendance at the game is also free, but arrive early if you want to be sure of getting a good seat.

7. A few changes have been made to our conference schedule. Because of a scheduling conflict, Professor Jamison will speak immediately following lunch instead of before. Morning coffee will be served in the front hall instead of in the dining room. The morning workshops will begin at ten o'clock, as originally scheduled, but the afternoon sessions won't begin until 1:30. And now Ms. Carter will give the opening talk.

8. The president left today for a visit to Latin America. He'll head first to a meeting in Mexico City with leaders from Colombia, Brazil, and Mexico. Following a few days of rest at a Mexican beach resort, he will go on to meetings with heads of state in Peru and Ecuador. In addition, he will tour factories and meet with union leaders in both countries.

9. Congratulations on becoming an owner of the Bread-o-riffic 2010 breadmaking machine. You're sure to enjoy the luxury of having fresh-baked bread every day right in your own home. It's easy to use your new bread machine. Simply choose a recipe from the instruction book, assemble and measure your ingredients, then place them in the machine. As the bread bakes, you won't be able to wait for your first taste.

10. Now you can register for classes by phone and avoid the long lines at the registration office. Just call 555-2445.

Press one if you are a new student, or press two if you are a returning student. Enter your Social Security number, then the class number. After you have selected all your classes, enter your credit card number, then hang up. You will receive a receipt by mail within five days.

Identifying the Audience (page 81)

1. Welcome to Introduction to Economics. The textbook for this course, *Economics for the New Millennium,* is available at the university bookstore. The price is a bit steep, but I think you will find it is well worth it. Please bring your books to the next class. There will be two exams—a midterm and a final—in addition to which you will write several short research papers.

2. All of you need to be aware of our return policy. Please don't accept any returns from customers without a dated receipt. Also make sure all returned items are in good condition before accepting them. Check the items carefully as we have had problems in the past with customers returning damaged goods. Remember we issue store credit, not cash, for returns. If you receive complaints about this, please let me know.

3. You have reached Dr. Galbraith's office. If this is an emergency, please hang up and call an ambulance. If you would like to make an appointment or ask for medical advice, please call back during our regular office hours. We are open from ten to six Monday through Friday, and from nine to twelve on the first Saturday of each month. You need to make an appointment because we don't accept walk-ins. Thank you.

4. Remind the passengers that we will be landing shortly. Check to make sure all seat belts are fastened and ask the passengers to turn off all cell phones and recording devices. Find out if there is anyone with small children requiring extra assistance or if anyone needs help getting to a connecting flight.

5. The following is a public service announcement, brought to you by Radio XYZ. Because of the drought, government officials are asking all city residents to conserve water. Residents are asked not to fill their swimming pools or water their gardens until further notice. Right now, the government is asking residents to do this on a voluntary basis, although if the situation becomes severe, it is possible that fines will be imposed. Stay tuned to Radio XYZ for all the latest updates.

6. Thank you for calling the city hotline, your information source for all city events. For theater schedules and ticket orders, press one. For museum information, including information on special exhibits, the lecture series at the art museum, and the foreign film series at the history museum, press two. To hear about upcoming sports events at the city stadium, press three. To speak to an operator, please stay on the line.

7. The history museum is our last stop today. We will spend two hours here. Recorded tours are available at the front desk for a small fee. I also have free informational brochures about the permanent exhibits for anyone who is interested. You are asked to return to the bus no later than 5:30. The bus will take us to our hotel, where we will enjoy dinner and an evening program.

8. We have heavy traffic this morning because of a car breakdown on Route One near the airport. Avoid Route One if at all possible. In addition, road construction is slowing traffic over the City Bridge. Be prepared for a long, slow drive to work this morning. If you can, take the bus or subway.

9. Is your company looking to hire skilled computer technicians? Do you want to hire technicians who have been trained with state-of-the-art equipment? Look no more. Graduates of the Computer Technology Institute are highly trained and skilled technicians able to handle all your routine technical problems. All institute graduates are eligible to become certified computer technicians. Hire one today.

10. Buying a house can be confusing, especially in today's market. The first step is obtaining a loan from the bank. To apply for a home mortgage, you'll need to get the necessary paperwork from a bank officer. You will have to have proof of your income and financial assets. This will help the officer determine how large a loan you qualify for.

Identifying a Situation (page 83)

1. We are having a sale on specialty coffee. Today only you can get two pounds of coffee for the price of one. All of our South American and Central American blends are on sale. Our coffee is available whole bean or ground. Coffee is located on aisle five next to the produce section. There is a limit of four pounds per customer.

2. Good morning, passengers. This is the green line train to the airport. Please remember that the specially marked seats next to the doors are reserved for physically challenged passengers. Smoking, eating, and drinking are not allowed. Next stop, Central Square. Transfer there to the blue line for all uptown destinations.

3. All members of the soccer team are reminded that the bus to the out-of-town game will leave from the front of the school at 3:15. Please be on the bus and ready to go by then. The computer club will meet in the auditorium today and the Spanish Club will meet in the cafeteria. Due to the illness of several of its members, the graduation dance committee meeting has been postponed until next week.

4. Hi, it's Martha. I guess you've already left home. OK, well, I'm leaving the gym now. I had a great workout and now I'm really hungry and looking forward to dinner. So you'd better not be late. It'll probably take me about twenty minutes to get to the restaurant. I'm walking because I don't want to have to park the car. See you soon.

5. Move to the back, move to the back, please. The fare's $1.50, exact change only. Please stand behind the white line. Move away from the door, please. I can't

go anywhere until you let me close the door. Thank you. Next stop, Fifth Avenue, Fifth Avenue and the downtown shopping district.

6. To your right are several paintings by Picasso. Close examination shows the fine brushwork he used. These paintings represent some of Picasso's lesser-known work and are among our more recent acquisitions. We'll take a restroom break next, then continue on to the second floor galleries, where we'll view works by nineteenth-century artists. We'll start in the East Room, which houses our collection of pastoral landscapes.

7. Smith, party of four, your table is ready now. Follow me, please. Sorry to have kept you waiting. As you can see, we're very busy tonight. We reserved a place for you by the window with a view of the water. Here we are. You can hang your coats right over here. Would you like to order drinks and appetizers first?

8. All swimmers, get out of the water immediately. Dangerous thunderstorms are approaching. Parents, keep an eye on your children. There will be no running and no horsing around near the pool, or we may have to ask you to leave. Stay away from the pool until the lifeguard indicates that it is safe to return to the water.

9. May I have your attention, please? We will be closing in a few minutes. Please bring the books you wish to borrow to the checkout desk now. Remember, all books checked out today are due back on April 15th. There is a late fee of twenty-five cents a day, but you can renew your books before their due date by calling 555-0923. Thank you for your patronage and please come back again soon.

10. Hi Sam, it's Donna. I've been waiting for you here at the airport. You were supposed to pick me up. What happened? Well, you're not at the airport and you're not at your office, so where are you? I hope you're not on your way here now because I'm going to take a taxi to the office. See you soon, I hope.

Identifying the Topic (page 86)

1. I am pleased to introduce Mr. Lee Kim, author of *Amazon Adventure*. Mr. Kim, a retired lawyer, amateur photographer, and now a writer, spent the last year traveling by canoe down the Amazon River. He will discuss his travels in the Amazon region on which he based his book, and show some of the photographs he took during his trip. He's sure to have some amazing stories, so hold on to your seats.

2. Thank you all for taking the time to attend this meeting. I'd like to keep it brief, so let me get straight to the point. Staff members have been making unauthorized charges to the office expense account for things like lunches and taxi rides that are not related to your jobs. As a result of this, in the future, all charges to the office expense account must be approved by me ahead of time.

3. All schools will be closed today because of last night's snowstorm. The streets are still icy and dangerous for cars and buses. It is possible that schools will remain closed for several days as it could take some time to get all the streets cleared and safe for travel. Listen to the evening news to find out tomorrow's school schedule.

4. Do you get your sports news from television? Are you getting tired of all the commercial interruptions on TV? You don't have to be annoyed by commercials any more. Our magazine gives you all the latest sports news commercial-free. Read it to find out what's happening in the world of football, baseball, and basketball.

   Learn all about your favorite athletes. Our magazine gives you all this and more. Subscribe today.

5. Let Services, Inc. plan your next conference. We take care of it all— reserving rooms, printing schedules, ordering food, arranging entertainment. Our experienced planners take the headache out of conferences. Services, Inc. guarantees that your next conference will be a success. Call today for your free initial consultation.

6. Winter weather got you down? Chase those winter blues away by taking a trip to a sun-filled island. We offer both weekend and weeklong packages to the Sunshine Islands. Choose a cruise, stay at a resort, or relax at a quaint village inn. Take a fast-paced tour of the island hot spots, or opt for a slow-paced, low-key visit to the beach. You'll love our luxury accommodations and our economical prices. Call today to book your tour.

7. Believe it or not, breakfast is the most important meal of the day. Some people skip breakfast as part of a weight-reducing plan, but this is not a good idea. Studies have shown that people who don't eat a complete meal, including fruit, every morning actually end up gaining weight. They also often feel tired later in the day and compensate for this by eating unhealthy food. Healthy people never skip breakfast.

8. Does your health insurance cover all your needs? Will it pay for hospitalization? Will it cover you if you have an accident far from home? Will it pay for prescription medicine? Does it provide coverage for your husband or wife and other family members? Don't spend your life worrying as your insurance rates get higher and higher. Our insurance plan covers all your medical expenses at reasonable rates, wherever you may be.

9. We have a new schedule here at Radio 2000. We begin this afternoon with three solid hours of classic rock music. That's three solid hours with no commercial interruptions. That'll be followed by an exciting new interview show in which we talk with all your favorite rock musicians, both past and current. We'll have the weather report at five before we move on to our new evening news analysis program.

10. A protest against the increase in the sales tax took place in front of the presidential

palace yesterday. Protesters say the sales tax isn't fair to business owners or consumers. Our newly elected mayor supports the tax increase. She says it will help, not harm, small businesses and strengthen the city's economy. The new tax goes into effect next month.

Identifying a Request (page 88)

1. Next stop, Greenwich. Please remain seated until the train has come to a complete stop. Again, we ask all passengers not to stand up until we have stopped at the station. This is for your own safety. Please check around your seat to make sure you have left nothing behind. Thank you for riding the commuter rail service and have a pleasant trip.

2. Welcome to the Franklin Theater. Tonight's performance is the opening show of our twenty-fifth season. As a courtesy to those around you, members of the audience are asked to turn off all cell phones, pagers, and recording devices before the show begins. Also, the use of cameras is not permitted while the actors are on stage. This includes video and digital cameras. Information on upcoming shows is available in the lobby.

3. You have reached the voice mail of Martin Schwartz. I am either away from my desk or out of the office. If you'd like to make an appointment, please press one to speak with my assistant. Otherwise, wait for the beep and leave a message. I'll return your call as soon as I can.

4. Flight 15 is now ready for boarding. All passengers please line up at the gate and have your boarding pass ready to show to the flight attendant. Let a flight attendant know if you are traveling with small children or need special assistance boarding the plane. If your carry-on bags are too large, you may be asked to check them. We'd like to remind you that this is a nonsmoking flight.

5. A traffic accident downtown is causing major delays on several main roads. Drivers are asked to avoid North State Street. Use Constitution Avenue instead if you must drive downtown. Even on Constitution Avenue, however, you may still experience some delays. Officials expect the delays to last for several hours.

6. Thank you for calling Countway Computers. We value your call. All of our lines are busy now. If you want to reach technical support, hang up and dial 555-3456. If you wish to speak to a customer service representative, please stay on the line and your call will be answered in turn. Right now there is a wait of approximately five minutes.

7. Springfield was struck by a hurricane last week that left millions of dollars of property damage in its wake. Thousands of people have been left homeless and can expect to spend several weeks living in shelters. The city is seeking donations of food and clothing for hurricane victims. If you would like to help, please send your donations to the Springfield Rescue Committee.

8. I'm happy to introduce Mrs. Jackson, who has just joined our staff as the new manager's assistant. I ask all staff members to please help her out during her first few days here, as she learns our office routines. I know you are all ready to help her feel welcome to our office and I appreciate your cooperation in this matter.

9. Attention staff. The fire alarm system is being tested this morning. You may hear the alarm go off several times in the course of the morning. When you hear the alarm, please remain calm. There is no need to leave the building or to avoid using the elevator. Just continue with your usual routine. Thank you for your patience.

10. Will the driver of the white car that is parked near the back entrance please

move your car? You are parked illegally. You need to move your car immediately or it will be ticketed and towed. You can park in the visitor parking area that is located near the front of the building. The parking area by the back entrance is for delivery vehicles only.

Strategy Practice (page 91)

Questions 1 through 3 refer to the following announcement.

We hope you enjoyed this evening's talk by author Marvin Howard. If you would like to hear more, Mr. Howard will be interviewed on radio station PQR tomorrow morning at 11:30. If you would like a copy of Mr. Howard's book, we will have some available for sale up front. Mr. Howard will remain here a short while to sign books and answer questions.

Questions 4 through 6 refer to the following announcement.

Get out your winter coats and scarves because this morning's rain will turn to snow by early afternoon. You can expect three to four inches of snow before it ends this evening, so be careful on the drive home from work and be prepared for possible traffic delays. Tomorrow will be cold and windy, and the roads will probably be very icy. Fortunately, schools will be closed for the holiday, so we don't have to worry about the safety of our children. Expect warmer weather by the weekend.

Questions 7 through 9 refer to the following message.

Hi Charles. It's Mary. I just called to say that my plane arrives at the airport at four tomorrow. I'll probably want to go straight to the hotel, so I'll just take a taxi and meet you there at seven, OK? That'll give me a chance to rest a bit. I made

dinner reservations at the Colonial Restaurant. It's not far from the hotel. Also, I know you mentioned going to the movies after dinner, but I think I'd prefer to just sit and talk. We haven't seen each other for so long. Hope that's OK. Can't wait to see you. Bye.

Questions 10 through 12 refer to the following announcement.

Good evening, everyone. I'm your hostess, Matilda Wimple, and I am happy to welcome you to this evening's program, the third in the After Dinner lecture series. This evening we will begin with a brief musical performance by students from the City School of Music. Then we will hear Dr. Arthur James speak on Italian Art, and he has a fascinating slide show to accompany his talk. During the refreshment break, wine and cheese will be served in the cafeteria, and, of course, we will finish the evening with the usual question and answer session.

Questions 13 through 15 refer to the following talk.

Welcome to the Palm Breeze Hotel. We have a room ready for you on the third floor, for two nights as you requested. I've given you a room with an ocean view, but if you'd prefer to look over the pool, I also have a pool view room available. No? All right, ocean view. You can leave your car by the front door while you unload your luggage, then please park it in the lot by the side of the building. I'm sorry, but the garage is full. All hotel guests are invited to a free breakfast, served in the dining room from 7 to 9. If you'd like to use the fitness room or sauna, there is a small charge. Here's your key.

Audioscript Listening Comprehension Review

Part 1 (page 94)

1. Look at the picture marked number 1 in your book.
   - (A) He's photocopying a document.
   - (B) He's opening a drawer.
   - (C) He's buying more paper.
   - (D) He's handing over the file.

2. Look at the picture marked number 2 in your book.
   - (A) They're raking the leaves.
   - (B) They're climbing the trees.
   - (C) They're wading through water.
   - (D) They're walking beside the wall.

3. Look at the picture marked number 3 in your book.
   - (A) The cycles are stopped at the light.
   - (B) The motorbikes are parked in the lot.
   - (C) The bicycles are stored in the garage.
   - (D) The drivers are crowded in the park.

4. Look at the picture marked number 4 in your book.
   - (A) They're waiting to cross the street.
   - (B) They're shopping for bags.
   - (C) They're getting into a car.
   - (D) They're writing a greeting card.

5. Look at the picture marked number 5 in your book.
   - (A) The patrons are eating a meal.
   - (B) The waiters are serving the customers.
   - (C) The chefs are cooking with chopsticks.
   - (D) The diners are paying the bill.

6. Look at the picture marked number 6 in your book.
   - (A) She's watching her boys.
   - (B) She's talking on the phone.
   - (C) She's looking into a microscope.
   - (D) She's making a speech.

7. Look at the picture marked number 7 in your book.
   - (A) The snow covers the highway.
   - (B) The road is lined with trees.
   - (C) The path is crowded with pedestrians.
   - (D) The forest is by the sea.

8. Look at the picture marked number 8 in your book.
   - (A) She's watering the plants.
   - (B) She's cleaning her clothes.
   - (C) She's taking a bath.
   - (D) She's washing dishes.

9. Look at the picture marked number 9 in your book.
   - (A) The pilots are packing their suitcases.
   - (B) The passengers are closing the overhead bins.
   - (C) The travelers are checking in for the flight.
   - (D) The attendants are shutting the door to the plane.

10. Look at the picture marked number 10 in your book.
    - (A) The architect is drawing up the specifications.
    - (B) The construction manager is looking at the plans.
    - (C) The supervisor is taking a break.
    - (D) The road crew is stopping the traffic.

Part 2 (page 100)

11. What time is Ms. Sanchez arriving?
    - (A) On the corner.
    - (B) At three o'clock.
    - (C) For twenty minutes.

12. Have you found out when the flight gets in?
    (A) No, but I'll call the airline now.
    (B) Yes, I found it on the desk.
    (C) I'll get it in a light color.

13. I'll need to be picked up on Saturday morning.
    (A) We picked up the room.
    (B) I'll come get you at ten.
    (C) Yes, it's on Saturday.

14. Where should we have the office party this year?
    (A) I think we should have it at my house.
    (B) There's a party there every year.
    (C) My office is very near.

15. What's the name of the accounting firm we use?
    (A) The accounts are in order.
    (B) It's a firm offer.
    (C) I think it's Sanderson Accounting.

16. I think we're getting close.
    (A) You buy the clothes.
    (B) I think we're lost.
    (C) I got it the last time.

17. Haven't they located the problem yet?
    (A) Not that I know of.
    (B) Yes, though not at this location.
    (C) No, I don't have that kind of problem yet.

18. Will the seminar be held here or at the main office?
    (A) Yes, they're planning a long meeting.
    (B) No, they can't hear from so far away.
    (C) As far as I know, it'll be held at this office.

19. Who are the board members this year?
    (A) They're not as bored as you think.
    (B) They're the same as last year.
    (C) They're staying aboard the plane.

20. How much will this project cost the firm?
    (A) About thirty-eight hundred dollars.
    (B) I lowered the figures by ten percent.
    (C) The project will be finished soon.

21. This bus is really crowded.
    (A) Let's hope everybody gets off at the next stop.
    (B) At least no one is on it.
    (C) I like really cloudy days.

22. Are the board minutes ready for distribution?
    (A) No, they weren't distributed last Friday.
    (B) Not yet. I haven't read the final draft.
    (C) Yes, they're meeting in about an hour.

23. How about a long lunch break if we finish early?
    (A) Sounds good to me!
    (B) We finished earlier than expected.
    (C) Our lunch break is over already.

24. How far do you think the convention center is from our hotel?
    (A) Yes, the center sure is inconvenient.
    (B) I think I'll stay at the hotel for now.
    (C) I'd say about a fifteen-minute walk.

25. Save my seat. I'll be right back.
    (A) Try the left side.
    (B) You better hurry. The show's about to start.
    (C) You are never wrong.

26. Your vacation time was approved, wasn't it?
    (A) It's about time I took a vacation.
    (B) No, I have to pick new dates.
    (C) I didn't have time to approve it.

27. Doesn't our company get a special price on cell phones?
    (A) Yes, if we buy in quantity.
    (B) Yes, I'd appreciate your company on the trip.
    (C) No, I'll phone you at your office.

28. Would you like to come to our picnic on Sunday?
    (A) We picked out some clothes for Sunday.
    (B) Yes, it sure was a fun picnic.
    (C) Sorry, I have to work that day.

29. Where do you suggest I stay in Singapore?
    (A) Your best bet is the Hotel International.
    (B) I always suggest places to stay.
    (C) Your stay in Singapore is paid for.

30. Have you ordered the supplies I asked for?
    (A) I've run out of staples and paper.
    (B) Yes, they should arrive tomorrow.
    (C) No, I had to pay for them on my own.

31. When can you move the copy machine?
    (A) Right after lunch.
    (B) I moved last month.
    (C) About ten to twenty minutes.

32. Are you our new committee chairperson?
    (A) Yes, we bought several new chairs.
    (B) No, you aren't on the committee.
    (C) No, I'm new to this organization.

33. These pants are too big on me.
    (A) You should learn to dance.
    (B) France is a large country.
    (C) It looks like you've lost some weight.

34. How can I get more information about health insurance?
    (A) Talk to Mrs. Durfee in Human Resources.
    (B) I already have car insurance.
    (C) You're in good health.

35. The manager was present at yesterday's staff meeting, wasn't he?
    (A) No, it wasn't a staff meeting.
    (B) No, he didn't attend.
    (C) Yes, he gave everyone a present.

36. Why didn't you tell your supervisor?
    (A) I thought I could handle it myself.
    (B) I didn't tell her why.
    (C) No problem.

37. Isn't this the same place we had lunch last Tuesday?
    (A) The race is on Tuesday.
    (B) I always have the same thing for lunch.
    (C) Do you want to eat somewhere else?

38. It's very cold in here.
    (A) Put on a sweater.
    (B) She's not very old.
    (C) Turn off the heat.

39. Why does Michael always watch the news during coffee break?
    (A) He knew he broke his watch.
    (B) He always drinks coffee for breakfast.
    (C) He likes to be informed of events.

40. Isn't this suit already discounted?
    (A) Yes, I think it suits you very well.
    (B) There are discounts to suit everyone.
    (C) Yes, that's the sale price you're looking at.

PART 3 (PAGE 101)

Questions 41 through 43 refer to the following conversation.

Woman:	You've been at your computer all morning.
Man:	I have lots of e-mail to answer.
Woman:	Well, it's lunchtime. Let's go eat.
Man:	You go ahead. I'll see you in the cafeteria in 15 minutes.

Questions 44 through 46 refer to the following conversation.

Man:	Did you put your laptop in the overhead compartment?
Woman:	Yes. I didn't think I could use it on board.
Man:	Sure you can. I always use mine when I fly.
Woman:	I'm too tired for that. I think I'll take a nap.
Man:	Well, I'm hungry. I hope they serve a meal on this flight.

Questions 47 through 49 refer to the following conversation.

Man:	Good afternoon. May I help you?
Woman:	I have an appointment with Mr. Wong at one o'clock. I hope I'm not late for it.
Man:	Not at all. Please have a seat, and I'll tell him you're here.
Woman:	Thank you. You're very kind.

Questions 50 through 52 refer to the following conversation.

Woman:	I plan to invite a few people for dinner on Thursday.
Man:	Thursday? What's wrong with a weekend evening like Friday or Saturday?
Woman:	People are usually busy then.
Man:	Who will you invite? People from school?
Woman:	No, just some neighbors. I'm planning for six guests.

Questions 53 through 55 refer to the following conversation.

Man:	When does the cooking demonstration begin?
Woman:	There are two presentations—one at nine and another at eleven.
Man:	Let's go to the later one. Then we can have lunch. We'll be hungry.
Woman:	Fine. Then we'll be able to catch the two o'clock train home.

Questions 56 through 58 refer to the following conversation.

Woman:	I had thought the new expense report was due Wednesday.
Man:	Me, too. The manager said it was due the middle of the week.
Woman:	I know. But when I asked again, he said Tuesday, before the meeting.
Man:	That makes me mad. Now we'll have to work late on Monday to finish it.

Questions 59 through 61 refer to the following conversation.

Man:	I'm sure glad we decided to come here. This resort has everything!
Woman:	You can say that again. Good restaurants. Huge pool. And best of all, comfortable beds.
Man:	I plan to spend all day in the fitness room. I want to get a lot of exercise.

Questions 62 through 64 refer to the following conversation.

Woman:	Do you have self-adhesive envelopes? I need a box of 500.
Man:	Yes, but I only have the small size.
Woman:	That's too bad. I need the business-letter size.
Man:	If you like, I could place an order for you.
Woman:	I can't wait for that. I'll have to buy them elsewhere.

Questions 65 through 67 refer to the following conversation.

Man:	I can't believe all the work we did today—we wrote several letters, read e-mail, answered about ten phone calls . . .
Woman:	And I'm still expecting a package. When it comes, I'll have to work on the contents immediately.
Man:	Really? I was hoping for your help writing this report.
Woman:	I can help you now. Let's use the computer in your office. It's cleaner there.

Questions 68 through 70 refer to the following conversation.

Man:	I'm sorry, we don't take credit cards, just cash and money orders.
Woman:	I'll have to check if I have cash.
Man:	If you'd like, I can keep the shoes on hold for you for a few days.
Woman:	Just let me look in my purse. Yes, here's a $100 bill.
Man:	The shoes are $75, so here's your $25 change.

PART 4 (PAGE 104)

Questions 71 through 73 refer to the following announcement.

This is your captain. I hope you're enjoying the flight. It's a beautiful day out there. Off the left of the aircraft you can see Mt. Rushmore, and on the right, the approach to Deadwood, South Dakota. Our radar indicates some turbulence ahead, so I'm going to ask you all to fasten your seat belts and stay in your seats.

Questions 74 through 76 refer to the following announcement.

Welcome aboard our Tropical Garden Tour. I'm Kathy, your tram operator and tour guide. Please remain seated in the tram for the duration of the tour. I also ask that you please keep from leaning out the windows. Sometimes I'll be taking us very close to some large tree branches, and I don't want anyone getting hurt. Also, please refrain from picking any leaves or flowers. Our plants are for everyone to enjoy! So much for the precautions. Our first stop is coming up on your left. It's our rare orchid collection. About half of these plants are in full bloom. Some give off a very pleasant scent, and they're all colorful.

Questions 77 through 79 refer to the following message.

Next week is our community clean-up drive. Last year it was a dismal failure. Only fifteen people showed up. This year we hope to do better—much better. I want to see all of you at this year's event. To help convince you to participate, I remind you that making our neighborhood clean of trash and litter is for *your* benefit. Also, to help you convince members of your family to join the drive, remind them that when we finish, there will be free hot dogs and refreshments as well as games for the kids. See you next Saturday. We'll start at ten in the morning and finish at one in the afternoon.

Questions 80 through 82 refer to the following radio show.

Hello. Welcome to Sunday Evening Radio News Talk. Our guest this evening is Dr. Quimby Jones, professor of economics at National University. During the first half hour of the show, Dr. Jones will talk about the current economic situation in our country, especially about the problems in the agricultural sector, and answer your questions about the economy. So please call us at 649-555-2594 to speak with Dr. Jones. Following that, we will have our usual weekly news review. During the last ten minutes of the show we will read from your letters and e-mails commenting on last week's show. So settle in for the next hour to enjoy Sunday Evening Radio News Talk.

Questions 83 through 85 refer to the following lecture.

Good afternoon, class. Today we'll continue our discussion of ancient Chinese history. I'm sorry, the video I planned to show is unavailable. Instead, I have some slides to show you. These slides show some examples of ancient Chinese art and architecture, some views of the Great Wall, and some other things. If you read the assignment in your textbook, then you already have some background on the building of the Great Wall. Speaking of assignments, I have some articles for you to read for next week, some of the best written on the subject of Chinese history, in my opinion. Also, don't forget that next week we have a special guest, Dr. Smith, our own university president, who will talk about his recent trip to China.

Questions 86 through 88 refer to the following weather report.

This is a special weather report. Please be aware that the entire region is under a flood watch. We are currently experiencing heavy rains, which we expect to continue for the next twenty-four hours. While there is little wind now, heavy winds may move into the area overnight, bringing even more rain and possibly hailstorms with them. By tomorrow, flooding is expected in low-lying areas and may become widespread if the heavy rain continues. Everyone living within a mile of the Green River should listen tomorrow for evacuation orders.

Questions 89 through 91 refer to the following speech.

Welcome to our annual sales review luncheon meeting. I hope you enjoyed the delicious food as much as I did. We were able to provide such good food thanks to a slight increase in revenue over the past year. The purpose of my talk today is to review the past year and plan for the future. First of all, Internet sales last year did not account for the increase in revenue that we expected. Therefore, in the year to come, I want our sales force to concentrate once again on a more traditional means to get new customers and keep current ones. By this I mean everything from increasing media exposure of our products through television and radio ads to more door-to-door customer contact. This afternoon we'll meet in groups to discuss the specifics.

Questions 92 through 94 refer to the following announcement.

I'm very happy to announce that the company is building a new parking garage. It'll replace the parking lot we've used for so many years. Employees and visitors have always complained about the parking lot. If it rained hard, people couldn't stay dry when they had to walk from the lot to the building. In the summertime, their car interiors became like ovens. Construction will start next week and should be finished by the end of the year. During construction, all employees should park their cars across the street. We've made special arrangements with the shopping center to use one of their lots. We apologize for the inconvenience, but it'll be worth it!

Questions 95 through 97 refer to the following advertisement.

We buy houses, offering you fast cash and quick closings. Do you own an unwanted house or are you relocating? Need to sell quickly? Is your house vacant or in need of major repairs? These are common problems that can happen to anyone. We buy houses from people in situations just like yours. We can pay all cash and close quickly. We'll handle all the paperwork and make all the arrangements. We're not realtors. We're real estate investors that buy houses like yours. You'll get a quick sale with no hassles and your worries will be behind you. Call now to find out how we can solve your problem. 603-555-9000. That's 603-555-9000. Call today!

Questions 98 through 100 refer to the following announcement.

Attention shoppers! A lost cell phone has been found in the frozen food section, aisle 10. If you think this cell phone may be yours, please go to the customer service office to claim it. Don't forget shoppers, there's a special sale today on apples and pears. They're fresh from the farm and are selling at the low, low price of just one dollar a kilo. So hurry to the produce section and load up on apples and pears. Parents, don't forget that your children need to eat plenty of fresh fruit to stay healthy. Only customers with a Shoppers' Club membership card can take advantage of this special sale. If you don't have a card, hurry to the customer service office to sign up for your shoppers' club membership today.

AUDIOSCRIPT
PRACTICE TEST ONE

PART 1—PHOTOS (PAGE 210)

1. Look at the picture marked number 1 in your book.
    (A) The carts are by the road.
    (B) The cars are on the road.
    (C) The drivers are by the car.
    (D) The cards are on the shelf.

2. Look at the picture marked number 2 in your book.
    (A) The ship's officers are on the boat.
    (B) The sheep are in the field.
    (C) The sheets are on sale.
    (D) The sailors are playing bridge.

3. Look at the picture marked number 3 in your book.
    (A) She's talking on the phone.
    (B) She's opening a drawer.
    (C) She's writing in her book.
    (D) She's using her keyboard.

4. Look at the picture marked number 4 in your book.
    (A) The women are shopping before lunch.
    (B) The workers are preparing trays of food.
    (C) The technicians are building a kitchen.
    (D) The doctors are checking on their patients.

5. Look at the picture marked number 5 in your book.
    (A) They're sitting by the side of the road.
    (B) They're climbing over the fence.
    (C) They're watering the plants.
    (D) They're digging a hole in the ground.

6. Look at the picture marked number 6 in your book.
    (A) He's holding his head.
    (B) He's covering his glasses.
    (C) He's wiping his face with a napkin.
    (D) He's drinking a cup of tea.

7. Look at the picture marked number 7 in your book.
    (A) The office is large and spacious.
    (B) Three colleagues are talking to a fellow worker.
    (C) The men are looking at a computer game.
    (D) The headquarters is closed for the holiday.

8. Look at the picture marked number 8 in your book.
    (A) The men are all wearing hard hats.
    (B) The chorus is reading the score.
    (C) The crew is changing uniforms.
    (D) The recruits are taking off their ties.

9. Look at the picture marked number 9 in your book.
    (A) He's checking his bags at the counter.
    (B) He's ordering room service.
    (C) He's taking the elevator to his room.
    (D) He's checking into a hotel.

10. Look at the picture marked number 10 in your book.
    (A) She's covering her face.
    (B) She's faxing a document.
    (C) She's taking a photo of herself.
    (D) She's holding the door open for him.

PART 2—QUESTION-RESPONSE (PAGE 216)

11. When does your flight leave?
    (A) From the airport.
    (B) At 12:30.
    (C) From Gate 23.

12. Have we received that fax yet?
    (A) I've got it right here.
    (B) In about an hour.
    (C) I'll fax it now.

13. Ms. Pak, is it? How do you do?
    (A) It's my mistake.
    (B) I'm a lawyer.
    (C) How do you do?

14. Isn't it time for our meeting?
    (A) Sometimes I have meat.
    (B) A quarter to three.
    (C) Yes, but it's been rescheduled.

15. Is the boss in a good mood?
    (A) Yes, but he'll be right back.
    (B) I've seen him smiling all morning.
    (C) No, he's in the cafeteria.

16. I'm extremely tired.
    (A) I don't like extreme sports.
    (B) When did they fire you?
    (C) You should get more sleep.

17. Aren't we opening an office in Tokyo?
    (A) It's open from nine to five.
    (B) No, I'm not going to the office today.
    (C) That's what I've been told.

18. Why haven't we begun the conference?
    (A) We're having the meeting in my office.
    (B) We're still waiting for Mr. Carter to arrive.
    (C) It shouldn't take too long.

19. Hello. Uh . . . Who are you?
    (A) Fine, thank you.
    (B) The new secretary.
    (C) Downtown.

20. Whose computer can I use?
    (A) Ms. Hoffman's.
    (B) The blue one.
    (C) Sorry, I need it now.

21. That dripping faucet drives me crazy.
    (A) Relax. I'll drive you.
    (B) So call a plumber.
    (C) I tripped on that carpet, too.

22. How come you're late?
    (A) There was a lot of traffic.
    (B) No, I'll be there on time.
    (C) Yes, I eat very quickly.

23. Did you remember to invite everybody?
    (A) Thank you, but I can't come.
    (B) Yes, I sent the invitations yesterday.
    (C) I remember everyone I've ever met.

24. Have we placed all the newspaper ads?
    (A) Yes, they've all gone out.
    (B) It should be great for sales.
    (C) Yes, I picked up the newspaper.

25. When will the auditors be leaving?
    (A) An hour ago.
    (B) They're going now.
    (C) For an hour.

26. Why don't we take a fifteen-minute break?
    (A) No, I didn't break the plate.
    (B) It's working just fine.
    (C) Good. I need to make a call.

27. This article is poorly written.
    (A) There were a lot of errors in it.
    (B) You can't get rich riding around.
    (C) Art is not for the poor.

28. Where do you come from?
    (A) Canada.
    (B) The mailroom.
    (C) Only a few minutes ago.

29. How about joining us for lunch?
    (A) The employee cafeteria's downstairs.
    (B) I'd like to very much.
    (C) I didn't have time for breakfast.

30. I find this street plan confusing.
    (A) I found it for you.
    (B) You have the map upside down. That's why.
    (C) We planned to look for it tomorrow.

31. Would you mind if I asked you your age?
    (A) That's nice of you.
    (B) Not at all.
    (C) Certainly.

32. How long a trip is it from here to our Cairo office?
    (A) About twelve hours.
    (B) About seven thousand miles.
    (C) In Egypt.

33. Who are you sending that e-mail for?
    (A) The boss asked me to.
    (B) The boss. He's expecting it.
    (C) The boss. He asked me to.

34. Who are you sending that e-mail to?
    (A) The computer.
    (B) My new client.
    (C) More stamps.

35. Are we going to be offered stock options next year?
    (A) Yes, stocks should go up next year.
    (B) Yes, that's what the boss said.
    (C) No, but maybe next year.

36. You should take a vacation.
    (A) I take public transportation.
    (B) We took her to the station.
    (C) You're right. I work too hard.

37. Can you put in some overtime next week?
    (A) I can start work at four o'clock.
    (B) Sure. I'll put it in here next week.
    (C) It shouldn't be a problem.

38. How much farther is it?
    (A) About thirty minutes.
    (B) About thirty dollars.
    (C) About thirty kilometers.

39. Have you decided to ask for that transfer?
    (A) I'm putting in for vacation soon.
    (B) I have to think about it some more.
    (C) Yes, you could be right.

40. Will I be reimbursed for my expenses on that business trip?
    (A) Yes, if you give us your receipts.
    (B) Yes, business trips can be expensive.
    (C) If you can afford it.

PART 3—CONVERSATIONS (PAGE 217)

Questions 41 through 43 refer to the following conversation.

Woman: Please don't forget to mail those contracts to Mr. Park.

Man: It's already done. I mailed them this morning.

Woman: Great. OK, I'm off to the airport. My flight leaves in 45 minutes.

Man: When will we see you back here in the office?

Woman: Early next week. Look, it's 11 o'clock already. I have to run.

Questions 44 through 46 refer to the following conversation.

Man: Will the word processing classes start soon?

Woman: Yes. Are you interested in a beginners class, intermediate, or...?

Man: I'd like to take an advanced class. What's the basic cost?

Woman: Tuition is $500 for a six-month course.

Man: Fine. I'd like to register for a morning class.

Questions 47 through 49 refer to the following conversation.

Woman: Isn't Mr. Katz supposed to be here today?

Man: His flight was delayed because of the bad weather in New York. He'll be here tomorrow morning.

Woman: Oh, yes, I heard about that terrible rainstorm on the radio news.

Man: Well, at least it's not a snowstorm. That would be terrible.

Woman: Or an ice storm. That's the worst.

Questions 50 through 52 refer to the following conversation.

Man: Let's have Mr. Lee's retirement party in the conference room.

Woman: I don't think it's big enough for all fifty guests, even if we move the chairs and computers.

Man: Yes, you're right. We'd better have it at a restaurant. What day is the party?

Woman: Friday. That's just two days away, so we have to plan fast.

Questions 53 through 55 refer to the following conversation.

Man: I'm afraid you'll have to wait about 45 minutes for a table.

Woman: I don't think we can wait that long. We're starving.

Man: You could try that place around the corner. They serve good food.

Woman: We'll give it a try, then. I hope they don't require reservations.

Questions 56 through 58 refer to the following conversation.

Woman: I'm calling to speak with Mr. Curtis, please.

Man: Mr. Curtis is out of town on business. Would you like to leave a message?

Woman: Thank you, but . . . uh . . . I think I'd like to make an appointment for when he returns. I'd like him to take a look at some contracts for me.

Man: Well, Mr. Curtis will be returning tomorrow. I could schedule an appointment for you later in the week.

Woman: Thank you. That would be fine.

Questions 59 through 61 refer to the following conversation.

Man: Things just haven't been the same since Mr. Cho retired last month.

Woman: I know. Since he stopped working, there's no one here to tell us jokes.

Man: It's hard to work without Mr. Cho making us laugh.

Woman: Do you know what else isn't the same? Ms. Green didn't bring cookies today.

Man: That's because Ms. Green is on vacation this week. She's the one who always brings them.

Questions 62 through 64 refer to following conversation.

Woman: We've been waiting half an hour. What could've happened to Janet?

Man: She said she planned to stop at the store after work.

Woman: And she was late last time because she had a dentist appointment.

Man: She always has an excuse. It's really annoying.

Woman: Relax. She'll be here.

Questions 65 through 67 refer to the following conversation.

Man: This must be a mistake. I called to reserve the room a week ago.

Woman: I'm sorry, but I don't see anything here under your name.

Man: Don't you have some room you can give me? I need one for three days.

Woman: Let's see . . . I have a small one in back, and it costs just 165 dollars a night.

Questions 68 through 70 refer to the following conversation.

Woman: Did you hear about Carl's promotion?

Man: Yes, I did. I'm very happy for him.

Woman: I'm sure his wife doesn't feel too bad about it either.

Man: I think we should have a party to celebrate. Let's have it at my house and invite the whole office.

Part 4—Talks (page 220)

Questions 71 through 73 refer to the following report.

A careless man started a 520-acre forest fire not far from the town of White River, New York. The fire was 75 percent under control on Wednesday, according to firefighters. It has cost close to one million dollars so far to fight the fire. A spokesperson for the fire department said the cause was a smoker who threw his cigarette out his car window. The fire started in the state park and destroyed campgrounds and recreational areas there. Park visitors, including a group of boy scouts, took shelter in town. The fire also threatened houses just outside of White River. Five hundred people had to flee their homes at the height of the fire Monday night. Fortunately, firefighters were able to save that area. Authorities said the fire should be completely put out by today.

Questions 74 through 76 refer to the following announcement.

We're changing our name . . . but we're keeping our promises! For decades, Villa Hospitalis has been providing low-income and indigent people with the highest quality medical care. It's time to create a separate identity, so people will recognize what we do. That's why we're changing the name of our facility to the Albert Schweitzer Hospital. Inspired by the work of the great Dr. Schweitzer, we have renewed our commitment to excellence and quality, offering more services and setting new standards for medical treatment. The Albert Schweitzer Hospital . . . another name for positive results!

Questions 77 through 79 refer to the following restaurant review.

Fuji House is a Japanese restaurant full of wonderful aromas and tastes. The restaurant specializes in seafood, and its sushi is the best you can find anywhere. It also offers delicious tempura, several tasty chicken dishes, and a wonderful sweet and sour pork. The restaurant serves a variety of vegetarian dishes, too, and all the dishes are moderately priced. Fuji House is open for lunch and dinner seven days a week. It opens early for breakfast on Saturdays and Sundays only. A delicious and reasonably priced business lunch special is available Monday through Friday. If you like traditional Japanese cooking with a modern flair, visit Fuji House.

Questions 80 through 82 refer to the following talk.

I'd like to thank all of you for coming to this meeting. Once again it's time for us to elect the Employee of the Year. My assistants are now passing out ballot slips. Please use one to write down the name of your choice for Employee of the Year. Please consider someone who you feel has given 110 percent of him- or herself during this past year. Your choice should be someone who is not only a very hard worker, but is also someone who is kind, friendly, and helpful. In case you've forgotten, let me remind you that the winner will receive a $1,000 cash prize and a one-week vacation for two in the Bahamas. Okay, I'm now ready to take nominations from the floor.

Questions 83 through 85 refer to the following speech.

Good morning. My name is Norberto and I'll be your guide this morning as we tour the ruins of Machu Picchu. I hope all of you are wearing comfortable shoes because we'll be climbing up and down a great deal and covering a lot of ground during this tour. We'll start our walk at the main gate of the city, where you'll see the Temple of the Sun, and finish at the main plaza, which you can see in the distance behind me. I ask that you all stay close together as we proceed, and please don't worry; I'll give you plenty of time to ask questions and take pictures at our different stops. If there are no questions right now, let's begin. Please follow me.

Questions 86 through 88 refer to the following telephone message.

Hello. This is Mrs. Gail Winston. My phone number is 202-555-3434. I'm returning a call from a Mr. Max Amberson or Anderson. I couldn't get his name when he left his message. He wanted to verify my home address. My address is 3647 (thirty-six forty-seven) Delaware Lane. That's 3-6-4-7 Delaware Lane. Be sure to put Lane because there is also a Delaware Road and a Delaware Circle. If Mr. Amberson or Anderson has any further questions, he may call me after three this afternoon.

Questions 89 through 91 refer to the following report.

Now for the local news. Residents of Marlboro County are still without power. The heavy rains and strong winds that swept through the county last night tore down power lines and left 150,000 residents without electricity. Work crews have been working all night to restore power, but the winds, which remain strong, are making their work difficult. The Power Company expects that the western part of the county will be able to turn on their lights this evening, but the rest of the county will be lucky to have electricity by tomorrow night.

Questions 92 through 94 refer to the following announcement.

We are pleased to announce that the LaForce Fitness center will open the first of the month, November 1. Our year long renovation is complete and to celebrate, we are offering free orientation sessions for the citizens of our community. Come and see our 40,000 square-foot complex. Take a swim in our olympic-size pool. Play a round of golf on our championship golf course. Climb on our 60-foot rock wall. For a limited time, we're offering two-for-one memberships. Bring a friend to our orientation sessions. If one of you signs up, the other will receive a club membership free.

Questions 95 through 97 refer to the following train announcement.

Attention all passengers for Springdale. The 10:30 train to Springdale will begin boarding in five minutes. Reservations are required for this train. All passengers for Springdale, please go to track 15 now. Passengers with small children will be allowed to board first. If you haven't checked your luggage yet, please do so immediately. Each passenger is allowed to take only one small bag on the train. All other items, including large suitcases, boxes, bags, musical instruments, and pets must be checked in at the baggage office.

Questions 98 through 100 refer to the following introduction.

Good evening. Welcome to the first lecture in our series "The Wonders of Nature." In this seven-lecture series, we'll cover a variety of interesting topics such as insect life, exotic plants, desert ecology, life in the ocean, and more. We have a number of interesting speakers lined up. Now I'd like to introduce tonight's speaker, Patricia Mora, who will tell us about exotic butterflies of Central America. Before her talk, Ms. Mora will show us a video taken on her recent trip to Central America. And please don't forget, all the wonderful butterfly photos you saw on display when you came in will be on sale at the end of the talk. All proceeds will go to the Save the Butterfly Fund.

AUDIOSCRIPT
PRACTICE TEST TWO

PART 1—PHOTOS (PAGE 250)

1. Look at the picture marked number 1 in your book.
    (A) They're shaking out the sand.
    (B) They're greeting one another.
    (C) They're going out to sea.
    (D) They're running a mile.

2. Look at the picture marked number 2 in your book.
    (A) She's drawing on paper.
    (B) She's arranging the tiles.
    (C) She's filing her nails.
    (D) She's looking in the files.

3. Look at the picture marked number 3 in your book.
    (A) The telephones are on the wall.
    (B) The signs are under the phones.
    (C) The door is behind the sign.
    (D) The phones are to the left of the door.

4. Look at the picture marked number 4 in your book.
    (A) She's studying the X-rays.
    (B) She's looking at her vacation pictures.
    (C) She's watching a medical show on TV.
    (D) She's scanning a file.

5. Look at the picture marked number 5 in your book.
    (A) The uniformed guard is by the entrance.
    (B) The gate to the courtyard is open.
    (C) The pathway circles through the trees.
    (D) The tourists line up by the garden door.

6. Look at the picture marked number 6 in your book.
    (A) They're going down the stairs.
    (B) They're getting on the train.
    (C) They're boarding the plane.
    (D) They're checking their bags.

7. Look at the picture marked number 7 in your book.
    (A) The tables are set for lunch.
    (B) The diners are enjoying a break.
    (C) The customers are choosing their seats.
    (D) The chairs and tables are empty.

8. Look at the picture marked number 8 in your book.
    (A) The cargo is in the hold of the plane.
    (B) The boxes are loaded onto the container.
    (C) The goods are stacked in the warehouse.
    (D) The produce is on the back of the truck.

9. Look at the picture marked number 9 in your book.
    (A) They're staying on the platform.
    (B) They're opening the window.
    (C) They're waiting for the plane.
    (D) They're getting on the train.

10. Look at the picture marked number 10 in your book.
    (A) She's holding the cup with both hands.
    (B) She's walking in the pouring rain.
    (C) She's pointing up to the top shelf.
    (D) She's pouring a cup of coffee.

PART 2—QUESTION-RESPONSE (PAGE 256)

11. When did the director arrive?
    (A) Since this morning.
    (B) At the airport.
    (C) Late last night.

12. Do you know whose keys these are?
    (A) I left them on your desk.
    (B) I think they're Mr. Kim's.
    (C) They're the keys to the closet door.

13. Where did you put the packages for Ms. Sato?
    (A) Ms. Sato is over there.
    (B) They're on her desk.
    (C) She packed her bags.

14. Are you almost ready for the meeting?
    (A) I met him at the reception last night.
    (B) No, it's in the big conference room.
    (C) Yes, I just have to finish typing these notes.

15. Where do you usually park your car?
    (A) There's a beautiful park nearby.
    (B) In the garage across the street.
    (C) I had to take it to the mechanic last week.

16. When can I call you?
    (A) Tomorrow morning is a good time.
    (B) Most people just call me Maria.
    (C) My office is the best place to talk.

17. It's supposed to rain tomorrow.
    (A) You were supposed to come yesterday.
    (B) I'd better bring an umbrella.
    (C) Tomorrow's train is on time.

18. Who is going to meet Mr. Contini at the airport?
    (A) He's at the airport.
    (B) Mrs. Garcia will pick him up.
    (C) At ten o'clock.

19. Do you know what time the offices close?
    (A) I think everyone leaves by 5:30.
    (B) Yes, the offices are closed.
    (C) You really should buy some new clothes.

20. Why did Ms. Chen call a meeting today?
    (A) It's today.
    (B) At 2:30, I think.
    (C) Because we have to discuss the budget.

21. How often do you have to turn in financial reports?
    (A) Mrs. Gomez is our financial manager.
    (B) Once every month.
    (C) He's a very good reporter.

22. How long does the bus ride take?
    (A) It's only about fifteen minutes.
    (B) It's not a very big bus.
    (C) It's a very pleasant ride.

23. I don't feel very well.
    (A) You don't look sick.
    (B) She's fine, thank you.
    (C) You're welcome.

24. Where would you like to eat dinner?
    (A) As soon as I finish typing this document.
    (B) We could try that restaurant across the street.
    (C) Yes, I would like that very much.

25. Were you able to book a hotel for next week?
    (A) I've already read that book.
    (B) Yes, I got a room at a nice place downtown.
    (C) No, I didn't.

26. She's been waiting for over an hour.
    (A) My clock is broken.
    (B) Ask her if she wants to sit down and wait.
    (C) She's lost a lot of weight.

27. How can I make an appointment with Ms. Lee?
    (A) She's very happy about her new position.
    (B) You won't be disappointed.
    (C) You should speak with her assistant.

28. How long do you plan to stay in Tokyo?
    (A) Only about three or four days.
    (B) I haven't been there in a long time.
    (C) At one of the downtown hotels.

29. Would you like to go to a movie with us after work?
    (A) Yes, we took a long walk.
    (B) Yes, that's a great idea.
    (C) Yes, I worked all afternoon.

30. Did you notice whether Ms. Kovacs was at the reception?
    (A) Yes, I took thorough notes.
    (B) Yes, she was there.
    (C) Yes, she received it.

31. Where can I find Mr. Park?
    (A) He should be in his office now.
    (B) Usually after lunch.
    (C) At 10:45.

32. How many people work in this department?
    (A) Yes, it's quite a big apartment.
    (B) There are fifteen altogether.
    (C) I've worked here for several years.

33. When will you be free to meet for lunch?
    (A) In the cafeteria on the second floor.
    (B) It doesn't cost anything.
    (C) Next Monday is a good time.

34. Did you buy that newspaper downstairs?
    (A) Yes, we'll need some more paper.
    (B) Yes, at the newsstand in the lobby.
    (C) Yes, we said good-bye.

35. When will the new assistant manager start work?
    (A) In the office down the hall.
    (B) Next week, I think.
    (C) She has a lot of experience.

36. We're going to build a new house.
    (A) The new building is next to my home.
    (B) I'm going there, too.
    (C) I can recommend an architect.

37. Is there a discount on this furniture?
    (A) Yes, I can give you twenty-five percent off the regular price.
    (B) Yes, we counted it last night.
    (C) Yes, this is furniture.

38. Why hasn't Mr. Moreno signed those papers yet?
    (A) He buys the newspaper every morning.
    (B) Because he hasn't had a chance to read them.
    (C) No, he hasn't.

39. This grass is higher than ever.
    (A) I'm taller than you.
    (B) It's time to cut it.
    (C) The glass is never clean.

40. You aren't still working for the same company, are you?
    (A) No, I got a new job about a month ago.
    (B) No, I went there alone.
    (C) No, it was a different computer.

PART 3—CONVERSATIONS (PAGE 257)

Questions 41 through 43 refer to the following conversation.

Woman:	This package arrived for Mr. Ozawa this morning.
Man:	Who is it from? His boss?
Woman:	No, his secretary. It's the report he needs for his meeting with Ms. Jones tomorrow.
Man:	He's at lunch, but I'll put it on his desk with the rest of his mail.

Questions 44 through 46 refer to the following conversation.

Man:	Oh, no! I left my wallet at my desk!
Woman:	Don't worry about it. I'll pay for lunch.
Man:	Are you sure? I ate such a big meal.
Woman:	It's no problem. I'll use my credit card, and you can pay me later.

Questions 47 through 49 refer to the following conversation.

Man:	Do you have a table for three of us tonight? We don't have reservations.
Woman:	I can give you a table for three at nine o'clock, or at 8:45 I have a table next to the kitchen.
Man:	We'll take the nine o'clock. We'll just wait in the bar until then.

Questions 50 through 52 refer to the following conversation.

Woman:	White seems to be the best color for these walls, don't you think?
Man:	White is good for the windows, but you need a better color on the walls.
Woman:	You're right. How about yellow? Or blue? Blue would match the color of the rug and chairs.
Man:	Sounds good. I'll get the paints and we'll start the day after tomorrow. On Friday.

Questions 53 through 55 refer to the following conversation.

Man: Is Jim still working on that memo? I've got to see him before I leave.

Woman: Good luck. He missed the 3:00 meeting because he had to type the final copy.

Man: Well, I can't wait. I've got to catch the 6:00 train. I'm already late.

Questions 56 through 58 refer to the following conversation.

Man: We can't write this report here. Your office is too noisy. Aren't there desks somewhere where it's quieter?

Woman: Hmmm. We could take the elevator to the first floor conference room.

Man: OK. Let's just take this computer and that folder of papers with us.

Woman: Fine. We can leave the pens and notepads here. They have all that downstairs.

Questions 59 through 61 refer to the following conversation.

Woman: Sam, who will be in your office tomorrow to go over these accounts with me?

Man: I'll be at a conference, but my boss will be there after lunch. He'll help you.

Woman: Great. He's more helpful than your assistant. I'll take him out to dinner after work as a thank you.

Questions 62 through 64 refer to the following conversation.

Man: Look at this ad in the newspaper. Briefcases are on sale this week.

Woman: Wow! 15 percent off. That's a good deal. You should fax your order today.

Man: I think I'd rather call and order one over the phone.

Woman: Well, hurry, then. The sale ends tomorrow.

Man: No, it doesn't. Look, Saturday's the last day.

Questions 65 through 67 refer to the following conversation.

Man: This thing doesn't work. The copies come out too light.

Woman: I know. It's really old. It's always breaking down.

Man: I'm going to report this right away. I have to get these copies made.

Woman: I already called the company. A repair person will be here at noon.

Man: Great. Well, I guess I'll read my e-mail while I'm waiting.

Questions 68 through 70 refer to the following conversation.

Woman: We have to discuss the conference plans soon. Can we meet this week?

Man: Sorry, I'll be away on a business trip for the rest of this week.

Woman: How about next Monday then? I'll see you in your office at 11.

Man: Monday's fine, but let's make it at one. I have a morning class.

PART 4—TALKS (PAGE 260)

Questions 71 through 73 refer to the following announcement.

The 10:30 train to Paris will begin boarding in ten minutes at Gate 15. Passengers who still wish to check luggage should do so now. Passengers with small children or those needing special assistance are asked to arrive at the gate five minutes before boarding time. All other passengers will be boarded in the order that they arrive at the gate. Passengers without tickets can purchase them on the train. Please be advised that on board the train we can accept cash only. Credit cards and personal checks will not be accepted.

Questions 74 through 76 refer to the following report.

Welcome to the five o'clock weather report. I know you're all tired of this long day of rain, but the good news is that the skies will finally clear up tonight. By tomorrow morning there shouldn't be a cloud in the sky, and it'll be warm and sunny all day. For all you people who've been wanting to make a trip to the beach, tomorrow should be the perfect day for it.

Questions 77 through 79 refer to the following announcement.

Attention shoppers. Take advantage of today's special in the meat department. Ground beef is on sale at two pounds for the price of one. Don't forget to check out our produce department where we have fresh vegetables and a variety of fruit available. Shoppers purchasing fifteen or fewer items can use our express check-out lanes. Don't wait in line. Just follow the red signs to the express lanes at the front of the store.

Questions 80 through 82 refer to the following talk.

Good evening, class. I'm Dr. Compton. First, I'd like to explain the requirements of this course. We'll use just one textbook. It's available in the university bookstore and is called *Advanced Algebra*. I'll assign about ten algebra exercises a week for you to do as homework, and you'll have a midterm exam as well as a final exam. Class begins at seven o'clock and I expect everyone to be here on time.

Questions 83 through 85 refer to the following announcement.

Good afternoon. I hope you're all feeling well-rested and energetic after that delicious lunch. For our next stop, we'll visit the Bob Wilson House. Mr. Wilson is an important figure in our history and was our city's first mayor. The bus driver has informed me that we'll have an hour to spend at the Wilson House. Then we'll go on to see the war heroes monument. It'll be late by then, and we'll have to leave the art museum visit for another day.

Questions 86 through 88 refer to the following announcement.

Attention all employees. There are still a few tickets left for the year-end soccer tournament at the City Stadium. Anyone who wishes to join the company excursion to see the game should go to the front desk today to reserve your tickets. We've hired a bus which will leave from the front of the building on Saturday at six A.M. The bus ride is free. Join us on this exciting trip to watch your favorite players win the trophy.

Questions 89 through 91 refer to the following speech.

Good evening. I am pleased to introduce Ms. Lucy Park, the award-winning author of *You, Too, Can Become a Millionaire*. Ms. Park will read excerpts from her book and answer questions from the audience. Following that, she will be available to sign copies of her book. You can purchase the book at the back of the auditorium for twenty-five dollars. That's a special price available tonight only and is 10 percent off the usual cost.

Questions 92 through 94 refer to the following announcement.

You have reached the office of Pamela Jones, science reporter at the *Daily Times* newspaper. I'll be out of the office all week at the journalists' conference in New York. If you wish to speak to my assistant, press one. To reach the main switchboard, press two. To leave a message, please stay on the line. Start speaking at the sound of the beep. Thank you.

Questions 95 through 97 refer to the following recorded announcement.

You have reached the information hotline of Breezeway Airlines. The following updated flight information is available for this evening's arrivals. Flight 260 from Hong Kong will arrive twenty minutes late. Flight 75 from Sydney will arrive on time. Flight 186 from London will arrive one hour late. The delay is due to heavy rains over the British Isles. Flight 17 from Paris has been canceled due to a local blizzard. Now is the time to take advantage of our special sale. We still have sale-priced tickets available to selected destinations. Act now because the sale ends next week. Please note we will have a new flight schedule next month. Check our website for details. Thank you for choosing Breezeway Airlines.

Questions 98 through 100 refer to the following recorded announcement.

Thank you for calling the Starlight Cinema. Today we are showing the exciting action drama *Lost in the Storm*. We have shows today at 1, 3, 5, and 7:30 P.M. We will also have a special midnight showing of the mystery thriller *Black Night*. Tickets for this show will not be sold to anyone under the age of 18. All shows before five o'clock are half price. Cold drinks, hot popcorn, and other snacks are available for sale in the lobby. Please don't bring outside food into the theater.

ANSWER KEYS

ANSWER KEY
LISTENING COMPREHENSION

PART 1—PHOTOS

Photo 1 (page 4)

A.
1. (N)
2. (N)
3. (?)
4. (Y)
5. (?)
6. (Y)
7. (?)
8. (?)
9. (N)
10. (?)
11. (N)
12. (N)

B.
1. (Y)
2. (Y)
3. (N)
4. (N)
5. (N)
6. (Y)
7. (N)
8. (N)
9. (N)
10. (Y)
11. (N)
12. (N)

C.
1. taking
2. giving
3. facing
4. sitting
5. touching

D.
1. Neither man is wearing a jacket.
2. (Y)
3. (Y)
4. The man on the right has a watch on his left wrist.
5. There are few people in the office.
6. Both men are wearing white shirts.
7. The box is small and may or may not be heavy.
8. The man on the right is wearing a vest.

Photo 2 (page 7)

A.
1. (N)
2. (?)
3. (?)
4. (Y)
5. (?)
6. (?)
7. (?)
8. (N)
9. (N)
10. (N)
11. (N)
12. (N)

B.
1. (Y)
2. (N)
3. (Y)
4. (?)
5. (Y)
6. (Y)
7. (N)
8. (Y)
9. (N)
10. (Y)
11. (Y)
12. (N)

C.
1. addressing
2. listening
3. standing
4. expressing
5. sitting

D.
1. (Y)
2. Both men are wearing ties.
3. Neither of the men is wearing glasses.
4. Both men are dressed in suits.
5. The man behind the podium is not wearing a hat.
6. Both men are wearing dark suits.
7. One man is almost completely bald.
8. (Y)

Photo 3 (page 10)

A.
1. (N)
2. (?)
3. (Y)
4. (N)
5. (N)
6. (?)
7. (N)
8. (N)
9. (?)
10. (N)
11. (N)
12. (N)

B.
1. (Y)
2. (N)
3. (N)
4. (Y)
5. (N)
6. (N)
7. (Y)
8. (N)
9. (N)
10. (?)
11. (N)
12. (?)

C.
1. watching
2. constructing
3. holding
4. following
5. walking

D.
1. (Y)
2. (Y)
3. Both men are wearing shoes.
4. Both men are wearing gloves.
5. The man in front is wearing a uniform.
6. The man behind is wearing dark-colored pants.
7. Both men have light-colored hard hats.
8. Both men are wearing long pants.

Photo 4 (page 13)

A.
1.	(?)	7.	(?)
2.	(?)	8.	(N)
3.	(?)	9.	(N)
4.	(N)	10.	(Y)
5.	(N)	11.	(?)
6.	(N)	12.	(N)

B.
1.	(Y)	7.	(Y)
2.	(Y)	8.	(N)
3.	(Y)	9.	(N)
4.	(N)	10.	(Y)
5.	(Y)	11.	(N)
6.	(N)	12.	(N)

C.
1. styling
2. having
3. holding
4. looking
5. sitting

D.
1. Both women are wearing dark-colored clothing; one is wearing pants.
2. (Y)
3. (Y)
4. Both women have long hair.
5. (Y)
6. The woman on the left is wearing dark-colored pants.
7. Neither of the women is wearing glasses.
8. The woman sitting down has light hair.

Photo 5 (page 17)

A.
1.	(N)	7.	(Y)
2.	(Y)	8.	(Y)
3.	(Y)	9.	(Y)
4.	(N)	10.	(N)
5.	(N)	11.	(N)
6.	(N)	12.	(Y)

B.
1.	(Y)	7.	(N)
2.	(N)	8.	(Y)
3.	(N)	9.	(N)
4.	(Y)	10.	(Y)
5.	(N)	11.	(N)
6.	(Y)	12.	(Y)

C.
1. folded
2. took off
3. set
4. filled
5. placed

D.
1. (Y)
2. (Y)
3. The pitchers are different sizes.
4. The table is round.
5. The tablecloth is a light color.
6. (Y)
7. (Y)
8. The plates are clean.

Photo 6 (page 20)

A.
1.	(Y)	7.	(Y)
2.	(Y)	8.	(N)
3.	(?)	9.	(N)
4.	(?)	10.	(?)
5.	(Y)	11.	(N)
6.	(N)	12.	(Y)

B.
1.	(Y)	7.	(Y)
2.	(N)	8.	(N)
3.	(Y)	9.	(Y)
4.	(Y)	10.	(N)
5.	(Y)	11.	(Y)
6.	(Y)	12.	(Y)

C.
1. turned on
2. opened
3. cleaned
4. made up
5. placed

D.
1. The television is smaller than the dresser.
2. The lamps are different sizes.
3. The bed is made.
4. The chair has arms.
5. We do not know for sure if a window is behind the screen.
6. (Y)
7. The carpet is wall-to-wall.
8. (Y)

Photo 7 (page 23)

A.
1.	(Y)	7.	(N)
2.	(N)	8.	(Y)
3.	(N)	9.	(Y)
4.	(N)	10.	(?)
5.	(?)	11.	(?)
6.	(Y)	12.	(?)

B.
1.	(Y)	7.	(Y)
2.	(?)	8.	(N)
3.	(N)	9.	(Y)
4.	(?)	10.	(?)
5.	(Y)	11.	(?)
6.	(N)	12.	(N)

C. 1. leaning
2. hanging
3. closed
4. made up
5. painted

D. 1. (Y)
2. Curtains are hanging in the windows.
3. The small "open" sign is not straight.
4. (Y)
5. The windows are the same shape.
6. The wheels of the bicycle are the same size.
7. The window on the right is at the same height as the one on the left.
8. There is no basket on the handlebars of the bike.

Photo 8 (page 26)

A.
1.	(Y)	7.	(N)
2.	(Y)	8.	(Y)
3.	(N)	9.	(?)
4.	(N)	10.	(N)
5.	(?)	11.	(N)
6.	(Y)	12.	(?)

B.
1.	(Y)	7.	(Y)
2.	(Y)	8.	(Y)
3.	(N)	9.	(N)
4.	(Y)	10.	(N)
5.	(Y)	11.	(N)
6.	(Y)	12.	(Y)

C. 1. runs
2. separates
3. planted
4. strung
5. divides

D. 1. The walkway is above the canal.
2. (Y)
3. The bridge further away is larger.
4. The canal runs straight through the city.
5. The fence is not a solid fence.
6. (Y)
7. (Y)
8. There are no cars on the road.

Strategy Practice (page 32)

1.	(D)	6.	(D)
2.	(A)	7.	(B)
3.	(B)	8.	(C)
4.	(C)	9.	(A)
5.	(A)	10.	(B)

PART 2—QUESTION-RESPONSE

Identifying Time (page 39)

1.	(B)	6.	(C)
2.	(A)	7.	(A)
3.	(A)	8.	(B)
4.	(C)	9.	(C)
5.	(A)	10.	(A)

Identifying People (page 40)

1.	(B)	6.	(B)
2.	(B)	7.	(A)
3.	(A)	8.	(B)
4.	(B)	9.	(C)
5.	(C)	10.	(A)

Identifying an Opinion (page 42)

1.	(A)	6.	(C)
2.	(C)	7.	(B)
3.	(A)	8.	(A)
4.	(B)	9.	(C)
5.	(C)	10.	(B)

Identifying a Choice (page 43)

1.	(A)	6.	(B)
2.	(A)	7.	(C)
3.	(C)	8.	(A)
4.	(A)	9.	(C)
5.	(B)	10.	(B)

Identifying a Suggestion (page 45)

1.	(A)	6.	(C)
2.	(C)	7.	(B)
3.	(A)	8.	(A)
4.	(B)	9.	(B)
5.	(A)	10.	(C)

Identifying a Reason (page 46)

1.	(B)	6.	(C)
2.	(A)	7.	(A)
3.	(A)	8.	(B)
4.	(C)	9.	(A)
5.	(B)	10.	(C)

Identifying a Location (page 48)

1.	(B)	6.	(C)
2.	(A)	7.	(A)
3.	(B)	8.	(B)
4.	(B)	9.	(B)
5.	(A)	10.	(C)

Strategy Practice (page 50)

1.	(B)	11.	(B)
2.	(A)	12.	(C)
3.	(C)	13.	(B)
4.	(C)	14.	(A)
5.	(A)	15.	(C)
6.	(C)	16.	(C)
7.	(C)	17.	(A)
8.	(B)	18.	(B)
9.	(A)	19.	(A)
10.	(A)	20.	(B)

PART 3—CONVERSATIONS

Identifying Time (page 53)

1.	(A)	6.	(A)
2.	(A)	7.	(D)
3.	(B)	8.	(D)
4.	(A)	9.	(C)
5.	(B)	10.	(B)

Identifying People (page 56)

1.	(B)	6.	(D)
2.	(C)	7.	(A)
3.	(A)	8.	(B)
4.	(B)	9.	(C)
5.	(D)	10.	(C)

Identifying Intent (page 59)

1.	(C)	6.	(B)
2.	(C)	7.	(D)
3.	(A)	8.	(C)
4.	(B)	9.	(A)
5.	(D)	10.	(D)

Identifying the Topic (page 62)

1.	(D)	6.	(A)
2.	(B)	7.	(D)
3.	(C)	8.	(C)
4.	(A)	9.	(B)
5.	(C)	10.	(B)

Identifying a Reason (page 64)

1.	(C)	6.	(A)
2.	(A)	7.	(B)
3.	(C)	8.	(D)
4.	(B)	9.	(C)
5.	(D)	10.	(C)

Identifying a Location (page 67)

1.	(D)	6.	(B)
2.	(B)	7.	(A)
3.	(A)	8.	(B)
4.	(B)	9.	(D)
5.	(D)	10.	(D)

Identifying an Opinion (page 69)

1.	(B)	6.	(C)
2.	(D)	7.	(C)
3.	(A)	8.	(C)
4.	(D)	9.	(A)
5.	(A)	10.	(B)

Identifying Stress and Tone (page 72)

1.	(B)	6.	(B)
2.	(B)	7.	(D)
3.	(C)	8.	(C)
4.	(A)	9.	(C)
5.	(B)	10.	(A)

Strategy Practice (page 75)

1.	(B)	9.	(D)
2.	(A)	10.	(D)
3.	(D)	11.	(A)
4.	(C)	12.	(B)
5.	(B)	13.	(B)
6.	(D)	14.	(D)
7.	(B)	15.	(D)
8.	(B)		

PART 4—TALKS

Identifying the Sequence (page 79)

1.	(D)	6.	(D)
2.	(A)	7.	(B)
3.	(B)	8.	(B)
4.	(A)	9.	(B)
5.	(C)	10.	(A)

Identifying the Audience (page 81)

1.	(C)	6.	(A)
2.	(A)	7.	(D)
3.	(B)	8.	(C)
4.	(B)	9.	(A)
5.	(D)	10.	(B)

Identifying a Situation (page 83)

1.	(B)	6.	(C)
2.	(A)	7.	(A)
3.	(B)	8.	(C)
4.	(D)	9.	(C)
5.	(D)	10.	(C)

Identifying the Topic (page 86)

1.	(D)	6.	(B)
2.	(A)	7.	(A)
3.	(C)	8.	(A)
4.	(B)	9.	(B)
5.	(A)	10.	(D)

Identifying a Request (page 88)

1.	(B)	6.	(D)
2.	(C)	7.	(A)
3.	(C)	8.	(A)
4.	(A)	9.	(B)
5.	(C)	10.	(D)

Strategy Practice (page 91)

1.	(B)	11.	(D)
2.	(D)	12.	(D)
3.	(A)	13.	(A)
4.	(A)	14.	(B)
5.	(B)	15.	(C)
6.	(D)		
7.	(C)		
8.	(B)		
9.	(B)		
10.	(B)		

ANSWER KEY

LISTENING COMPREHENSION REVIEW

PART 1 (PAGE 94)

1. (A) The man is photocopying a document. Choice (B) tries to confuse you by providing incorrect details: He's *lifting the photocopier lid*, not *opening a drawer*. Choice (C) tries to confuse you by using the related word *paper*. Choice (D) tries to confuse you by using the related word *file* and provides incorrect details: The man's *hand is on the paper*, but he's not *handing it over* to anyone.

2. (D) The girls are walking through the leaves beside the wall. Choice (A) tries to confuse you by using the similar-sounding word *raking* for *walking*. Choice (B) tries to confuse you by using the similar-sounding word *trees* for *leaves* and provides incorrect details: They're *walking alongside the trees*, not *climbing the trees*. Choice (C) provides incorrect details: They're *wading* through the *leaves*, not the *water*.

3. (B) The motorbikes are parked in a lot. Choice (A) provides incorrect details: There is no light in the picture, and the cycles are *parked*, not *stopped*. Choice (C) tries to confuse you by using the similar-sounding word *bicycles* for *motorcycles*. Choice (D) uses the word *park* in a different context: The cycles are *parked*, but we do not see the driver and do not know if they're in a *park* (recreational area).

4. (A) We can assume the women on the sidewalk in front of the pedestrian crossing are waiting to cross the street. Choice (B) provides incorrect details: One woman is carrying a *handbag* and one has a *suitcase*, but they're not *shopping for bags*. Choice (C) provides incorrect details: While there are cars in the picture, the women are not getting into any of them. Choice (D) tries to confuse you by using the similar-sounding word *writing* for *waiting*.

5. (A) The patrons are eating a meal. Choice (B) tries to confuse you by using the related words *waiter*, *serving*, and *customers*. Choice (C) tries to confuse you by using the related words *chefs* and *cooking*. Choice (D) tries to confuse you by using the related word *diners*.

6. (D) The woman is making a speech. Choice (A) tries to confuse you by using the similar-sounding word *boys* for *voice*. Choice (B) tries to confuse you by using the similar-sounding word *phone* for *microphone*. Choice (C) tries to confuse you by using the similar-sounding word *microscope* for *microphone*.

7. (B) The road is lined with trees. Choice (A) provides incorrect details: There are *sand dunes* in the picture, not *snow*; the road is *small*, not a *highway*, and is not covered with snow. Choice (C) provides incorrect details: There is *only one* person on a bike on the road. Choice (D) tries to confuse you by using related words *forest* (many trees) and *sea* (sand).

8. (D) The woman is washing the dishes. Choice (A) provides incorrect details: She is *washing a water glass*, not *watering the plants*. Choice (B) provides incorrect details: She is cleaning the *dishes*, not her *clothes*. Choice (C) incorrectly infers she is taking a *bath*.

9. (B) The passengers are closing the overhead bins on the plane. Choice (A) tries to confuse you by using the related word *suitcases*. Choice (C) tries to confuse you by using the related word *flight*. Choice (D) provides incorrect details: They're shutting the *overhead bins*, not the *door to the plane*. All of the subjects are words associated with air travel.

10. (B) We can assume the man looking at the plans is the construction manager. Choice (A) tries to confuse you by using the related word *specifications*. Choice (C) tries to confuse you by using the related word *supervisor*. Choice (D) tries to confuse you by using the related word *crew*.

PART 2 (PAGE 100)

11. (B) *At 3 o'clock* answers *when* (what time). Choice (A) answers *where*. Choice (C) answers *how long*.

12. (A) *No, but I'll call the airline* answers the *yes/no* question and provides an action. Choice (B) repeats the word *found*. Choice (C) confuses similar sounds *light* and *flight*.

13. (B) *I'll come get you* responds to *need to be picked up*. Choice (A) repeats the words *picked up*. Choice (C) repeats the word *Saturday*.

14. (A) *At my house* answers *where*. Choice (B) repeats the words *party* and *year*. Choice (C) repeats the word *office* and confuses similar sounds *near* and *year*.

15. (C) *Sanderson Accounting* answers *what's the name of*. Choice (A) confuses similar sounds *accounts* and *accounting*. Choice (B) repeats the word *firm*.

16. (B) *I think we're lost* responds to the statement *We're getting close*. Choice (A) confuses the similar sounds of *close* and *clothes*. Choice (C) repeats forms of the verb *get/got*.

17. (A) *Not that I know of* answers *Haven't they located the problem yet*. Choice (B) confuses similar sounds *location* and *located*. Choice (C) repeats the words *have*, *problem*, and *yet*.

18. (C) *It'll be held at this office* answers *Will the seminar be held here or at the main office*. Choice (A) confuses *meeting* and *seminar*. Choice (B) confuses *hear* and *here*.

19. (B) *The same as last year* answers *Who are the board members this year*. Choice (A) confuses *bored* and *board*. Choice (C) confuses similar sounds *aboard* and *board*.

20. (A) *About thirty-eight hundred dollars* answers *how much*. Choice (B) associates *figures* with *cost*. Choice (C) repeats the word *project* and answers *when*.

21. (A) *Let's hope everybody gets off at the next stop* responds to the statement *This bus is really crowded*. Choice (B) contradicts the meaning of the statement. There are many people on the bus. Choice (C) repeats the word *really* and confuses the similar-sounding word *cloudy* for *crowded*.

22. (B) *Not yet* answers *Are the board minutes ready*. Choice (A) confuses similar sounds *distributed* and *distribution*. Choice (C) confuses the *board meeting* and the *board minutes*.

23. (A) *Sounds good to me* is an enthusiastic response to *How about a long lunch break*. Choice (B) confuses similar sounds *earlier* and *early*. Choice (C) repeats the phrase *lunch break* and confuses *over already* and *finish early*.

24. (C) *A fifteen-minute walk* answers *how far*. Choice (A) repeats the word *center* and confuses similar sounds *inconvenient* and *convention*. Choice (B) repeats the word *hotel* and confuses similar sounds *now* and *how*.

25. (B) *You better hurry. The show's about to start* responds to the request *Save my seat*. Choice (A) uses the associated word *left* for the direction *right*. However, in this context *right* means *very soon*. Choice (C) uses the associated word *wrong* for *right*. Again, *right* has a different meaning in this context.

26. (B) *No, I have to pick new dates* provides a negative response with a reason it wasn't approved. Choice (A) repeats the word *vacation*. Choice (C) repeats the word *approve*.

27. (A) *Yes, if we buy in quantity* answers the *yes/no* question *Doesn't our company get a special price*. Choice (B) confuses *company* (companionship) and *company* (business). Choice (C) confuses similar sounds *phone* and *phones* and associates *office* with *company*.

28. (C) *Sorry, I have to work that day* provides a response by giving the reason that the speaker cannot come. Choice (A) confuses similar sounds *picked* and *picnic* and repeats the word *Sunday*. Choice (B) repeats the word *picnic* and confuses similar sounds *fun* and *come*.

29. (A) *The Hotel International* answers *where*. Choice (B) repeats the words *suggest* and *stay*. Choice (C) confuses *stay* (n.) and *stay* (v.) and repeats the word *Singapore*.

30. (B) *Yes, they should arrive tomorrow* answers the *yes/no* question *Have you ordered the supplies*. Choice (A) associates *staples* and *paper* with *supplies*. Choice (C) repeats the word *for* and associates *pay* with *order*.

31. (A) *Right after lunch* answers *when*. Choice (B) confuses *When did you move* and *When can you move the copy machine*. Choice (C) associates *minutes* with *time* and answers *how long will it take*.

32. (C) *No, I'm new* answers the *yes/no* question *Are you our new committee chairperson*. Choice (A) confuses *chairs* and *chairperson*. Choice (B) repeats the word *committee* and answers *Am I on the committee*.

33. (C) *It looks like you've lost some weight* is an observation on the *pants that are too big*. Choice (A) uses similar-sounding *dance* for *pants*. Choice (B) uses the similar-sounding *France* for *pants* and the synonym *large* for *big*.

34. (A) *Talk to Mrs. Durfee in Human Resources* answers *how can I get more information*. Choice (B) confuses *car insurance* and *health insurance*. Choice (C) repeats the word *health*.

35. (B) *No, he didn't attend* answers the *yes/no* question *The manager was present at yesterday's staff meeting*. Choice (A) repeats the phrase *staff meeting*. Choice (C) confuses *present* (n.) and *present* (v.).

36. (A) *I thought I could handle it myself* answers *Why didn't you tell* by giving a reason. Choices (B) and (C) are not appropriate responses.

37. (C) *Do you want to eat somewhere else* answers *Isn't this the same place* by offering an alternative. Choice (A) confuses similar sounds *race* and *place* and repeats the word *Tuesday*. Choice (B) repeats the words *same* and *lunch*.

38. (A) *Put on a sweater* is the advice given to someone who thinks *It's very cold in here*. Choice (B) repeats the word *very* and uses the similar-sounding *old* for *cold* and the word *She* for a word that sounds like *her: here*. Choice (C) contradicts the meaning of the statement. If it is cold, you turn *on* the heat, not *off*.

39. (C) *He likes to be informed of events* answers *Why does Michael always watch the news*. Choice (A) confuses the similar sounds *knew* and *news*, and *broke* and *break*, and confuses *watch* (n.) and *watch* (v.). Choice (B) repeats the word *always* and confuses similar sounds *breakfast* and *break*.

40. (C) *Yes, that's the sale price you're looking at* answers *Isn't this suit already discounted*. Choice (A) confuses the similar words *suits* (v.) and *suit* (n.). Choice (B) confuses similar sounds *discounts* and *discounted* and *suit* (v.) and *suit* (n.).

PART 3 (PAGE 101)

41. (B) The man says *I have lots of e-mail to answer*. Choice (A) confuses *mailing a letter* with *e-mail*. Choice (C) confuses *answering the phone* with *e-mail to answer*. Choice (D) repeats the word *computer*, but the man is using the computer, not repairing it.

42. (A) The woman says *Let's go eat*. Choice (B) associates *coffee* with *cafeteria*. Choice (C) confuses *go to bed* with the similar-sounding *go ahead*. Choice (D) confuses the word *seat* with the similar-sounding word *eat*.

43. (D) The man says he'll be in the cafeteria in fifteen minutes. Choice (A) is not mentioned. Choice (B) confuses the *teen* of *fifteen* with the similar-sounding word *ten*. Choice (C) confuses *five* with *fifteen*.

44. (C) The speakers mention *overhead compartment, on board, fly,* and *flight,* so they are on a plane. Choice (A) confuses *apartment* with the similar-sounding word *compartment.* Choice (B) associates *office* with *laptop.* Choice (D) associates *hotel* with *nap* and *serve a meal.*

45. (A) The woman says *I'll take a nap.* Choice (B) associates *work* with *laptop.* Choice (C) associates *cook* with *meal.* Choice (D) is not mentioned.

46. (D) The man says that he is hungry. Choice (A) confuses *bored* with *board.* Choice (B) is how the woman feels. Choice (C) confuses *angry* with the similar-sounding word *hungry.*

47. (B) The man is helping a woman who has arrived for an appointment, so he is a receptionist. Choice (A) uses the word *clock* in a different context. Choice (C) is not mentioned. Choice (D) confuses the job of an usher with the man's offer to *have a seat.*

48. (A) The woman says she has an appointment at 1:00. Choice (B) confuses *four* with the similar-sounding word *for.* Choice (C) confuses *eight* with the similar-sounding word *late.* Choice (D) confuses *nine* with the similar-sounding word *kind.*

49. (B) The woman accepts the man's offer to have a seat. Choice (A) confuses *call* with the similar-sounding word *all.* Choice (C) confuses *ball* with the similar-sounding word *all.* Choice (D) repeats the word *appointment,* but the woman never says she wants a new one.

50. (B) Thursday is the day the woman plans to invite people for dinner. Choice (A) confuses *Tuesday* with the similar-sounding word *Thursday.* Choices (C) and (D) are days mentioned by the man.

51. (C) The woman plans to invite neighbors. Choice (A) confuses *business* with the similar-sounding word *busy.* Choice (B) is mentioned by the man. Choice (D) confuses *sisters* with the similar-sounding words *six guests.*

52. (C) The woman says that she is planning for six guests. Choice (A) confuses *two* with the similar-sounding word *to.* Choice (B) confuses *four* with the similar-sounding word *for.* Choice (D) confuses *ten* with the similar-sounding word *then.*

53. (B) The speakers agree to go to the later presentation, which begins at 11:00. Choice (A) is the time of the earlier presentation. Choice (C) uses the word *one* in a different context. Choice (D) is the time their train will leave.

54. (A) It is a cooking demonstration. Choice (B) confuses *books* with the similar-sounding word *cook.* Choice (C) repeats a word mentioned in another part of the conversation. Choice (D) confuses *games* with the similar-sounding word *train.*

55. (B) The man suggests having lunch. Choice (A) is what the woman suggests doing. Choice (C) confuses *watch* with the similar-sounding word *catch.* Choice (D) confuses *look* with the similar-sounding word *cook.*

56. (B) The manager said that the report is due Tuesday. Choice (A) is the day the speakers will work on the report. Choice (C) is the day the speakers thought that the report was due. Choice (D) confuses *Thursday* with the similar-sounding word *Tuesday.*

57. (C) The woman calls it an expense report. Choice (A) confuses *news* with *new.* Choice (B) confuses *management* with *manager.* Choice (D) repeats the word *meeting* in a different context.

58. (D) The man says that he is mad. Choice (A) confuses *sad* with the similar-sounding word *mad.* Choice (B) is not mentioned. Choice (C) confuses *ill* with the similar-sounding word *will.*

59. (A) The speakers mention a *resort, restaurants, pool, beds,* and *fitness room,* so they are in a hotel. Choice (B) repeats the word *restaurant.* Choice (C) associates *beach* with *resort.* Choice (D) associates *apartment building* with *beds, pool,* and *fitness room.*

60. (C) The woman says *And best of all, comfortable beds*. Choices (A), (B), and (D) are things mentioned by the speakers but none is mentioned as the woman's favorite.

61. (D) The man says he plans to spend the day in the fitness room. Choice (A) associates *sleep* with *beds*. Choice (B) associates *eat* with *restaurants*. Choice (C) associates *swim* with *pool*.

62. (B) The woman is shopping for envelopes in a store. Choice (A) confuses *waiting room* with the related word *wait*. Choice (C) associates *post office* with *letter*. Choice (D) associates *library* with *books* by confusing *books* with the similar-sounding word *box*.

63. (C) The woman is shopping for envelopes. Choice (A) confuses *book* with the similar-sounding word *box*. Choice (B) confuses *adhesive tape* with *self-adhesive envelopes*. Choice (D) confuses *letter paper* with *business letter size envelopes*.

64. (A) The man offers to order the kind of envelope that the woman wants. Choice (B) is the kind of envelope that is in the store. Choice (C) is what the woman says she will do. Choice (D) repeats the word *box*.

65. (D) The man says they answered ten phone calls. Choice (A) confuses *two* with *to*. Choice (B) confuses *four* with *for*. Choice (C) is not mentioned.

66. (C) The woman says that she is expecting a package. Choices (A), (B), and (D) are things the man mentioned when describing the work they had already done.

67. (A) The man asks the woman to help him write a report. Choice (B) associates *mail* with *letters*. Choice (C) is confused with the man's mention that his office had been cleaned this morning. Choice (D) repeats the word *computer*.

68. (C) The woman pays with a $100 bill. Choice (A) uses the word *check* in a different context. Choice (B) is the way the woman originally wants to pay.

Choice (D) is mentioned by the man as an acceptable form of payment.

69. (B) The woman is buying shoes. Choice (A) confuses *cards* with *credit cards*. Choice (C) confuses *book* with the similar-sounding word *look*. Choice (D) repeats the word *purse*.

70. (C) The man says that the shoes are $75. Choice (A) confuses $17.50 with the similar-sounding number $75. Choice (B) is the amount of change the man gives the woman. Choice (D) is the size of the bill the woman uses to pay for the shoes.

Part 4 (Page 104)

71. (C) The speaker is the *captain* and mentions *flight, radar, turbulence*, and *seatbelts*. Choice (A) is a different form of transportation. Choice (B) associates *airport* with *airplane*. Choice (D) is a different form of transportation.

72. (A) The speaker says *This is your captain*. Choice (B) associates *tour guide* with what the passengers can see from the plane. Choice (C) associates *weather forecaster* with *turbulence*. Choice (D) associates flying with *passenger*.

73. (D) The speaker says *You can see Mt. Rushmore*. Choice (A) confuses *cemetery* with *Deadwood*. Choice (B) uses *radar* in a different context. Choice (C) confuses *woods* with *Deadwood*.

74. (A) The speaker says *Welcome aboard our Tropical Garden Tour*. Choice (B) associates *forest* with *large tree branches*. Choice (C) associates *museum* with *collection*. Choice (D) associates *flower shop* with *flowers*.

75. (C) The speaker asks participants to *remain seated*. Choice (A) is what the tour guide asks participants not to do. Choice (B) confuses *close* with the similar-sounding *clothes*. Choice (D) associates *flower shop* with *flowers*.

76. (B) The speaker says the first stop is *on your left*. Choice (A) mentions trees in a different context. Choice (C) mentions *tree branches* not *river branches*. Choice (D) confuses *rear* with the similar-sounding *rare*.

77. (D) The speaker mentions a *community clean-up drive*. Choice (A) associates *garbage collectors* with *trash* and *litter*. Choice (B) repeats the word *community*. Choice (C) repeats the words *kids* and *Saturdays*.

78. (C) The speaker says the clean-up *was a dismal failure* and *only 15 people showed up*. Choice (A) is not mentioned in relation to last year's drive. Choice (B) confuses *50* with the similar-sounding *15*. Choice (D) is not correct because the speaker mentions *15 people*.

79. (A) The speaker says *We'll start at ten in the morning*. Choice (B) is when the drive will finish. Choice (C) confuses *three* with the similar-sounding *free*. Choice (D) confuses *three* with the similar-sounding *free* and repeats *15* in a different context.

80. (C) The speaker says that Dr. Jones is a *professor of economics*. Choice (A) is what the announcer is. Choice (B) associates *Dr.* with medicine. Choice (D) associates *farmer* with *agricultural sector*.

81. (B) The speaker says *We will read from your letters*. Choices (A) and (C) are topics the guest will talk about. Choice (D) will be another part of the guest portion of the show.

82. (C) The speaker mentions *the next hour*. Choice (A) is how long the announcer will read letters and e-mails. Choice (B) is how long the guest will be on the show. Choice (D) is not the correct total.

83. (C) The speaker says *Good afternoon, class.* Choice (A) will be next week's special guest. Choice (B) is who will come next week. Choice (D) confuses the speaker with the class.

84. (A) The speaker mentions ancient Chinese history. Choice (B) confuses *art history* with *art*. Choice (C) confuses *writing* with the related word *written*. Choice (D) confuses *travel* with the guest's *trip*.

85. (B) The speaker says they will see slides instead of the video. Choice (A) is not mentioned. Choice (C) is what they were going to do, but the *video* is unavailable. Choice (D) associates *art museum* with *art*.

86. (B) The speaker mentions heavy rains. Choices (A), (C), and (D) are all things that may happen.

87. (C) The speaker mentions problems during the next 24 hours. Choices (A), (B), and (D) are not mentioned.

88. (C) The speaker says to listen for evacuation orders. Choice (A) confuses *vacation orders* with the similar-sounding *evacuation orders*. Choice (B) confuses *train* with the similar-sounding *rain*. Choice (D) is not mentioned.

89. (B) The speaker mentions that the food was paid for thanks to a slight increase in revenue over the past year. Choice (A) is not mentioned. Choice (C) confuses *generosity* with *thanks*. Choice (D) is not mentioned.

90. (A) The speaker mentions that the purpose of the talk is to plan for the future. Choice (B) is not mentioned. Choice (C) is not the main purpose of the speech. Choice (D) is not mentioned.

91. (B) The speaker says in the afternoon they *will meet in groups*. Choice (A) confuses *write new ads* with *radio ads*. Choice (C) confuses *visit customers' homes* with *more door-to-door contact*. Choice (D) is not mentioned.

92. (C) The speaker says *people couldn't stay dry* and *interiors became like ovens*. Choices (A), (B), and (D) are not mentioned.

93. (A) The speaker says *by the end of the year.* Choice (B) is the beginning of another year. Choices (C) and (D) are not mentioned.

94. (D) The speaker mentions special arrangements with a shopping center to use one of their lots. Choices (A), (B), and (C) are not mentioned.

95. (C) The number is *603-555-9000*. Choices (B), (C), and (D) are incorrect.

96. (D) The speaker says *We're real estate investors*. Choice (A) confuses *investment bankers* with *investors*. Choice (B) confuses *real estate company* with *real estate investors*. Choice (C) is what the speaker says they are not.

97. (A) The speaker wants to buy houses from people. Choices (B), (C), and (D) are all people who might want to buy a house, not sell a house.

98. (C) The speaker mentions *frozen food, aisle 10, apples, pears,* and *fresh fruit,* all things in a grocery store. Choice (A) associates *a farm* with *apples, pears, and fresh fruit.* Choice (B) associates *theater* with *cell phone.* Choice (D) associates *cell phone store* with *cell phone.*

99. (D) The speaker mentions ancient Chinese history. Choices (A), (B), and (C) are all mentioned, but they are not the place to claim the lost cell phone.

100. (A) The speaker says *Only customers with a Shoppers' Club card.* Choices (B), (C), and (D) are mentioned, but they are not correct answers.

ANSWER KEY
READING

PART 5—INCOMPLETE SENTENCES

Word Families (page 110)

1.	(A)	6.	(D)
2.	(B)	7.	(C)
3.	(C)	8.	(B)
4.	(C)	9.	(A)
5.	(B)	10.	(C)

Similar Words (page 112)

1.	(C)	6.	(C)
2.	(D)	7.	(B)
3.	(C)	8.	(A)
4.	(B)	9.	(C)
5.	(D)	10.	(D)

Prepositions (page 114)

1.	(B)	6.	(C)
2.	(D)	7.	(A)
3.	(A)	8.	(D)
4.	(B)	9.	(B)
5.	(B)	10.	(A)

Conjunctions (page 116)

1.	(D)	6.	(B)
2.	(A)	7.	(A)
3.	(A)	8.	(C)
4.	(B)	9.	(B)
5.	(A)	10.	(A)

Adverbs of Frequency (page 118)

1.	(D)	6.	(C)
2.	(A)	7.	(A)
3.	(B)	8.	(B)
4.	(B)	9.	(D)
5.	(D)	10.	(C)

Causative Verbs (page 120)

1.	(D)	6.	(A)
2.	(B)	7.	(B)
3.	(C)	8.	(C)
4.	(C)	9.	(B)
5.	(B)	10.	(B)

Conditional Sentences (page 122)

1.	(A)	6.	(C)
2.	(D)	7.	(B)
3.	(B)	8.	(B)
4.	(C)	9.	(A)
5.	(C)	10.	(B)

Verb Tense (page 123)

1.	(B)	6.	(A)
2.	(C)	7.	(C)
3.	(C)	8.	(B)
4.	(D)	9.	(A)
5.	(C)	10.	(C)

Two-Word Verbs (page 125)

1.	(B)	6.	(C)
2.	(C)	7.	(B)
3.	(B)	8.	(A)
4.	(C)	9.	(C)
5.	(B)	10.	(A)

Strategy Practice (page 127)

1.	(C)	11.	(A)
2.	(B)	12.	(D)
3.	(D)	13.	(B)
4.	(C)	14.	(C)
5.	(B)	15.	(D)
6.	(B)	16.	(C)
7.	(A)	17.	(A)
8.	(D)	18.	(B)
9.	(B)	19.	(C)
10.	(C)	20.	(A)

PART 6—TEXT COMPLETION

Words in Context (page 130)

1.	(D)	6.	(A)
2.	(A)	7.	(B)
3.	(B)	8.	(B)
4.	(B)	9.	(D)
5.	(B)	10.	(C)

Pronouns (page 133)

1.	(D)	6.	(A)
2.	(D)	7.	(C)
3.	(C)	8.	(D)
4.	(A)	9.	(C)
5.	(C)	10.	(C)

Subject-Verb Agreement (page 136)

1.	(B)	6.	(C)
2.	(A)	7.	(A)
3.	(A)	8.	(B)
4.	(D)	9.	(A)
5.	(A)	10.	(B)

Modal Auxiliaries (page 139)

1.	(D)	6.	(B)
2.	(B)	7.	(B)
3.	(A)	8.	(A)
4.	(C)	9.	(D)
5.	(D)	10.	(A)

Adjective Comparisons (page 142)

1.	(B)	6.	(D)
2.	(D)	7.	(B)
3.	(A)	8.	(B)
4.	(B)	9.	(B)
5.	(C)	10.	(D)

Gerunds or Infinitives (page 144)

1.	(B)	6.	(A)
2.	(A)	7.	(B)
3.	(D)	8.	(A)
4.	(B)	9.	(D)
5.	(A)	10.	(C)

Strategy Practice (page 147)

1.	(A)	7.	(C)
2.	(D)	8.	(B)
3.	(A)	9.	(D)
4.	(C)	10.	(A)
5.	(A)	11.	(B)
6.	(D)	12.	(C)

PART 7—READING COMPREHENSION (PAGE 153)

1.	(B)	24.	(B)
2.	(D)	25.	(C)
3.	(A)	26.	(D)
4.	(D)	27.	(D)
5.	(C)	28.	(D)
6.	(C)	29.	(C)
7.	(D)	30.	(B)
8.	(A)	31.	(A)
9.	(A)	32.	(D)
10.	(C)	33.	(D)
11.	(C)	34.	(A)
12.	(B)	35.	(B)
13.	(B)	36.	(D)
14.	(D)	37.	(D)
15.	(B)	38.	(B)
16.	(D)	39.	(B)
17.	(B)	40.	(B)
18.	(C)	41.	(C)
19.	(D)	42.	(C)
20.	(B)	43.	(A)
21.	(B)	44.	(D)
22.	(B)	45.	(B)
23.	(C)		

Strategy Practice (page 169)
Single Passages

1.	(D)	11.	(A)
2.	(B)	12.	(C)
3.	(A)	13.	(C)
4.	(C)	14.	(A)
5.	(C)	15.	(D)
6.	(A)	16.	(B)
7.	(B)	17.	(D)
8.	(A)	18.	(C)
9.	(D)	19.	(D)
10.	(B)	20.	(A)

Double Passages

21.	(C)	26.	(A)
22.	(C)	27.	(A)
23.	(A)	28.	(C)
24.	(D)	29.	(D)
25.	(A)	30.	(C)

ANSWER KEY READING REVIEW

PART 5 (PAGE 180)

101. (D) A past participle is required after *were* to make the passive voice: *were organized.* Choices (A) and (B) are nouns. Choice (C) is the base verb form.

102. (C) A past participle adjective describes the noun *sales plan.* Choice (A) is the base verb form. Choice (B) is the simple present. Choice (D) is the present participle.

103. (B) The subordinate conjunction *because* is needed to explain why the action was taken. Choice (A) goes with the other clause: *There were many customer complaints; therefore, we withdrew the item from the market.* Choice (C) is contrary to the idea. Choice (D) doesn't make sense in this context.

104. (A) A past participle is required after *is* to make the passive voice: *is respected.* Choice (B) is the simple present. Choice (C) is the base verb form. Choice (D) is the present participle.

105. (C) *Increased,* which means "made more or longer" in this case, is the only idea that is logical for this sentence. Choice (A), *insisted,* means "demanded" or "required." Choice (B), *installed,* means "put in place." Choice (D), *intruded,* means "put or forced in without being asked or wanted."

106. (B) A noun used as an adjective, *sales,* is required to explain what the report is about. Choice (A) is a present participle. Choice (C) is the base verb form. Choice (D) is the simple present.

107. (B) A singular noun is required because of the article *a.* Choice (A) is a gerund but has a different meaning. Choice (C) is a plural noun. Choice (D) is the simple past.

108. (C) *At* is the preposition used when specifying an exact time. Choices (A) and (B) are prepositions that are not used with time phrases containing hours and minutes. Choice (D) is used with nouns that represent a period of time: *the winter, the war, the meeting.*

109. (A) *Instructions,* which means "how to do something," is the only noun that is logical for this sentence. Choice (B), *delays,* means "postponements." Choice (C), *reservations,* means "something to be set aside for future use." Choice (D), *adjustments,* means "changes made to correct something."

110. (C) A past participle is required here. It represents a reduced passive voice: *any other project that has been undertaken.* Choice (A) is a present participle. Choice (B) is the simple past. Choice (D) is the base verb form.

111. (A) An adverb is required to describe the adjective *changing.* Choice (B) is a gerund. Choice (C) is the simple present. Choice (D) is the simple past.

112. (C) The preposition *beyond* is the only one that is logical in this sentence. In this case it means "more/greater than." Choice (A), *outside,* means "not related to" in this context. Choice (B), *inside,* means "agrees with" in this context. Choice (D), *before,* is not logical in this idea.

113. (A) An adjective is required to describe the noun *demands.* Choice (B) is an adverb. Choice (C) is a noun. Choice (D) is a gerund.

114. (D) The noun which means "the people who plan something " is required as the subject in this sentence. Choice (A) is the noun for things. Choice (B) is the present participle. Choice (C) is the simple past.

115. (B) The third person singular, masculine possessive adjective is required. Choice (A) is the direct object form. Choice (C) is the subject form. Choice (D) is the reflexive pronoun.

116. (A) *Indications,* which means "things that show you something," is the only logical idea for this sentence. Choice (B), *solutions,* means "ways to solve a problem." Choice (C), *proposals,* means "suggestions." Choice (D), *revisions,* means "changes to improve something."

117. (D) *Enter,* which means "putting information into a computer," is the only logical idea for this sentence. Choice (A), *submerge,* means "to put or go under water." Choice (B), *propose,* means "to suggest." Choice (C), *admit,* means "to allow to enter or pass."

118. (C) The subordinate conjunction *although* is required to introduce this clause. It means that what follows is contrary to a logical conclusion. Choices (A) and (D), which carry the idea of *but,* would work at the beginning of the second clause. Choice (B) is illogical in this context.

119. (A) When negative adverbs of frequency are used at the beginning of a sentence, there is a word inversion that looks like a question form: *Never have the employees complained . . .* Choices (B), (C), and (D) are not negatives and are also illogical for this idea.

120. (D) The preposition *from* explains where these people are originating. Choices (A), (B), and (C) are not logical prepositions for describing these people.

121. (B) An adverb is required to describe how the crew worked. Choice (A) is an adjective. Choice (C) is a noun or verb. Choice (D) is a comparative adjective phrase.

122. (C) An adjective is required to describe the noun phrase *job performance.* Choice (A) is a preposition. Choice (B) is a noun. Choice (D) is an adverb.

123. (B) A noun is required after the definite article *the.* In this case we need the noun that means "the event." Choice (A) is the simple past. Choice (C) is the noun for a person. Choice (D) is the simple present.

124. (A) The expression *to have a clue* means "to understand" or "to have an idea about something." Choices (B), (C), and (D) carry the basic idea needed but are not used in this expression.

125. (C) The preposition *without* is required with the noun phrase *a good credit history.* Choices (A) and (D) are illogical in this idea. Choice (B) is a conjunction.

126. (C) A verb is required after the subject of the sentence. Choices (A) and (D) are nouns. Choice (B) is the present participle.

127. (A) The reflexive pronoun is used here to show that the subject does the action alone. Choice (B) is a subject pronoun. Choice (C) is an object pronoun. Choice (D) is a possessive pronoun.

128. (D) *Minimize,* which means "to make as little or small as possible," is the only verb that is logical in this sentence. Choice (A), *criticize,* means "to judge the good or bad points of something." Choice (B), *localize,* means "to restrict to a particular area." Choice (C), *sanitize,* means "to make clean and hygienic."

129. (C) *Impatient,* which means "not willing to wait," is the only adjective that is logical in this sentence. Choice (A), *evident,* means "obvious, clear." Choice (B), *extraordinary,* means "more than usual, special." Choice (D), *inconclusive,* means "not completely sure or proven."

130. (C) A noun is required before the verb *broke down.* Choice (A) is an adjective. Choice (B) is the simple past. Choice (D) is the base verb form.

131. (D) The pronoun *what*, which means "the particular thing that . . . ," is required as the subject. Choice (A) is a pronoun but means something already indicated, so it doesn't work here. Choice (B) is a pronoun but means a particular thing in a selection, so it doesn't work here. Choice (C) is a pronoun referring to people, so it doesn't work here.

132. (A) *Proposed*, which means "suggested" or "asked to be considered," is the only one of these past participles that is logical for the idea of this sentence. Choice (B), *propelled*, means "caused to be set in motion." Choice (C), *preferred*, means "liked the most." Choice (D), *preordained*, means "made to be someone's fate or destiny."

133. (B) The subject of this sentence must be a noun. Choice (A) is an adjective. Choice (C) is both the simple past and the past participle adjective. Choice (D) is the present participle.

134. (A) *Refrain*, which means "to keep or stop from doing something," is the only logical idea for this sentence. Choice (B), *respect*, means "to have high regard or esteem for." Choice (C), *reserve*, means "to keep for a special use." Choice (D), *restore*, means "to bring back to the original condition."

135. (C) The present participle, or –*ing*, adjective is required to describe *the news*. Use this adjective form when the person or thing described is creating the feeling. Choice (A) is the base verb form. Choice (B) is the simple past or past participle adjective. Choice (D) is the simple present.

136. (D) *Inadequate*, which means "insufficient" or "not enough," is the only adjective that is logical to complete the idea of this sentence. Choice (A), *improper*, means "not correct or appropriate." Choice (B), *unlikely*, means "improbable." Choice (C), *unlucky*, means "not having luck."

137. (B) *Attitude*, which means "a state of mind" or "feeling," is the only noun that is logical to complete the idea of this

sentence. Choice (A), *alteration*, means "a change, making something different." Choice (C), *anxiety*, means "a state of uneasiness and worry." Choice (D), *ambivalence*, means "feeling two different ways about something or somebody at the same time."

138. (C) The construction *so . . . that . . .* quantifies how something was. *So* is always followed by an adjective or adverb. Choice (A) has the same construction, *such . . . that . . .* , but *such* is followed by a noun phrase: *such a hot day; such a well-written report*. Choices (B) and (D) are not logical for the idea of this sentence.

139. (D) A noun for a thing must be used as the subject of this sentence. Choice (A) is a noun but means the person. Choice (B) is the base verb form. Choice (C) is an adjective.

140. (C) *Therefore* is a conjunction meaning "because of what I have just said" or "for this reason." Choices (A), (B), and (D) are conjunctions but are not logical for the idea of this sentence.

PART 6 (PAGE 185)

141. (C) We know that the writer is currently at his new job because of the use of the present perfect tense in the first sentence: *My first week . . . has been very good.* Therefore, the present progressive form *am enjoying* is correct. Choice (A) is simple past. Choice (B) is future. Choice (D) is past progressive.

142. (A) *First* introduces the first problem that the writer mentions. Choices (B), (C), and (D) are words to introduce items that follow the first item on a list.

143. (B) The adverb *slowly* describes how the computer works. Choice (A) is an adjective. Choice (C) is a comparative adjective. Choice (D) is a noun.

144. (B) *In* is the correct preposition to use with *the afternoon*. Choices (A), (C), and (D) cannot be used with this phrase.

145. (B) This announcement is about helping *people who have suffered* during a disaster,

in other words, *victims*. Choice (A) means "people who watch something." Choice (C) means "people who plan something." Choice (D) means "people who tell about what happened."

146. (D) A noun is needed here as an object of the verb *lost*. Choice (A) is a present tense verb. Choice (B) is a past tense verb. Choice (C) is a present participle.

147. (D) The announcement asks people to give money, or a *donation*, to help the flood victims. Choices (A), (B), and (C) are things one could *make*, but they do not fit the context.

148. (C) From the context of the announcement, we know that people in the office will continue to collect money until Friday, and then they *will send* it, that is, in the future. Choice (A) is the base verb form. Choice (B) is past tense. Choice (D) is a future idea, but it means "maybe."

149. (D) Mr. Miser's prices are compared to all the other prices in town, so the superlative form of the adjective is required here. Choice (A) is a simple adjective form. Choice (B) is a comparative adjective. Choice (C) looks like a comparative adjective but is actually a present tense verb.

150. (C) This part of the ad talks about the *places*, or *locations*, where you can find Mr. Miser's agencies. Choices (A), (B), and (D) mention other aspects of Mr. Miser's car rental business.

151. (C) Adverbs of frequency follow the verb *to be*. Choices (A), (B), and (D) do not have correct word order.

152. (A) This is an imperative sentence, which uses the base form of the verb. Choice (B) is the simple tense. Choice (C) is the present participle. Choice (D) is the future.

PART 7 (PAGE 189)

153. (B) *Professionals* is the correct answer because all the specific information given is about professionals. Choice (A) associates *laborers* with work. Choice (C) is incorrect because the information is specifically about professional workers. Choice (D) is the people who did the study.

154. (A) The report states that *Ten years ago, most professional people worked 40 hours a week or less*, so the correct answer is *40 or less*. Choices (B), (C), and (D) confuse other numbers in the report.

155. (B) The numbers were released last week, so the correct answer is *7 days ago*. Choice (A) is not mentioned. Choices (C) and (D) confuse other times mentioned in the report.

156. (C) *100* is the correct answer. Choices (A), (B), and (D) are the number of liters sold in other months.

157. (C) *May* is the correct answer. Choices (A), (B), and (D) are amounts of ice cream during other months.

158. (B) *February* is the correct answer. Ike sold only 90 liters of ice cream during that month, but he sold larger amounts during all the other months. Choices (A), (C), and (D) are other months on the graph.

159. (C) The graph covers the six months from January through June, so the correct answer is *half a year*. Choices (A), (B), and (D) are incorrect.

160. (A) In the first sentence of the letter, Charles Chung states *I am interested in working at the Worldwide Travel Agency*, so *He wants a job* is the correct answer. Choice (B) confuses *experience working with computers* with wanting to buy a computer. Choice (C) associates the travel agency with taking a trip. Choice

(D) confuses *enclosing my résumé* with writing a résumé.

161. (D) The letter states *I have five years' experience as a travel agent*, so the correct answer is *He worked as a travel agent*. Choice (A) is incorrect because we don't know how long he studied computers. Choice (B) is incorrect because he wants to work with Ms. Greene in the future, but he hasn't worked with her yet. Choice (C) associates the travel agency with traveling.

162. (C) The announcement says *Our new address, starting April 12*, so the correct answer is *April 12*. Choices (A), (B), and (D) confuse 12 with similar-looking numbers.

163. (A) *On Oakland Avenue* is the correct answer. Choice (B) confuses the street address with the suite number. Choice (C) is a nearby street. Choice (D) confuses *across the street from a bank* with *next to a bank*.

164. (C) The announcement says *Our phone number will stay the same*, so the correct answer is *the telephone number*. Choices (A), (B), and (D) are all things that will change.

165. (B) *Three hours* is the correct answer. Choices (A) and (C) confuse other periods of time mentioned in the article. Choice (D) is the length of the trip on the regular train.

166. (C) *Four* is the correct answer. Choices (A), (B), and (D) confuse other numbers mentioned in the article.

167. (B) The article states *Many people will prefer the regular trains because the tickets are cheaper*, so *The tickets are less expensive* is the correct answer. Choices (A), (C), and (D) mention things that are true about the express trains, not the regular trains.

168. (C) The train will start operating between the two cities. The other options do not fit the context.

169. (A) The business sells fruit and meat by the kilo and cookies by the bag, which are things sold at *a grocery store*. Choice

(B) associates the name of the market *ABC* with *school*. Choice (C) associates food with *restaurant*. Choice (D) associates *cookies* with *bakery*.

170. (C) The sale is *this weekend only*, so the correct answer is *Saturday and Sunday*. Choices (A), (B), and (D) confuse the days the store is open.

171. (C) Fresh produce is produce that has just been picked. The other options do not fit the context.

172. (B) *$2.50 a bag* is the correct answer. Choices (A) and (C) are not mentioned. Choice (D) is incorrect because a customer has to pay for two bags before getting one bag for free.

173. (D) *45%* chose soccer as their favorite sport. Choices (A), (B), and (C) have lower percentages.

174. (B) *20%* prefer basketball. Choices (A), (C), and (D) match other sports on the chart.

175. (C) This is a form for subscribing to something that will arrive in your home monthly, so the correct answer is *a magazine*. Choices (A), (B), and (D) are things that one does not normally subscribe to.

176. (B) Helena Bishop is ordering a one-year subscription. The cost for one year is *$45*. Choice (A) is the cost for six months. Choice (C) is the cost for two years. Choice (D) is not mentioned.

177. (C) Helena marked *credit card* on the form, so the correct answer is *credit card*. Choices (A), (B), and (D) are methods she did not choose.

178. (D) Employees who wish to smoke must go outdoors but not near the main entrance. Choice (A) associates *picnic area* with *outdoors*. Choices (B) and (C) are not mentioned.

179. (B) Employees who smoke feel like they are being treated like second-class citizens. Choice (A) is not mentioned. Choice (C) is incorrect because there is no employee lounge; it is something that's being suggested. Choice (D) confuses *the*

weather making it hard to work and *having to smoke outdoors in the bad weather.*

180. (B) Ms. Dunnaway is requesting a meeting with Ms. Fagan for the employees who smoke. Choice (A) confuses the request and Ms. Fagan's decision to make the mill off limits to smokers. Choice (C) is incorrect because she suggests one employee lounge in her letter. Choice (D) is incorrect because the location of the meeting is not mentioned.

181. (D) The e-mail reports that the location of the meeting was changed to the lounge. Choice (A) was the original location of the meeting. Choice (B) is not mentioned. Choice (C) is confused with the agenda item about conference plans.

182. (C) The e-mail says that the third item on the agenda was discussed first. By looking at the agenda, we see the *new hiring policy* is the third item. Choices (A), (B), and (D) are the other agenda items.

183. (A) The e-mail, which is sent to Sam Blair, states that *everyone was there, except you.* Choice (B) wrote the e-mail. Choices (C) and (D) are names mentioned on the meeting agenda who attended the meeting.

184. (D) According to the agenda, the meeting was planned to start at 4:00. The e-mail says that the meeting started on time and lasted two and a half hours. Therefore, it ended at 6:30. Choices (A), (B), and (C) are not correct times.

185. (D) The e-mail says that next month's meeting will be held on the 18th. We see on the agenda that this month is April, so the next meeting will take place on May 18th. Choices (A), (B), and (C) are not correct.

186. (D) The schedule lists Monday–Wednesday classes, Tuesday–Thursday classes, and one Saturday class. That adds up to five days. Choices (A), (B), and (C) are not correct.

187. (B) The instructions following the class schedule say to mail a completed registration form to the school. Choices (A), (C), and (D) are not mentioned.

188. (A) Elizabeth's class begins at 6:00, and she says that that gives her half an hour to get there after leaving work, so she leaves work at 5:30. Choices (B), (C), and (D) are not correct.

189. (D) Elizabeth says that she wants to take a word processing class that begins at 7:30 on Tuesdays and Thursdays. By looking at the schedule we see that the only word processing class at that time is Level IV. Choices (A), (B), and (C) are not correct.

190. (D) Elizabeth mentions two classes that she wants to take. By looking at the schedule, we see that each class costs $275, making the total cost for two classes $550. Choices (A), (B), and (C) are not correct.

191. (A) Although the memo says that both conference rooms need painting, it only mentions one that will actually be painted now. Choice (B) is the number of conference rooms that need painting. Choices (C) and (D) are other rooms mentioned in the memo and e-mail.

192. (A) The memo states that the painting *should take no more than two days.* Choices (B), (C), and (D) are not correct.

193. (D) In the e-mail, George explains why he needs to use the conference room and then asks the question *Would it be possible to schedule the painting so that it begins on Wednesday or Thursday?* Choice (A) is confused with George wanting to use the conference room for a meeting. Choice (B) is confused with George's mention of his office. Choice (C) is confused with George's explanation of why he can't use other rooms.

194. (A) In his e-mail George says that his meeting is planned for *the day painting begins.* We know from the first memo that the painting will begin on Tuesday. Choices (B) and (C) are the days George suggests that the painting begin. Choice (D) is confused with *Conference Room 2 is already booked through Friday.*

195. (C) In his e-mail George says the *meeting place you suggest is too informal*. By looking at the first memo, we see that Luis suggests using the cafeteria for meetings while the conference room is being painted. Choices (A), (B), and (D) are places mentioned in the memo and e-mail, but they are not the correct answers.

196. (B) The ad gives Ms. Kovacs' title as *Director of Human Resources*. Choice (A) is the title of the advertised position. Choice (C) is confused with the *team of market researchers*. Choice (D) is confused with Ms. Choi's psychology degree.

197. (D) The letter states that *the position that we advertised has already been filled.* Choice (A) is not correct because we can tell that Ms. Kovacs has read the résumé by her knowledge of Ms. Choi's background. There is nothing to indicate that choice (B) is true. Choice (C) is not true because Ms. Kovacs points out several qualifications in the letter.

198. (C) The letter states *you have the educational level we require*. By looking at the ad, we see that the required educational level is a Master's in Business Administration. Choice (A) is confused with Ms. Choi's *Bachelor's* degree in Psychology. Choice (B) is confused with the business degree and the title of the position *associate* researcher. Choice (D) is confused with the *Master's* degree in Business Administration.

199. (D) The letter states that Ms. Choi has *more years of experience in the field than we asked for*, and we see in the ad that three to five years are required. Choices (A), (B), and (C) are confused with the actual number of years required.

200. (B) At the end of the letter Ms. Kovacs suggests that Ms. Choi call her in six months. Choices (A), (C), and (D) are confused with other things mentioned in the letter.

ANSWER KEY
PRACTICE TEST ONE

PART 1 (PAGE 210)

1. (B) The cars are on the road. Choice (A) tries to confuse you by using the similar-sounding word *carts* for *cars*. Choice (C) provides incorrect details: The drivers are inside driving the cars, they're not by the car. Choice (D) tries to confuse you by using the similar-sounding *cards* for *cars*.

2. (A) We can assume the men in uniform are the ship's officers and they are on the boat. Choice (B) tries to confuse you by using the similar-sounding word *sheep* for *ship*. Choice (C) tries to confuse you by using the similar-sounding word *sheets* for *ship* and by confusing *sale* for *sail*.

3. (A) The woman is talking on the phone. Choice (B) provides incorrect details: An *open book* is on the table, but there is no *open drawer*. Choice (C) provides incorrect details: She has a *pen in her hand* and an open *book in front of her,* but she is not *writing* in it. Choice (D) provides incorrect details: There is a keyboard in the background, but she is not using it.

4. (B) The kitchen workers are preparing trays of food. Choice (A) tries to confuse you by using the related word *lunch.* Choice (C) tries to confuse you by using the related word *kitchen.* Choice (D) incorrectly infers the women are doctors.

5. (D) The men are digging a hole in the ground. Choice (A) provides incorrect details: They're *standing,* not *sitting.* Choice (B) provides incorrect details: They're *digging near the fence,* not *climbing the fence.* Choice (C) incorrectly infers they're *admiring the garden,* but they're *digging in the garden.*

6. (D) The man is drinking from a teacup. Choice (A) provides incorrect details: He is *holding a cup,* not *holding his head.* Choice (B) provides incorrect details: He is *wearing glasses,* not *covering his glasses.* Choice (C) provides incorrect details: There are napkins on the table, but he is not using them.

7. (B) The three men are talking to a female colleague. Choice (A) provides incorrect details: The office is small and cramped. Choice (C) provides incorrect details: The men are *looking at the woman,* not a *computer game.* Choice (D) tries to confuse you by using the similar-sounding word *headquarters* for *heads.*

8. (A) The men are all wearing hard hats. Choice (B) incorrectly infers the men are in a chorus: The men are *reading plans,* not *reading music.* Choice (C) tries to confuse you by using the related words *crew* and *uniforms.* Choice (D) incorrectly infers the men are recruits. Incorrect details are provided: The men are *wearing ties,* not *changing ties.*

9. (D) The man is checking into a hotel. Choice (A) tries to confuse you by using the related words *checking* and *counter.* Incorrect details are provided: There are no *bags* in the picture. Choice (B) provides incorrect details: The man is not looking at the art on the walls. Choice (C) tries to confuse you by using related words *elevator* and *room.*

10. (B) The woman is faxing a document. Choice (A) provides incorrect details: the woman's *hair covers her face,* but the woman is not *covering her face.* Choice (C) confuses *photocopy machine* for *fax machine.* Choice (D) provides incorrect details: She's *putting the document in the document feeder,* not *holding open a door.*

PART 2 (PAGE 216)

11. (B) *At 12:30* answers *when.* Choice (A) associates *airport* with *fight* and answers *where.* Choice (C) associates *Gate* with *flight* but answers *where.*

12. (A) *I've got it [the fax] right here* answers *have we received the fax?* Choice (B) *In about an hour* answers *when.* Choice (C) repeats the word *fax* but answers *when will you fax it?*

13. (C) *How do you do* answers the question. Choice (A) confuses similar sounds *mistake* and *Ms. Pak.* Choice (B) answers *what do you do.*

14. (C) *Yes, [it is time for our meeting] but it's been rescheduled* answers the question. Choice (A) confuses similar sounds *meat* and *meeting.* Choice (B) answers *when is our meeting.*

15. (B) *I've seen him smiling* answers the *yes/no* question by associating *smiling* with *being in a good mood.* Choice (A) answers *has the boss left.* Choice (C) answers *where.*

16. (C) *You should get more sleep* responds to the statement *I'm extremely tired.* Choice (A) repeats the word *extreme.* Choice (B) uses the similar-sounding word *fire* for *tired.*

17. (C) *That's what I've been told* answers the *yes/no* question by confirming the man heard the Tokyo office would be opened. Choice (A) uses the word *open* but answers with the hours of operation. Choice (B) repeats the word *office* but answers *where are you going.*

18. (B) *We're still waiting* answers *why.* Choice (A) associates *meeting* with *conference* but answers *where.* Choice (C) answers *when.*

19. (B) *The new secretary* answers *Who are you.* Choice (A) answers *how are you.* Choice (C) answers *where are you.*

20. (A) *Ms. Hoffman's* answers *whose computer.* Choice (B) answers *which.* Choice (C) answers *can I use it.*

21. (B) *So call a plumber* identifies the occupation of the person who can fix a *dripping faucet.* Choice (A) repeats the word *drive* but not in the idiomatic sense of being *driven crazy.* Choice (C) uses the similar-sounding word *tripped* for *dripping.*

22. (A) *There was a lot of traffic* is a reason for being late. Choice (B) answers *will you be late.* Choice (C) confuses similar sounds *ate* and *late* and the opposites *quickly* and *late.*

23. (B) *Yes, I sent the invitations yesterday* answers the *yes/no* question and provides the day they were sent. Choice (A) is a possible response to an invitation. Choice (C) repeats the word *remember* and *every[body]* but does not answer the question.

24. (A) *Yes, they've all gone out* answers the *yes/no* question. Choice (B) associates *sales* with *ads.* Choice (C) repeats the word *newspaper* and answers *did you pick up the newspaper.*

25. (B) *They're going now* answers *when will the auditors be leaving.* Choice (A) answers *when did they leave.* Choice (C) answers *how long have they been here.*

26. (C) is an affirmative response to the suggestion. Choice (A) confuses *break* (chip or crack) with *break* (rest from work or activity). Choice (B) confuses *break* (not working) with *break* (rest from work or activity).

27. (A) *There were a lot of errors in it* responds to the opinion about the *article being poorly written.* Choice (B) uses the word *rich* for its opposite *poor.* However, in this context *poorly* means *not well.* This choice also uses the similar-sounding word *riding* for *written.* Choice (C) uses the similar-sounding word *art* for *article* and repeats the word *poor.*

28. (A) *Canada* answers *Where do you come from?* Choice (B) answers *where did you come from* specifically within the building. Choice (C) answers *when.*

29. (B) *I'd like to* answers the invitation. Choice (A) *The employee cafeteria's downstairs* answers *where should we eat.* Choice (C) associates the meals *breakfast* with *lunch.*

30. (B) *You have the map upside down* is a possible reason that the *street plan* is *confusing.* Choice (A) repeats a form of the verb *find, found.* Choice (C) repeats

the word *plan* and the associated phrase *to look for* for something you want to *find*.

31. (B) *Not at all* is a polite response to the question. Choices (A) and (C) are not appropriate responses to the question.

32. (A) *About 12 hours* answers *how long*. Choice (B) answers *how far*. Choice (C) associates *Egypt* with *Cairo* and answers *where*.

33. (C) *The boss asked me to* answers *Who are you sending that e-mail for*. Choice (A) answers *who asked you to send the e-mail*. Choice (B) answers *who are you sending the e-mail to*.

34. (B) *My new client* answers *who*. Choice (A) answers *where are you sending the e-mail from*. Choice (C) associates *stamps* with *e-mail*.

35. (B) *Yes, that's what the boss said* answers the yes/no question. Choice (A) answers *will stocks go up next year*. Choice (C) repeats the phrase *next year*.

36. (C) *You're right. I work too hard* responds to the opinion *You should take a vacation*. Choice (A) repeats the words *I take* and tries to confuse you with the similar-sounding word *transportation* for *vacation*. Choice (B) uses a form of the verb *take* and the similar-sounding word *station* for *vacation*.

37. (C) *Working overtime shouldn't be a problem*. Choice (A) answers *when the man can start work* but not if he *can stay and work overtime*. Choice (B) repeats the word *put* but is in a different context.

38. (C) *About 30 kilometers* answers *how much farther*. Choice (A) answers *how much longer*. Choice (B) answers *how much does it cost*.

39. (B) *I have to think about it some more* is an appropriate response to the question. Choice (A) confuses *vacation* with *transfer*. Choice (C) is a yes/no response but does not fit the context.

40. (A) *Yes, if you give us your receipts* answers *will I be reimbursed*. Choice (B) repeats the words *business trips* and confuses similar sounds *expensive* with *expenses*.

PART 3 (PAGE 217)

41. (C) The man says *back here in the office*. Choice (A) associates *mail* with *post office*. Choice (B) confuses a *park* with *Mr. Park*. Choice (D) is where the woman is going.

42. (D) The man says he mailed the contracts *this morning*. Choice (A) confuses you with *early next week*, which is when the woman will return. Choice (B) repeats the word *morning*. Choice (C) is not mentioned.

43. (C) The woman says it's *11 o'clock already*. Choices (A) and (B) confuse *11* with the similar-sounding number *7*. Choice (D) repeats the number *11*.

44. (D) The man wants to take the advanced-level class. Choices (A), (B), and (C) repeat other words mentioned in the conversation but are not correct answers.

45. (C) The woman says the tuition is *$500*. Choice (A) confuses *90* with the similar-sounding word *fine*. Choice (B) confuses *$400* with the similar-sounding word *for*. Choice (D) confuses *$600* with *six-month*.

46. (A) The man will *register for a morning class*. Choices (B) and (C) confuses you with the similar-sounding word *noon*. Choice (D) is not mentioned.

47. (C) The man says *He'll be here tomorrow morning*. Choice (A) is when the woman thought Mr. Katz would arrive. Choices (B) and (D) are not mentioned.

48. (A) The woman heard about that *terrible rainstorm*. Choices (B) and (C) are other types of weather mentioned by the speakers. Choice (D) confuses *nice* with the similar-sounding word *ice*.

49. (B) The woman says she heard about the storm *on the radio news*. Choice (A) repeats a name mentioned elsewhere in the conversation. Choice (C) confuses *newspaper* with *news*. Choice (D) is not mentioned.

50. (D) is the correct answer. Choice (A) is the place the speakers consider but reject. Choice (B) repeats the name of the party honoree, but the party will not be held in his office. Choice (C) repeats the word *party*.

51. (C) is the correct number of guests. Choices (A), (B), and (D) confuse the correct answer with other similar-sounding numbers.

52. (D) The woman says the party will be on Friday. Choice (A) confuses *Tuesday* with *two days away*. Choice (B) confuses *Wednesday* with *What day?* Choice (C) is not mentioned.

53. (A) The speakers are talking about *a table*, the woman says they *are starving*, and the man mentions *good food*, so they are in a restaurant. Choices (B), (C), and (D) are places where people might have to wait and might need reservations.

54. (D) is the amount of time mentioned by the man. Choices (A) and (C) confuse the correct answer with other similar-sounding numbers. Choice (B) confuses *ten* with the similar-sounding word *then*.

55. (C) The man says *You could try that place around the corner.* Choices (A) and (B) repeat other words mentioned in the conversation. Choice (D) is not mentioned.

56. (B) The man says that *Mr. Curtis is out of town on business.* Choice (A) confuses *busy* with the similar-sounding word *business*. Choice (C) confuses *downtown* with *out of town*. Choice (D) associates *calling*, which is what the woman is doing, with *phone*.

57. (C) is what the woman says she will do. Choice (A) is what the man suggests she do. Choice (B) repeats the word *return*. Choice (D) repeats the word *call*.

58. (A) The woman says she'd like him *to look at some contracts.* Choice (B) confuses *book* with the similar-sounding word *look*. Choice (C) confuses *bank* with the similar-sounding word *thank*. Choice (D) confuses *a boat* with the similar-sounding word *about*.

59. (D) Mr. Cho retired. Choice (A) confuses *tired* with the similar-sounding word *retired*. Choice (B) repeats the word *vacation*, which refers to Ms. Green, not Mr. Cho. Choice (C) confuses *fired* with the similar-sounding word *retired*.

60. (D) Last month is when Mr. Cho retired. Choices (A) and (B) confuse *two days* and *Tuesday* with the similar-sounding word *today*. Choice (C) repeats the word *week*.

61. (A) The woman says that without Mr. Cho, *there's no one here to tell us jokes.* Choice (B) confuses *worked hard* with *It's hard to work*. Choice (C) confuses *clean* with the similar-sounding word *Green*. Choice (D) is incorrect because it is Ms. Green, not Mr. Cho, who brings cookies.

62. (A) The woman says they have been waiting for *half an hour.* Choice (B) repeats the word *hour*. Choice (C) confuses *8* with the similar-sounding word *late*. Choice (D) confuses *9* with the similar-sounding word *time*.

63. (C) The man tells us that Janet *planned to stop at the store.* Choice (A) was Janet's reason for being late last time. Choice (B) repeats the words *work* and *late* in a different context. Choice (D) confuses *exercise* with the similar-sounding word *excuse*.

64. (B) The man says *It's really annoying.* Choice (A) confuses *happy* with the similar-sounding word *happened*. Choice (C) confuses *sad* with the similar-sounding word *mad*. Choice (D) repeats the word *relax* out of context.

65. (A) The speakers are discussing a hotel reservation and the woman says *I don't see anything here under your name.* Choices (B), (C), and (D) are not mentioned.

66. (C) The man says *I need one for three days.* Choice (A) repeats the word *one* out of context. Choice (B) is not mentioned. Choice (D) confuses *four* with the word *for*.

67. (D) *$165* is the price the woman mentions. Choices (A), (B), and (C) confuse similar-sounding numbers with the correct answer.

68. (A) The woman mentions Carl's promotion. Choice (B) repeats the word *house*, but it is the speaker's house that is mentioned, not Carl's. Choice (C) associates *got married* with *wife*. Choice

(D) repeats the word *office*, but nothing is mentioned about Carl painting an office.

69. (B) The man says that he is *happy* for Carl. Choice (A) confuses *unhappy* with *happy*. Choice (C) confuses *fearful* with the similar-sounding word *feel*. Choice (D) confuses *mad* with the similar-sounding word *bad*.

70. (D) The man suggests having a party. (A) Carl's wife is mentioned in the conversation, but nothing is said about meeting her. (B) The office staff is mentioned, but leaving the office isn't. (C) It is the speaker's house that is mentioned, not Carl's.

Part 4 (page 220)

71. (D) A smoker started the fire. Choice (A) associates *park ranger* with *park*. Choices (B) and (C) are mentioned in the talk but not as people responsible for the fire.

72. (A) The fire destroyed campgrounds in the park. Choice (B), *houses*, are mentioned as threatened by the fire but not destroyed. (C) The smoker's *car* is mentioned, but it wasn't destroyed. Choice (D), *a town*, White River, is mentioned as being close to the fire, but not destroyed.

73. (C) They expect the fire to be completely put out by today. Choice (A) is the day people had to flee their homes. Choice (B) is the day the fire was 75 percent under control. Choice (D) confuses *two days* with the similar-sounding word *today*.

74. (D) It is a place that provides *medical care*, so it is a *hospital*. Choices (A) and (B) are other types of places where people can receive services. Choice (C) is confused with the former name of the place *Villa Hospitalis*.

75. (A) The hospital provides care for *low-income* and *indigent people*. These are poor people. Choices (B) and (C) do not fall into the low-income or indigent category. Choice (D) is not mentioned.

76. (C) They are changing the name because they would like to have a separate

identity. Choice (A) is not correct because the new name is longer than the old one. Choice (B) may be true but is not the reason for the name change. Choice (D) is not mentioned.

77. (A) The restaurant specializes in seafood. Choices (B), (C), and (D) are dishes served at the restaurant, but they aren't mentioned as specialties.

78. (C) The speaker says that the restaurant is *full of wonderful aromas and tastes*. Choice (A) is incorrect because the speaker says *the dishes are moderately priced*. Choice (B), *vegetarian dishes*, are mentioned, but meat dishes are mentioned as well. Choice (D) is incorrect because the restaurant serves Japanese food only.

79. (A) The speaker says that the restaurant is open *seven days a week*. Choice (B) is not correct. Choice (C) confuses you with the days that breakfast is served. Choice (D) confuses you with the days the business lunch is offered.

80. (C) They are meeting to elect the *Employee of the Year*. Choices (A), (B), and (D) are not correct.

81. (A) Employees will vote by writing the names of their choice on ballot slips. Choice (B), (C), and (D) are not mentioned.

82. (B) The winner will receive two prizes: a cash prize and a vacation. Choices (A), (C), and (D) are not correct.

83. (A) The tour takes place in the morning. Choices (B), (C), and (D) are contradicted by the tour guide's greeting, *good morning*.

84. (C) The tour will finish at the main plaza. Choice (A) is where the tour starts. Choice (B) is the place they are touring. Choice (D) is what they will see from the main gate.

85. (B) The tour guide requests that the tourists *all stay close together*. Choices (A), (C), and (D) are not mentioned.

86. (A) The speaker says that she is returning a phone call. Choice (B) confuses you

with the speaker giving her own address. Choice (C) is incorrect because it is her address, not her phone number, that Max wanted her to verify. Choice (D) is incorrect because an appointment is never mentioned.

87. (D) The speaker is not sure whether Max's last name is Amberson or Anderson. Choice (A) is incorrect because she knows that Max called to verify her address. Choice (B) confuses you with the speaker giving Max a time to call her back. Choice (C) is incorrect because the speaker clearly states the name of her street.

88. (C) The speaker says to call her back *after three this afternoon*. Choices (A) and (B) confuse *noon* with *afternoon*. Choice (D) confuses *after three days* with *after three this afternoon*.

89. (A) According to the talk, *The heavy rains and strong winds . . . tore down power lines*. Choice (B) repeats the word *residents*. Choice (C) repeats *work crews*. Choice (D) repeats *Power Company*.

90. (D) According to the talk, 150,000 residents were without electricity. Choices (A), (B), and (C) are numbers that sound similar to the correct answer.

91. (B) The speaker says *The western part of the county will be able to turn on their lights this evening*. Choice (A) repeats the words *Power Company*. Choice (C) repeats the word *lucky*. Choice (D) repeats the word *county*.

92. (B) The opening of LaForce Fitness Center is being announced. Choice (A) confuses a *golf tournament* and *golf course* being offered at the center. Choice (C) confuses similar-sounding *renovation* and *orientation*. Choice (D) is contradicted by *free orientation sessions*.

93. (A) The fitness center will open on November 1. Choices (B), (C), and (D) are dates that sound similar to the correct answer.

94. (C) For a limited time, two-for-one memberships are being offered. Choices (A), (B), and (D) are not mentioned.

95. (D) It is the *10:30 train to Springdale*. Choice (A) is when boarding of the train will begin. Choice (B) confuses you with the track number. Choice (C) confuses *seven* with the similar-sounding number *ten*.

96. (B) The speaker says *Passengers with small children will be allowed to board first*. Choice (A) is incorrect because all passengers must have reservations. Choice (C) repeats the word *bags*. Choice (D) repeats the word *pets*.

97. (B) According to the speaker, *Each passenger is allowed to take only one small bag on the train*. Choice (A) confuses you with the long list of things passengers are not allowed to take. Choices (C) and (D) are mentioned as things passengers are not allowed to take.

98. (A) There are seven lectures in the series. Choices (B), (C), and (D) are numbers that sound similar to the correct answer.

99. (A) Tonight's speaker will talk about butterflies. Choices (B), (C), and (D) are mentioned as the topics of other lectures in the series.

100. (D) The speaker says that photos will be on sale at the end of the talk. Choice (A) confuses you with the topic of the video. Choice (B) confuses you with the photos of butterflies on display. Choice (C) is what will happen before the talk.

PART 5 (PAGE 223)

101. (B) A noun is needed after the definite article. *Deductions*, which means "money taken out," is logical here. Choice (A) is a verb. Choice (C) is a noun but isn't logical here because it deals with insurance. Choice (D) is a gerund but isn't logical here.

102. (A) A past participle is required for the passive voice. Choice (B) is a noun. Choice (C) is the basic verb form. Choice (D) is the simple present.

103. (D) The adverb *yet* is used with a negative verb in the present perfect and is always placed after the verb phrase: *hasn't arrived yet*. Choice (A) is an

affirmative adverb used with present perfect. Choice (B) works the same as *yet* but is always placed before the verb phrase: *still hasn't arrived.* Choice (C) is illogical in this idea.

104. (C) A past participle is required with the auxiliary *has* to form the present perfect. Choice (A) is the simple present. Choice (B) is the basic verb form. Choice (D) is the present participle.

105. (A) *Requested*, which means "asked to do something," is the only logical choice for this idea. Choice (B), *referred*, means "directed to a source of help or information." Choice (C), *rejected*, means "refused, denied." Choice (D), *reported*, means "told about."

106. (D) The noun *remarks* is needed to go with the possessive adjective *our*. Choice (A) is a gerund but isn't logical here. Choice (B) is an adjective. Choice (C) is the simple past.

107. (C) The present participle, or *–ing*, adjective *amazing* is needed to describe the noun *advice*. Use the present participle adjective when describing what causes or creates the feeling: *My cousin's amazing advice.* Choice (A) is an adverb. Choice (B) is the simple past. It can also be the past participle adjective, which describes the person or people receiving the feeling: *We were amazed.* Choice (D) is a noun.

108. (B) A preposition is needed: *to be surprised at.* Choices (A), (C), and (D) don't go with *to be surprised.*

109. (D) *Refund*, which means "cash or credit received for a return," is the only logical choice for this sentence. Choice (A), *reimbursement*, means "money you paid that is repaid." Choice (B), *premium*, means "an amount you pay for insurance." Choice (C), *duplication*, means "copying something."

110. (A) *So that* is a conjunction that explains the purpose or intention of doing something for a future result. Choice (B), *because*, explains the past or current situation that causes something to

happen. Choices (C) and (D) are not logical in this sentence.

111. (C) The adverb *surprisingly* modifies the adjective *large*: *surprisingly large*. Choice (A) is the simple past. Choice (B) is an adjective. Choice (D) is a noun.

112. (A) The preposition *within* means "in." It can be used for concrete things (*within the room; within the city*) or with abstract things (*within his job description; within the court's jurisdiction*). Choice (B), *into*, is a preposition of movement and doesn't work in this case. Choice (C), *about*, does not make sense in this context. Choice (D), *inside*, is mostly used with concrete things: *inside the room; inside the city.*

113. (B) *Realistic* is an adjective that means "concerned with facts as they really are" and is appropriate for this sentence. In addition, an adjective is required after the predicate *isn't*. Choice (A) is an adjective but has the wrong meaning for this sentence. It means "not false, not artificial." Choices (C) and (D) are adverbs.

114. (B) The adjective *collaborative* modifies the noun *effort*. Choices (A) and (C) are nouns. Choice (D) is an adverb.

115. (D) The possessive pronoun *yours* is the object of the preposition *of*. Choice (A) is a possessive adjective. Choice (B) is the subject pronoun. Choice (C) is the reflexive pronoun and does not make sense in this context.

116. (D) *Research* means "looking into scientific information" and fits the idea of this sentence. Choice (A), *investigation*, means "looking into information, usually by the police or government." Choice (B), *investing*, means "putting money into a company." Choice (C), *planning*, means "deciding how to do something in the future."

117. (D) *Prepare* means "to make ready" and fits the idea of this sentence. Choice (A), *compensate*, means "to make payment." Choice (B), *deliver*, means "to bring something for business reasons." Choice (C), *apply*, means "to ask for in a formal way, usually in writing."

118. (A) The comparative adjective *different* is always followed by the preposition *from*. Choices (B), (C), and (D) are therefore incorrect.

119. (B) When a sentence begins with a negative adverb of frequency, there is a word inversion like the word order for a *yes/no* question: *Never has there been . . . .* Choices (A), (C), and (D) are not negative adverbs of frequency and are therefore incorrect.

120. (C) The preposition *by* means "before or at, but not later than." Choices (A), (B), and (D) are not used in this context with the phrase *the end of the year*.

121. (C) The noun *accuracy* is needed after the adjective *utmost*. Choice (A) is an adjective. Choice (B) is an adverb. Choice (D) is a quantifying phrase but is not logical after *utmost*.

122. (B) The adjective *periodic* modifies the noun *questionnaires*. Choice (A) is a noun. Choice (C) is an adverb. Choice (D) is a noun.

123. (D) The adverb *anxiously* modifies the verb *awaiting*. Choice (A) is a noun. Choice (B) is an adjective. Choice (C) is a noun.

124. (C) *Report* means "a document about something" and fits the idea of this sentence. Choice (A), *accounting*, means "managing the books and taxes for companies or individuals." Choice (B), *documentation*, means "written proof of something." Choice (D), *observance*, means "celebrating a holiday or tradition."

125. (A) *On* is the preposition used after the verb *elaborate*. Choices (B), (C), and (D) are illogical.

126. (B) *It is recommended that* requires the basic verb form *seek out*. Choice (A) is the present progressive. Choice (C) is the infinitive verb. Choice (D) is the simple past.

127. (A) The reflexive pronoun *itself* means "alone" in this context. Choice (B) is the subject pronoun. Choice (C) is used with the preposition *on: on its own*. Choice (D) is an incorrect form.

128. (C) *Expand* means "to increase, get larger," and fits the idea of this sentence. Choice (A), *extrapolate,* means "to infer unknown information from known information." Choice (B), *exhibit*, means "to show." Choice (D), *exhale*, means "to breathe out."

129. (C) *Aggressive* means "assertive, bold," and fits the idea of this sentence. Choice (A), *outrageous,* means "disgraceful, offensive, shameless." Choice (B), *lucrative,* means "profitable." Choice (D), *astounding,* means "very amazing, surprising."

130. (D) A noun is needed after the adjective *every. Intention* is the correct choice here because it means "a plan of action or a design" and it fits the idea. Choice (A) is a noun, but its meaning is "a purpose" and it doesn't fit this idea. Choice (B) is an adverb. Choice (C) is a verb.

131. (B) With prepositions, we need to use the direct object form of pronouns. *Whom* is the direct object form. Choice (A) is the subject pronoun. Choice (C) is used for things, not people. Choice (D) is the incorrect pronoun.

132. (B) *Screened* means "investigated" and fits the idea of this sentence. Choice (A), *screamed,* means "shouted, yelled." Choice (C), *scrawled,* means "not written clearly." Choice (D), *scraped,* means "rubbed with a lot of pressure."

133. (A) Because of the possessive, *Mr. Hansen's,* the gerund noun *resigning* must be used. Choice (B) is the simple past. Choice (C) is the simple present. Choice (D) is the basic verb form.

134. (C) *Predictions* means "saying what you think will be in the future" and fits the idea of this sentence. Choice (A), *predicaments,* means "trouble, problems." Choice (B), *predilections,* means "preferences." Choice (D), *predicates,* means "the parts of sentences that include the verb and object."

135. (B) The present participle, adjective, *exciting,* modifies the noun *possibilities*. Present participle adjectives describe the person or thing creating the feeling.

Choice (A) is the past participle adjective, which describes the person or thing receiving the feeling. Choice (C) is a noun. Choice (D) is an adjective but means "easily excited."

136. (D) *Unimaginable* means "something we couldn't have imagined before" and fits the idea of this sentence. Choice (A), *unacceptable*, means "something nobody can agree to or accept." Choice (B), *implacable*, means "cannot be pleased." Choice (C), *inadvertent*, means "accidental, unintentional."

137. (A) *Events* means "important occurrences" and fits the idea of this sentence. Choice (B), *reunions*, means "people meeting after a long separation." Choice (C), *councils*, means "groups of experts called together for consultation." Choice (D), *invocations*, means "prayers."

138. (A) The construction *such . . . that . . .* is used to quantify how much of a success the blood drive was. *Such* is always used with a noun phrase: *such a success*. Choice (B), *so*, is used with adjectives or adverbs. Choices (C) and (D) do not make sense in this context.

139. (B) The adjective *collective* means "acting as one," which is appropriate for the idea of this sentence. Choice (A) is the past participle adjective," and it doesn't work in this idea. Choice (C) is a present participle adjective. Choice (D) is an adjective that means "something worth collecting for its value," so it does not make sense in this context.

140. (D) The subordinate conjunction *despite* is used with a direct object. Choice (A) is missing the preposition *of*. Choice (B) does not make sense in this context. Choice (C) requires a noun and verb phrase after it, and it does not make sense in this context.

PART 6 (PAGE 227)

141. (B) The bank branch will open at a future date, so a future verb is required when describing it. Choice (A) is present perfect tense. Choice (C) is a present participle. Choice (D) is simple past tense.

142. (D) *There* plus *to be* is followed by a noun or list of nouns, so the noun form *entertainment* is correct. Choice (A) is a verb. Choice (B) is a noun, but it refers to a person. Choice (C) is a gerund.

143. (C) The announcement is directed at customers, who usually go to a bank to open an *account*. Choices (A), (B), and (D) are things that would more likely be opened by bank employees.

144. (D) People usually go to a bank to take care of their financial needs. Choices (A), (B), and (C) are needs that people may have but that are normally not taken care of at a bank.

145. (C) The article mentions computer, software, and communications companies, in other words, *technology* companies. Choices (A), (B), and (D) are sectors of the economy but are not mentioned in the article.

146. (A) The preposition *to* correctly follows the verb *compared*. Choices (B), (C), and (D) are prepositions which cannot follow *compared*.

147. (D) The paragraph talks about a rise in *profits*, which means the same as *earnings*. Choice (A) is something a company would not hope to increase. Choices (B) and (C) are things a company might increase but are not the subject of the paragraph.

148. (B) *Costly* is an adjective, and an adjective is required, describing the wireless service. Choice (A) is a noun or a verb. Choice (C) is a verb form of another word with a different meaning. Choice (D) is a gerund.

149. (C) The writer is addressing Ms. Harwood about Ms. Harwood's staff, so the second person possessive adjective *your* is the correct form. Choice (A) is the first person singular form. Choice (B) is the first person plural form. Choice (D) is the third person plural form.

150. (C) *Departed* means "left a place." Choices (A) and (B) mean "left a job." Choice (D) means "left school."

151. (D) An adverb is required here to describe how the job was done. Choice (A) is an adjective. Choice (B) is a past tense verb. Choice (C) is a gerund.

152. (A) The writer of the letter was a guest at the hotel, and *stay* is what hotel guests do. Choice (B) is what a hotel employee would do. Choices (C) and (D) are not important activities at a hotel.

PART 7 (PAGE 231)

153. (B) The announcement talks about *relaxing, full bodywork,* and *chair for neck, shoulders, and back;* the announcement is about massages. Choice (A) confuses *length of breaks* with needing a *real break.* Choice (C) associates *furniture* with *table* and *chair.* Choice (D) confuses similar sounds *language* and *lounge.*

154. (B) The service is free of charge for employees. Choice (A) confuses $15 for 15 minutes and the 15 minutes the massage takes. Choice (C) is not mentioned. Choice (D) confuses Human Resources having the rates and Human Resources offering the service.

155. (C) Employees must give up two days of pay to end the budget crisis. Choices (A), (B), and (D) are not mentioned.

156. (B) Because of poor profits, the budget is short by about $13 million. Choice (A) is the opposite of a shortage. Choices (C) and (D) are contradicted by poor profits causing a shortage.

157. (A) It is necessary for all employees to give up two days' pay by scheduling the two days they do not report to work. Choice (B) confuses *June 30* with the *date by which the budget must be balanced.* Choice (C) is contradicted by the plan announced. Choice (D) is contradicted by having to balance the budget by this fiscal year.

158. (D) The two left lanes on the north side will be closed. Choices (A), (B), and (C) are contradicted by the *two left lanes on the north side will be closed.*

159. (B) Miami-Dade County, the issuer of the notice, is authorizing the lane closures.

Choices (A), (C), and (D) are not mentioned.

160. (C) The NE 151st exit falls outside of the NE 79th St. to NE 135th St. area that will be affected. Choices (A), (B), and (D) fall within the area that will be affected.

161. (D) The article is about how much money old covers of *Movie Goer Magazine* are worth. Choice (A) confuses *literary value* with *monetary value.* Choice (B) is incorrect because although Mr. Boulis is mentioned, he is not the main subject of the article. Choice (C) confuses *issues* with *covers.*

162. (B) The writer assumes readers have old issues in the basement. Choices (A), (C), and (D) are not mentioned.

163. (A) The cover of the first issue, the premier issue, of the magazine is the most valuable. Choice (B) is the opposite of the *first one.* Choices (C) and (D) are valued at less than the value of the first one.

164. (B) *Financial Success* is on the air for one hour, from 8:00 to 9:00. Choices (A), (C), and (D) are incorrect.

165. (C) There are six different business shows being televised; one is being shown twice. Choices (A), (B), and (D) are incorrect.

166. (A) *Business Week in Review* is being repeated. Choices (B), (C), and (D) are not financial/business shows.

167. (B) BPL is the only station that shows only business programs. Choices (A) and (C) show different types of programs. Choice (D) shows only movies.

168. (C) A department within an organization such as a police department is often called a unit. The other options do not fit the context.

169. (B) Michael O'Brien was freed by a group of judges in the Court of Appeals. Choice (A) associates the *Queen* with *Great Britain.* Choice (C) is who is deciding on his compensation. Choice (D) is not mentioned.

170. (C) Mr. O'Brien was convicted of industrial espionage. Choices (A), (B), and (D) are crimes but not the one he was convicted for.

171. (D) To commit a crime is to carry out a crime. The other options do not fit the context.

172. (A) Mr. O'Brien is upset because he has to reimburse the prison for room and board. Choice (B) confuses *paying money to the Home Office* and the *Home Office ruling that he would have to reimburse the prison.* Choices (C) and (D) are not mentioned.

173. (D) There are four ways to buy merchandise at "Trendy Male": at their stores, by phone, by mail, and online. Choices (A), (B), and (C) are incorrect.

174. (B) If you buy an item on sale, the second item will be 50% off. You would pay $23 for the second shirt if you buy the first for $46. Choices (A), (C), and (D) are not correct.

175. (C) The offer lasts 21 days, from June 17 though July 7. Choices (A), (B), and (D) are contradicted by the dates given.

176. (C) These instructions are for a cellular phone. Choice (A) confuses *portable phone* with *cellular phone.* Choices (B) and (D) are associated with the technical terms mentioned in the article but are incorrect.

177. (A) If the battery is not charging, check that it is connected to an approved charging device. Choice (B) is not mentioned. Choice (C) is what you should do after you check the connection to the charger device. Choice (D) repeats the words *normal operating*: this is not one of the steps.

178. (B) If the device fails to charge properly, contact your dealer. Choices (A), (C), and (D) are not mentioned.

179. (D) You can study at home in your spare time. Choices (A), (B), and (C) are times you can study if those are considered your individual spare times.

180. (D) You could get an accounting degree in as little as two years. Choice (A) is how long it takes to get a career degree as a private investigator or medical

transcriptionist. Choice (B) is how long it takes to get a high school diploma. Choice (C) confuses similar sounds *18 months* and *8,000,000 men and women.*

181. (C) The first e-mail says that it is a *department meeting,* so *department members* will attend. Choice (A) confuses you with the location of the meeting (conference room). Choice (B) is incorrect because the meeting is only for department members. Choice (D) is the person with whom Mr. Richards will meet on Friday.

182. (A) The e-mail says that the meeting will take place in *Conference Room 2.* Choices (B) and (C) confuse you with the lunch that will be served at the meeting. Choice (D) is the original location of the meeting, but according to the e-mail, that location was changed.

183. (B) *Thursday* is the day Mr. Richards will leave for Sydney. Choice (A) is the day people must notify Ms. Santelli if they can't attend the meeting. Choice (C) is the day Mr. Richards will meet with Mr. Lockerman. Choice (D) is the day Mr. Richards will send his report about his meeting with Mr. Lockerman.

184. (D) In his e-mail, Mr. Richards mentions that *Peter worked with me on this,* in reference to his report. By looking at the addressees of the first e-mail, we can see that *Peter's* last name is Kim. Choices (A), (B), and (C) are the other addressees of the first e-mail, but none of them is named *Peter.*

185. (A) Mr. Richards' e-mail says he will leave *figures you'll need for the second item on the meeting agenda.* By looking at Ms. Santelli's e-mail, we see that the second item is the *budget.* Choice (B) is the person with whom Mr. Richards will meet in Sydney, but nothing is mentioned about his address. Choices (C) and (D) are mentioned in the e-mail but are not the correct answer.

186. (A) In this letter, H. J. Simpson says that he received the shipment on November 18. It was shipped on November 15. Choice (B) is based on the date the letter was written. Choice (C) is not mentioned. Choice (D) is not mentioned.

187. (A) The letter states *the items we received were not the same* as *the items we ordered.* Choices (B), (C), and (D) are not mentioned.

188. (B) The letter states that the model D is half the price of the model B. The invoice shows that the model B costs $150, so the model D must cost $75. Choice (A) is not mentioned. Choice (C) is the price of the model B, not D, shown on the invoice. Choice (D) is double, not half, the price of the model B.

189. (B) The letter states *At least the watercooler was correct.* By looking at the invoice, we see that one watercooler was shipped. Choices (A), (C), and (D) are not mentioned.

190. (D) The letter states that when he tried calling, *the line is always busy.* Choices (A), (B), and (C) are possible outcomes but are not the correct answer.

191. (D) The earliest train arrives at 10:30 in the morning. Choices (A), (B), and (C) refer to times listed on the schedule in bold, meaning that they are afternoon and evening arrival times.

192. (B) The trip lasts four hours and twenty minutes. Choice (C) is the length of the trip when intermediate stops are made. Choices (A) and (D) are not mentioned.

193. (C) This is the second train on Tuesday morning. Choice (A) is the first train. Choice (B) is the second train on Monday, Wednesday, and Friday only. Choice (D) is a later train and also leaves only on Monday, Wednesday, and Friday.

194. (D) Ms. Heinz wants to travel business class. A one-way ticket is $175, so a round-trip ticket is $350. Choice (A) is the price for a one-way tourist class ticket. Choice (B) is the price for a one-way

business class ticket. Choice (C) is the price for a round-trip tourist class ticket.

195. (D) Ms. Heinz says that she wants to return about *5 or 6 in the afternoon.* Choices (A), (B), and (C) are not mentioned.

196. (A) The ad says to *contact Cathy Chang, Events Manager,* and the e-mail is addressed to Cathy Chang. Choice (B) is the name of the hotel's Head Manager. Choice (C) is the name of the person who wants to host a banquet, and choice (D) is her assistant.

197. (B) The e-mail states *I am planning the annual employee appreciation banquet for my company.* Choices (A), (C), and (D) are other reasons a company might have a banquet but are not the correct answer.

198. (D) The e-mail states *Our banquet is scheduled for the evening of July 15.* Choice (A) confuses you with May 23, the date the ad appeared in the paper. Choice (B) is the date the ad appeared in the paper. Choice (C) July 5 confuses you with July 15.

199. (B) The ad says that the hotel has room for 250 guests, and the e-mail states *We only plan to have half the number of guests mentioned in your ad.* Choice (A) is not mentioned. Choice (C) is the number of guests mentioned in the ad. Choice (D) is double, not half, the number of guests mentioned in the ad.

200. (D) The banquet planner mentions that she wants both vegetarian and meat choices. Choice (A) is incorrect because she wants vegetarian food as well as meat. Choice (B) is incorrect because she says *I think a five-course dinner would be too much.* Choice (C) is incorrect because the banquet is planned for the evening, which would mean dinner, not lunch.

ANSWER KEY
PRACTICE TEST TWO

PART 1 (PAGE 250)

1. (B) The men are greeting one another. Choice (A) tries to confuse you by using the similar-sounding phrase *shaking out the sand* for *shaking the man's hand*. Choice (C) tries to confuse you by using *sea* for *see*. Choice (D) tries to confuse you by using the similar-sounding phrase *putting on a smile* and *running a mile*.

2. (D) The woman has the file cabinet drawer open and is looking in the files. Choice (A) tries to confuse you by using the similar-sounding word *drawing* for *drawer*. Choice (B) tries to confuse you by using the similar-sounding word *tiles* for *files*. Choice (C) uses the word *filing* in a different context. The woman may be filing (putting in order) documents, but she's not filing (smoothing) her nails.

3. (A) The telephones are on the wall. Choice (B) gives incorrect details: the signs are above the phones. Choice (C) gives incorrect details: the door is to the left of the phones. Choice (D) provides incorrect details: the phones are to the right of the door.

4. (A) The woman is studying the X-rays. Choice (B) tries to confuse you by using the related word *pictures*. Choice (C) provides incorrect details: *she's looking at X-rays posted on a lighted screen*, not *watching TV*. Choice (D) provides incorrect details: *she's holding a clipboard or file*, not *scanning a file*.

5. (B) The gate to the courtyard is open. Choice (A) provides incorrect details: there is no guard in the picture; and tries to confuse you by using the related word *entrance*. Choice (C) provides incorrect details: the *pathway is straight*, but the *entrance is circular*. Choice (D) tries to confuse you by using the related word *garden* and provides incorrect details: there are no tourists lined up at the door.

6. (C) The people are boarding a plane. Choice (A) provides incorrect details: they're going up the stairs. Choice (B) tries to confuse you by using the similar-sounding word *train* for *plane*. Choice (D) provides incorrect details: people are *carrying bags*, not *checking bags*.

7. (D) The chairs and tables are empty. Choice (A) provides incorrect details: the tables are empty. Choice (B) tries to confuse you by using the related word *diners* and provides incorrect details: there are no diners. Choice (C) tries to confuse you by using the related word *customers* and provides incorrect details: there are no customers.

8. (C) The goods are in cartons stacked in the warehouse. Choice (A) tries to confuse you by using the similar-sounding and related word *cargo* for *cartons*. Choice (B) tries to confuse you by using the related words *boxes* and *container*. Choice (D) provides incorrect details: we do not know if there is produce in the boxes and the boxes are on the front of a forklift, not on the back of a truck.

9. (D) They are getting on the train. Choice (A) tries to confuse you by using the related word *platform*. Choice (B) tries to confuse you by using the related word *window*; there are windows on the train, but they're not being opened. Choice (C) tries to confuse you by using the similar-sounding word *plane* for *train*.

10. (D) The woman is pouring coffee into the cup. Choice (A) provides incorrect details: she's holding the cup with one hand and pouring the coffeepot with the other. Choice (B) uses the word *pouring* in a different context. Choice (C) tries to confuse you by using the similar-sounding word *pointing* for *pouring*.

PART 2 (PAGE 256)

11. (C) *Late last night* answers *when*. Choice (A) answers *how long*. Choice (B) answers *where*.

12. (B) *Mr. Kim's* answers *whose?* Choice (A) answers *where*. Choice (C) confuses similar sounds *they're keys* and *these are* and answers *where*.

13. (B) *On her desk* answers *where*. Choice (A) confuses *where is Ms. Sato* and *where are her packages*. Choice (C) confuses similar sounds *packed* and *packages*.

14. (C) *Yes, I just have to finish typing these notes* answers the *yes/no* question. Choice (A) uses the similar-sounding word *met*. Choice (B) answers *where*.

15. (B) *In the garage* answers *where do you usually park*. Choice (A) confuses *park* (n.) and *park* (v.). Choice (C) associates *mechanic* with *car*.

16. (A) *Tomorrow morning* answers *when*. Choice (B) answers *what can I call you*. Choice (C) associates *talk* and *call* and answers *where*.

17. (B) *I'd better bring an umbrella* responds to the idea *It's supposed to rain tomorrow*. Choice (A) repeats the word *supposed* and uses the associated words *yesterday* for *tomorrow*. Choice (C) repeats the word *tomorrow* and the similar-sounding word *train* for *rain*.

18. (B) *Mrs. Garcia* answers *who*. Choice (A) answers *where is Mr. Contini*. Choice (C) answers *when*.

19. (A) *Everyone leaves by 5:30,* so the office is considered closed by then. Choice (B) repeats *the offices are closed*. Choice (C) confuses similar sounds *clothes* and *close*.

20. (C) *Because we have to discuss the budget* answers *why*. Choices (A) and (B) answer *when*.

21. (B) *Once every month* answers *how often*. Choice (A) answers *who*. Choice (C) confuses similar sounds *reporter* and *reports*.

22. (A) *About 15 minutes* answers *how long*. Choice (B) answers *how big*. Choice (C) answers *how is the ride*.

23. (A) *You don't look sick* responds to the speaker's *not feeling well*. Choice (B) uses the similar-meaning word *fine* for *well*. Choice (C) uses the similar sounding *welcome* for *well*.

24. (B) *That restaurant across the street* answers *where*. Choice (A) answers *when*. Choice (C) answers *would you like to eat*.

25. (B) *Yes, I got a room at a nice place downtown* answers *were you able to book a hotel*. Choice (A) confuses the similar words *book* (n.) and *book* (v.). Choice (C) answers *did you book a hotel*.

26. (B) *Ask her if she wants to sit down and wait* addresses the topic of someone who has been *standing and waiting for an hour*. Choice (A) tries to confuse you by using the time words *clock* for an *hour*. Choice (C) uses *weight* for *wait*.

27. (C) *You should speak with her assistant* answers *how can I make an appointment*. Choice (A) associates *position* and *appointment*. Choice (B) confuses similar sounds *disappointed* and *appointment*.

28. (A) *Only about 3 or 4 days* answers *how long*. Choice (B) answers *how long has it been since you were last there*. Choice (C) answers *where will you stay*.

29. (B) *Yes, that's a great idea* answers *would you like to go*. Choice (A) confuses similar sounds *walk* and *work*. Choice (C) repeats the word *worked*.

30. (B) *Yes, she was there* answers *did you notice whether Ms. Kovacs was at the reception*. Choice (A) confuses similar sounds *notes* and *notice*. Choice (C) confuses similar sounds *received* and *reception*.

31. (A) *In his office* answers *where*. Choices (B) and (C) answer *when*.

32. (B) *There are 15* answers *how many*. Choice (A) confuses similar sounds *apartment* and *department*. Choice (C) answers *how long*.

33. (C) *Next Monday* answers *when*. Choice (A) associates *cafeteria* with *lunch*. Choice (B) associates *cost* with *free*.

34. (B) *Yes, at the newsstand* answers *did you buy that newspaper downstairs.* Choice (A) repeats the word *paper.* Choice (C) confuses similar sounds *good-bye* and *buy.*

35. (B) *Next week* answers *when.* Choice (A) answers *where.* Choice (C) describes the new assistant manager.

36. (C) *I can recommend an architect* responds with the type of occupation involved in building a home. Choice (A) repeats the word *building* and uses the similar word *home* for *house.* It also repeats the word *new.* Choice (B) repeats the verb *going.*

37. (A) *25% off the regular price* answers *is there a discount.* Choice (B) confuses similar sounds *counted* and *discount.* Choice (C) repeats the word *furniture.*

38. (B) *Because he hasn't had a chance to* answers *why.* Choice (A) confuses similar sounds *newspaper* and *papers.* Choice (C) answers *has he signed those papers.*

39. (B) *It's time to cut it* responds to the topic of the high grass. Choice (A) uses the similar word *taller* for *higher* and repeats the word *than.* Choice (C) uses the similar sounding word *glass* for *grass* and *never* for *ever.*

40. (A) *No, I got a new job* answers *you aren't still working for the same company.* Choice (B) does not answer the question. Choice (C) confuses similar sounds *computer* and *company.*

PART 3 (PAGE 257)

41. (D) The woman says that the secretary sent the package. Choice (A) is incorrect because the package is for Mr. Ozawa, not from him. Choice (B) is the person with whom Mr. Ozawa will meet tomorrow. Choice (C) is mentioned as a person who did not send the package.

42. (D) The meeting is tomorrow. Choice (A) is not mentioned. Choice (B) is when the package arrived. Choice (C) confuses *tonight* with the similar-sounding word *right.*

43. (A) The man says that Mr. Ozawa is at lunch. Choice (B) is where the man will put the package. Choice (C) is where Mr.

Ozawa will go tomorrow. Choice (D) associates *mailroom* with *mail.*

44. (D) They have just finished lunch at a restaurant. Choice (A) is where the man's wallet is. Choice (B) associates *bank* with *pay.* Choice (C) is not mentioned.

45. (B) The woman will pay for lunch with her credit card. Choice (A) confuses *card* with *credit card.* Choice (C) confuses *play* with the similar-sounding word *pay.* Choice (D) associates *cook a meal* with *lunch.*

46. (A) The man says that he will pay the woman back. Choice (B) confuses *letters* with the similar-sounding word *later.* Choice (C) is what the man left at home. Choice (D) associates *meal* with *lunch.*

47. (B) The man wants dinner reservations for three people. Choice (A) is not mentioned. Choice (C) confuses *eight* with the time *8:45.* Choice (D) confuses *you* with the time they will eat dinner.

48. (C) The man says that he will take the 9:00 table. Choice (A) is not mentioned. Choice (B) is another option the woman offered. Choice (D) confuses *ten* with the similar-sounding word *then.*

49. (C) The man says that they will sit in the bar until 9:00. Choice (A) repeats the word *kitchen.* Choice (B) repeats the word *table.* Choice (D) confuses *car* with the similar-sounding word *bar.*

50. (C) The speakers are discussing putting colors on the walls and windows. Choice (A) *windows* is mentioned, but washing them is not. Choice (B) *chairs* is mentioned, but buying them is not. Choice (D) the *rug* is mentioned, but cleaning it is not.

51. (D) The woman says that blue would match the color of the rug. Choice (A) confuses *green* with the similar-sounding word *seems.* Choices (B) and (C) are possible colors the woman mentions for the walls.

52. (C) The woman says they will start work on Friday. Choices (A), (B), and (D) are not mentioned.

53. (B) Jim missed the meeting because he had to type his report. Choices (A) and (C) are not mentioned. Choice (D) confuses *copy machine* with *final copy*.

54. (A) It was a 3:00 meeting. Choice (B) is not mentioned. Choice (C) is the time of the woman's train. Choice (D) confuses *eight* with the similar-sounding word *late*.

55. (D) The man is afraid that he will miss his train. Choice (A) repeats the word *meeting*, but the meeting is already over. Choice (B) confuses *letter* with the similar-sounding word *later*. Choice (C) confuses *rain* with the similar-sounding word *train*.

56. (A) The woman suggests going to the conference room and the man agrees. Choice (B) confuses *business office* with *noisy* office. Choice (C) is how they will get to the conference room. Choice (D) is where they are now, but they can't work there because of the noise.

57. (C) The man suggests taking a computer with them. Choices (A) and (B) are the things that the woman says they don't need. Choice (D) associates *computer paper* with *computer*, but *paper* is never mentioned.

58. (D) The man says *We can't write this report here* and wants to find another place to do the work. Choice (A) associates *pens and notepads* with *office supplies*. Choice (B) confuses *planning a conference* with *the conference room*. Choice (C) confuses *fixing a computer* with the computer the speakers are using for their work.

59. (B) The man, Sam, says that his boss will be in the office tomorrow. Choice (A) is incorrect because Sam says that he will be at a conference. Choice (C) is not mentioned. Choice (D) is mentioned but is not being helpful.

60. (C) The woman says that she needs someone to go over accounts with her. Choice (A) confuses *cooking lunch* with looking for the boss after lunch. Choice (B) confuses *book* with the similar-sounding word *look*. Choice (D) confuses *planning a conference* with the conference that Sam will attend.

61. (B) The woman will look for the boss in his office after lunch. Choice (A) is when she will take the boss to dinner. Choice (C) repeats the word *lunch*. Choice (D) repeats the word *dinner*.

62. (D) He is talking about a sale on briefcases. Choice (A) refers to the woman's suggestion that he fax his order to the store. Choice (B) is where he read the ad. Choice (C) is how he will make his order.

63. (B) The briefcases are 15% off. Choice (A) confuses *ten* with the similar-sounding word *then*. Choice (C) is not mentioned. Choice (D) confuses *50* with the similar-sounding number *15*.

64. (C) The man says that Saturday is the last day of the sale. Choice (A) is when the woman suggests making the order. Choice (B) is when the woman believes the sale is over. Choice (D) confuses *next week* with *on sale this week*.

65. (B) The copies are coming out too light because the photocopier is broken. Choice (A) confuses similar-sounding *come* and *conditioner*. Choice (C) associates *telephone* with *call*. Choice (D) uses the word *light* in a different context.

66. (A) The woman says that the repair person will be here at noon. Choice (B) confuses *week* with the similar-sounding word *work*. Choice (C) is when the man wants to report the problem. Choice (D) confuses *afternoon* with *noon*.

67. (B) The man says that he will read his e-mail. Choice (A) confuses *eat a meal* with the similar-sounding word *e-mail*. Choice (C) uses the word *report* in a different context. Choice (D) is what the woman already did.

68. (C) The man can't meet this week because he will be away on a business trip. Choice (A) repeats the word *meet*. Choice (B) confuses *rest this week* with *the rest of this week*. Choice (D) repeats the word *office*.

69. (A) The woman says that she wants to meet to discuss conference plans. Choice (B) is not mentioned. Choice (C) confuses

money with the similar-sounding word *Monday*. Choice (D) is where the man will be Monday morning.

70. (D) 1:00 is the time that they agree on. Choice (A) confuses *9* with the similar-sounding word *fine*. Choice (B) confuses *10* with the similar-sounding word *then*. Choice (C) is the woman's original suggestion for a meeting time.

PART 4 (PAGE 260)

71. (C) The train will leave at 10:30. Choice (A) confuses *10:10* and *10 minutes*. Choice (B) confuses *10:15* and *Gate 15*. Choice (D) incorrectly assumes it's 10:30 now, and since boarding starts in 10 minutes, the train would leave at 10:40.

72. (D) Passengers with small children should arrive five minutes before boarding time. Choice (A) confuses *offer help* and *needing special assistance*. Choice (B) is contradicted by *passengers who still wish to check luggage should do so now*. Choice (C) is not mentioned.

73. (A) The speaker says that only cash is accepted on board the train. Choices (B) and (C) are mentioned as unacceptable forms of payment. Choice (D) uses the word *order* out of context.

74. (B) A weather forecaster is talking. Choice (A) associates *news reporter* with *good news*. Choice (C) associates *pilot* with *skies*. Choice (D) associates *travel agent* with *trip to the beach*.

75. (C) The speaker announces the *5:00 weather report* and mentions *the long day of rain*; it must be in the evening. Choice (A) is contradicted by *long day of rain*. Choice (B) confuses similar-sounding *noon* and *news*. Choice (D) is when the rain will stop.

76. (C) The speaker says *By tomorrow morning. . . it'll be warm and sunny all day*. Choice (A) is the weather today. Choice (B) confuses *you* with *not a cloud in the sky*. Choice (D) confuses *cold* with the similar-sounding word *cloud*.

77. (A) You would hear this announcement at a grocery store. Choice (B) confuses *department store* with *meat department* and

produce department. Choice (C) associates *restaurant* with the food that's mentioned. Choice (D) associates *library* with *check out*.

78. (A) There is a sale on ground beef. Choices (B) and (C) repeat items that are mentioned in the talk but that are not on sale. Choice (D) confuses *suits* with the similar-sounding word *fruit*.

79. (D) Shoppers purchasing 15 or fewer items can use the express check out lanes. Choices (A), (B), and (C) are possible but only if they have 15 or fewer items.

80. (B) A professor is talking to his class. Choice (A) is who he is speaking to. Choice (C) associates *author* with *textbook*. Choice (D) associates *medical doctor* with *Dr.*

81. (A) The subject of the class is algebra. Choice (B) confuses similar sounds *computers* and *Compton*. Choice (C) confuses similar-sounding *finance* and *advanced*. Choice (D) associates *health* with *Dr.*, *exercises*, and *exams*.

82. (B) There will be two tests: a midterm and a final. Choice (A) is how many textbooks they will use. Choice (C) is what time the class starts. Choice (D) is the number of exercises that will be assigned each week.

83. (A) Bob Wilson was the city's first mayor. Choice (B) is who is keeping time. Choice (C) confuses *war hero* with *an important figure in our history* and the *war heroes monument*. Choice (D) associates *artist* and *art museum*.

84. (B) The speaker says *We'll have an hour to spend*. Choice (A) confuses *half an hour* with the similar-sounding *have an hour*. Choice (C) confuses the number *ten* with the similar-sounding word *spend*. Choice (D) confuses *two* with *to*.

85. (C) They will see the war heroes monument after visiting the Wilson House. Choice (A) is where they went before the Wilson House. Choice (B) confuses *bus station* and *bus driver*. Choice (D) is where they will go another day.

86. (C) The tickets are for the year-end soccer tournament. Choice (A) confuses similar

sounds *tour* with *tournament,* and *bus tour* with *bus ride.* Choice (B) confuses similar sounds *theater* and *there are.* Choice (D) associates *awards ceremony* with *trophy.*

87. (B) Tickets can be reserved at the front desk. Choices (A), (C), and (D) are not mentioned as a place to get tickets.

88. (B) The bus leaves at *6:00 A.M.* Choices (A) and (C) confuse *three* with the similar-sounding word *free.* Choice (D) confuses *6:00 P.M.* with *6:00 A.M.*

89. (C) *You, Too, Can Become a Millionaire* is most likely about making money. Choice (A) is what Ms. Park is doing now. Choice (B) is not likely. Choice (D) confuses *retail business* with selling books.

90. (C) Ms. Park will read excerpts from her book. Choice (A) is what the speaker is doing. Choice (B) confuses *receive an award* and *award-winning author.* Choice (D) confuses *make copies* and *sign copies.*

91. (A) You can purchase the book at the back of the auditorium. Choice (B) confuses similar words *signs* (n.) and *sign* (v.). Choice (C) confuses *You, Too, Can Become a Millionaire* with a game. Choice (D) is what Ms. Park will do after reading.

92. (D) Pamela Jones is the science reporter at the *Daily Times* newspaper. Choice (A) associates *telephone operator* with the phone message. Choice (B) confuses *scientist* and *science reporter.* Choice (C) confuses *an assistant* and *my assistant.*

93. (A) She can't answer the phone because she is at a conference. Choices (B), (C), and (D) are contradicted by *out of the office all week at the journalists' conference.*

94. (C) To leave a message, stay on the line. Choices (A) and (B) are mentioned but are contradicted by *to leave a message, stay on the line.* Choice (D) is not mentioned.

95. (B) The flight from Sydney will arrive on time. Choices (A), (C), and (D) are flights which are delayed or canceled.

96. (B) The flight from Paris was canceled because of a blizzard. Choice (A) is confused with the reason for the delay of the London flight. Choice (C) is confused with the sale on tickets. Choice (D) is confused with the schedule change next month.

97. (C) The message says that the sale *ends next week.* Choice (A) is confused with *this evening's arrivals.* Choice (B) is confused with *ends next week.* Choice (D) is when the schedule will change.

98. (D) The message announces shows at 1, 3, 5, 7:30, and midnight. Choices (A) and (C) are confused with show times. Choice (B) confuses *two* with the similar-sounding word *today.*

99. (C) The message says *All shows before five o'clock are half price.* Choices (A) and (D) are mentioned but not at half price. Choice (B) is confused with people who will not be admitted to the midnight show.

100. (D) This is the only item mentioned as not allowed. Choices (A), (B), and (C) are things sold inside the theater.

PART 5 (PAGE 263)

101. (D) The noun is needed as the subject of the sentence. Choice (A) is the past participle adjective. Choice (B) is the present participle adjective. Choice (C) is the basic verb form.

102. (C) The past participle adjective is required to describe the subject, which is receiving the feeling. Choice (A) is the present participle adjective, which describes the person or thing creating the feeling. Choice (B) is the simple present. Choice (D) is the basic verb form.

103. (D) *Yet* is a negative adverb with present perfect. It can be placed after the first auxiliary *(haven't yet been made)* or at the end of the sentence *(haven't been made yet).* Choice (A) is affirmative, so it won't work. Choice (B) can be used in a negative present perfect, but it must be placed before the verb phrase: *still haven't been made.* Choice (C) does not make sense in this context.

104. (B) The past participle is required to make a present perfect verb form. Choice

(A) is the present participle. Choice (C) is the basic verb form. Choice (D) is the simple present.

105. (A) *Admitted* means "allowed to enter" and fits the idea of this sentence. Choice (B), *omitted*, means "left or taken out." Choice (C), *permitted*, means "allowed" and does not make sense in this context. Choice (D), *submitted*, means "given to."

106. (D) The noun meaning the act of serving is required to fit the idea of this sentence. Choice (A) is a noun meaning people who serve. Choice (B) is the gerund. Choice (C) is the basic verb form.

107. (B) The present participle adjective is required to describe the thing that is creating the feeling. Choice (A) is the simple present. Choice (C) is the adverb. Choice (D) is the simple past or past participle adjective, which describes the person receiving the feeling.

108. (B) The preposition always used with the phrase *to be interested* is *in*. Choices (A), (C), and (D) are the wrong prepositions.

109. (C) Crops (vegetables or fruit) are raised (cultivated). Choice (A), *grown up*, means "become adult" and is used for children or young animals. Choice (B), *increased*, means "made or become more." Choice (D), *enlarged*, means "made larger, bigger."

110. (A) The subordinate conjunction *although* is used when the idea of the sentence is the opposite of what you would expect to hear or read, and it fits this idea. Choice (B), *because*, explains why something has happened and does not make sense in this context. Choice (C), *so*, works like *because*. In addition, it cannot be used at the beginning of the sentence with this meaning. Choice (D), *in spite of*, requires a gerund phrase after it because of the preposition: *In spite of her working* . . . .

111. (B) An adverb is used to describe an adjective. Choice (A) is a past participle adjective. Choice (C) is the basic verb form. Choice (D) is the simple present.

112. (A) *Past* means "after" and fits the idea of this sentence. Choice (B), *over*, means

"during" with time phrases and does not make sense in this context. Choice (C), *later*, could work with the preposition *than*. Choice (D), *above*, does not make sense in this context.

113. (C) The adjective is required in this context to describe the reports. Choice (A) is the simple present. Choice (B) is the noun. Choice (D) is the basic verb form.

114. (A) The noun is required as the subject of this sentence. Choice (B) is the simple past. Choice (C) is the adjective. Choice (D) is the simple present.

115. (B) The object pronoun is required. Choice (A) is the subject pronoun. Choice (C) is the possessive adjective. Choice (D) is the possessive pronoun.

116. (A) *Current* means "present, now" and fits the idea of this sentence. Choice (B), *abundant*, means "a very large amount" and does not make sense in this context. Choice (C), *actual*, means "real." Choice (D), *eventual*, means "something that will happen at some unspecific time in the future."

117. (D) *Assist* mean "to help," and fits the idea of this sentence. Choice (A), *resist*, means "to work against" and does not make sense in this context. Choice (B), *desist*, means "to stop" or "to cease," Choice (C), *insist*, means "to demand."

118. (D) *As . . . as.* is a comparative phrase showing that two things are equal. The adverb *well* is used because the sentence discusses how something acts: *as well as.* Choice (A) does not contain the second *as.* Choice (B) uses the wrong comparative. Choice (C) uses an adjective instead of an adverb.

119. (C) A negative adverb of frequency at the beginning of a sentence causes a word inversion to follow: *have market conditions been.* Choice (A), *reliably*, means "able to depend on" and does not make sense in this context. Choices (B) and (D) cannot create the word inversion in this sentence.

120. (A) The preposition *of* always follows *most* if an optional preposition is used. This rule applies to *many* as well. Choices (B), (C), and (D) are incorrect prepositions.

121. (D) The adverb is required to describe how the action should be done. Choice (A) is the simple past. Choice (B) is the basic form of the verb. Choice (C) is the noun.

122. (B) The adjective is required to describe the subject. Choice (A) is the noun and does not make sense in this context. Choice (C) is an adverb. Choice (D) is a verb.

123. (A) The noun is required with the comparative adjective. Choice (B) is the present participle adjective. Choice (C) is the past participle adjective. Choice (D) is the adverb.

124. (C) The preposition *throughout* means "all over," "in all parts of" and fits the idea of this sentence. Choice (A) is an adjective. Choice (B), *during,* is used only with nouns that refer to periods of time *(our vacation; the war; the night).* Choice (D) is an adjective.

125. (C) *Against* is a negative preposition that fits in with the idea of this sentence. You *advise somebody to do something;* you *advise somebody against doing something.* Choices (A), (B), and (D) are incorrect prepositions for this idea.

126. (B) The basic verb form must be used together with *to,* the shortened form of *in order to,* to show the reason for doing something. Choice (A) is a noun. Choice (C) is the simple past. Choice (D) is the gerund.

127. (B) The possessive adjective is required. Choice (A) is the contraction of *she is* or *she has.* Choice (C) is the subject pronoun. Choice (D) is the possessive pronoun.

128. (A) *Expectations* means "what you think will happen" and fits in with the idea of this sentence. Choice (B), *experiences,* means "what has happened to somebody." Choice (C), *experiments,* means "trying something to see if it

works." Choice (D), *expressions,* means "communicating an idea, especially by words."

129. (D) *Removed* means "taken out" or "taken away" and fits the idea of this sentence. Choice (A), *reminded,* means "made somebody remember." Choice (B), *remarked,* means "said." Choice (C), *remodeled,* means "changed the interior design, usually of a house."

130. (A) An adjective is required to describe the noun. *Admirable* means "very good" and fits the idea of this sentence. Choice (B) is the past participle adjective describing the person or thing receiving the feeling and does not fit the idea here. Choice (C) is an adverb. Choice (D) is a noun meaning "an officer in the navy."

131. (A) The object pronoun referring to a person is required after the preposition. Choice (B), *which,* refers to things, not people. Choice (C), *who,* is the subject pronoun. Choice (D), *where,* does not make sense in this context.

132. (D) *Opinion* means "personal thoughts or feelings" and fits into the idea of this sentence. Choice (A), *reaction,* could work if followed by the preposition *to.* Choice (B), *mind,* does not make sense in this context. Choice (C), *reason,* might work if followed by the preposition *for.*

133. (A) The adjective is required to describe the noun *advice.* Choice (B) is a noun. Choice (C) is a verb. Choice (D) is the gerund.

134. (C) *Consider* means "to think about" and fits the idea of this sentence. Choice (A), *confuse,* means "to mix up" and does not make sense in this context. Choice (B), *convince,* means "to make somebody believe something." Choice (D), *concur,* means "to agree."

135. (B) An adjective is needed to describe the noun *director.* Choice (A) is a verb or the noun for this action. Choice (C) is a noun, the person who does this action. Choice (D) is the simple past.

136. (B) *Attitude* means "a state of mind" or "feeling" and fits the idea of this

sentence. Choice (A), *assertion*, means "a declaration" or "a statement" and does not make sense in this context. Choice (C), *assignment*, means "a job or responsibility one needs to do." Choice (D), *attendant*, means "somebody who takes care of something."

137. (A) *Impossible* means "not possible" and fits the idea of this sentence. Choice (B), *impatient*, means "not willing to wait" and does not make sense in this context. Choice (C), *improper*, means "not correct." Choice (D), *impolite*, means "rude" or "not polite."

138. (B) The construction *so . . . that* quantifies how something was. *So* is always followed by an adjective or adverb. Choice (A), *too*, is a negative idea and does not make sense in this context. Choice (C), *such*, has the same construction as (B), *such . . . that*, but *such* is followed by a noun phrase: *such a hot day; such a well-written report*. Choice (D), *a lot*, must be followed by a comparative adjective (*a lot happier*) or a comparative adverb (*a lot more quickly*).

139. (C) A noun is required as the subject of this sentence. Choice (A) is an adjective. Choice (B) is the simple past. Choice (D) is an adverb.

140. (C) The subordinate conjunction *because of* explains the reason that something is done and fits the idea of this sentence. Choice (A), *although*, means the opposite of what you expect to happen, so it does not make sense in this context. Choice (B), *in spite of*, is incorrect for the same reason that (A) is incorrect. Choice (D), *consequently*, is in the wrong clause.

Part 6 (page 267)

141. (A) The announcement is about an art show, or *exhibit*. Choices (B), (C), and (D) are things that could happen at a museum but are not the subject of the announcement.

142. (B) *Such* is an adverb describing the adjective *wide*, meaning "to a large degree." Choices (A), (C), and (D) cannot be correctly used in this context.

143. (B) The paragraph discusses something for which there are prices and which are used for admission to the museum, in other words, *tickets*. Choices (A), (C), and (D) are things you could get at a museum but do not fit the description.

144. (D) A future verb is required since this sentence describes something that will happen *during the show*, which is *upcoming*, that is, in the future. Choice (A) is present perfect. Choice (B) is simple past. Choice (C) is simple present.

145. (C) This is a recommendation letter, or *reference*. Choice (A) is described in the letter but is not the entire purpose of the letter. Choices (B) and (D) are other types of job-related letters.

146. (D) The writer is referring to himself here, so the first person possessive adjective is needed. Choice (A) is the second person form. Choices (B) and (C) are third person forms.

147. (C) This gives the correct position for an adverb of frequency used with the present perfect tense. Choices (A), (B), and (D) give incorrect word order.

148. (A) This refers to a new job, which is the subject of the letter. Choices (B), (C), and (D) are not related to the subject of the letter.

149. (A) This is the correct preposition to follow the noun *result*. Choices (B), (C), and (D) cannot correctly follow this word.

150. (C) A noun follows the article *the*. Choice (A) is a present tense verb. Choice (B) is a past tense verb. Choice (D) is the present participle.

151. (D) Company employees will use their own money to pay for travel expenses. Then they will receive money back, or *reimbursement*, from the company. Choices (A), (B), and (C) are not correct in this context.

152. (C) The department head will approve, or *authorize*, expenses that are work-related. Choices (A), (B), and (D) are not correct in this context.

PART 7 (PAGE 271)

153. (B) The job fair offers the opportunity to meet people currently working in a variety of fields and who have job openings. Choice (A) confuses *learn to write a résumé* and *bring your résumé*. Choice (C) confuses similar sounds *conference* with *convention* and *commerce*. Choice (D) confuses *buy things on sale* with *marketing* and *commerce*.

154. (A) The job fair will be held in the Downtown Convention Center. Choice (B) is the street by which you can reach the convention center. Choice (C) is the street on which the convention center is located. Choice (D) is the sponsor of the job fair.

155. (D) To make a long distance call, dial 1—which is the front desk—to ask for assistance. Choice (A) is provided as a local number of interest. Choice (B) would be able to connect you with food but not be able to connect you to a long distance number. Choice (C) is provided as a local number of interest.

156. (A) Dialing 9 is how you make a local call, and 567-555-1014 is the number for City Public Transport. Choice (B) would be 9-567-555-2113. Choice (C) would be 9-567-555-3456 or 2 for room service. Choice (D) confuses *how to make a local call* with *dialing 9 to make a local call*.

157. (B) To reach maid service, dial 3. Choices (A), (C), and (D) would not connect you to maid service.

158. (A) The letter asks for feedback on Mary Matta's experience with Technical Support. Choice (B) confuses *offering support* and *evaluating the support given*. Choice (C) associates selling *computers* with *technical support*. Choice (D) confuses *advertising a website* and *completing the customer survey form on the website*.

159. (B) The customer is asked to mail the completed form or complete it online. Choices (A), (C) and (D) are not correct.

160. (B) Ms. Matta, the customer, spoke with Joan Kim, a Technical Support representative. Choice (A) is the person writing the letter and asking for feedback. Choice (C) is who should be called with questions about the form. Choice (D) is who they would like feedback from.

161. (A) The notice serves to let tenants know that service work will be performed on the fire alarm system. Choice (B) confuses *an actual fire* with *service on the fire alarm system*. Choices (C) and (D) repeat the word *fire* but are not the purpose of the notice.

162. (C) If tenants hear the alarm during 8:30 and 10, they should not be concerned because it is only part of the normal service routine. Choice (A) is what tenants should do if the alarm goes off at a time outside of 8:30–10:00. Choice (B) is what tenants should do if they have questions. Choice (D) confuses *wait patiently* and *thank you for your patience*.

163. (B) This notice is aimed at homeowners who are thinking about selling their homes. Choice (A) is who issued the notice. Choice (C) associates *researchers* with *research* and *market*. Choice (D) associates *marketing experts* with *real estate market*, and confuses similar sounds *experts* and *experience*.

164. (C) Ms. Ortiz will give a lecture on the real estate market and strategies. Choice (A) confuses *estate sale* and *real estate*. Choice (B) associates a *party* with *refreshments* and *event*. Choice (D) confuses similar sounds *competition* and *competitive*.

165. (D) You must reserve your space by calling Mr. Jones if you want to attend. Choice (A) is why people would want to attend. Choice (B) is incorrect because the event is free. Choice (C) is who will speak at the event.

166. (B) These instructions would be found enclosed in a package with a product that was ordered. Choice (A) is where the product was purchased from. Choice (C) associates *post office* with *mail, package, return postage*, and *shipping label*. Choice (D) associates store with *buying, product*, and *merchandise*.

167. (C) The condition of something is the state of something. The other options do not fit the context.

168. (A) To return a product within 30 days, repack it in the same box and mail it back. Choice (B) would not be wise because after 30 days the refund process becomes more difficult. Choice (C) is what you should do to return a product after 30 days. Choice (D) is not mentioned.

169. (C) You will get a full refund, no questions asked, if you return a product within 30 days. Choice (A) is contradicted by *no questions asked*. Choices (B) and (D) are contradicted by *you will get a full refund, no questions asked*.

170. (C) They are asked to notify the staff in advance of their arrival if they wish to make changes in the room arrangements. Choices (A), (B), and (D) are contradicted by *in advance of your arrival*.

171. (B) A complete itinerary will be distributed when the participants meet for dinner. Choice (A) confuses the *tour schedule* with the enclosed *airport shuttle schedule*. Choice (C) is when they should mention they are with the tour so that the staff can inform the tour leader. Choice (D) is unknown.

172. (D) The itinerary will be printed and sent around to the members of the tour group. The other options do not fit the context.

173. (B) George Harris, the Assistant Director of Tours of World Travel Tours, wrote the letter. Choices (A), (C), and (D) are contradicted by Mr. Harris's title.

174. (B) Participation in this training seminar is mandatory for all staff of the Finance Office. Choice (A) is who the memo is addressed to. Choice (C) is contradicted by *mandatory for all staff of the Finance Office*. Choice (D) confuses *people contacted by Mr. Oh* and *contacting Mr. Oh if you would like to attend*.

175. (C) The seminar will take place in Conference Room B. Choices (A), (B), and (D) are not correct.

176. (C) Mr. James will not speak tonight because there is a problem with the heating system in the auditorium. Choices (A) and (B) are not mentioned. Choice (D) is contradicted by them having to close the auditorium to repair the heating system.

177. (B) Sharon Rockford will give a talk next Monday. Choice (A) confuses *closing at 8:00 P.M.* and the *talk starting at 8:00 P.M.* Choice (C) is not mentioned. Choice (D) confuses similar sounds *résumés* (n.) and *resume* (v.).

178. (D) The World Wide Cafe in Terminal 6 provides Internet connection. Choices (A), (B), and (C) do not offer Internet connection.

179. (B) Business Centers do not offer fax service. Choices (A), (C), and (D) are available.

180. (C) Taxi stands and bus stops are located in the front of each terminal. Choice (A) can only be found in Terminals 1, 4, and 7. Choice (B) can't be found in Terminal 5. Choice (D) can only be found in Terminal 2.

181. (D) The ad lists *making appointments* among the office assistant's responsibilities. Choice (A) is confused with *typing documents*. Choice (B) is confused with *answering phones*. Choice (D) is confused with *maintaining database*.

182. (C) Ms. Wang's letter states that she has the required computer skills which, according to the letter, include *word processing*. Choices (A) and (B) are not mentioned. Choice (D) is confused with the fact that the position is in an architectural firm.

183. (A) Ms. Wang's letter states *I would like to enter your profession*. The letter is addressed to Mr. Woo, who, we know from the ad, is an *architect*.

184. (B) In her letter, Ms. Wang states *I am taking a night class at the university now*. Choice (A) is confused with Ms. Wang's mention of her high school record. Choice (C) is confused with her goal of

becoming an architect. Choice (D) is confused with her application for the job of office assistant.

185. (A) Ms. Wang states that she has enclosed her résumé. Choice (B) is not mentioned. Choice (C) is not enclosed; Mr. Woo is asked to call the high school to obtain it. Choice (D) is confused with Ms. Wang's mention of the university class she is taking.

186. (D) The party is a farewell for Martha Cunningham, who is moving to another city. Choices (A), (B), and (C) are people mentioned in the invitation and e-mail but are not the correct answer.

187. (D) The invitation says that the party is on Thursday, and in his e-mail Tom apologizes for not attending the party *yesterday*, so he wrote the e-mail on *Friday*. Choice (A) is the day to reply to the invitation. Choice (B) is not mentioned. Choice (C) is the day of the party.

188. (A) In his e-mail Tom states *I had a family emergency*. Choice (B) is confused with Tom's statement that he *had planned* to attend the party. Choice (C) is confused with the upcoming meeting Tom mentions at the end of the e-mail. Choice (D) is confused with the accounting office mentioned in the invitation.

189. (D) In the invitation, Susan said she hoped to raise $300. By Tom's e-mail, we know that she was able to raise *$75 more than expected*, so the total raised was $375. Choice (A) is the amount Susan asks each person to contribute. Choice (B) is the extra amount of money raised. Choice (C) is the amount Susan hoped to raise.

190. (C) Tom mentions that he sent a cake to the party. Choice (A) is confused with the money raised for the gift. Choice (B) is confused with Tom's mention of signing a card. Choice (D) is confused with the gift bought for Martha with everyone's contributions.

191. (A) *Cash* is the only form of payment not mentioned in the notice.

192. (A) The office is open Monday through Friday. 555-9754 is the number to call on days when the office is closed. Choice (B) is the number to call when the office is open. Choices (C) and (D) are Mr. Wilson's phone numbers.

193. (B) In his e-mail, Mr. Wilson says that he has to attend a meeting in the afternoon. Choice (A) is what Mr. Wilson will not be able to do. Mr. Wilson will not do Choice (C) because he is using e-mail to make a new appointment. Choice (D) is confused with the assistant sending a check to the dentist's office.

194. (B) According to the notice, the cancellation fee is $40. This is the amount Jim Wilson will pay for his missed appointment. Choices (A) and (C) are confused with the 24 hours notice required to avoid the cancellation fee. Choice (D) is confused with the $40 cancellation fee.

195. (D) Mr. Wilson asks for an evening appointment. From the office hours listed on the notice, we know that the Friday is the only day of the week that evening appointments are available.

196. (C) Ms. Lopez is making travel arrangements for Mr. Pak, so she is a travel agent. Choice (A) is not mentioned. Choice (B) is incorrect because Ms. Lopez is arranging airline flights as well as a hotel room. Choice (D) is incorrect because she is arranging a hotel room as well as airline flights.

197. (C) According to the first message, 11:15 was the time of Ms. Lopez's call. Choice (A) is the time she wants Mr. Pak to return her call. Choice (B) is the time that Mr. Pak wants to return from his trip. Choice (D) is the time that Mr. Pak called Ms. Lopez.

198. (D) In his phone message, Mr. Pak says that he prefers *the second option*. The second option mentioned in Ms. Lopez's message is Wednesday morning. Choice (A) is the time he wants to return from his trip. Choice (B) is the time that there

is no flight available. Choice (C) is the first option mentioned.

199. (A) In his message, Mr. Pak says that he'll *stay with his first choice*, or request for a hotel. From Ms. Lopez's message we know that Mr. Pak requested the Grand Hotel. Choices (B) and (C) are other hotel options mentioned in Ms. Lopez's

message. Choice (D) is confused with the name of Ms. Lopez's company.

200. (C) In his message, Mr. Pak says that *he has a vacation next month*. Choices (A) and (B) are confused with times mentioned in reference to Mr. Pak's upcoming business trip. Choice (D) is not mentioned.